Lecture Notes in Artificial Intelligence   2663

Edited by J. G. Carbonell and J. Siekmann

Subseries of Lecture Notes in Computer Science

Springer

Berlin
Heidelberg
New York
Barcelona
Hong Kong
London
Milan
Paris
Tokyo

Ernestina Menasalvas   Javier Segovia
Piotr S. Szczepaniak (Eds.)

Advances in
Web Intelligence

First International Atlantic Web Intelligence Conference
AWIC 2003
Madrid, Spain, May 5-6, 2003
Proceedings

Springer

Series Editors

Jaime G. Carbonell, Carnegie Mellon University, Pittsburgh, PA, USA
Jörg Siekmann, University of Saarland, Saarbrücken, Germany

Volume Editors

Ernestina Menasalvas
Javier Segovia
Universidad Politécnica de Madrid
Facultad de Informática
Campus de Montegancedo, Boadilla del Monte, 28660 Madrid, Spain
E-mail: {emenasalvas/fsegovia}@fi.upm.es

Piotr S. Szczepaniak
Technical University of Lodz
Institute of Computer Science
ul.Sterlinga 16/18, 90-217 Lodz, Poland
E-mail: office@ics.p.lodz.pl
Cataloging-in-Publication Data applied for

A catalog record for this book is available from the Library of Congress.

Bibliographic information published by Die Deutsche Bibliothek
Die Deutsche Bibliothek lists this publication in the Deutsche Nationalbibliografie;
detailed bibliographic data is available in the Internet at <http://dnb.ddb.de>.

CR Subject Classification (1998): I.2, H.3, H.4, C.2, H.5, J.1, J.2

ISSN 0302-9743
ISBN 3-540-40124-5 Springer-Verlag Berlin Heidelberg New York

Springer-Verlag Berlin Heidelberg New York
a member of BertelsmannSpringer Science+Business Media GmbH

http://www.springer.de

© Springer-Verlag Berlin Heidelberg 2003
Printed in Germany

Typesetting: Camera-ready by author, data conversion by PTP-Berlin GmbH
Printed on acid-free paper   SPIN: 10930601   06/3142   5 4 3 2 1 0

Preface

We are pleased to present the proceedings of the 2003 Atlantic Web Intelligence Conference, AWIC 2003. The conference was located in Madrid, Spain during May 5–6, 2003, organized locally by the Technical University of Madrid.

AWIC 2003 aimed to be the first of a series of conferences on Web Intelligence, to be celebrated annually, alternatively in Europe and America, starting in Madrid. It was born as an activity of the recently created WIC-Poland Research Centre and the WIC-Spain Research Centre, both belonging to the Web Intelligence Consortium (WIC) (http://wi-consortium.org). AWIC 2003 was supported with grants from the Spanish Ministry for Science and Technology and the European Network of Excellence in Knowledge Discovery, KDNet.

AWIC 2003 brought together scientists, engineers, computer users, and students to exchange and share their experiences, new ideas, and research results about all aspects (theory, applications, and tools) of artificial intelligence techniques applied to Web-based systems, and to discuss the practical challenges encountered and the solutions adopted. Almost 70 contributions were submitted. After a preliminary evaluation, 60 of these papers were accepted to the conference and were assigned at least two reviewers from the international program committee. Out of this 60, 33 were conditionally accepted, and 32 of them were finally accepted after the conditions set by the reviewers had been met, which resulted in an acceptance ratio of 45%.

AWIC 2003 had a general session with 9 papers, and the others were organized into special sessions on areas such as:

- Web security,
- Semantic Web,
- Web authoring and design,
- Web information retrieval,
- Agents for the web, and
- User behavior

During AWIC 2003 we were pleased to have some important invited speakers. Prof. Lotfi Zadeh, who does not need any introduction, was the honorary chair and gave a talk about the transition of search engines to question-answering systems. This book contains what could be considered an extended abstract of his actual lecture. Prof. Ning Zhong, President of WIC, who can be considered as one of the fathers of the term "Web Intelligence," gave a talk about the past, present, and future of the area. Finally, Prof. Ryszard Tadeusiewicz spoke about the application of artificial intelligence techniques for information retrieval.

We thank all the authors for contributing to what in our minds was a more than interesting program in Web Intelligence. We also want to thank the remarkable effort made by Coro Perez, secretary of the conference, and the rest of the local committee. We hope to see all of them, and many others at AWIC 2004.

May 2003

E. Menasalvas
J. Segovia
P.S. Szczepaniak

AWIC 2003 Organization

Honorary Chair

Lotfi A. Zadeh (University of California, USA)

Conference Co-chairs

Javier Segovia (Universidad Politécnica de Madrid, Spain)
Piotr Szczepaniak (Technical University of Lodz, Poland)

Steering Committee

Ning Zhong (Maebashi Institute of Technology, Japan)
Enric Trillas (Universidad Politécnica de Madrid, Spain)
Jiming Liu (Hong Kong Baptist University)
Janusz Kacprzyk (Systems Research Institute, Polish Academy of Sciences, Warsaw, Poland)

Organizing Committee

Ernestina Menasalvas (Universidad Politécnica de Madrid, Spain)
Jesús Favela (Centro de Investigación Científica y de Educación Superior de Ensenada, México)

Local Committee

José M. Peña (Universidad Politécnica de Madrid, Spain)
Oscar Marbán (Universidad Carlos III de Madrid, Spain)
Ángel Lucas (Universidad Politécnica de Madrid, Spain)
Sonia Frutos (Universidad Politécnica de Madrid, Spain)
Javier Crespo (Universidad Carlos III de Madrid, Spain)
Eugenio Santos (Universidad Politécnica de Madrid, Spain)

Organization of the Special Track on Uncertainty, Hypermedia and the Web: Search, Personalization and Usability

José Angel Olivas (Universidad de Castilla-La Mancha, Spain)
Miguel-Ángel Sicilia (Universidad Carlos III, Spain)

AWIC 2003 Program Committee

Table of Contents

Special Session: Web Security

Special Session: Semantic Web

Special Session: Web Authoring and Design

Special Session: Web Information Retrieval

Special Session: Agents for the Web

Special Session: User Behavior

Toward Web Intelligence

Ning Zhong

Department of Information Engineering
Maebashi Institute of Technology
460-1 Kamisadori-Cho, Maebashi-City 371-0816, Japan
zhong@maebashi-it.ac.jp

Abstract. Web Intelligence (WI) presents excellent opportunities and challenges for the research and development of new generation of Web-based information processing technology, as well as for exploiting Web-based advanced applications. Based on two perspectives of WI research: an intelligent Web-based business-centric schematic diagram and the conceptual levels of WI, we investigates various ways to study WI and potential applications.

1 Introduction

The concept of Web Intelligence (WI for short) was first introduced in our papers and books [19,35,38,41,45,46]. Broadly speaking, Web Intelligence is a new direction for scientific research and development that explores the fundamental roles as well as practical impacts of Artificial Intelligence (AI)[1] and advanced Information Technology (IT) on the next generation of Web-empowered systems, services, and environments. The WI technology revolutionizes the way in which information is gathered, stored, processed, presented, shared, and used by electoronization, virtualization, globalization, standardization, personalization, and portals.

With the rapid growth of the Web, research and development on WI have received much attention. There is great potential for WI to make useful contributions to e-business (include e-commerce), e-science, e-learning, e-government, and so on. Many specific applications and systems have been proposed and studied. In particular, the e-business activity that involves the end user is undergoing a significant revolution [29]. The ability to track users' browsing behavior down to individual mouse clicks has brought the vendor and end customer closer than ever before. It is now possible for a vendor to personalize his product message for individual customers at a massive scale. This is called *direct marketing* (or *targeted marketing*) [32,47]. Web mining and Web usage analysis play an important role in e-business for customer relationship management (CRM) and direct marketing. Web mining is the use of data mining techniques to automatically discover and extract information from Web documents and services [15,29,36,

---

[1] Here the term of AI includes classical AI, computational intelligence, and soft computing etc.

E. Menasalvas et al. (Eds.): AWIC 2003, LNAI 2663, pp. 1–14, 2003.

40]. A challenge is to explore the connection between Web mining and the related agent paradigm such as Web farming that is the systematic refining of information resources on the Web for business intelligence [10].

The paper investigates various ways to study WI and potential applications. Section 2 discusses how to develop an intelligent enterprise portal for e-business intelligence by using WI technology. Based on the discussion in Sect. 2, an intelligent Web-based business-centric schematic diagram of WI-related topics is given in Sect. 3, and conceptual levels of WI for developing the Wisdom Web are provided in Sect. 4, respectively. Section 5 describes various ways for studying WI, which include the semantics in the Web and the Web as social networks, as well as proposes new approaches for developing semantic social networks and for creating Web mining Grids. Finally, Sect. 6 gives concluding remarks.

2 How to Develop Intelligent Enterprise Portals?

As an example for developing enterprise portals by using WI technology, we here discuss how to construct an intelligent virtual industry park (VIP) that has been developing in our group. The VIP portal is a website in which all of the contents related to the mid-sized/small-scale companies in Maebashi city can be accessed.

The construction process can be divided into three phases. We first constructed a basic system including the fundamental functions such as the interface for dynamically registering/updating enterprise information, the database for storing the enterprise information, the automatic generation/modification of enterprise homepages, and the domain-specific, keyword-based search engine. When designing the basic system, we also started by analyzing customer performance: what has each customer bought, over time, total volumes, trends, and so on.

Although the basic system can work as a whole-one, we now need to know not only past performance on the business front, but also how the customer or prospect enters our VIP portal in order to target products and manage promotions and marketing campaigns. To the already demanding requirement to capture transaction data for further analysis, we now also need to use the Web usage mining techniques to capture the clicks of the mouse that define where the visitor has been on our website. What pages has he or she visited? What is the semantic association between the pages he or she visited? Is the visitor familiar with the Web structure? Or is he or she a new user or a random one? Is the visitor a Web robot or other users? In search for the holy grail of "stickiness", we know that a prime factor is *personalization* for:

- making a dynamic recommendation to a Web user based on the user profile and usage behavior,
- automatic modification of a website's contents and organization,
- combining Web usage data with marketing data to give information about how visitors used a website for marketers.

Therefore, we need to extend the basic VIP system by adding more advanced functions such as Web mining, the ontologies-based search engine, as well as automatic email filtering and management.

Finally, a portal for e-business intelligence can be implemented by adding e-business related application functions such as electronic data interchange (EDI) and security solution.

3   An Intelligent Web-Based Business-Centric Schematic Diagram of WI-Related Topics

From the example stated in the previous section, we can see that developing an intelligent enterprise portal needs to apply results from existing disciplines of AI and IT to a totally new domain. On the other hand, WI is also expected to introduce new problems and challenges to the established disciplines on the new platform of the Web and Internet. That is, WI is an enhancement or an extension of AI and IT.

In order to study advanced WI technology systematically, and develop advanced Web-based intelligent information systems, we provide a schematic diagram of interrelated research topics from a Web-based, business intelligence centric perspective in Fig. 1.

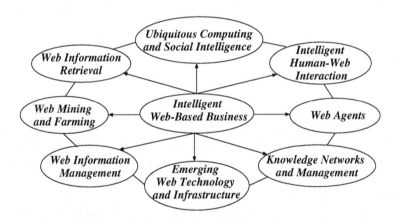

Fig. 1. An intelligent Web-based business-centric schematic diagram of WI-related topics

4   The Wisdom Web vs. Levels of WI

In previous papers [19,45], we argued that the next paradigm shift in the Web is towards *wisdom* and developing the Wisdom Web will become a tangible goal for WI research. The new generation of the WWW will enable humans to gain wisdom of living, working, playing, in addition to information search and knowledge queries.

In order to develop a Wisdom Web, WI needs to be studied in at least four conceptual levels as shown by Fig. 2. The four-level framework ranges from the lower hardware-centered level to the higher application-centered level. It builds upon the fast development as well as application of various hybridization of AI and WWW technologies.

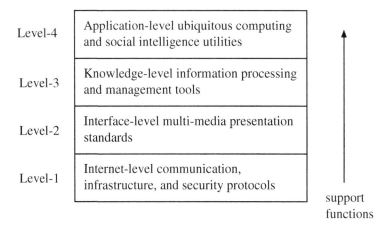

Fig. 2. Levels of WI

1. **Internet-level communication, infrastructure, and security protocols**. The Web is regarded as a *computer-network system*. WI techniques for this level include, for instance, Web data prefetching systems built upon Web surfing patterns to resolve the issue of Web latency. The intelligence of the Web prefetching comes from an adaptive learning process based on observations of user surfing behavior.
2. **Interface-level multimedia presentation standards**. The Web is regarded as an *interface* for human-Internet interaction. WI techniques for this level are used to develop intelligent Web interfaces in which the capabilities of adaptive cross-language processing, personalized multimedia representation, and multimodal data processing are required.
3. **Knowledge-level information processing and management tools**. The Web is regarded as a *distributed data/knowledge base*. We need to develop semantic markup languages to represent the semantic contents of the Web available in machine-understandable formats for agent-based autonomic computing, such as searching, aggregation, classification, filtering, managing, mining, and discovery on the Web [4].

4. **Application-level ubiquitous computing and social intelligence environments**. The Web is regarded as a *basis for establishing social networks* that contain communities of people (or organizations or other social entities) connected by social relationships, such as friendship, coworking or information exchange with common interests. They are Web-supported social networks or virtual communities. The study of WI concerns the important issues central to social network intelligence (social intelligence for short) [28]. Furthermore, the multimedia contents on the Web are not only accessible from stationary platforms, but increasingly from mobile platforms [30,31]. Ubiquitous Web access and computing from various wireless devices needs adaptive personalization for which WI techniques are used to construct models of user interests by inferring implicitly from user behavior and actions [2,5].

The social intelligence approach presents excellent opportunities and challenges for the research and development of WI, as well as a Web-supported social network that needs to be supported by all levels of WI as mentioned above. This is based on the observation that the Web is now becoming an integral part of our society and that scientists should be aware of it and take much care about handling social issues [23]. Study in this area must receive as much attention as Web mining, Web agents, ontologies, and related topics.

5   Ways for Studying the Web Intelligence

With respect to different levels of WI mentioned previously, the Web can be studied in several ways.

5.1   Studying the Semantics in the Web

One of the fundamental issues of WI is to study the *semantics* in the Web, called the semantic Web, with respect to level 3 of WI, that is, modeling *semantics* of Web information. Advantages of the semantic Web include:

- allowing more of the Web content (not just form) to become machine readable and processible,
- allowing for recognition of the semantic context in which Web materials are used,
- allowing for the reconciliation of terminological differences between diverse user communities.

Thus, information will be machine-processible in ways that support intelligent network services such as information brokers and search agents [4,7,8].

The semantic Web is a step towards Web intelligence. It is based on languages that make more of the semantic content of the page available in machine-readable formats for agent-based computing.

The main components of semantic Web techniques include:

- a unifying data model such as RDF,

- languages with defined semantics, built on RDF, such as OWL (DAML+OIL),
- ontologies of standardized terminology for marking up Web resources, used by semantically rich service-level descriptions (such as DAML-S, the DAML-based Web Service Ontology), and support tools that assist the generation and processing of semantic markup.

Ontologies and agent technology can play a crucial role in Web intelligence by enabling Web-based knowledge processing, sharing, and reuse between applications. Generally defined as shared formal conceptualizations of particular domains, ontologies provide a common understanding of topics that can be communicated between people and agent-based systems.

An ontology can be very high-level, consisting of concepts that organize the upper parts of a knowledge base, or it can be domain-specific such as a chemical ontology. We here suggest three categories of ontologies: *domain-specific*, *task*, and *universal* ones.

A *domain-specific* ontology describes a well-defined technical or business domain.

A *task* ontology might be either a quite domain-specific one, or a set of ontologies with respect to several domains (or their reconstruction for that task), in which relations between ontologies are described for meeting the requirement of that task.

A *universal* ontology describes knowledge at higher levels of generality. It is a more general-purpose ontology (or called a common ontology) that is generated from several domain-specific ontologies. It can serve as a bridge for communication among several domains or tasks.

The Roles of Ontologies. Generally speaking, a domain-specific (or task) ontology forms the heart of any knowledge information system for that domain (or task). Ontologies will play a major role in supporting information exchange processes in various areas. The roles of ontologies for Web intelligence include:

- communication between Web communities,
- agents communication based on semantics,
- knowledge-based Web retrieval,
- understanding Web contents in a semantic way,
- and social network and Web community discovery.

More specifically, new requirements for any exchange format on the Web are:

- Universal expressive power. A Web based exchange format must be able to express any form of data.
- Syntactic interoperability. Applications must be able to read the data and get a representation that can be exploited.
- Semantic interoperability. One of the most important requirements for an exchange format is that data must be understandable. It is about defining mappings between terms within the data, which requires content analysis.

The semantic Web requires interoperability standards that address not only the syntactic form of documents but also the semantic content. Ontologies serve as metadata schemes for the semantic Web, providing a controlled vocabulary of concepts, each with explicitly defined and machine-processable semantics.

A semantic Web also lets agents utilize all the (meta) data on all Web pages, allowing it to gain knowledge from one site and apply it to logical mappings on other sites for ontology-based Web retrieval and e-business intelligence. For instance, ontologies can be used in e-commerce to enable machine-based communication between buyers and sellers, vertical integration of markets, description reuse between different marketplaces. Web-search agents use ontologies to find pages with words that are syntactically different but semantically similar.

Ontology Languages. Ontologies provide a way of capturing a shared understanding of terms that can be used by human and programs to aid in information exchange. Ontologies have been gaining popularity as a method of providing a specification of a controlled vocabulary. Although simple knowledge representation such as Yahoo's taxonomy provides notions of generality and term relations, classical ontologies attempt to capture precise meanings of terms. In order to specify meanings, an ontology language must be used. So far, several ontology languages such as OIL and DAML have been proposed.

OIL (Ontology Inference Layer) is an Ontology Interchange Language for the Web [7,9]. It is an effort to produce a layered architecture for specifying ontologies. The major functions of OIL include:

- It provides the modelling primitives commonly used in frame-based ontologies.
- It has a simple, clean, and well defined semantics based on description logics.
- Automated reasoning support may be specified and provided in a computationally efficient manner.

DAML (DARPA Agent Markup Languages) is a new DARPA research program. One of main tasks of this program is to create an Agent Mark-Up Language (DAML) built upon XML. It is a *semantic* language that ties the information on a page to machine readable semantics (ontology). It is a step toward a "semantic Web" where agents, search engines and other programs can read DAML markup to decipher meaning rather than just content on a website [11,12].

Currently, a sub-dialect of OIL and DAML called OWL is the starting point of a Web ontology language standardization group of the W3C.

Automatic Construction of Ontologies. Although ontology engineering has been studied over the last decade, few of (semi) automatic methods for comprehensive ontology construction have been developed. Manual ontology construction remains a tedious, cumbersome task that can easily result in a bottleneck for Web intelligence. Learning and construction of domain-specific ontology from Web contents is one of important tasks in both text mining and WI.

Maedche et al proposed an ontology learning framework as semi-automatic with human intervention, adopting the paradigm of balanced cooperative modeling for constructing ontologies for the semantic Web [22]. Their framework extends typical ontology engineering environments by using semi-automatic ontology construction tools.

Missikoff et al developed an integrated approach and a tool called OntoLearn, for extracting domain concepts and to detect semantic relationships among them, from websites and more generally from documents shared among the members of virtual organizations, to support the construction of a domain ontology [24].

Zhong et al proposed a process of construction of task (or domain-specific) ontologies [44]. It is a multi-phase process in which various text mining techniques and natural-language understanding methods are used. The major steps in the process of construction of a task ontology include content collection, morphological analysis, text (domain) classification, generation of classification rules, conceptual relationship analysis, as well as generation, refinement, conceptual hierarchy, and management of ontologies. A thesaurus is necessary to be used as a background knowledge base in the process. We emphasize that the process is iterative, and may repeat at different intervals when new/updated data come.

5.2   Studying the Web as Social Networks

We can view the Web as a directed network in which each node is a static Web page to another. Thus, the Web can be studied as a *graph* that connects a set of people (or organizations or other social entities) connected by a set of social relationships, such as friendship, co-working or information exchange with common interests [16,28].

Social Network Analysis. The main questions about the Web graph include:

- How big is the graph?
- Can we browse from any page to any other?
- Can we exploit the structure of the Web?
- What does the Web graph reveal about social dynamics?
- How to discover and manage the Web communities?

Modern social network theory is built on the work of Stanley Milgram [33]. Milgram found so-called the *small-world phenomenon*, that is, typical paths took only six hops to arrive. Ravi Kumar and colleagues observed there is a strong structural similarity between the Web as a network and social networks [16]. The small-world phenomenon constitutes a basic property of the Web, which is not just interesting but also useful.

Current estimates suggest that the Web graph has several billion nodes (pages of content) and an average degree of about 7. A recurrent observation on the Web graph is the prevalence of power laws: the degree of nodes are distributed according to inverse polynomial distribution [1,13,14,20].

The Web automatically captures a rich interplay between hundreds of millions of people and billions of pages of content. In essence these interactions embody a *social network* involving people, the pages they create and view, and even the Web pages themselves. These relationships have a bearing on the way in which we create, share, and manege knowledge and information. It is our hope that exploiting these similarities will lead to progress in knowledge management and business intelligence.

The *broader* social network is a self-organizing structure of users, information, and communities of expertise [2,28]. Such social networks can play a crucial role in implementing next-generation enterprise portals with functions such as data mining and knowledge management for discovery, analysis, and management of social network knowledge.

The social network is placed at the top of a four-level WI infrastructure as described in Sect. 4 and is supported by functions, provided in all levels of WI, including security, prefetching, adaptive cross-language processing, personalized multimedia representation, semantic searching, aggregation, classification, filtering, managing, mining, and discovery.

Semantic Social Networks for Intelligent Enterprise Portals. One of the most sophisticated applications on the Web today is *enterprise information portals* operating with state-of-the-art markup languages to search, retrieve and repackage data. The enterprise portals are being developed into an even more powerful center based on component-based applications called Web Services [2, 28].

WI researchers must to study both centralized and distributed information structures. Information/knowledge on the Web can be either globally distributed throughout the Web within multi-layer over the infrastructure of Web protocols, or located locally, centralized on an intelligent portal providing Web services (i.e. the intelligent service provider) that is integrated to its own cluster of specialized intelligent applications. However, each approach has a serious flaw. As pointed out by Alesso and Smith [2], the intelligent portal approach limits uniformity and access, while the global semantic Web approach faces combinatory complexity limitations.

A way to solve the above issue is to develop and use the *Problem Solver Markup Language* (PSML), for collecting globally distributed contents and knowledge from Web-supported, semantic social networks and incorporating them with locally operational knowledge/databases in an enterprise or community for local centralized, adaptable Web intelligent services.

The core of PSML is distributed inference engines that can perform automatic reasoning on the Web by incorporating contents and meta-knowledge autonomically collected and transformed from the semantic Web with locally operational knowledge-data bases. A feasible way to implement such PSML is to use existing Prolog-like logic language plus dynamic contents and meta-knowledge collection and transformation agents.

In our experiments, we use KAUS for representation local information sources and for inference and reasoning. KAUS is a knowledge-based system developed in our group which involves knowledge-bases on the basis of Multi-Layer Logic and databases based on the relational data model [25,26,34]. KAUS enables representation of knowledge and data in the first-order logic with data structure in multi-level and can be easily used for inference and reasoning as well as transforming and managing both knowledge and data.

By using this information transformation approach, the dynamic, global information sources on the Web can be combined with the local information sources in an enterprise portal together for decision-making and e-business intelligence.

5.3   Creating Web Mining Grids

As mentioned at the previous sections, Web mining, the knowledge discovery from the Web, is one of core techniques of WI technology. Web mining is the application of data mining techniques to large, distributed, Web-based data repositories such as Web documents, Web logs, databases linked to the Web, and services. Web mining research is at the cross road of research from several research communities, such as database, information retrieval (IR), artificial intelligence (AI), especially the sub-areas of machine learning (ML), natural language processing (NLP), and intelligent agent technology (IAT). Web mining is expected to play an increasingly important role in the future intelligent Web information services.

However, it has been recently recognized that the Web mining process for real-world applications is extremely complicated [39]. There are several levels, phases and large number of steps and alternative Web mining techniques in the process, iteration can be seen in anywhere and at any time, and the process may repeat at different intervals when new/updated data comes. The major questions include

- How to plan, organize, control, and manage the Web mining process dynamically for different tasks for multi-aspect analysis in distributed, multiple Web data sources;
- How to get the system to know it knows and impart the knowledge to decide what tools are appropriate for what problems and when.

Solving such issues needs a new infrastructure and platform as the middleware to develop and support such functions. Our methodology is to create a grid-based, organized society of Web mining agents, called *Web Mining Grid* [3, 6]. This means

- To develop many kinds of Web mining agents for different tasks;
- To organize the Web mining agents into a grid with multi-layer under the Web as a middleware that understands the user's questions, transforms them to Web mining issues, discovers the resources and information about the issues, and get a composite answer or solution;

- To use the grid of Web mining agents for multi-aspect analysis in distributed, multiple Web data sources;
- To manage the grid of Web mining agents by a distributed cooperative multi-level control authority.

That is, the Web Mining Grid is made of many smaller components that are called *Web mining agents*. Each agent by itself can only do some simple thing. Yet when we join these agents in a *grid*, this leads to implement more complex Web mining tasks.

5.4 Soft Computing for WI

Another challenging problem in WI is how to deal with uncertainty of information on the wired and wireless Web. Adapting existing soft computing solutions, when appropriate for Web intelligence applications, must incorporate a robust notion of learning that will scale to the Web, adapt to individual user requirements, and personalize interfaces. There are ongoing efforts to integrate logic (including non-classical logic), artificial neural networks, probabilistic and statistical reasoning, fuzzy sets, rough sets, granular computing, genetic algorithm, and other methodologies in the soft computing paradigm [43], to construct a hybrid approach/system for Web intelligence.

6 Concluding Remarks

Web Intelligence (WI) is a newly recognized, very dynamic field. It is the key as well as the most urgent research field of IT in the era of the World Wide Web, knowledge Web, grid computing, intelligent agent technology, and ubiquitous social computing. WI technology will produce the new tools and infrastructure components necessary to create intelligent enterprise portals that serves its users wisely for e-business intelligence.

To meet the strong demands for participation and the growing interests in WI, the Web Intelligence Consortium (WIC) was formed in spring 2002. The WIC (http://wi-consortium.org/) is an international non-profit organization dedicated to promoting world-wide scientific research and industrial development in the era of Web and agent intelligence. The WIC specializes in the development and promotion of new WI-related research and technologies through collaborations with WI research centers throughout the world and organization/individual members, technology showcases at WI conferences and workshops, WIC official book and journal publications, the WIC newsletter, and WIC official releases of new industrial solutions and standards.

In addition to various special issues on WI published or being published by several international journals, including IEEE Computer, a WI-focused scientific journal, Web Intelligence and Agent Systems: An International Journal (http://wi-consortium.org/journal.html), has been successfully launched as the official journal of the WIC.

The interest in WI is growing very fast. We would like to invite everyone, who are interested in the WI related research and development activities, to join the WI community. Your input and participation will determine the future of WI.

Acknowledgments. I would like to thank Jiming Liu and Yiyu Yao who are my colleagues introduced Web Intelligence (WI) with me together. The contents of this paper include their contributions. I am very grateful to people who have joined or supported the WI community, in particular, the WIC Advisory Board members: Edward A. Feigenbaum, Setsuo Ohsuga, Benjamin Wah, Philip Yu, and Lotfi A. Zadeh, all the WIC Technical Committee Members, as well as the IEEE TCCI Chair: Xindong Wu. I thank them for their strong support.

References

1. R. Albert, H. Jeong, A.L. Barabasi: Diameter of the World-Wide Web, Nature, 410, 130–131 (1999)
2. H.P. Alesso, C.F. Smith (2002): *The Intelligent Wireless Web* (Addison-Wesley, 2002)
3. F. Berman: From TeraGrid to Knowledge Grid, *CACM*, 44, 27–28 (2001)
4. T. Berners-Lee, J. Hendler, O. Lassila: The Semantic Web, Scientific American, 284, 34–43 (2001)
5. D. Billsus et al.: Adaptive Interfaces for Ubiquitous Web Access, *CACM*, 45, 34–38 (2002)
6. M. Cannataro and D. Talia: The Knowledge Grid, *CACM*, 46, 89–93 (2003)
7. S. Decker, S. Melnik, et al.: The Semantic Web: the Roles of XML and RDF, *IEEE Internet Computing*, 4(5), 63–74 (2000)
8. S. Decker, P. Mitra, S. Melnik: Framework for the Semantic Web: an RDF Tutorial, *IEEE Internet Computing*, 4(6), 68–73 (2000)
9. D. Fensel: *Ontologies: A Silver Bullet for Knowledge Management and Electronic Commerce* (Springer, 2001)
10. R.D. Hackathorn: *Web Farming for the Data Warehouse* (Morgan Kaufmann, 2000)
11. J.A. Hendler: Agent Based Computing and DAML, http://www.daml.org/ (2000)
12. J.A. Hendler and E.A. Feigenbaum: Knowledge Is Power: The Semantic Web Vision. In N. Zhong, Y.Y. Yao, J. Liu, S. Ohsuga (eds.): *Web Intelligence: Research and Development*, LNAI 2198 (Springer, 2001) 18–29
13. B.A. Huberman, P.L.T. Pirolli, J.E. Pitkow, R.M. Lukose: Strong Regularities in World Wide Web Surfing, Science, 280, 96–97 (1997)
14. B.A. Huberman, L.A. Adamic: Growth Dynamics of the World-Wide Web, Nature, 410, 131 (1999)
15. R. Kosala and H. Blockeel: Web Mining Research: A Survey, *ACM SIGKDD Explorations Newsletter*, 2, 1–15 (2000)
16. R. Kumar, P. Raghavan, S. Rajagopalan, A. Tomkins: The Web and Social Networks. IEEE Computer Special Issue on Web Intelligence, 35(11) 32–36 (November 2002)
17. J. Liu, N. Zhong (eds.): *Intelligent Agent Technology: Systems, Methodologies, and Tools* (World Scientific, 1999)

18. J. Liu, N. Zhong, Y.Y. Tang, P.S.P. Wang (eds.): *Agent Engineering* (World Scientific, 2001)
19. J. Liu, N. Zhong, Y.Y. Yao, Z.W. Ras: The *Wisdom Web*: New Challenges for Web Intelligence (WI), Journal of Intelligent Information Systems, Kluwer Academic Publishers, 20(1) 5–9 (2003)
20. J. Liu, S. Zhang, Y. Ye: Agent-Based Characterization of Web Regularities. In N. Zhong, J. Liu, Y.Y. Yao (eds.) *Web Intelligence*, 19–36 (Springer, 2003)
21. Z. Lu, Y.Y. Yao, N. Zhong: Web Log Mining. In N. Zhong, J. Liu, Y.Y. Yao (eds.) *Web Intelligence*, 172–194 (Springer, 2003)
22. A. Maedche and S. Staab: Ontology Learning for the Semantic Web *IEEE Intelligent Systems*, 16(2) 72–79 (2001)
23. T. Nishida: Social Intelligence Design for the Web. IEEE Computer, 35(11) 37–41 (November 2002)
24. M. Missikoff, R. Navigli, P. Velardi: Integrated Approach to Web Ontology Learning and Engineering, IEEE Computer, 35(11) 60–63 (November 2002)
25. S. Ohsuga and H. Yamauchi: Multi-Layer Logic - A Predicate Logic Including Data Structure as Knowledge Representation Language. New Generation Computing, 3(4) 403–439 (Springer, 1985)
26. S. Ohsuga: Framework of Knowledge Based Systems – Multiple Meta-Level Architecture for Representing Problems and Problem Solving Processes. Knowledge Based Systems, 3(4) 204–214 (Elsevier, 1990)
27. N. Porter (ed.): Webster's Revised Unabridged Dictionary, G&C. Merriam Co., (http://humanities.uchicago.edu/forms_unrest/webster.form.html) (1913)
28. P. Raghavan: Social Networks: From the Web to the Enterprise, IEEE Internet Computing, 6(1), 91–94 (2002)
29. J. Srivastava, R. Cooley, M. Deshpande, P. Tan: Web Usage Mining: Discovery and Applications of Usage Patterns from Web Data. *SIGKDD Explorations, Newsletter of SIGKDD*, 1, 12–23 (2000)
30. M. Weiser: The Computer for the Twenty-First Century, Scientific American, September, 94–10 (1991)
31. M. Weiser: The Future of Ubiquitous Computing on Campus, CACM 41(1), 41–42 (1998)
32. A.R. Simon, S.L. Shaffer: *Data Warehousing and Business Intelligence for e-Commerce* (Morgan Kaufmann, 2001)
33. S. Wasserman, K. Faust: *Social Network Analysis* (Cambridge University Press, 1994)
34. H. Yamauchi and S. Ohsuga: Loose coupling of KAUS with existing RDBMSs. Data & Knowledge Engineering, 5(4) 227–251 (North-Holland, 1990)
35. Y.Y. Yao, N. Zhong, J. Liu, S. Ohsuga: Web Intelligence (WI): Research Challenges and Trends in the New Information Age. In: N. Zhong, Y. Y. Yao, J. Liu, S. Ohsuga (eds.) *Web Intelligence: Research and Development*, LNAI 2198, (Springer, 2001) 1–17
36. Y.Y. Yao, N. Zhong, J. Huang, C. Ou, C. Liu: Using Market Value Functions for Targeted Marketing Data Mining, International Journal of Pattern Recognition and Artificial Intelligence, 16(8) 1117-1131 (World Scientific, 2002)
37. Y. Ye, J. Liu, A. Moukas: Agents in Electronic Commerce. *Special Issue on Intelligent Agents in Electronic Commerce, Electronic Commerce Research Journal* (2001)
38. N. Zhong, J. Liu, Y.Y. Yao, S. Ohsuga: Web Intelligence (WI), *Proc. 24th IEEE Computer Society International Computer Software and Applications Conference (COMPSAC 2000)*, (IEEE CS Press, 2000) 469–470

39. N. Zhong, C. Liu, S. Ohsuga: Dynamically Organizing KDD Process in a Multi-Agent Based KDD System, in J. Liu, N. Zhong, Y.Y. Tang, P. Wang (eds.) Agent Engineering (World Scientific, 2001) 93–122

40. N. Zhong: Knowledge Discovery and Data Mining, *The Encyclopedia of Microcomputers*, 27(Supplement 6) 235–285 (Marcel Dekker, 2001)

41. N. Zhong, Y.Y. Yao, J. Liu, S. Ohsuga (eds.): *Web Intelligence: Research and Development*, LNAI 2198 (Springer, 2001)

42. N. Zhong, J. Liu, S. Ohsuga, J. Bradshaw (eds.): *Intelligent Agent Technology: Research and Development* (World Scientific, 2001)

43. N. Zhong, J.Z. Dong, C. Liu, and S. Ohsuga: A Hybrid Model for Rule Discovery in Data, *Knowledge Based Systems, An International Journal*, Elsevier Science, 14(7) 397–412 (2001)

44. N. Zhong: Representation and Construction of Ontologies for Web Intelligence, *International Journal of Foundations of Computer Science (IJFCS)*, 13(4) 555–570 (World Scientific, 2002)

45. N. Zhong, J. Liu, Y.Y. Yao: In Search of the Wisdom Web. IEEE Computer, 35(11) 27–31 (2002)

46. N. Zhong, J. Liu, Y.Y. Yao (eds.): *Web Intelligence* (Springer, 2003)

47. N. Zhong, J. Liu, Y.Y. Yao: Web Intelligence (WI): A New Paradigm for Developing the Wisdom Web and Social Network Intelligence. In N. Zhong, J. Liu, Y.Y. Yao (eds.): *Web Intelligence*, 1–16 (Springer, 2003)

From Search Engines to Question-Answering Systems – The Need for New Tools

Lotfi A. Zadeh[*]

Professor in the Graduate School and Director, Berkeley initiative in Soft Computing (BISC)
Computer Science Division and the Electronics Research Laboratory, Department of EECS
University of California, Berkeley, CA 94720-1776
Tel.: 510-642-4959; Fax: 510-642-1712;
zadeh@cs.berkeley.edu

Search engines, with Google at the top, have many remarkable capabilities. But what is not among them is the deduction capability – the capability to synthesize an answer to a query by drawing on bodies of information which are resident in various parts of the knowledge base. It is this capability that differentiates a question-answering system, Q/A system for short, from a search engine.

Construction of Q/A systems has a long history in AI. Interest in Q/A systems peaked in the seventies and eighties, and began to decline when it became obvious that the available tools were not adequate for construction of systems having significant question-answering capabilities. However, Q/A systems in the form of domain-restricted expert systems have proved to be of value, and are growing in versatility, visibility and importance.

Search engines as we know them today owe their existence and capabilities to the advent of the Web. A typical search engine is not designed to come up with answers to queries exemplified by "How many Ph.D. degrees in computer science were granted by Princeton University in 1996?" or "What is the name and affiliation of the leading eye surgeon in Boston?" or "What is the age of the oldest son of the President of Finland?" or "What is the fastest way of getting from Paris to London?"

Upgrading a search engine to a Q/A system is a complex, effort-intensive, open-ended problem. Semantic Web and related systems for upgrading quality of search may be viewed as steps in this direction. But what may be argued, as is done in the following, is that existing tools, based as they are on bivalent logic and probability theory, have intrinsic limitations. The principal obstacle is the nature of world knowledge.

The centrality of world knowledge in human cognition, and especially in reasoning and decision-making, has long been recognized in AI. The Cyc system of Douglas Lenat is a repository of world knowledge. The problem is that much of world knowledge consists of perceptions. Reflecting the bounded ability of sensory organs, and ultimately the brain, to resolve detail and store information, perceptions are intrinsically imprecise. More specifically, perceptions are f-granular in the sense that (a) the

---

[*] Research supported in part by ONR N00014-00-1-0621, ONR Contract N00014-99-C-0298, NASA Contract NCC2-1006, NASA Grant NAC2-117, ONR Grant N00014-96-1-0556, ONR Grant FDN0014991035, ARO Grant DAAH 04-961-0341 and the BISC Program of UC Berkeley.

E. Menasalvas et al. (Eds.): AWIC 2003, LNAI 2663, pp. 15-17, 2003.
© Springer-Verlag Berlin Heidelberg 2003

boundaries of perceived classes are fuzzy; and (b) the perceived values of attributes are granular, with a granule being a clump of values drawn together by indistinguishability, similarity, proximity or functionality. What is not widely recognized is that f-granularity of perceptions put them well beyond the reach of computational bivalent-logic-based theories. For example, the meaning of a simple perception described as "Most Swedes are tall," does not admit representation in predicate logic and/or probability theory.

Dealing with world knowledge needs new tools. A new tool which is suggested for this purpose is the fuzzy-logic-based method of computing with words and perceptions (CWP), with the understanding that perceptions are described in a natural language. A concept which plays a key role in CWP is that of Precisiated Natural Language (PNL). It is this language that is the centerpiece of our approach to reasoning and decision-making with world knowledge.

A concept which plays an essential role on PNL is that of precisiability. More specifically, a proposition, p, in a natural language, NL, is PL precisiable, or simply precisiable, if it is translatable into a mathematically well defined language termed precisiation language, PL. Examples of precisiation languages are: the languages of propositional logic; predicate logic; modal logic; etc.; and Prolog; LISP; SQL; etc. These languages are based on bivalent logic. In the case of PNL, the precisiation language is a fuzzy-logic-based language referred to as the Generalized Constraint Language. (GCL). By construction, GCL is maximally expressive.

A basic assumption underlying GCL is that, in general, the meaning of a proposition, p, in NL may be represented as a generalized constraint of the form X isr R, where X is the constrained variable; R is the constraining relation, and r is a discrete-valued variable, termed modal variable, whose values define the modality of the constraint, that is, the way in which R constrains X. The principal modalities are; possibilistic (r=blank); probabilistic (r=p); veristic (r=v); usuality (r=u); random set (r=rs); fuzzy graph (r=fg); and Pawlak set (r=ps). In general, X, R and r are implicit in p. Thus, precisiation of p, that is, translation of p into GCL, involves explicitation of X, R and r. GCL is generated by (a) combining generalized constraints; and (b) generalized constraint propagation, which is governed by the rules of inference in fuzzy logic. The translation of p expressed as a generalized constraint is referred to as the GC-form of p, GC(p). GC(p) may be viewed as a generalization of the concept of logical form. An abstraction of the GC-form is referred to as a protoform (prototypical form) of p, and is denoted as PF(p). For example, the protoform of p: "Most Swedes are tall" is Q A's are B's, where A and B are labels of fuzzy sets, and Q is a fuzzy quantifier. Two propositions p and q are said to be PF-equivalent if they have identical protoforms. For example, "Most Swedes are tall," and "Not many professors are rich," are PF-equivalent. In effect, a protoform of p is its deep semantic structure. The protoform language, PFL, consists of protoforms of elements of GCL.

With the concepts of GC-form and protoform in place, PNL may be defined as a subset of NL which is equipped with two dictionaries: (a) from NL to GCL; and (b) from GCL to PFL. In addition, PNL is equipped with a multiagent modular deduction database, DDB, which contains rules of deduction in PFL. A simple example of a rule of deduction in PFL which is identical to the compositional rule of inference in fuzzy logic, is: if X is A and (X, Y) is B then Y is A∘B, where A∘B is the composition of A and B, defined by

$$\mu_B(v) = \sup_u (\mu_A(u) \wedge \mu_B(u,v)),$$

where μ_A and μ_B are the membership functions of A and B, respectively, and $\wedge$ is min or, more generally a T-norm. The rules of deduction in DDB are organized into modules and submodules, with each module and submodule associated with an agent who controls execution of rules of deduction and passing of results of execution.

In our approach, PNL is employed in the main to represent information in the world knowledge database (WKD). For example, the items:

- If X/Person works in Y/City then it is likely that X lives in or near Y
- If X/Person lives in Y/City then it is likely that X works in or near Y

are translated into GCL as:

Distance (Location (Residence (X/Person), Location (Work (X/Person) isu near

where isu, read as ezoo, is the usuality constraint. The corresponding protoform is:

F (A(B(X/C), A(E(X/C)) isu G.

A concept which plays a key role in organization of world knowledge is that of an epistemic (knowledge-directed) lexicon (EL). Basically, an epistemic lexicon is a network of nodes and weighted links, with node i representing an object in the world knowledge database, and a weighted link from node i to node j representing the strength of association between i and j. The name of an object is a word or a composite word, e.g., car, passenger car or Ph.D. degree. An object is described by a relation or relations whose fields are attributes of the object. The values of an attribute may be granulated and associated with granulated probability and possibility distributions. For example, the values of a granular attribute may be labeled small, medium and large, and their probabilities may be described as low, high and low, respectively. Relations which are associated with an object serve as PNL-based descriptions of the world knowledge about the object. For example, a relation associated with an object labeled Ph.D. degree may contain attributes labeled Eligibility, Length.of.study, Granting.institution, etc. The knowledge associated with an object may be context-dependent. What should be stressed is that the concept of an epistemic lexicon is intended to be employed in representation of world knowledge – which is largely perception-based – rather than Web knowledge, which is not.

As a very simple illustration of the use of an epistemic lexicon, consider the query "How many horses received the Ph.D. degree from Princeton University in 1996." No existing search engine would come up with the correct answer, "Zero, since a horse cannot be a recipient of a Ph.D. degree." To generate the correct answer, the attribute Eligibility in the Ph.D. entry in EL should contain the condition "Human, usually over twenty years of age."

In conclusion, the main thrust of the fuzzy-logic-based approach to question-answering which is outlined in this abstract, is that to achieve significant question-answering capability it is necessary to develop methods of dealing with the reality that much of world knowledge is perception-based. Dealing with perception-based information is more complex and more effort-intensive than dealing with measurement-based information. In this instance, as in many others, complexity is the price that has to be paid to achieve superior performance.

Artificial Intelligence Techniques in Retrieval of Visual Data Semantic Information

Ryszard Tadeusiewicz and Marek R. Ogiela

University of Mining and Metallurgy, Institute of Automatics
Al. Mickiewicza 30, PL-30-059 Kraków, Poland
{rtad,mog}@biocyb.ia.agh.edu.pl

Abstract. The development of the information society results in the fact that an ever increasing amount of information is stored in computer databases, and a growing number of practical activities depend on efficient retrieval and association of the data. In the case of textual information, the problem of retrieving the information on a specific subject is comparatively simple (although it has not been fully solved from a scientific point of view). On the other hand, the application of databases that store multimedia information, particularly images, causes many more difficulties. In such cases, the connection between the subject-matter of the content (i.e. the meaning of the image) and its form is often very unclear; while the retrieving activities as a rule aim at the image content, the accessible methods of searching refer to its form. With the aim to partially solve those emerging problems this paper presents new opportunities for applying linguistic algorithms of artificial intelligence to undertake tasks referred to by the authors as the automatic understanding of images. A successful obtaining of the crucial semantic content of an image thanks to the application of the methods presented in this paper may contribute considerably to the creation of intelligent systems that function also on the basis of multimedia data. In the future the technique of automatic understanding of images may become one of the effective tools for storing visual data in scattered multimedia databases and knowledge based systems. The application of the automatic understanding of images will enable the creation of automatic image semantic analysis systems which make it possible to build intelligent multimedia data retrieval or interpretation systems. This article proves that structural techniques of artificial intelligence may be useful when solving a given problem. They may be applied in the case of tasks related to automatic classification and machine perception of semantic pattern content in order to determine the semantic meaning of the patterns. This article paper presents ways of applying such techniques in the creation of web based systems and systems for retrieving and interpreting selected medical images. The proposed approach will be described in selected examples of medical images obtained in radiological and MRI diagnosis, however the methodology under consideration has general applications.

1 Introduction

The intelligent multimedia Internet applications that are created within the framework of specialist intelligent information systems belong to the most dynamically developing areas in computer science and technology. Such systems have increasingly wide

E. Menasalvas et al. (Eds.): AWIC 2003, LNAI 2663, pp. 18-27, 2003.

applications practically in all fields of life and it would be impossible to list them here. In order to focus the reader's attention on one particular problem, this paper will deal with multimedia information systems in medicine, especially with the medical image databases (X-ray, MR, ultrasonographic ones and many others). Such databases store and offer image medical data mainly within the hospital PACS systems. However, the methods of the image semantic content intelligent discovering and coding that are described in this paper may be also used by medical advisory systems, for elements of telemedical techniques and for the systems of analysis and medical diagnosis support.

Due to the possibility to store, apply and process a significantly large amount of multimedia information included in specialist databases, a rapid semantic interpretation of the data being analyzed has become crucially important. In the case of medical images it often happens that the same illnesses are visualized in various forms of images that are registered and processed (Fig. 1)

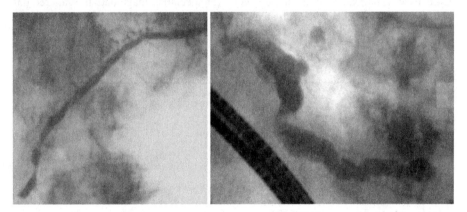

Fig. 1. Two images carrying the same message (in both images symptoms of cancer of pancreas are visible)

This is the reason why attempts have been made for a long time to create a system that would automatically find the message (i.e. the content) carried by analyzed medical images. The aim has been both to be able to classify and diagnose them (e.g. for the needs of medical diagnosis) and to carry out the automatic indexation tasks (followed by intelligent retrieval) of multimedia databases. Such a system should be differentiated from better known (and generally much simpler) systems of automatic image recognition that are occasionally applied in similar tasks (especially in diagnosis support). The difference between image recognition and perception lies mainly in the fact that in the case of recognition in the course of computer analysis the belonging of objects in an image (or its main feature, e.g. its texture) to some defined classes is determined. The perception of an image requires a deeper analysis aimed at the determination of significant semantic features. Such features enable a further semantic image interpretation or a semantically oriented indexation when in images objects are retrieved that come from various diagnostic examinations or determine different disease entities. Due to the fact that the number of combinations of features that characterize images is by no way limited, it can be assumed that perception may refer the image to potentially unlimited number of classes. This indicates that when understanding an image one should refer to a tool that can currently generate its descriptions and not just select a suitable item from a prepared list. Therefore in the course of creating techniques of automatic image perception, specified languages of image description must be a natural tool, and the whole field must be based on mathematical linguistics.

2 A General Overview of the System

An intelligent pattern understanding information system should enable us to conduct a fully automatic semantic analysis. Such an analysis is directed not only at simple recognition but also at a deeper understanding and determining the semantic content of the analysed images. A synthesis of the thus obtained information which specifies the medical meaning of the analysed images allows one also to create effective mechanisms used in indexation tasks and to search for specialist image data in scattered databases. A general scheme of such an analysis is presented in Fig. 2.

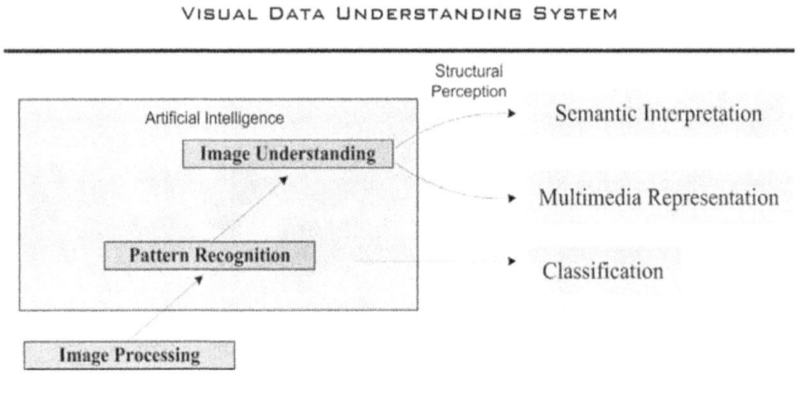

Fig. 2. General schema of medical pattern analysis and semantic classification in Visual Data Understanding Systems

In image perception systems the image understanding process is characterised by a two-way flow of information. The stream of empirical data, which originates from the sub-system, registers and analyses the image, interferes with the stream of expectations. The expectations can have features with some postulates specifying the important features of the analysed image with the assumption that the content of the image corresponds to one possible variant of its semantic interpretation (interpretation of its meaning). It is assumed that the system understating images has a set of generators for the previously mentioned expectations at its disposal; the generators are connected with various hypothetical methods of the meritorious interpretation of the image content [2]. Such a structure of the image understanding system generally corresponds to one of the psychological models of visual perception which is based on the concept of the use of knowledge about objects perceived.

Constructing those systems is extremely efficient in the case of the structural analysis of complex shapes of chest or abdominal cavity organs which are characterised by an occurrence of morphological lesions typical of developing disease processes.

A possibility to conduct such a cognitive analysis will be presented on the examples of analysis of patterns received during the diagnostic examinations of renal pelvis, pancreatic ducts and the spinal cord (Fig. 3).

Patterns and semantic descriptions

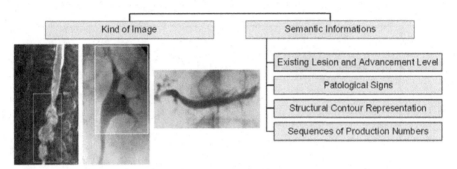

Fig. 3. Analysed images of the spinal cord (left) urinary tracts (middle) and pancreatic duct (right) and semantic information necessary to understand the medical meaning of the pathologies visible in them.

For the analysis of the mentioned structures and for the verification of lesions advancement level, a graph grammar of type EDT [1, 2] and an attributed context-free grammars of type LALR (1) have been proposed. These method formalisms have been applied to detect changes in the width of different structures which are visible in graphs. These graphs are obtained thanks to applications at the image pre-processing stage, a straightening transformation, which allows for the production of graphs of straightened structures while preserving the morphological changes occurring in them.

3   Retrieving Visual Data Semantic Information

Specifying the semantic content of medical image data is possible due to the use of various formalisms which constitute both the sequential and the graph methods of structural image analysis. In particular, these are context-free attributed grammars, languages of description of shape features and tree or graph grammars.

A general approach in the application of structural pattern classification algorithms for the creation of perceptual descriptions for analyzed structures follows. Starting from defining a simple shape elements a general grammar description of the considered organ is built. Such descriptions in the form of sequences of terminal symbols belong to the languages generated by the introduced grammar. The main analysis and recognition of pathological signs are based on parsing algorithms which analyze input sequences and reduce them to one of the known categories. Such an analysis provides both the diagnosis concerning the type and the progression degree of a discovered irregularity and the additional information and parameters that make it possible to create a description of the external morphology of the structure under examination and the generation paths of the description with the application of derivating rules of a defined formal grammar. Before coming to the recognition of the changes it is necessary to preserve the sequence of operations, which are included in the image pre-processing [3, 6]. The goal of this analysis is to obtain new representation in the form of width graphs, which show the pathological changes occurring in these structures.

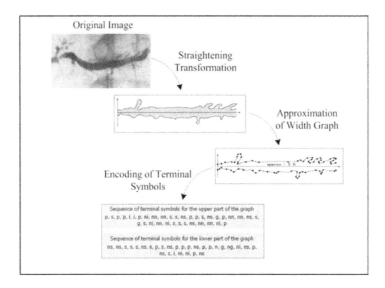

Fig. 4. An example of the application of preliminary processing stages, and the way of creating syntactic descriptions for the outer boundaries.

During the initial analysis of visualisations, the following operations are executed: segmentation and skeletonisation of the research structures, the application of a straightening transformation to transform the contour of the analysed structure in two-dimensional space into one-dimensional graph form which shows a profile of a straightened organ [1]. The graphs obtained in a such way are the starting point in the classification of morphological features by using context-free grammars.

In order to define primary components on the obtained width graphs as terminal symbols describing these components, an algorithm of line approximation was used [3]. As a result, sequence of terminal symbols for every graph was received, which constitute an input to syntax analysers and semantic classifiers. An example of application of such operations is presented on Fig. 4.

4   An Understanding of the Nature of Changes in the Renal Pelvis Shape

An example of understanding the gist of morphological lesions of the shape with the use the graph grammars will be presented on an actual task in which an analysis of the correctness of the renal pelvis and renal calyxes is to be made on the visualised uro-graph images (Fig. 5). For this purpose a grammar of the EDT class has been pro-posed [2].

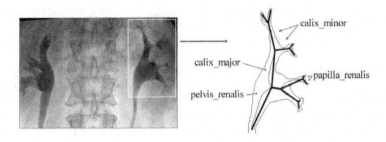

Fig. 5. Attempt at automatic understanding of the shape of renal pelvises. A urogram of healthy renal pelvis and calyxes together with a skeleton and graph description obtained after approxi-mating the skeleton

Although these structures are characterized by unusual shape variations, it is possi-ble to distinguish certain common features which characterize all proper structures us-ing a number of smaller and bigger calyxes revealed in the renal sinus [5]. To de-scribe the shapes of these structures we have suggested an expansive graph grammar defined with the aim of analyzing the skeleton morphology of investigated renal pel-vises and renal calyxes. A graph grammar describing the skeletons of renal pelvises and renal calyxes is defined in such a way that the root of the graph is defined by the location bifurcation in the bigger calyxes. Next, its consequents are determined by branch points of the second degree which is the beginning of the smaller calyxes. The last layer of vertices is defined by branch points of the third degree, that is, branches which appear in a case when the renal papillae has a concave shape.

To characterize the original components which are used in graph grammar, an ap-proximation algorithm for the skeleton branches in the pelvis and the renal calyxes can be applied. Then each branch can be identified with a single section whose ends are determined by the ends of the approximated branch. Next, to each determined segment are assigned edge terminal labels, depending on the angle of its inclination.

To diagnose morphological changes in renal pelvises the following graph grammar was used: $G_{EDT}=(\Sigma, \Gamma, r, P, Z)$, where $\Sigma = \Sigma_N \cup \Sigma_T$ is a set of terminal and non-terminal vertex labels defined in the following way:

$\Sigma_T = \{pelvis\_renalis, calix\_major, calix\_minor, papilla\_renalis\}$
$\Sigma_N = \{PELVIS\_RENALIS, CALIX\_MAJOR, CALIX\_MINOR\}$
r - is a function which assigns to the graph vertex the number of its consequents
$\Gamma = \{x, y, z\}$ - is a set of edge labels for $y \in (-30°, 30°), x \in (30°, 180°), z \in (-30°, -180°)$
Z={PELVIS_RENALIS} - is a finite set of starting graphs

P- is a set of production:

1. PELVIS_RENALIS → pelvis_renalis(xCALIX_MAJOR yCALIX_MAJOR zCALIX_MAJOR)
    → pelvis_renalis(xCALIX_MAJOR yCALIX_MAJOR)
    → pelvis_renalis(xCALIX_MAJOR zCALIX_MAJOR)
    → pelvis_renalis(yCALIX_MAJOR zCALIX_MAJOR)
2. CALIX_MAJOR → calix_major(xCALIX_MINOR yCALIX_MINOR zCALIX_MINOR)
    → calix_major(xCALIX_MINOR yCALIX_MINOR)
    → calix_major(xCALIX_MINOR zCALIX_MINOR)
    → calix_major(yCALIX_MINOR zCALIX_MINOR)
3. CALIX_MINOR → calix_minor($x$papilla_renalis) | calix_minor($y$papilla_renalis)
    → calix_minor($z$papilla_renalis) | calix_minor($x$papilla_renalis $y$papilla_renalis)
4. CALIX_MINOR → calix_minor($x$papilla_renalis $z$papilla_renalis)
    → calix_minor($y$papilla_renalis $z$papilla_renalis)

The first group of productions defines the different kinds of normal renal pelvises i.e. having two or three smaller calyxes. The succeeding productions define the form of bigger calyxes formed from two or more smaller calyxes. The last group defines the proper form of renal papillae which obtains a fork form during the skeletonisation, which means that it finishes with short branches which arise only when it is concave to the interior of a smaller calyx. Convex forms during skeletonisation are thinned to the line without end branches, which results from the properties of skeletonisation algorithms.

5   Interpretation of Spinal Cord Visualizations

The application of sequential methods to extract important semantic information from images will be shown in the example of syntactic analysis of spinal cord images.

In the case of the spine and spinal cord MRI image analyses, the aim of the diagnosis is to find changes that may be evidence of several disease entities such as encephalomeningocele, different inflammatory states, ischaemia of the meninges or the spinal cord, and the most serious cases of intraspinal and extraspinal tumours. An unambiguous identification of all entities with the application of the diagnostic program is extremely difficult due to rather subtle differences that are decisive in a correct classification. However, it turns out that a structural analysis may be very useful when determining the degree of the progression of an illness entity by means of defining the level of changes in the spinal cord morphology and determining the degree of the spinal cord and spinal compression [5].

For an analysis of this structure a context-free grammar was prepared which allows us to identify symptoms, and to draw diagnostic conclusions concerning the essence of visible pathology. The general form of the context-free grammar is the following: $G = (V_N, V_T, SP, STS)$, where V_N - set of non-terminal symbols, V_T - set of terminal symbols, SP - set of production, STS - starting symbol of grammar.

In the case of the analysis of the spinal cord image, the grammar was defined in the following way:

V_N = {LESION, NARROWING, ENLARGEMENT, N, U, D}
V_T = {n, u, d} for n∈[-10°, 10°], u∈(10°, 180°), d∈(-10°, -180°)
STS = LESION
SP:

1. LESION → NARROWING   Lesion=narrowing
2. LESION → ENLARGEMENT   lesion=enlargement
3. NARROWING → D N U | D U | D N
4. ENLARGEMENT → U N D | U D | U N
5. N → n | n N $w_{sym}:=w_{sym}+w_n$; $h_{sym}:=h_{sym}+h_n$
6. U → u | u U $w_{sym}:=w_{sym}+w_u$; $h_{sym}:=h_{sym}+h_u$
7. D → d | d D $w_{sym}:=w_{sym}+w_d$; $h_{sym}:=h_{sym}+h_d$

This grammar permits us to detect different forms of narrowing and enlargements which characterise the different disease units (neoplasm or inflammation processes). Using the attributes permits us to calculate the numerical parameters of detected morphological changes which allows us in turn to characterize the degree of lesions.

The simplicity of this grammar results mainly from the big generation capacity of context-free grammars which are understood mainly as possibilities to describe complex shapes by means of a small number of introductory rules that are grammar productions. A totally different situation is in the analysis of pathological lesions in the main pancreatic ducts where a bigger number of symptoms and the variety of their shapes result in the necessity to introduce more complex grammar [1].

6 Selected Results

Thanks to the application of the presented context-free grammars it is possible quite precisely to detect different kinds of irregularities in the investigated structures. In the case of the syntactical analysis using context-free or graph grammars, a recognition program delivers almost complete information concerning the visual morphological irregularities of investigated organs.

An analysis of the morphological changes was carried out on the basis of a set of a dozen or so images (urograms, pancreatic, and spinal cord images). With regard to the graph and context-free grammars, parsers were constructed to serve the syntactical analysis. Because of the analysis of these images in each case we have obtained the kind of recognized symptom and a sequence of production numbers, which lead to grammar derivations of the shape description of such lesions. Such sequences create a proper description of analyzed shapes and have been stored in an indexing record.

The results obtained because of the application of the characterized methods, confirm the importance of syntactical methods in the perceptual analysis and understanding of medical visualizations. The efficiency of gaining recognition of information with semantic character, in all cases exceeded the threshold of 90%. In the pancreatic duct image analysis, owing to the additional use of procedures based on languages of description of shape features, the efficiency reached 95%. The grammar for the analysis of pancreas images was presented in [1, 2].

In Fig. 6 are presented examples which show the description of the changes in question for pancreatic duct and spinal cord images. The recognition process is based on production numbers generated as an output string by syntax analyzers. Recognized symptoms are marked by the bold line.

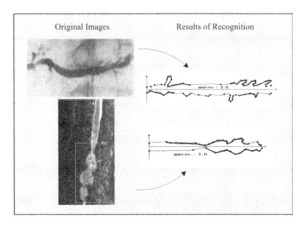

Fig. 6. Results of disease symptom recognition and understanding using syntactical methods of pattern recognition. Width diagrams show the place in which the looked-for lesion was diagnosed. Its structural description with the use of terminal symbols and the proper production sequences constitutes theirs unambiguous descriptions.

7   Conclusion

The development of the Internet and techniques of visual data storing (including medical data) made access to practically any database, with the information coming from diagnostic research, extremely easy. However, the automatic analysis and intelligent interpretation of the data by the information system is still a significant problem. In order to solve this problem advanced techniques of artificial intelligence must be applied that will enable the creation of systems that can both recognize and understand (to some degree, of course) processed data in the form of images. Man has such abilities and this is the reason why he can quickly conduct various analyses which results in a quick and meaningful perception of certain crucial elements of an image. At the same time he has the ability not to concentrate on elements that do not have any special semantic meaning.

Thus the aim of the presented algorithms was to show an innovative concept of the application of structural algorithms of artificial intelligence in the creation of Internet intelligent systems aimed at understanding and determining the semantic meaning of medical images of certain classes. It is worth mentioning that machine perception using such methods may lead to an automatic interpretation of medical images in the way it is done by a specialist. It may enable the determination of not only crucial changes but also the consequences of existing irregularities and finally the optimal directions and methods of conducting a suitable therapy.

As a result of our research we discovered possibilities for applying linguistic algorithms to syntactic pattern analysis and classification, and it was possible to construct an intelligent information system allowing us to recognise and understand important diagnostic lesions which were visible on analysed patterns. These methods have turned out to be not only very efficient in the direct morphological deformation recognition of various medical images, but they also allow us to introduce very effective methods of creating meaningful descriptions of examined images as well as semantic representations. Research conducted proves that the systems discussed in this paper enable us to reach such an intelligent understanding of a pattern. Owing to this, they allow us to efficiently detect pathological lesions of dangerous diseases.

Understanding the image content may be used to effectively support the diagnostic process. Automatic understanding of the image content can have numerous further applications: for example such information can be used to monitor therapeutic processes or to forecast disease development as well as the patient's future state of health.

Furthermore, by gaining an efficient method of guaranteeing an automatic understanding of the medical image content we can treat results obtained by this method as special description indexing images in a big multimedia database. In order for this type of indexing to be prepared, first images must be stored in a data base and then images in the form of queries addressed to that data base will allow one to enhance the process of context search for image information. Currently this process of context-data search in multimedia databases cannot be completely done.

Acknowledgements. This work was supported by University of Mining and Metallurgy under Grant No. 10.10.120.39.

References

1. Ogiela, M.R., Tadeusiewicz, R.: Syntactic pattern recognition for X-ray diagnosis of pancreatic cancer. IEEE Engineering In Medicine and Biology Magazine, 19 (2000) 94–105
2. Ogiela, M.R., Tadeusiewicz, R.: Image Understanding Methods in Biomedical Informatics and Digital Imaging, Journal of Biomedical Informatics, Vol. 34, No. 6 (2001) 377–386
3. Ogiela, M.R., Tadeusiewicz, R.: Advanced image understanding and pattern analysis methods in Medical Imaging, Proceedings of the Fourth IASTED International Conference SIGNAL and IMAGE PROCESSING (SIP 2002), Kaua'i, Hawaii, USA (2002) 583–588
4. Sonka, M., Fitzpatrick, J.M. (eds.): Handbook of Medical Imaging: Vol. 2- Medical image processing and analysis. SPIE PRESS, Bellingham WA (2000)
5. Burgener, F.A., Meyers, S.P., Tan, R.: Differential diagnosis in Magnetic Resonance Imaging. Thieme, Stuttgart (2001)
6. Javidi, B. (ed.): Image Recognition and Classification. Marcel Dekker, Inc., New York (2002)

A Framework to Integrate Business Goals in Web Usage Mining

E. Hochsztain[1*], S. Millán[2], B. Pardo[3], J.M. Peña[3], and E. Menasalvas[3+]

[1]Facultad de Ingeniería - Universidad ORT Uruguay
[2]Facultad de Ingeniería. Universidad del Valle. Cali. Colombia
[3]Facultad de Informática UPM. Madrid Spain
esthoc@adinet.com.uy
millan@eisc.univalle.edu.co
bpardo@teldat.es
jmpena@fi.upm.es
emenasalvas@fi.upm.es

Abstract. Web mining is a broad term that has been used to refer to the process of information discovery from Web sources: content, structure, and usage. Information collected by web servers and kept in the server log is the main source of data for analyzing user navigation patterns. Notwithstanding, knowing the most frequent user paths is not enough: it is necessary to integrate web mining with the company site goals in order to make sites more competitive. The concept of **Web Goal Mining** is introduced in this paper to refer to the process information discovery of the relationship between site visitors and sponsor goals.

1 Introduction

Explosive growth in size and usage of the World Wide Web has made it necessary for web site administrators to track and analyze the navigation patterns of web site visitors. The web is a rich source of information about user navigation patterns, content of pages and site structures making it a perfect target for data mining. Web mining is a broad term that has been used to refer to the process of information discovery from Web sources (Web content), discovery of the structure of the Web servers (Web structure) and mining for user browsing and access patterns through logs analysis (Web usage) [2,12]. Information collected by web servers and kept in the server log is the main source of data for analyzing user navigation patterns. Web servers commonly record an entry in a Web log file for every access. Common components of a log file include: IP address, access time, request method, URL of the object or page accessed, data transmission protocol, return code and number of bytes transmitted.

Nevertheless, these data have to be enhanced with information about the business, so that patterns can be extracted to provide the company with information about users and their activities. Adaptive web sites are web sites in which information is custom-

---

* Research has been partially supported by Programa de Desarrollo Tecnológico (Uruguay).
+ Research has been partially supported by UPM (Spain) under project WEBP-RT.

E. Menasalvas et al. (Eds.): AWIC 2003, LNAI 2663, pp. 28–36, 2003.

ized according to the user. Most of the approaches to build this kind of servers are based on the user's identity and profile.

A lot of approaches [9,11–13,15–20] propose to track and analyze clickstream data to obtain most frequent paths. Most of these approaches calculate user profiles taking into account this information. Many companies have focused more on web site traffic than on their profitability. However, the number of visitors does not necessarily correlate with the number of customers ("those who purchase at the site"). Though marketing has generally focused on the former campaigns should also be focused on customers, those who ultimately determine profits.

Thus, knowing the most frequent user paths is not enough. But, it is necessary to integrate web mining with the company site goals in order to make sites more competitive. One of the reasons web mining may fail is that most of the web mining firms concentrate exclusively on the analysis of clickstream data that contain information about users, their page views, and the timing of their page views. In order to solve this problem, in [7] authors propose an algorithm that considers information on both server logs and business goals to improve traditional web analysis. The focus is on the business and its goals, and this is reflected on the computation of link values, integrating server logs analysis with both the background that comes from the business goals and the available knowledge about the business area. They do not, however, explicitly show how to compute or implement the approach. Taking their proposal as the underlying idea, it is possible to establish that, through web site analysis, both visitors and web site sponsors have to be taken into account.

Other authors [22] present different session reconstruction strategies in terms of either proactive or reactive behavior. They also include a set of different metrics for the evaluation of the reconstruction process. And in [23] a more semantic and context-rich approach based on ontologies is proposed.

It has been shown that web mining must help both users and sponsors of a web site to achieve their goals. Our proposal, unlike traditional web mining approaches, sets the focus on the achievement of site sponsors goals.

A Web site is designed to serve the company needs. Thus, the way the site is used must add value not only for users but also for the company [26]. Former Web Mining approaches focus on site usage: tracking how many visitors there are and how well the site fits their needs. Summing up, the only point of view taking into account is the user's one.

These approaches are based on the idea that if users do not feel comfortable while navigating the company's site, they will not become customers. So, in order to turn users into customers and to avoid current customers to churn, it is necessary to fulfill users' needs.

However, achieving visitors satisfaction is not enough. It must be kept in mind that the site main goal is not just customer satisfaction, but contributing to company success [26]. It is possible that visitors do not use the site in the way it is intended to, nor responding to company needs. For instance, visitors to an electronic book shop may use the site as a catalog to look for books, read some reviews, and then go to a traditional, non web-based book shop to buy the selected items. Probably, that user feels that the site is very useful for him/her, but the goals of the site sponsor (selling books) are not being fulfilled.

Traditionally, clickstream data have been used to measure web sites success. However, using number of hits and page views to evaluate sites success is much like evaluating music quality by its length. Web advertising is another example. Advertising cost (through banners, for instance) is calculated counting clickthroughs. So, the advertiser pays each time a user clicks on the banner. Consequently, many companies use the same way to measure advertising effectiveness: number of visitors clicking the ad. But customers or sales are not being considered in this measure. In [21], authors state that, if the company goal is selling, the site must attract customers instead of mere visitors. According to this, it is not worth to track user's behavior and sponsor goals separately: it is necessary to analyze how the site is being used and how this usage affects the company's goals as a whole.

Traditional classification of Web Mining into three areas (content, structure and usage) does not consider sites sponsors or companies. Existing approaches do not explicitly consider that web sites are used by sponsor companies as a way to achieve their business goals, and consequently, it is necessary for these companies to measure site effectiveness from that point of view.

Hence, in order to consider this point of view, we introduce a new web mining approach over those already proposed in [2,12] called **Web Goal Mining**. We use the term Web Goal Mining to refer to the process of discovering information about the relationship between site visitors and site goals. The objective of Web Goal Mining is to evaluate the effectiveness of a web site according to the company's goals. In spite of the huge volume of data stored in the web, it is difficult to understand the relationship between user navigation data and site effectiveness in terms of site goals when trying to design "good pages" from the site users' point of view.

Based on navigation pattern discovery, a methodology to improve the success of web sites is proposed in [1, 9]. To improve the success of a site, the authors propose a model that measures and improve the success of the site. The proposed model takes into account the owner's corporate objectives, categorizes users according to their activities in pursuing those goals, and evaluates the site's success. The model can also be used on a regular basis.

In order to evaluate the success of the site, two measures (contact and conversion efficiency) are proposed in [3]. The success of the site is defined by the author in terms of its efficiency for transforming visitors into customers. On the other hand, Eighmey [4] presents a diagnostic method, Website Response Profile, for website planners and designers, that can be used to evaluate visitor reactions to the experience of any website.

The main purpose of this paper is to propose a framework to add value to already existing approaches [24]. Decision-making criteria related to design and content of web sites are needed, so that user behavior matches the objectives and expectations of web site owners. We are proposing therefore a set of criteria (elements) to evaluate web user behavior in terms of web site owners' objectives and to improve web content and design.

The proposed framework takes into account traditional commerce features. In traditional commerce, when a customer arrives at a particular business, her/his acquiring goods/services intention can be easily inferred. Therefore, arriving action has high value. However, if we find that the same customer (or profile) frequently visits the site but never buys anything, the arriving customer action will reduce its value. In the same way, we propose to analyze data of site visitors in order to discover the best ones according to the site business success criteria.

The paper has been organized as follows: Sect. 2 introduces the concept of Web Goal Mining. In Sect. 3 a description of the Web Goal Mining Framework is introduced. Section 4 presents both conclusions and future research lines.

2 Web Goal Mining

In the previous section, the need for considering the business's point of view when performing Web Mining task was presented, and the concept of Web Goal Mining to address this problem has been proposed. Nevertheless, it is necessary to define this concept in a more formal manner.

Web Goal Mining is defined as the process of discovering information formerly unknown and useful for making decisions. These decisions should allow the sponsor company to improve the effectiveness of its web site. Effectiveness is measured in terms of how well the company achieves its (business) goals through its web site. Web Mining has been traditionally divided into three interrelated areas: Web Content Mining, Web Usage Mining and Web Structure Mining [2,12]. In this sense, Web Content Mining has been used to refer to the process of extracting information from web pages content. Web Structure Mining makes reference to the process of information extraction from web topology based on existing links between web pages. Finally, Web Usage Mining has been used in reference to the process of information extraction on how the web is being used. This has been the traditional classification of web mining.

In none of these areas business goals are explicitly considered. This is to say that web sites sponsors use web sites as means for obtaining business's goals. Hence, sponsors need an accurate measure of Web site effectiveness according to the business's goals point of view. The purpose of a web site is to help companies reach the proposed target. Thus, we consider that any of these approaches can be enriched taking into account business's goals

We propose to analyze how well users' navigation fits company aims, how accurate Web site content reflects company's purposes and how much Web site structure contribute to achieve company's goals.

Hence, Web Goal Mining like Web Mining, may be divided into three main areas: Web Usage Goal Mining, Web Content Goal Mining and Web Structure Goal Mining, bringing information regarding the company and its goals together with traditional Web Mining areas.

- Clickstream data (Web logs) + Metadata + (Company + Company Goals) = Web Usage Goal Mining
- Links data + Metadata + (Company + Company Goals) = Web Structure Goal Mining
- Sites content data + Metadata + (Company + Company Goals) = Web Content Goal Mining

Once the Web Goal Mining concept has been defined more accurately, it is necessary to present more comprehensive definitions of what is meant when we refer to goals. We assume definitions for terms regarding objectives like the ones presented in [25]:

- Objective: An objective is a desired end result or condition expressed in measurable terms that can be achieved by the successful performance of one or more business or functional processes.
- Goal: A goal (or target) is the criterion by which you measure the accomplishment of an objective. Every objective must have a quantifiable goal or target.
- Strategy: A strategy is a method or procedure for accomplishing the related objective and achieving the desired goal.
- Performance Measure: A performance measure is an indicator built into a strategy that can measure progress toward satisfying the related strategy.
- Critical Success Factor (CSF): A CSF is a business function or activity that must be performed correctly and completely.
- Key Indicator: A key indicator is a measurement that is readily obtained by observation of a business process or activity, which provides data on how well a process or activity is performed.
- Variance or limits: The degree to which a key indicator can vary and still be within tolerance.

Last, incorporating data regarding the company and its goals to evaluate the web site leads us to consider the following subjects:

- Creating a representation model for company data
- Defining ways to represent company aims
- Analyzing goals at different levels of granularity: company wide goals or department wide ones; short, medium or long term ones and based on users' profiles, for instance.
- Finding the relationship between the web site and company objectives.
- Defining metrics to evaluate whether the site contributes to company goals, and how.

Once Web Goal Mining has been introduced we present an approach than can be categorized as a Web Goal Mining approach overlapping with Web Usage Mining. The approach assumes a webhouse in which information about users, goals, web site, and clickstream data is stored.

3   Web Goal Mining Framework

The proposed framework tries to increase Web Mining effectiveness adding information about business's goals. Web Goal Mining architecture is formed by the modules, depicted by Fig. 1:

- **Business Data**: This module incorporates gathering, preprocessing, modeling and storing data regarding business (goals, different points of view to evaluate those goals and company environment).
- **Web Data**: Module that gathers, preprocesses and stores web data (web logs, user profiles, web environment, navigational patterns, etc.). This module is also present in traditional Web Mining.
- **Web Enrichment Criteria**: This component gathers data on both web and business. Then it generates a common model that will be the base for Web Goal Mining analysis.
- **On-line Access Analysis**: This element applies the former model to current sessions in order to estimate how valuable the session will be for achieving company's goals.
- **Web Server Response**: Decisions and operational strategies to address user navigation towards more profitable web pages or services. These decisions would be mechanisms like special web-page contents, improvement/tuning of web server performance, special offers or advertisements, to name a few.

Web Enrichment Criteria should be reviewed as new decisions are proposed. This feedback data allow web site owner to review how data are integrated and which information is useful in terms of the business's goals. New information and the result of different proposed decisions should be included in a continuous iterative cycle.

The following table represents each module, the inputs it needs and the outputs it must produce.

Module	Input	Output
Business Data Harvesting	Interviews Focus groups Documentation Market Analysis	 Goals Sets Points of View Sets Environment Sets
Web Data Retrieving	Site topology Web Logs Relational Database Data Webhouse	Refined Web Logs
Web Logs Enrichement	Logs Taget, points of view, environments	Link values Page values

4 Conclusions

Under the assumption that "What it is interesting for the web user could not be profitable for the web site company", the Web Goal Mining approach has been defined. The objective of Web Goal Mining, differing from the traditional Web Mining concept, is to evaluate the effectiveness of a web site according to the company's goals.

In this paper we had introduced Web Goal Mining as a new and integrated web mining approach in which the relationship between Web Site and Company's Goals is considered. This contribution defines a new framework for how Business Objectives and Navigation Analysis should be combined. The purpose of this combination is to label web sessions in terms of profit-related criteria, closer to the objectives requested by the web site sponsors/owners. This innovative approach opens new and challenging research lines on the mechanisms and metrics appropriate to merge this information, as well as new decisions and strategies to redirect and seduce potentially profitable clients.

Our contribution identifies the different Web Goal Mining steps and the main targets to be provided for each of the phases this process is divided into. These phases are complex and their procedures require collaboration between both market-analysts and web development experts.

New challenges and future research directions are proposed. These open issues could be developed and addressed by multiple alternatives and the forecoming work on this framework will present them.

References

[1] Spiliopoulou M, Pohle C . Data Mining for Measuring and Improving the Success of Web Sites. Data mining and Knowledge Discovery, (5)1–2, 2001

[2] Han J. and Kamber M. (2001) Data Mining: Concepts and Techniques. Morgan Kaufmann Publishers.

[3] Berthon P., Pitt L., Watson R. The World Wide Web as an advertising medium. Journal of Advertising Research 36(1) pp. 43–54,1996

[4]   Eighmey J. On the Web: It's What You Say and How You Say It. Greenlee School of
      Journalism and Communication, Iowa State University
      http://www.Eighmey.Website.Response.Profile.htm
[5]   The CRM Handbook Jill Dyché – Addison Wesley 2001
[6]   Hu X., Cercone N. An OLAM Framework for Web Usage Mining and Business Intelli-
      gence Reporting – WCCI 2002
[7]   Menasalvas E. Hochsztain E. Sessions Value as measure of web site goal achievement.
      SNPD'2002. Madrid July 2002
[8]   Kimball R. Merz, R.The Data Webhouse Toolkit Wiley, 2000
[9]   Spiliopoulou M., Pohle C., Faulstich L. (1999) Improving the efectiveness of a web site
      with web usage mining. In Proceedings WEBKDD99.
[10] Menasalvas E, Millán S, Hochsztain E. (2002) A Granular Approach for Analyzing the
      Degree of Afability of a Web Site. In International Conference on Rough Sets and Current
      Trends in Computing RSCTC2002
[11] Mobasher B., Jain N., Han E. and Srivastava J. (1997) Web mining: Pattern discovery
      from WWW transaction. In Int Conference on Tools with Artificial Intellgence, pages
      558–567, New Port.
[12] Srivastava J. , Cooley R., Deshpande M. , and Pang-Ning Tan. (2000) Web usage mining:
      Discovery and applications of usage patterns from web data. SIGKDD Explorations,
      1:12–23.
[13] Florescu D., Levy A. , and Mendelzon A. (1998) Database techniques for the World-Wide
      Web: A survey. SIGMOD Record (ACM Special Interest Group on Management of
      Data), 27(3):59.
[14] Menasalvas E, Millán S, Hadjimichael M, Hochsztain E (2002) An algorithm to calculate
      the expected value of an ongoing user session In The 2002 IEEE Data Mining Conference
      ICDM '02
[15] Shahabi C., Zarkesh A.M. , Adibi J., and Shah V. (1997) Knowledge discovery from user's
      web-page navigation. In Proceedings of the Seventh International Workshop on Research
      Issues in Data Engineering, High Performance Database Management for Large-Scale
      Applications (RIDE'97), pages 20–1, Washington – Brussels – Tokyo, IEEE.
[16] Nasraoiu O., Krisnapuram R., and Joshi A. Mining web access logs using a fuzzy rela-
      tional clustering algorithm based on a robust estimator.
[17] Mobasher B., Dai H., Luo T., Nakagawa M., and Witshire J.. (2000) Discovery of aggre-
      gate usage profiles for web personalization. In Proceedings of the WebKDD Workshop.
[18] Borges J. and Levene M. (2000) A heuristic to capture longer user web navigation pat-
      terns. In Proc. Of the First International Conference on Electronic Commerce and Web
      Technologies, Greenwich, U.K., September.
[19] Pei J., Han J., Mortazavi-Asl B. , and Zhu H. (2000) Mining access patterns eficiently
      from web logs. In Proceedings Pacific-Asia Conference on Knowledge Discovery and
      Data Mining (PAKDD'00).
[20] Wolfang G. and Lars S. Mining web navigation path fragments. In Workshop on Web
      Mining for E-Commerce – Challenges and Opportunities Working Notes (KDD2000),
      pages 105–110, Boston, MA, August 2000.
[21] Ansari S. and Kohavi R. and Mason L. and Zheng Z. Integrating E-commerce and Data
      Mining: Architecture and Challenges. In Workshop on Web Mining for E-Commerce -
      Challenges and Opportunities Working Notes (KDD2000), pages, Boston, MA, August
      2000.
[22] Spiliopoulou M., Mobase B., Berent B. and Nakagawa M. A Framework for the evalua-
      tion of session reconstruction heuristics and web Usage Analysis, in I. Journal on Com-
      puting pp 1–20, 2002
[23] Berent B. Detail and Context in Web Usage Mining: Coarsing and Visualazing Se-
      quences, In Proc. WEBKDD 2001
[24] Mobasher B. Integrating Web Usage and Content Mining for More Effective Personaliza-
      tion, In Proc. ECWeb 2000

[25] Department of Defense, Framework for Managing Process Improvement, On-line guide: `http://www.c3i.osd.mil/bpr/bprcd/policy/fr_toc.html`. Dec 2001

[26] Mobasher B., Berent B., Spiliopoulou M.and Wiltshire J. Measuring the Accuracy of Sessionizers for Web Usage Analysis. In Proceedings of the Web Mining Workshop at the First SIAM International Conference on Data Mining, April 2001

Clustered Organized Conceptual Queries in the Internet Using Fuzzy Interrelations

Pablo J. Garcés [1], José A. Olivas [1], and Francisco P. Romero [2]

[1] Dep. of Computer Science, University of Castilla-La Mancha, Paseo de la Universidad 4,
13071-Ciudad Real, SPAIN
pgarces@upco, JoseAngel.Olivas@uclm.es
[2] Soluziona Software Factory, C/ Pedro Muñoz 1, 13071-Ciudad Real, SPAIN
fromero@uf-isf.es

Abstract. This paper introduces a new application of the FIS-CRM model (Fuzzy Interrelations and Synonymy based Concept Representation Model) in order to define a mechanism to achieve the conceptual matching between the concepts contained in a web page and the implicit concepts in the user's query, that is, the proposed system is able to retrieve the web pages that contain the concepts (not the words) specified in the query (called clustered organized conceptual queries in this paper). FIS-CRM may be considered a fuzzy extension of the vector space model that is based on fuzzy interrelations between terms (fuzzy synonymy and fuzzy generality at the moment). The FISS metasearcher was the first system integrating this model and, in that system, the model was used to extract the concepts contained in the snippets retrieved by the search engine (Google) making possible to cluster the results of the query into groups of conceptually related web pages.

1 Introduction

Nowadays, the big amount of web links retrieved by any searcher surpasses the user's expectations and also the patience needed to navigate looking for the links really related to the user's aim.

On other occasions, the use of polysemic words and generic words in the query make impossible to inspect the resulting links in a logical way.

In most cases we find the problem that searchers only retrieve the pages that contain words that exactly match the words in the query, ignoring the pages that contain related words to the ones in the query. These related words could be synonyms, more specific words, more general words, antonyms,...

In a more general way, we can affirm that the real cause of all of these problems is that information retrieval (IR) systems only take into account the lexicographical aspects of the words, and do not consider the semantic ones [1].

Definitively, web searching is widely recognized as a growing problem that is being approached in different ways [2–4] such as natural language processing trends,

E. Menasalvas et al. (Eds.): AWIC 2003, LNAI 2663, pp. 37–45, 2003.

new extensions of the vector space model [5–7], soft computing techniques [8–11] and fuzzy techniques [12–19].

Some representative approaches of the vector space model extensions are the ones based on WordNet [6,7], a semantic net of word groups. These systems require a special matching mechanism (ontomatching algorithm [7]) when comparing the associated concepts of the words.

A very interesting use of fuzzy techniques to information retrieval is the one proposed by Takagi [18,19]. In this case, Conceptual Fuzzy Sets (CFS) are used to represent the concepts contained in a document and Hopfield networks algorithms are used when matching the words in the query and the words in the CFS.

On the contrary of the system proposed in this paper, the approaches mentioned before require special search engines implementing specific matching algorithms.

In this context, the main objective of this work is to achieve the "clustered organized conceptual (COC) queries", first obtaining the pages that contain the concepts specified in the user query and later organizing the resulting pages into clusters of conceptually related pages, using a metasearcher that implements the standard vector space model matching algorithm.

The key of this process is to extract the concepts of all the items involved in a web search system, and this was the aim of the FIS-CRM model that was presented in [15]. The FISS metasearcher (also presented in [15]) was the first system integrating the FIS-CRM model and its main characteristic is the ability to cluster the pages retrieved by a search engine (Google) into conceptual groups, that is, the second aspect of the COC queries.

In order to complete the global process of the COC queries, this work is focused on the retrieving of the pages that conceptually match the query, that is, the pages that contain words that represent the same concept that the words specified in the query.

This way, the proposed system faces up to all the search problems mentioned before, using for its purpose soft computing metodologies applied to a fuzzy extension of the vector space model.

In Sect. 2 FIS-CRM is briely reviewed. This model can be used to represent the concepts contained in any kind of document and is supported by a fuzzy dictionary of synonyms (an adapted version of the one presented in [20]) and fuzzy ontologies of terms (automatically built using the algorithm presented in [17]). The fuzzy dictionary provides the fuzzy degrees of the synonymy interrelation, whereas the fuzzy ontologies provide the fuzzy degrees of the generality interrelation.This section also includes new considerations about the properties (symmetrical and transitive) of the synonymy interrelation and the generality interrelation.

In Sect. 3 we present the architecture of the global system able to make the COC queries, describing the four main components of the system: the web crawler, the query input component, the search engine and the clustering component.

Section 4 contains some examples to show the eficiency of the results obtained with the global system and finally, in Sect. 5, conclusions are described.

2   FIS-CRM Review

FIS-CRM may be considered as an extension of the vector space model [5], which is totally compatible with the matching mechanisms of most IR systems, given that the base vector of a FIS-CRM document is merely a single term weigth vector.

FIS-CRM is based on the idea that if a word appears in a document, then its synonyms (representing the same concept) underly it, and if a word appears in a document, the words that represent a more general concept also underly it.

The fundamental basis of FIS-CRM is to "share" the occurrences of a contained word among the fuzzy synonyms that represent the same concept and to "give" a fuzzy weight to the words that represent a more general concept that the contained one.

The construction of the document vectors takes two steps:

- Representing documents by their base weight vectors (based on the occurrences of the contained words).
- Weights readjusting (obtaining vectors based on concept occurrences). This way, a word may have a fuzzy weight in the new vector even if it is not contained in it, as long as the referenced concept underlies the document.

The readjustment process is implemented with an iterative algorithm that is repeated until no changes in the vector are produced. In each step, the weights of the contained words and the weights of their synonyms and more general words are readjusted (using FIS-CRM formulae [15]) taking into account the type of the words involved (weak words – polysemic – and strong words – one meaning) and the fuzzy synonymy and generality degrees provided by the fuzzy dictionary and the fuzzy ontologies. Obviously, the context of the document plays a fundamental role when determining the meaning of a weak word in a document.

Concerning the properties of the fuzzy synonymy interrelation, it is widely assumed that it has a non symmetrical behaviour, that is to say, word A may be a synonym of word B with a fuzzy certainty degree of X, and word B may be a synonym of word A with a different fuzzy certainty degree.

On the other hand, the synonymy relationship is not transitive, but it would be such if strong words were involved. Only in this case, if C is synonym of B and B is synonym of A, we can affirm that C is synonym of A.

The study of these properties on the fuzzy generality interrelation concludes that it is non symmetrical, given that if a word A is more general than a word B (with a given certainty degree), B is not possible to be more general than A. However, it can be considered to satisfy the transitivity property when the chain of words belongs to the same ontology.

It is important to point out that despite the readjustment process being iteratively carried out, some restrictions are defined to avoid undesired transitive synonyms to be applied, while transitive chains of applications of the generality readjustment are applied until the top word node of the tree (the most general word) is reached.

3   COC Query System Architecture

The clustered organized concept query system has four main components that correspond with the four main steps of the global process carried out in this system. They are the web crawler (showed in Fg.1), the query input component, the search engine and the clustering component (these later ones showed in Fig. 2).

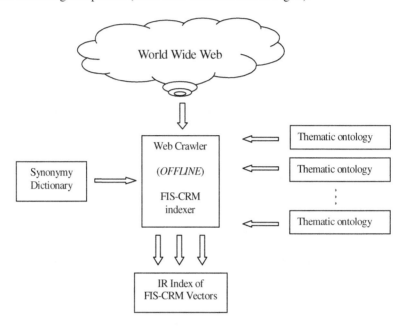

Fig. 1. Web crawling offline process

- **Web Crawler**. The process carried out by this component is offline. It includes the crawling of all the accesible web pages in the Internet and the construction of the IR index. The main characteristic of this component is that documents are indexed using the FIS-CRM model instead of using the standard vector space model. Figure 1 shows the items involved in this step.
- **Query Input Component.** This module allows the user to make a query. The user is also required to enter the thematic ontology (if wanted) and the similarity threshold used to cluster the resulting links. This component generates new queries using the synonyms of the words contained in the query. Each one of the new queries has a fuzzy compatibility degree with the original query that is calculated from the synonymy degree between the words included in it and the words specified in the original query. This value is later used when ordering the retrieved links. All the items involved in the query online processing are shown in Fig. 2.
- **Search Engine**. It is the responsible for retrieving the links of the web pages that match the generated queries. Although the documents are indexed using

the FIS-CRM model, the matching mechanism is the standard one implemented in most IR systems. As the vectors are formed by fuzzy weights, the matching function provides a fuzzy value for every page that represents the matching degree. Just as the compatibility degree obtained previously, this value is also used when ordering the retrieved links, in the same way that the page rank obtained by the number of links to the web page is also used.

- **Clustering Component**. This module implements a soft-clustering algorithm to organize the resulting links into clusters of conceptually related web pages. FIS-CRM is applied to the snippets retrieved by the search engine. The similarity function contemplates the co-occurrence of words and phrases, size of the snippets, rarety of words and the co-occurrence of concepts (in an implicit way). In this step groups are also labelled with the words that represent the concepts inside the groups documents.

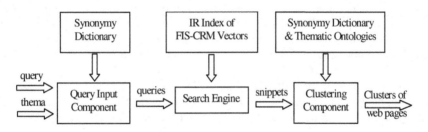

Fig. 2. Query online process

4   COC Query Processing

The complete COC query process is clearly divided in two phases: The offline modelling and indexing process carried out by the web crawler and the online process carried out by the query input component, the search engine and the clustering component.

FIS-CRM algorithms are used in the first phase in the same way FISS uses them to represent the snippets and are explained in detail in [15]. The only difference is that, in the system presented in this work, FIS-CRM is applied to model the whole web pages instead of the snippets retrieved by the search engine.

The other three steps carried out by the corresponding online components are very similar to the ones implemented in FISS [15]. The main difference between FISS and the new proposed system is that, the FISS metasearher uses Google search engine and so, the web pages indexes of Google (modelled with the standard vector space model), and the system we propose uses its own search engine that is fed up with its own web crawler that uses FIS-CRM to model the web pages.

The best way of showing the efficiency of this system is to follow the complete process of a clustered organized conceptual query example. Let's see what happens if we make a query with the word "memory".

Before studying the online query processing, we must take into account that the system needs a previous offline indexing process that captures the whole web pages links, indexing them using FIS-CRM techniques. So, let´s consider some examples of FIS-CRM vectors obtained after applying this model to some web pages. In this case we will only consider the pages related to some degree with the word "memory", but we must not forget that this model is offline applied to the whole web pages.

A piece of the corresponding indexed vector to a web page concerning the components of a computer could be this one:

cache	chipset	CPU	device	memory	Pentium	SDRAM
1	1	**1.2**	**0.5**	**0.6**	2	1

The bold weight values correspond to words not contained in the web page ("device", "memory" and "CPU"). These have been obtained due to the presence of the referred concepts and thanks to the thematic ontologies used by FIS-CRM. These words would never take a value in a vector space model IR system and so, this web page would not be retrieved by a basic IR system as result of a query with the words "device", "memory" or "CPU".

The following vector is the one obtained for a web page concerning the way of improving human capacity of memorizing. In this case, the word "brain" and "memory" has got a weigth because of their ontology interrelation with "memorizing".

acronym	brain	memory	memoryzing	mnemonic	remember	technique
1	**0.5**	**0.6**	1	1	2	1

The next vector represents a web page related to the remembrance of the first walk on the moon.

Apollo	Armstrong	commemoration	memory	moon	remembrance	rocket	space
1	1	**0.577**	**0.577**	1	0.577	**0.6**	**0.7**

The words "rocket" and "space" obtain their weight thanks to the words "Apollo" and "moon", while the word "memory" and "commemoration" get a value by their synonymy relationship with "remembrance" (that loses part of its weight in favour of these words).

As it can be observed, these three pages do not have any occurrence of the word "memory", that is why they will never be obtained by a vector space model based IR system when processing a query with this word.

Studying these vectors in detail we can also observe that the first web page will not be retrieved by a query with the word "computer" (when using a basic IR system), just as the second web page will not be obtained by a query with the word "brain", and neither will be the third one for the words "rocket", "space" or "commemoration".

That is, despite these three web pages containing the concepts associated to the words specified in these hypothetical queries, they will never be retrieved by a basic IR system.

Let's now study the complete online process when making the query with the word "memory".

First of all, the user will be asked for optionally entering the thema of the query. Although that informaion could be used for refining the aim of the query, in this case it will only be used by the Clustering Component for extracting the concepts of the retrieved snippets.

When introducing the query, the Query Input Component will generate other queries with the synonyms of the word "memory", that is, "remembrance", "commemoration", "memorial", "memorandum", etc. The generated queries will then have a compatibility degree with the original one (obtained by the synonymy degrees) that will determine the membership degree of the retrieved links to the whole group of retrieved links.

In this case, the Search Engine, using the offline indexed FIS-CRM vectors and the standard matching mechanism, will retrieve all the vectors having a value for the word "memory", that is, the vectors that contain some occurrence of the concept represented by this word (despite not containing the word itself). So, the three example web pages mentioned before will be retrieved.

Finally, the Clustering Component will process all the snippets produced by the generated queries. In order to extract the semantic component of these snippets, FIS-CRM is applied (using the ontology associated to the user entered thema). This way, this Clustering Component, using a similarity function based on the coocurrence of concepts, will be able to make groups of conceptually related snippets. That is, the pages related to "computer memory" will be grouped together, and the same will occur to the "memorizing techniques" web pages and the ones concerning any kind of "commemoration". Moreover, each one of the first level groups can be expanded and explored through the lower level groups that compound it, that is, the resulting links are presented to the user in a hierarchical structrure of conceptual clusters that will facilitate the user to explore and find the really desired web pages. It is important to point out that the resulting clusters are labelled with their most representative words.

5 Conclusions

Despite conceptual queries having been considered an uthopy for a long time, the proposed COC query system is an easily implementing approach that provides a way of managing this kind of queries.

Although the FIS-CRM model is capable of improvement in some of its aspects (mainly exploiting the context of the documents), FIS-CRM capability of representing the concepts contained in any kind of document makes it a very useful element when managing the vaguity of the Internet information.

The most important advantage for any searcher of using the FIS-CRM model to represent web pages is that the matching mechanism does not need to be changed and, best of all, without reducing either the performance or the efficiency.

Unlike other metasearchers that first try to reduce the scope of the query implementing refinement techniques, in this sytem the query is first spread using its synonyms (not caring about the meaning of each one of them). Although it could be considered a way of putting some noise in the search process, this is not the consequence, as the clustering component later groups conceptually the retrieved links in order to facilitate the user the exploration of the results. The shown query example with the word "memory" (a polysemic word) is a good proof of it.

To get an idea of the efficiency of the system when retrieving pages let's take into consideration the number of pages that would have never be retrieved by a basic IR system but they would be obtained by this system. As an example datum, Google search engine has more than 500.000 links to web pages containg the word "SDRAM" but not containing the word "memory", that is, none of these pages would be retrieved by this searcher when making a query with the word "memory", but the COC query system would.

In this sense, considering the benefits of implementing FIS-CRM in the web crawler component (not forgetting that this is only an approach to a very complex problem) and taking into account that any search engine could manage FIS-CRM vectors without having to adapt its matching mechanism without affecting its efficiency, we sincerily think that the proposed system should be considered to be implemented in any searcher.

Acknowledgements. This research is supported by CIPRESES (TIC 2000-1362-C02-02) Project, MCYT, Spain.

References

1. I. Ricarte, F. Gomide, A reference model for intelligent information search, Proceedings of the BISC Int. Workshop on Fuzzy Logic and the Internet, (2001) 80–85.
2. M. Nikravesh, Fuzzy conceptual-based search engine using conceptual semantic indexing, Proceedings of the 2002 NAFIPS annual meeting, (2002) 146–151.
3. M. Kobayashi, K. Takeda, Information retrieval on the web, ACM Computing Surveys 32(2), (2000) 144–173.
4. G. Pasi, Flexible information retrieval: some research trends, Mathware and Soft Computing 9, (2002) 107–121.
5. G. Salton, A. Wang, C.S.A. Yang, Vector space model for automatic indexing, Communications of the ACM 18, (1975) 613–620.
6. J. Gonzalo, F. Verdejo, I. Chugur, J. Cigarran, Indexing with WordNet synsets can improve retrieval, Proc. of the COLING/ACL Work. on usage of WordNet in natural language processng systems, (1998).
7. A.K. Kiryakov, K.I. Simov, Ontologically supported semantic matching, Proceedings of "NODALIDA'99: Nordic Conference on Computational Linguistics", Trondheim, (1999).
8. Y. Tang, Y. Zhang, Personalized library search agents using data mining techniques, Proceedings of the BISC Int. Workshop on Fuzzy Logic and the Internet, (2001) 119–124.
9. O. Zamir, O. Etzioni, Grouper: A dynamic clustering interface to web search results, Proceedings of the WWW8, (1999).
10. F. Cresatani, G. Pasi, Soft computing in information retrieval: Techniques and applications, Physica Verlag, Series studies in fuzziness, 2000.

11. L. King-ip, K. Ravikumar, A similarity-based soft clustering algorithm for documents, Proc. of the Seventh Int. Conf. on Database Sys. for Advanced Applications, (2001).

12. D. Choi, Integration of document index with perception index and its application to fuzzy query on the Internet, Proceedings of the BISC Int. Workshop on Fuzzy Logic and the Internet, (2001), 68–72.

13. T.H. Cao, Fuzzy conceptual graphs for the semantic web, Proceedings of the BISC Int. Workshop on Fuzzy Logic and the Internet, (2001) 74–79.

14. G. Bordogna, G. Pasi, Flexible representation and querying of heterogenous structured documents, Kibernetica, Vol. 36, N. 6, (2000), 617–633.

15. Olivas J.A, Garces P.J., Romero F.P., FISS: Application of fuzzy technologies to an Internet metasearcher, Proceedings of the 2002 NAFIPS annual meeting, (2002) 140–145.

16. M.J. Martin-Bautista, M. Vila, D. Kraft, J. Chen, User profiles and fuzzy logic in web retrieval, Proc.of the BISC Int. Workshop on Fuzzy Logic and the Internet, (2001), 19–24.

17. D. Widyantoro, J. Yen, Incorporating fuzzy ontology of term relations in a serach engine, Proceedings of the BISC Int. Workshop on Fuzzy Logic and the Internet, (2001), 155–160.

18. T. Takagi, M. Tajima, Proposal of a search engine based on conceptual matching of text notes, Proc. of the BISC Int. Workshop on Fuzzy Logic and the Internet, (2001), 53–58.

19. R. Ohgaya, T. Takagi, K. Fukano, K. Taniguchi, Conceptual fuzzy sets- based navigation system for Yahoo!, Proceedings of the 2002 NAFIPS annual meeting, (2002) 274–279.

20. S. Fernandez, A contribution to the automatic processing of the synonymy using Prolog, PhD Thesis, University of Santiago de Compostela, Spain, 2001.

Collaborative Filtering Using Interval Estimation Naïve Bayes

V. Robles[1], P. Larrañaga[2], J.M. Peña[1], O. Marbán[3], J. Crespo[3], and M.S.Pérez[1]

[1] Department of Computer Architecture and Technology, Technical University of Madrid, Madrid, Spain
{vrobles,jmpena,mperez}@fi.upm.es
[2] Department of Computer Science and Artificial Intelligence, University of the Basque Country, San Sebastián, Spain
ccplamup@si.ehu.es
[3] Department of Computer Science, University Carlos III of Madrid, Madrid, Spain
{omarban,jcrespo}@inf.uc3m.es

Abstract. Personalized recommender systems can be classified into three main categories: content-based, mostly used to make suggestions depending on the text of the web documents, collaborative filtering, that use ratings from many users to suggest a document or an action to a given user and hybrid solutions. In the collaborative filtering task we can find algorithms such as the naïve Bayes classifier or some of its variants. However, the results of these classifiers can be improved, as we demonstrate through experimental results, with our new semi naïve Bayes approach based on intervals. In this work we present this new approach.[1]

1 Introduction

Nowadays, the volume of information on the World Wide Web has been arising in an exponential way [2] and the number of pages will be even bigger in a near future. Therefore, people need technology to avoid the problems that this amount of information generates. Due to it, web mining has arose to facilitate the user's information access.

Web mining is a broad term that has been used to refer to the process of information discovery from sources in the Web (Web content), to the process of discovery of the structure of the web servers (Web structure) and to the process of mining for user browsing and access patterns through logs analysis (Web usage) [4].

Three phases [6] are identified in Web using mining: Collecting and preprocessing of data, pattern discovery and pattern analysis.

In the first phase data can be gathered from different sources [9]. On one hand, we can collect data directly from the user. We can ask information through surveys, polls or asking directly to the user. On the other hand, we can obtain information without the user intervention. There are two different ways we can use to gather this user's unconscious information:

---

[1] The work presented in this paper has been partially supported by UPM project RT-Webp – ref.14495

E. Menasalvas et al. (Eds.): AWIC 2003, LNAI 2663, pp. 46–53, 2003.

- Direct pursuit maintains a registry of user's activities, normally located on the client-side such as cookies, beacons, etc.
- Indirect pursuit using log files. Log files can be used in order to find association patterns, sequential patterns and trends of Web accesses.

Therefore, information can be collected and preprocessed depending on its usage. Thus, it would be used to consider the user's preferences, to generate new pages with greater acceptance, for recommendations in the selection of a new product, to diagnose his desires of an information, etc.

In the second phase, once the data have been preprocessed, there are several approaches that can be performed depending on the needs. Many approaches have focused on applying intelligent techniques to provide user personal recommendations. These personalized recommender systems can be classified into three main categories:

1. Content Based Filtering
   In content-based filtering, a user's preference model is constructed for the individual based upon the user's ratings and descriptions (usually, textual expressions) of the rated items. Such systems try to find regularities in the descriptions that can be used to distinguish highly rated items from others. There are three kinds of content based filtering systems: Pure information systems [17], survey or polling or social information systems [16] and content-wise examination information systems [14].
2. Collaborative Filtering
   The main idea of collaborative filtering is to recommend new items of interest for a particular user based on other users' opinions. A variety of collaborative filtering algorithms have been reported and their performance has been evaluated empirically [1] [13] [17] [10]. These algorithms are based on a simple intuition: predictions for a user should be based on the preference patterns of other people who have similar interest.
3. Unified or Hybrid Solution
   Several authors [15] suggest methods for a hybrid solution. They present a combination between collaborative filtering and content-based filtering. They propose a generative probabilistic model for combining collaborative and content-based recommendations in a normative manner.

In this work we present a new approach to collaborative filtering with naïve Bayes. We have developed a new semi naïve Bayes approach based on intervals. This new approach outperforms the simple naïve Bayes classifier and other variants specifically defined for collaborative filtering [10]. We evaluated this algorithm using a database of Microsoft Anonymous Web Data from the UCI repository [12].

The outline of this paper is as follows. Section 2 presents the state of the art in collaborative filtering with naïve Bayes. Section 3 presents a new semi naïve Bayes approach, interval estimation naïve Bayes. Section 4 illustrates the results obtained with the UCI dataset. Section 5 gives the conclusions and suggests further future work.

2 Naïve Bayes Classifiers in Collaborative Filtering

The naïve Bayes classifier [3] [5] is a probabilistic method for classification. It can be used to determine the probability that an example belongs to a class given the values of variables. The simple naïve Bayes classifier is one of the most successful algorithms on many classification domains. In spite of its simplicity, it is shown to be competitive with other complex approaches specially in text categorization and content based filtering.

This classifier learns from training data the conditional probability of each variable X_k given the class label c_i. Classification is then done by applying Bayes rule to compute the probability of C given the particular instance of $X_1, \ldots, X_n$,

$$P(C = c_i | X_1 = x_1, \ldots, X_n = x_n) \tag{1}$$

As variables are considered independent given the value of the class this probability can be calculated as follows,

$$P(C = c_i | X_1 = x_1, \ldots, X_n = x_n) \propto P(C = c_i) \prod_{k=1}^{n} P(X_k = x_k | C = c_i) \tag{2}$$

This equation is well suited for learning from data, since the probabilities $P(C = c_i)$ and $P(X_k = x_k | C = c_i)$ can be estimated from training data. The result of the classification is the class with highest probability.

In [10] Pazzani and Miyahara two variants of the simple naïve Bayes classifier for collaborative filtering are defined:

1. **Transformed Data Model** After selecting a certain number of features, absent or present information of the selected features is used for predictions. That is:

$$P(C = c_i | S_1 = s_1, \ldots, S_n = s_n), \tag{3}$$

   where $r \leq n$ and $S_i \in X_i, \ldots, X_n$. S_i variables are selected using a theory based approach to determinate the most informative features. This is accomplished by computing the expected information gain that the presence of absence of a variable gives toward the classification of the labelled items.
2. **Sparse Data Model** In this model, authors assume that only known features are informative for classification. Therefore, only known features are used for predictions. That is:

$$P(C = c_i | X_1 = 1, X_3 = 1, \ldots, X_n = 1) \tag{4}$$

3 A New Semi-naïve Bayes Approach: Interval Estimation Naïve Bayes

We propose a new semi naïve Bayes approach named interval estimation naïve Bayes. In this approach, in spite of calculate the punctual estimation of the conditional probabilities from data, as simple naïve Bayes does, we calculate interval estimations. After that, by searching for the best combination of values into these intervals, we seek to break the assumption of independence among variables in the simple naïve Bayes. Although we have used this algorithm for collaborative filtering, it can be used in the same problems we use the simple naïve Bayes.

The approach is based on two different steps:

In the **first step**, each parameter is estimated by intervals. Thus, we consider the next interval for the conditional probabilities $\hat{p}_{k,i}^r = \hat{P}(X_k = x_k^r | C = c_i)$

$$\left(\hat{p}_{k,i}^r - z_\alpha \sqrt{\frac{\hat{p}_{k,i}^r (1 - \hat{p}_{k,i}^r)}{N}}, \hat{p}_{k,i}^r + z_\alpha \sqrt{\frac{\hat{p}_{k,i}^r (1 - \hat{p}_{k,i}^r)}{N}} \right) \tag{5}$$

where

r is the possible values of the variable X_k
$\hat{p}_{k,i}^r$ is the punctual estimation of the conditional probability $P(X_k = x_k^r | C = c_i)$
z_α is the $(1 - \alpha)$ percentile in the $\mathcal{N}(0,1)$
N is the number of cases in dataset.

In the **second step** we make a heuristic search to obtain the best combination of conditional probabilities that maximize a predefined evaluation function. The values for each of this conditional probabilities are found inside each corresponding interval. The evaluation function depends on each specific problem. It does not matter which algorithms we use for the search: Genetic algorithms, simulated annealing, tabu search, etc.

It is important to emphasize three key aspects in interval estimation naïve Bayes:

– In the heuristic search, we take into account all the conditional probabilities at the same time, searching for the best combination. This means that we are breaking the assumption of independence among the variables.
– As validation method we are using leave-one-out cross validation. This method guarantees that no overfitting will occur for these data.
– Normally, the evaluation function will be the percentage of successful classified. However, sometimes, as occurs in this approach, we need a different evaluation function.

Figure 1 shows the pseudocode of interval estimation naïve Bayes.

To make the heuristic search in this work we have used EDAs – estimation of distribution algorithms –. EDAs [11,8] are non-deterministic, stochastic heuristic search strategies that form part of the evolutionary computation approaches, where number of solutions or individuals are created every generation, evolving once and again until a satisfactory solution is achieved. In brief, the characteristic that most differentiates EDAs from other evolutionary search strategies such as GAs is that the evolution from a generation to the next one is done by estimating the probability distribution of the fittest individuals, and afterwards by sampling the induced model. This avoids the use of crossing or mutation operators, and the number of parameters that EDAs requires is reduced considerably.

Interval Estimation naïve Bayes

Calculate every interval estimation $\hat{p}_{k,i}^r$ for $P(X_k = x_k^r | C = c_i)$ from data

$$\left(\hat{p}_{k,i}^r - z_\alpha \sqrt{\frac{\hat{p}_{k,i}^r (1 - \hat{p}_{k,i}^r)}{N}}, \hat{p}_{k,i}^r + z_\alpha \sqrt{\frac{\hat{p}_{k,i}^r (1 - \hat{p}_{k,i}^r)}{N}} \right)$$

For $k = 1, \ldots, n \wedge i = 1, \ldots, \|C\| \wedge r = 1, \ldots, \|X_k\|$

Make a heuristic search to obtain the combination of values that maximize a predefined evaluation function

---

Fig. 1. Pseudocode for interval estimation naïve Bayes

4   Experimentation

4.1   Dataset

For the evaluation of our new approach (internal estimation naïve Bayes) for collaborative filtering we have used a dataset of Microsoft Anonymous Web Data from the UCI repository [12].

This data was created by sampling and processing the www.microsoft.com logs. The data records the use of www.microsoft.com by 32711 anonymous, randomly-selected users. For each user, the data lists all the areas that the user visited in a one week timeframe. Thus, each instance in the dataset represents an anonymous user and each attribute is an area of the www.microsoft.com web site. There are a total of 294 areas.

This dataset shows instance independence among each of the records of the database. Taking this into account our leave one out evaluation method will not have overtraining problem.

In this case we have a very sparse data, so areas visited are explicit while non-visited are implicit. Thus, an attribute will have a value 1 if the area has been visited, and a value 0 in other case.

Our task is to predict the areas of www.microsoft.com that a user will visit, based on data on what other areas he or she visited.

After the learning and validation we will evaluate prediction accuracy, learning time and speed of predictions. The accuracy will be measured via the leave one out method [7].

4.2   Measuring Prediction Accuracy – Evaluation Function

Most of the times quality of classifiers can be measured by the percentage of successful predictions. However, this measure is not a good idea in this dataset due to the lack of balance between positive and negative cases. Let's see an example.

Suppose that from the 32711 users only 1000 have visited an especific page and the next confusion matrix (see table 1) coming from our classifier, where all the users have been classified as non potential visitors.

Table 1. An example of a confusion matrix

	Classified as	
Real	*0*	*1*
0	31711	0
1	1000	0

Table 2. A generic confusion matrix

	Classified as	
Real	*0*	*1*
0	a	b
1	c	d

Everybody can appreciate that this classifier is really bad, however the accuracy is $31711/32711 = 96.94\%$. That means that % of successful predictions is not a good reference. As we can see in table 3 simple naïve Bayes has this problem in collaborative filtering.

Thus, given a generic confusion matrix (see Table 2), the measure we will use is

$$\left(\frac{a}{a+b} + \frac{d}{c+d}\right)/2 \tag{6}$$

This measure is much better and realistic because we are evaluating the percentage of visitors classified as visitors and the % of non-visitors classified as non-visitors independently. Then we calculate the average of both.

This formula (6) will be used as the evaluation function in interval estimation naïve Bayes. Besides, for calculating the probabilities we have used the idea exposed in the variant Sparse Data Model (see equation 4) defined by Pazzani and Miyahara and only known features are used for predictions.

4.3 Experimental Results

We have run the algorithm in the 18 more visited pages. The most visited page has 10836 visitors and the less visited has 1087 visitors. This range of visitors is enough to analyze the behavior of our new approach.

Table 3 contains the experiment results for simple naïve Bayes, the variant Sparse Data Model defined by Pazzani and Miyahara and interval estimation naïve Bayes approaches. The first two columns in the table have the identifier of the area and the number of visitors in that area. The next two columns have the results for the simple naïve Bayes. The first one with the symbol % is the percentage of successful predictions and the second one the value of the evaluation function. After that we have two columns with the results for the variant Sparse Data Model and the last two columns with the results for interval estimation naïve Bayes.

We must remember that the most significant columns are those with the values of the evaluation function.

Evaluation of interval estimation naïve Bayes:

Table 3. Experiment results for Interval Estimation naïve Bayes

		simple NB		PazzaniNB		IENB Max(feval)	
Area	*Visitors*	*%*	*f_eval*	*%*	*f_eval*	*%*	*f_eval*
'1008'	10836	72.34	63.03	70.94	70.59	71.23	71.73
'1034'	9383	74.47	64.72	72.35	54.56	72.38	55.93
'1004'	8463	72.31	54.12	72.48	53.95	72.01	55.75
'1018'	5330	86.70	72.08	78.85	75.60	79.52	77.49
'1017'	5108	83.94	62.39	76.68	68.96	77.92	71.15
'1009'	4628	88.45	71.16	84.32	72.11	85.21	73.12
'1001'	4451	88.24	71.75	86.31	77.49	86.42	78.58
'1026'	3220	92.22	71.41	91.78	83.68	91.84	85.84
'1003'	2968	90.03	72.21	86.58	78.39	86.95	79.54
'1025'	2123	91.99	67.24	91.85	55.53	91.88	57.53
'1035'	1791	94.15	75.97	89.22	88.64	88.60	89.54
'1040'	1506	94.89	68.06	92.71	75.45	92.61	79.36
'1041'	1500	94.89	71.74	89.36	79.61	89.44	80.77
'1032'	1446	95.98	57.27	95.98	57.23	96.02	58.47
'1037'	1160	94.22	68.40	90.27	79.26	90.38	80.99
'1030'	1115	94.91	65.26	89.61	71.69	89.24	73.51
'1038'	1110	95.54	73.52	92.55	80.58	92.57	83.66
'1020'	1087	95.40	62.71	92.88	68.60	92.80	70.97
Average		88.93	**67.39**	85.82	**71.77**	85.95	**73.55**

- Prediction accuracy: About the evaluation function the results are clear. The variant of Pazzani and Miyahara outperforms simple naïve Bayes in 4.38% and our new approach, interval estimation naïve Bayes, outperforms the variant in 1.78% and the simple naïve Bayes in 6.16%.
- Learning time: simple naïve Bayes and the variant of Pazzani and Miyahara have a really short learning time. Few seconds are enough for the learning. However, interval estimation must make a heuristic search of the conditional probabilities. The evaluation of each individual takes the same time than the evaluation of the simple naïve Bayes classifier. In conclusion, as thousand of evaluation are needed in interval estimation, the learning time is some hours. However, as learning should be done only once, this is not a relevant issue.
- Speed of predictions: The speed of the predictions is exactly the same for the three algorithms.

5 Conclusion and Further Work

In this work we have presented a new semi naïve Bayes approach named interval estimation naïve Bayes. We have used this new approach for collaborative filtering. Experimental results shown that our approach outperforms the simple naïve Bayes and other variants specifically defined for collaborative filtering.

As this is the first time we use this approach for collaborative filtering many issues remain for future research. For instance, it is possible to change the objective of the heuristic search. We can try to maximize the area under the ROC curve. Another viable idea is to combine interval estimation naïve bayes with a feature subset selection. On a first phase it is possible to make a subset selection, and on a second phase to apply interval estimation to the previous results.

References

1. J. Breese, D. Heckerman, and C. Kadie. Empirical analysis of predictive algorithm for collaborative filtering. Technical report, Microsoft Corporation, Redmond,WA 98052, May 1998. One Microsoft Way.
2. P. Bruemmer. Google: Search technology for the millennium. Search Engine Guide, February 2002. Every 28 days, Google indexes 3 billion Web Documents.
3. R. Duda and R. Hart. *Pattern Classification and Pattern Analysis*. Wiley, New York, 1973.
4. J. Han and M. Kamber. *Data Mining: Concepts and Techniques*. Morgan Kaufmann publisher, 2001.
5. D.J. Hand and K. Yu. Idiot's Bayes - not so stupid after all? *International Statistical Review*, 69(3):385–398, 2001.
6. M. Deshpande J. Srivastava, R. Cooley and P. Tan. Web usage mining: Discovery and applications of usage patterns from web data. *SIGKDD Explorations*, 1:12–23, 2000.
7. R. Kohavi. A study of cross-validation and bootstrap for accuracy estimation and model selection. In *IJCAI*, pages 1137–1145, 1995.
8. P. Larrañaga and J. A. Lozano. *Estimation of Distribution Algorithms: A New Tool for Evolutionary Computation*. Kluwer Academic Publisher, 2001.
9. O. Marbán, E. Menasalvas, C. Montes, and J. Segovia. *Book: E-Commerce and Intelligent Methods in the Studies in Fuzziness and Soft Computing Series*, chapter CRM in e-Business: a client's life cycle model based on a neural network, pages 61–77. Springer-Verlag, 2002.
10. K. Miyahara and M.J. Pazzani. Collaborative filtering with the simple Bayesian classifier. In *Pacific Rim International Conference on Artificial Intelligence*, pages 679–689, 2000.
11. H. Mühlenbein. The equation for response to selection and its use for prediction. *Evolutionary Computation*, 5:303–346, 1998.
12. P. M. Murphy and D. W. Aha. UCI repository of machine learning databases. `http://www.ics.uci.edu/~mlearn/`, 1995.
13. P. Resnick, I. Neophytos, S. Mitesh, P. Bergstrom and J. Rieldd. Grouplens: An open architecture for collaborative filtering of netnews. In *CSCW94: Conference on Computer Supported Cooperative Work*, pages 175–186, 1994.
14. M. Pazzani and D. Billsus. Learning and revising user profiles: The identification of interesting web sites. *Machine Learning*, 27:313–331, 1997.
15. A. Popescul, L. Ungar, D. Pennock, and S. Lawrence. Probabilistic models for unified collaborative and content-based recommendation in sparse-data environments. In *17th Conference on Uncertainty in Artificial Intelligence*, pages 437–444, Seattle, Washington, August 2–5 2001.
16. G. Salton and M. J. McGill. Introduction to modern information retrieval, 1983.
17. U. Shardanand and P. Maes. Social information filtering: Algorithms for automating "word of mouth". In *Proceedings of ACM CHI'95 Conference on Human Factors in Computing Systems*, volume 1, pages 210–217, 1995.

DJ-Boids: Flocks of DJ's to Program Internet Multichannel Radio Stations

Jesus Ibanez[1], Antonio Gomez-Skarmeta[2], and Josep Blat[3]

[1] Centre for Virtual Environments, University of Salford
Business House, Salford, Manchester, M5 4WT, UK
jesus.ibanez@tecn.upf.es
[2] Departamento de Ingenieria de la Informacion y las Comunicaciones
Universidad de Murcia, 30001 Murcia, Spain
skarmeta@dif.um.es
[3] Departamento de Tecnologia, Universidad Pompeu Fabra
Passeig de Circumvallacio, 8, 08003 Barcelona, Spain
josep.blat@tecn.upf.es

Abstract. In this paper we propose to apply emergent collective behavior ideas to automatically program Internet multichannel radio stations. The proposed model simulates n virtual Dj's (one per channel) playing songs at the same time. Every virtual Dj takes into account the songs played by the other ones, programming a sequence of songs whose order is also coherent. That is, every song played in a channel takes into account both, the song previously played in the same channel and the songs being played in the other channels at the same time.

1 Introduction

Radio station services are currently flourishing on the Internet. Most of these Internet radio stations are specialized in programming music. These are usually streaming media servers with several channels, every one of them playing songs according to a particular musical style. In this way, the radio stations intend to maximize the number of listeners. Therefore the listeners have to choose the musical style they prefer to listen.

Although every listener may have her favorite musical style, it is usual that she prefers listening to music in a more eclectic way. In fact, reading specialized musical magazines or chatting with friends, we can find many more intuitive and natural adjectives to qualify a song than just its musical style (for example fresh, obscure, slow, etc). Furthermore, any good Dj knows that after playing a particular song, there are a lot of them that should not be played. The sequence order of the songs is really important, however this order cannot be obtained just from the musical style.

On the other hand, we have recently seen the success of several optimization techniques and mechanisms that imitate biological principles (evolutionary algorithms [1], ant algorithm [3]).

E. Menasalvas et al. (Eds.): AWIC 2003, LNAI 2663, pp. 54–61, 2003.

In this sense, the collective behavior of flocks, herds and schools has been studied in the artificial life [10] and complex systems [5] areas. This kind of behavior seems complex, however Reynolds suggested [15] that this behavior could be modeled by applying a few simple rules to every individual. In his so-called model boids every individual (boid) tries to fulfill three conditions: collision avoidance (avoid collisions with nearby flockmates), velocity matching (attempt to match velocity with nearby flockmates) and flock centering (attempt to stay close to nearby flockmates). This model has been successfully applied to animate the behavior of flocks in several famous films.

In this paper we propose to apply these ideas to automatically program Internet multichannel radio stations. The structure of this paper is as follows. Firstly we describe related work. Then we describe the overall idea. Next we describe the DJ-Boids algorithm [8]. Finally we show experiments carried out and provide the conclusions.

2   Related Work

There are various very recent works that try to cope with the problem of automatic generation of music playlists. AutoDJ [13] is a system for automatically generating music playlists based on one or more seed songs selected by a user. AutoDJ uses Gaussian Process Regression to learn a user preference function over songs. Flycasting [6] [7] is a method for using collaborative filtering techniques to generate a playlist for an online radio in real-time based on the request histories of the current listening audience. PersonalDJ [4] tries to automatically generate good playlists for individual listeners by matching information about the users with information about the music. PersonalDJ categorizes the songs according to moods while the usual Internet based radio system use genre based categories. Flytrap [2] is a group music environment that knows its users' musical tastes and can automatically construct a playlist that tries to please everyone in the room where it is played. The system works by paying attention to what music people listen to on their computers. The system tries to satisfy the tastes of people in the room, but it also makes a playlist that fits its own notion of what should come next. mpME! [11] introduces users to new music and interweaves old music the listener has heard of before and enjoys. mpME! uses a feature intersection algorithm to make recommendations for artists using features of artists found on the web. MUSICFX [12] is a group preference arbitration system that allows the members of a fitness center to influence, but not directly control, the selection of music in the fitness center.

On the other hand, some research groups have been working in the application of the idea of emergence to different problems. In particular, the boids algorithm, which was initially conceived to simulate flocks, has also been used [14] as the core of a novel method of visualising data in such a way that the new technique allows the user to see complex correlations between data items through the amount of time each boid spends near others.

3   DJ-Boids

Three song characteristics are selected. These characteristics have to be such that they allow for a sequential classification of the songs (i.e. musical style is not a possible characteristic). Both extreme values of every characteristic usually correspond to linguistic terms. Possible extreme pairs for characteristics are: slow-quick, somber-happy, light-heavy, simple-complex, etc.

The songs of the radio station are annotated according to the selected characteristics. This task is certainly subjective. Reference values can be fixed, in order to make things easy on the annotation process. For example, if the songs are going to be annotated with values between 0 and 1, various reference songs can be annotated with values 0, 0.25, 0.5, 0.75 and 1, to be taken into account during the annotation process. Then every annotated song is located in a three-dimensional space. If a radio station uses the speed, lightness level, and happiness level as characteristics to annotate every song, the corresponding three-dimensional space is the one shown in Fig. 1.

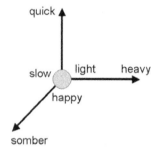

Fig. 1. A sample three-dimensional space

A user interface presents this three-dimensional space to the human DJ, including an interactive simulation of a flock of n boids. The boids are limited to fly into the virtual box defined by the extreme values of the three characteristics. Every boid, which we call dj-boid, corresponds to a channel of the radio station and its behavior programs the list of songs of its corresponding channel.

The user interacts with the simulation, by intuitively varying the three parameters (collision avoidance, velocity matching and flock centering) of the individual behavior of the dj-boids, in order to get the desired global behavior of flock. Once the simulation is configured as desired, it can be used to automatically program the channels of the radio station.

When the simulation is run to program the channels of the radio station, the successive locations occupied by every dj-boid determine the songs of its corresponding channel.

Note that every location occupied by a dj-boid corresponds to concrete values for the three chosen characteristics (speed, lightness level and happiness level in the example). These values determine the next song to be programmed. The procedure that determines the concrete song to be programmed from these three characteristics is described in subsection *Algorithm*.

In this way, by intuitively interacting with the simulation through the visual feedback of the tool, it is possible to get simulation parameters of particular interest. We show two examples of it in subsection *Experiments*. Note also that the speed factor determines the degree of softness with which the songs are mixed, that is, it regulates the coherence of the order of the programmed song sequence.

3.1   Algorithm

The classic boids algorithm involves vector operations on the positions of the boids. Each of the boid rules works independently, therefore, for each boid, it is calculated how much it will get moved by each of the three rules [15], giving us three velocity vectors. Then these three vectors are added to the current velocity of the boid to work out its new velocity. Interpreting the velocity as how far the boid moves per time step we simply add it to the current position. A simplified version of the algorithm is as follows.

```
PROCEDURE boids()
        Vector v1, v2, v3
        Boid b
        FOR EACH BOID b
            v1 = rule1(b)
            v2 = rule2(b)
            v3 = rule3(b)
            b.velocity = b.velocity + v1 + v2 + v3
            b.position = b.position + b.velocity
        END
END PROCEDURE
```

However, this algorithm is not well suited for our case because it calculates a new location for all the boids every time step, while we should calculate the location of just a boid every time step. This is because we take into account that different songs usually have different lengths.

We have designed and developed an algorithm that programs the list of songs to be played by every channel of the radio station during a particular time period.

We describe the data structures and some functions before we show the algorithm. Firstly we describe the data structures.

- MAX_SONG is the maximum number of songs in the system.
- $NUM\_DJBOIDS$ is the number of dj-boids in the system, corresponding to the number of channels in the radio station.
- $TOTAL\_LENGTH$ is the lenght of the time period to be programmed.
- $songs[1.. MAX\_SONG]$ is an array of records with five fields:

- *id* (the name of the song),
- *length* (the length of the song),
- *characX* (the value of the song for the characterisitic corresponding to the X axis),
- *characY* (the value of the song for the characterisitic corresponding to the Y axis) and
- *characZ* (the value of the song for the characterisitic corresponding to the Z axis).

- $djb[1..NUM\_DJBOIDS]$ is an array of records with five fields (note that $djb[i]$ models the i-th dj-boid):
  - *songList* (a list which saves the sequence of programmed songs),
  - *programmedTime* (the total time programmed, i.e. the sum of the length of all the songs in *songList*),
  - *x* (the current location of the dj-boid in the X axis),
  - *y* (the current location of the dj-boid in the Y axis) and
  - *z* (the current location of the dj-boid in the Z axis).
- *currentMoment* indicates the current moment.
- *minX* and *maxX* are respectively the minimum and maximum possible values in the axis X.
- *minY* and *maxY* are respectively the minimum and maximum possible values in the axis Y.
- *minZ* and *maxZ* are respectively the minimum and maximum possible values in the axis Z.

Next we describe some functions.

- *random(min, max)* is a function which returns a random value between *min* and *max*.
- *add(i, l)* is a function which adds the item *i* to the list *l*.
- *selectSong(x, y, z)* is a function that selects a song according to three values *x*, *y*, *z* corresponding respectively to the three characteristics. The process is as follows: select randomly a song among all the ones whose three characteristics correspond to x, y, and z. If there is no song that fulfills this requirement, select the song that minimizes the distance between the point represented by x, y, z and the point corresponding to the three characterisitc values of the song. If there are various songs with the same distance value, select randomly one of them.
- *boids(i)* is a function that calculates a new location for the dj-boid $djb[i]$ according to the boids algorithm.

Then the algorithm is as follows.

```
// INITIALIZATION
currentMoment = 0 for i = 1 to NUM_DJBOIDS
    djb[i].x = random(minX, maxX)
    djb[i].y = random(minY, maxY)
```

```
djb[i].z = random(minZ, maxZ)
song = selectSong(djb[i].x,djb[i].y,djb[i].z)
add(song, djb[i].songList)
djb[i].programmedTime = song.length

// MAIN LOOP
while currentMoment < TOTAL_LENGTH
    select dj (1 <= dj <= NUM_DJBOIDS) such that
    minimizes djb[dj].programmedTime

    currentMoment = djb[dj].programmedTime
    boids(dj)
    song= selectSong(djb[dj].x,djb[dj].y,djb[dj].z)
    add(song, djb[dj].songList)
    djb[dj].programmedTime = currentMoment
                          + song.length
```

We have developed a simple version of this algorithm using VRML [9] and Java. The *boids* function is based on the Anthony Steed's boids implementation [16]. The user interface allows regulating the inertia factor, the pull factor, the proximity distance to be maintained between every pair of boids, the proximity factor and the maximum allowed velocity. The DJ-Boids interface is shown in Fig. 2.

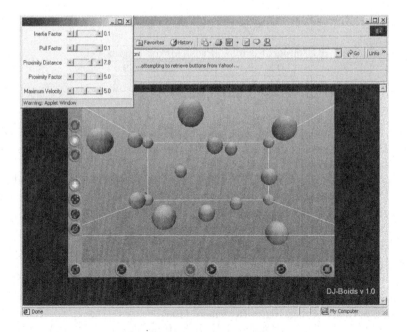

Fig. 2. DJ-Boids interface

In this way, when the program execution finishes we have a list of songs for every channel of the radio station. Note that all the channels should start to play their related list at the same time.

3.2   Experiments and Conclusions

We have found two sets of simulation parameters of particular interest, by intuitively interacting with the simulation through the visual feedback of the tool.

- The case A (see Table 1) in which all the dj-boids are uniformly distributed in the three-dimensional space, while each of them maintains the ability to reach any point in the space. This case guarantees that the songs being played by all the channels of the radio station at any time are varied enough to cover a great number of potential listeners. It also guarantees that the songs being played by a particular channel along the time are varied enough to not bore its listeners.
- The case B (see Table 1) in which all the dj-boids are uniformly distributed in the three-dimensional space, while each of them is contained in a zone in which it can move itself but from which it cannot exit. This case guarantees that the songs being played by all the channels of the radio station are at any time varied enough to cover a great number of potential listeners. It also guarantees that the songs being played by a particular channel maintain a certain trend.

Table 1. Interesting Cases

Case	Inert.F	Pull F.	Prox.D.	Prox.F.	Max.Vel.
A	0.1	0.1	5.3	9.5	9.5
B	0.1	0.1	7.8	5.0	5.0

In Table 1, $Inert.F.$ indicates the inertia factor, $PullF.$ the pull factor, $Prox.D.$ the proximity distance, $Prox.F.$ the proximity factor and $Max.Vel.$ the maximum velocity.

The results obtained up to now with the application of the proposed algorithm show the suitability of emergent collective behavior ideas to automatically program Internet multichannel radio stations. We will continue working in this direction of research.

References

1. Biethahn, J., Nissen, V. (ed.): Evolutionary Algorithms in Management Applications. Springer-Verlag, Berlin Heidelberg (1995)
2. Crossen, A., Budzik, J., Hammond, K. J.: Flytrap: Intelligent Group Music Recommendation. In Proceedings of Intelligent User Interfaces 2002. ACM Press (2002)

3. Dorigo, M., Maniezzo, V., Colorni, A.: The Ant System: Optimization by a Colony of Cooperating Agents. IEEE Transactions on Systems, Man, and Cybernetics-Part B. Vol. 26. Num. 1 (1996) 29–41

4. Field, A., Hartel, P., Mooij, W.: Personal DJ, an Architecture for Personalised Content Delivery. Tenth International World Wide Web Conference (2001) 1–7

5. Flake, G. W.: The Computational Beauty of Nature : Computer Explorations of Fractals, Chaos, Complex Systems, and Adaptation. MIT Press (1999)

6. French, J. C., Hauver, D.B.: Flycasting: On the Fly Broadcasting. DELOS Workshop: Personalisation and Recommender Systems in Digital Libraries (2001)

7. Hauver, D. B., French, J. C.: Flycasting: Using Collaborative Filtering to Generate a Playlist for Online Radio. International Conference on Web Delivering of Music (WEDELMUSIC'2001) (2001)

8. Ibanez, J., Gomez-Skarmeta, A. F., Blat, J.: DJ-Boids: Emergent Collective Behavior as Multichannel Radio Station Programming. International Conference on Intelligent User Interfaces 2003 (IUI'03). ACM Press (2003): 248–250

9. Joint Technical Committee ISO/IEC JTC 1 and The VRML Consortium, Inc.: The Virtual Reality Modeling Language. International Standard ISO/IEC 14772-1:1997. (1997)

10. Langton, C.: Artificial Life: An Overview. MIT Press, Cambridge, MA (1995)

11. Lapat, L., Dunne, J., Flury, M., Shabib, M., Warner, T., Budzik, J., Hammond, K., Birnbaum, L.: mpME!: Music Recommendation and Exploration. In Proceedings of Intelligent User Interfaces 2002. ACM Press (2002)

12. McCarthy, J. F., Anagnost, T. D.: MUSICFX: An Arbiter of Group Preferences for Computer Supported Collaborative Workouts. In Proceedings of the ACM 1998 Conference on Computer Supported Cooperative Work (CSCW 98) (1998) 363–372

13. Platt, J., Burges, C., Swenson, S., Weare, C., Zheng, A.: Learning a Gaussian Process Prior for Automatically Generating Music Playlists. Advances in Neural Information Processing Systems. Vol. 14 (2002) 1425–1432

14. Proctor, G., Winter, C.: Information Flocking: Data Visualisation In Virtual Worlds Using Emergent Behaviours. Proceedings of First International Conference on Virtual Worlds, VW'98. Lecture Notes in Computer Science, Vol. 1434 (1998)

15. Reynolds, C. W.: Flocks, Herds, and Schools: A Distributed Behavioral Model. Comp. Graph. Vol. 21. Num. 4 (1987) 25–34

16. Steed, A.: Steed's Boids Page. Available at
http://www.cs.ucl.ac.uk/staff/A.Steed/boids.html

Evaluating the Informative Quality of Web Sites by Fuzzy Computing with Words

Enrique Herrera-Viedma, Eduardo Peis, María Dolores Olvera,
Juan Carlos Herrera, and Yusef Hassan Montero

School of Library Science Studies, Univ. of Granada, Spain

Abstract. In this paper we present a method based on fuzzy computing with words to measure the informative quality of Web sites used to publish information stored in XML documents. This method generates linguistic recommendations on the informative quality of Web sites. This method is made up of both an evaluation scheme to analyze the informative quality of such Web sites and a generation method of linguistic recommendations. The evaluation scheme presents both technical criteria of Web site design and criteria related to the content of information of Web sites. It is oriented to the user because the chosen criteria are user friendly, in such a way that visitors to a Web site can assess them by means of linguistic evaluation judgements. The generation method generates linguistic recommendations of Web sites based on those linguistic evaluation judgements using the LOWA and LWA operators. Then, when a user looks for information on the Web we can help him/her with both recommendations on Web sites which store the retrieved documents and also recommendations on other Web sites which store other documents of interest related to his/her information needs. With this proposal information filtering and evaluation possibilities on the Web are increased.

1 Introduction

The networked world contains a vast amount of data. The exponential increase in Web sites and Web documents is contributing to Internet users not being able to find the information they require in a simple and efficient manner. There exists much debate on the quality of the information available on the Web, and how to recognize useful and quality information in an unregulated market place such as the Internet is becoming a serious problem. Therefore, users require tools to enable them to deal with the vast amount of content available on the Web [9, 10].

Recommender systems evaluate and filter the great amount of information available on the Web to assist people in their search process [13]. In a typical recommender system people provide evaluation judgements or annotations about documents as inputs, which the system then aggregates obtaining recommendations that are stored. Later, these recommendations can be reused to assist other people in their search process. In this sense, recommendations are a kind of plausible measure of the informative quality of Web documents. However, the

E. Menasalvas et al. (Eds.): AWIC 2003, LNAI 2663, pp. 62–72, 2003.

importance of Web sites that provide information should not be underestimated. Therefore, an interesting proposal to improve the performance of recommender systems also consists in generating recommendations on the informative quality of Web sites that store Web documents.

Usually, the quality of Web sites is measured using criteria focused on the effective Web site design (e.g. clear ordering of information, consistent navigation structure, ...). However, from the information consumer's perspective the quality of a Web site may not be assessed independently of the quality of the information content that it provides. The evaluation of Web sites focusing on the quality of the information that it provides is a difficult task that has rarely been studied [12]. In [8] an evaluation scheme of the information quality for analyzing personal Web sites which combines both informative and technical design aspects was proposed. This model is based on the *information quality framework* for the design of information systems defined in [7,11,14,15].

On the other hand, in typical recommender systems is assumed that people express their evaluation judgements by means of numerical values [13]. Sometimes, a person cannot express his/her judgements with an exact numerical value. Then, a more realistic approach may be to use linguistic assessments to express the evaluation judgements instead of numerical values. The *fuzzy linguistic approach* is a tool to manage linguistic information, which is based on the concept of *linguistic variables* [17]. It allows us to model qualitative values typical of human communication for representing qualitative concepts such as "importance" [4,5].

In this paper, we present an evaluation method of informative quality of the Web sites based on fuzzy linguistic techniques. This method allows us to generate linguistic recommendations on quality Web sites. We consider Web sites that have information stored in multiple kinds of documents structured in the XML-format, e.g. scientific articles, opinion articles,... The idea consists in evaluating a Web site according to the evaluations aported by all its visitors. After visiting a Web site to examine a stored document users are invited to complete an evaluation questionnaire about the informative quality of the site. Using the information quality framework proposed in [7,11,14,15], we develop a particular evaluation scheme of Web sites which is oriented to the user. This evaluation scheme considers both technical criteria of Web site design and criteria related to the information content of Web sites. The chosen criteria are easily comprehensible to the users such that Web visitors can easily assess them. Visitors provide their evaluation judgements by means of linguistic terms assessed on linguistic variables [17]. Given an area of interest, the recommendation of a Web site is obtained by combining the linguistic evaluation judgements provided by different visitors to the site. To do this, we use the operators for *fuzzy computing with words* LOWA [3] and LWA [2]. The recommendations obtained are linguistic values that express qualitatively the informative quality of the Web site with respect to the area of interest. Then, when a user requires information together with retrieved documents we can also provide him/her with both recommendations on the informative quality of Web sites that store these documents and recommendations on other Web sites that could store other documents of interest. In such a way, the filtering of information and evaluation possibilities in the Web are increased.

The paper is set out as follows. The foundation of fuzzy computing with words is presented in Sect. 2. The evaluation scheme for analyzing the informative quality of Web sites is defined in Sect. 3. The generation method of linguistic recommendations is defined in Sect. 4. Finally, in Sect. 5 we present our conclusions.

2   Foundation of Fuzzy Computing with Words

The *ordinal fuzzy linguistic approach* [2,3] is a very useful kind of fuzzy linguistic approach used for modeling the computing with words process as well as linguistic aspects of problems. It is defined by considering a finite and totally ordered label set $S = \{s_i\}, i \in \{0, \ldots, \mathcal{T}\}$ in the usual sense, i.e., $s_i \geq s_j$ if $i \geq j$, and with odd cardinality (7 or 9 labels). The mid term represents an assessment of "approximately 0.5", and the rest of the terms being placed symmetrically around it. The semantics of the label set is established from the ordered structure of the label set by considering that each label for the pair $(s_i, s_{\mathcal{T}-i})$ is equally informative. For example, we can use the following set of nine labels to provide the user evaluations: $\{T = Total, EH = Extremely\_High, VH = Very\_High, H = High, M = Medium, L = Low, VL = Very\_Low, EL = Extremely\_Low, N = None\}$.

In any linguistic approach we need management operators of linguistic information. An advantage of the ordinal fuzzy linguistic approach is the simplicity and quickness of its computational model. It is based on the symbolic computation [2,3] and acts by direct computation on labels by taking into account the order of such linguistic assessments in the ordered structure of labels. Usually, the ordinal fuzzy linguistic model for computing with words is defined by establishing i) a negation operator, ii) comparison operators based on the ordered structure of linguistic terms, and iii) adequate aggregation operators of ordinal fuzzy linguistic information. In most ordinal fuzzy linguistic approaches the negation operator is defined from the semantics associated to the linguistic terms as $Neg(s_i) = s_j \mid j = \mathcal{T} - i$; and there are defined two comparison operators of linguistic terms: i) *Maximization operator*, $MAX(s_i, s_j) = s_i$ if $s_i \geq s_j$; and ii) *Minimization operator*, $MIN(s_i, s_j) = s_i$ if $s_i \leq s_j$. In the following subsections, we present two operators based on symbolic computation.

2.1   The LOWA Operator

The *Linguistic Ordered Weighted Averaging* (LOWA) is an operator used to aggregate non-weighted ordinal linguistic information, i.e., linguistic information values with equal importance [3].

Definition 1. *Let $A = \{a_1, \ldots, a_m\}$ be a set of labels to be aggregated, then the LOWA operator, ϕ, is defined as $\phi(a_1, \ldots, a_m) = W \cdot B^T = \mathcal{C}^m\{w_k, b_k, k =$*

$1, \ldots, m\} = w_1 \odot b_1 \oplus (1 - w_1) \odot \mathcal{C}^{m-1}\{\beta_h, b_h, h = 2, \ldots, m\}$, where $W = [w_1, \ldots, w_m]$, is a weighting vector, such that, $w_i \in [0, 1]$ and $\Sigma_i w_i = 1$. $\beta_h = w_h / \Sigma_2^m w_k, h = 2, \ldots, m$, and $B = \{b_1, \ldots, b_m\}$ is a vector associated to A, such that, $B = \sigma(A) = \{a_{\sigma(1)}, \ldots, a_{\sigma(m)}\}$, where, $a_{\sigma(j)} \leq a_{\sigma(i)} \ \forall \ i \leq j$, with σ being a permutation over the set of labels A. $\mathcal{C}^m$ is the convex combination operator of m labels and if m=2, then it is defined as $\mathcal{C}^2\{w_i, b_i, i = 1, 2\} = w_1 \odot s_j \oplus (1 - w_1) \odot s_i = s_k$, such that, $k = min\{\mathcal{T}, i + round(w_1 \cdot (j - i))\}$ $s_j, s_i \in S, (j \geq i)$, where "round" is the usual round operation, and $b_1 = s_j$, $b_2 = s_i$. If $w_j = 1$ and $w_i = 0$ with $i \neq j \ \forall i$, then the convex combination is defined as: $\mathcal{C}^m\{w_i, b_i, i = 1, \ldots, m\} = b_j$.

The LOWA operator is an "or-and" operator [3] and its behavior can be controlled by means of W. In order to classify OWA operators in regard to their localisation between "or" and "and", Yager [16] introduced a measure of orness, associated with any vector W:$orness(W) = \frac{1}{m-1} \sum_{i=1}^{m}(m - i)w_i$. This measure characterizes the degree to which the aggregation is like an "or" (MAX) operation. Note that an OWA operator with $orness(W) \geq 0.5$ will be an orlike, and with $orness(W) < 0.5$ will be an andlike operator.

An important question of the OWA operator is the determination of W. A good solution consists of representing the concept of fuzzy majority by means of the weights of W, using a non-decreasing proportional fuzzy linguistic quantifier [18]Q in its computation [16]:$w_i = Q(i/m) - Q((i - 1)/m), i = 1, \ldots, m$, being the membership function of Q: $Q(r) = \begin{cases} 0 & \text{if } r < a \\ \frac{r-a}{b-a} & \text{if } a \leq r \leq b \\ 1 & \text{if } r > b \end{cases}$ with $a, b, r \in [0, 1]$.

When a fuzzy linguistic quantifier Q is used to compute the weights of LOWA operator, ϕ, it is symbolized by ϕ_Q.

2.2 The LWA Operator

The Linguistic Weighted Averaging (LWA) operator is another important operator which is defined to aggregate weighted ordinal linguistic information, i.e., linguistic information values with non equal importance [2].

Definition 2. The aggregation of a set of weighted linguistic opinions, $\{(c_1, a_1), \ldots, (c_m, a_m,)\}$, $c_i, a_i \in S$, according to the LWA operator Φ is defined as $\Phi[(c_1, a_1), \ldots, (c_m, a_m)] = \phi(h(c_1, a_1), \ldots, h(c_m, a_m))$, where a_i represents the weighted opinion, c_i the importance degree of a_i, and h is the transformation function defined depending on the weighting vector W used for the LOWA operator ϕ, such that, $h = MIN(c_i, a_i)$ if $orness(W) \geq 0.5$ and $h = MAX(Neg(c_i), a_i)$ if $orness(W) < 0.5$.

3 Evaluation Scheme of Informative Quality of Web Sites

3.1 Brief Background about Information Quality Framework

In [7,11,14,15] it was proposed an information quality framework by considering that the quality of the information systems cannot be assessed independently of the information consumers' opinions (people who use information). This framework establishes four major information quality categories to classify the different evaluation dimensions [7,11,14,15]:

1. *Intrinsic information quality*, which emphasizes the importance of the informative aspects of the information itself. It implies that information has quality in its own right. The main dimension of this category is the accuracy of the information. If a reputation for inaccurate information becomes common knowledge for a particular information system, this system is viewed as having little added value and will result in a reduction of use. Other dimensions of this category are: believability, reputation and objectivity.
2. *Contextual information quality,* which also emphasizes the importance of the informative aspects of the information but from a task perspective. It highlights the requirement that information quality must be considered within the context of the task in hand; it must be relevant, timely, complete, and appropriate in terms of amount, so as to add value to the tasks for which the information is provided. Therefore, some dimensions of this category are: value-added, relevance, completeness, timeliness, appropriate amount.
3. *Representational information quality,* which emphasizes the importance of the technical aspects of the computer system that stores the information. It requires information systems to present their information in such a way that it is interpretable, easy to understand, easy to manipulate, and is represented concisely and consistently. Some of its dimensions are: understandability, interpretability, concise representation, consistent representation.
4. *Accessibility information quality,* which emphasizes the importance of the technical aspects of the computer system that provides access to information. It requires the information system to be accessible but secure. Some dimensions of this category are: accessibility and secure access.

Using this quality framework, in [8] a tool to evaluate the informative quality of personal Web sites was proposed, which includes the following dimensions:

1. *Intrinsic quality of Personal Web sites:* i) accuracy and errors of the content, and ii) accurate, workable and relevant hyperlinks.
2. *Contextual quality of Personal Web sites:* provision of author's information.
3. *Representational quality of Personal Web sites:* i) organization, visual settings, typographical features, and consistency, ii) vividness and attractiveness, and iii) confusion of the content.
4. *Accessibility quality of Personal Web sites:* navigational tools provided.

3.2   Definition of the Evaluation Scheme of Documental Web Sites

Using the above information quality framework we develop an evaluation scheme for analyzing the informative quality of Web sites that provide information stored in XML documents. It is defined from the information consumers' perspective, and for this reason we can say that it is oriented to the user. Before presenting it, we will take into account two considerations: i) We want to generate recommendations on Web sites from the evaluations provided by different visitors to Web sites. Therefore, the evaluation scheme requires the inclusion of subjective dimensions easily comprehensible to the information consumers (e.g. relevance, understandability) rather than dimensions that can be objectively measured independently of the consumers (e.g. accuracy measured by the number of spelling or grammatical errors). And ii) we analyze Web sites that store information in multiple kinds of documents structured in the XML format (e.g. scientific articles, opinion articles) when users visit them occasionally because they store documents which meet their information needs. Therefore, user opinions on the informative quality of these documents (e.g. the relevance) must be an important dimension in the evaluation scheme. Taking into account these considerations, we define an evaluation scheme of Web sites oriented to the user that contemplates four quality categories with the following evaluation dimensions:

1. *Intrinsic quality of Web sites.* Accuracy of information is the main determinant of the intrinsic information quality of information systems. We discuss accuracy of Web sites by considering what visitors think about the believability of the information content that the Web site provides. Given that we consider Web sites as information sources that are visited occasionally, we are not interested in evaluating the accuracy by means of grammatical and spelling errors or relevant hyper-links existing on the Web site.
2. *Contextual quality of Web sites.* This is the most important category in the evaluation scheme. In our evaluation scheme neither the dimension of author's information, as in [8], nor the appropriate amount of information are meaningful. We propose to evaluate this category by considering what visitors think about the relevancy, timeliness and completeness of documents that the Web site provides them with when they search for information about particular topic, i.e., if documents are relevant to the search topic, if documents are sufficiently current and up-to-date with regards to the search topic, and if documents are sufficient complete with regards to the topic.
3. *Representational quality of Web sites.* We analyze this category for the Web sites that provide information stored in XML documents from two aspects: i) representational aspects of Web site design and ii) representational aspects of documents stored in the Web site. In the first case, we consider what visitors think about the understandability of the Web site, i.e., whether or not the Web site is well organized in such a way that visitors can easily understand how to access stored documents. In the second one, we consider what visitors think about the understandability, originality and conciseness of the information content of XML documents used.
4. *Accessibility quality of Web sites.* As in [8] we consider that this category must be assessed as to whether or not the Web site provides enough navigation mechanisms so that visitors can reach their desired documents faster and easier. Lacking effective paths to access the desired documents would handicap visitors, therefore navigation tools are necessary to help users locate the information they require. We evaluate this category by considering

what visitors think about the navigational tools of the Web site. The security dimension is not a key aspect on the Web sites that we are considering.

The evaluation scheme is summarized in Table 1.

Table 1. Evaluation scheme of Web sites oriented to the user

Information Quality Categories	Evaluation Dimensions
Intrinsic quality of Web sites	believability
Contextual quality of Web sites	relevancy, timeliness, completeness
Representational quality of Web sites	understandability of Web sites, originality, understandability of documents, conciseness
Accessibility quality of Web sites	navigational tools

4   Evaluating the Informative Quality of Web Sites

In this section, we present a generation method of linguistic recommendations for evaluating the informative quality of Web sites. These linguistic recommendations are obtained from the linguistic evaluation judgements provided by a non-determined number of Web visitors. After a visitor has used an XML document stored in a Web site, he/she is invited to complete a quality evaluation questionnaire as per the quality dimensions established in the above evaluation scheme. The recommendations are obtained by aggregating the linguistic evaluation judgements by means of the LWA and LOWA operators.

4.1   Development of the Quality Evaluation Questionnaire

The quality evaluation questionnaire provides questions for each one of the dimensions proposed in the evaluation scheme, i.e., there are nine questions: $\{q_1, \ldots, q_9\}$. For example for the quality dimension *believability* the question q_1 can be: "What is the degree of believability of this Web site in your opinion?". The concept behind each question is rated on a linguistic term set S. For example, we can use the set of nine linguistic terms proposed in Sect. 2 to rate all the questions. Furthermore, we assume that each quality dimension does not have the same importance in the evaluation scheme, i.e., it is assigned a relative linguistic importance degree for each quality dimension: $\{I(q_1), \ldots, I(q_9)\}$, $I(q_i) \in S$. To assign these degrees, the quality dimensions related to the Web site content it-self (those included in the first and second category of evaluation scheme) should have more importance than the remaining ones. In particular, the *relevancy* has the greatest degree of relative importance.

As we pointed out in Sect. 3.2 and in the above paragraph, the question $q_2 = relevancy$ is very important in our evaluation scheme. For this reason, we propose to evaluate the relevance of the XML documents provided by the Web site for a particular search topic in a more meticulous way. We do not evaluate it directly by means of a particular value supplied by a user. The idea consists in evaluating it from the evaluation of the relevance of the parts that make up the structure of XML documents. To do so, we associate with each XML document an evaluation questionnaire of relevance that depends on the kind of document. For example, if the XML document is a "scientific article" with the DTD,

```
<!DOCTYPE article [
<!ELEMENT article (title, authors, abstract?, introduction, body, conclusions,
bibliography)>
<!ELEMENT title (#PCDATA)>
<!ELEMENT authors (author+)>
<!ELEMENT (author | abstract | introduction) (#PCDATA)>
<!ELEMENT body (section+)>
<!ELEMENT section (titleS, #PCDATA)>
<!ELEMENT titleS (#PCDATA)>
<!ELEMENT conclusions (#PCDATA)>
<!ELEMENT bibliography (bibitem+)>
<!ELEMENT bibitem (#PCDATA)> ]
```

then, we can establish the relevance evaluation questionnaire on the following set of elements of DTD : "title, authors, abstract, introduction, body, conclusions, bibliography". In this case, the relevance evaluation questionnaire would have 7 questions, and for example, a question could be "What is the relevance degree of the title with respect to the search topic?". In other kinds of XML documents we have to choose the set of elements of DTD, $\{p_1, \ldots, p_n\}$, to be considered in the relevance evaluation questionnaire. We assume that each component p_k has a distinct informative role, i.e., each one affects the overall relevance eval-uation of XML document in a different way. This is modeled by assigning to each p_k a relative linguistic importance degree $I(p_k) \in S$. As we did in [6], this peculiarity is added in the DTD using the XML syntax [1] to define an attribute of importance "rank" for each meaningful component of DTD, which contains a relative linguistic importance degree. Then, given a search topic (e.g. "recommender systems"), the relevance for an XML document is obtained by combining the linguistic evaluation judgements provided by the visitor regarding the meaningful components of its DTD.

Summarizing, the quality evaluation questionnaire that a visitor must com-plete is comprised of 8 questions and a relevance evaluation questionnaire which is associated with the document accessed and depends on the kind of docu-ment.

4.2 Generation Method of Linguistic Recommendations

Suppose that we want to generate a recommendation database for qualifying the informative quality of a set of Web sites $\{Web_1, \ldots, Web_L\}$ which stores information in XML documents. These Web sites can be evaluated from a set of different areas of interest or search topics, $\{\mathcal{A}_1, \ldots, \mathcal{A}_M\}$. Suppose that D_l represents the set of XML documents stored in the Web site Web_l. We consider that each XML document $d_j \in D_l$ presents an evaluation scheme composed of a finite set of elements of its DTD, $\{p_1, \ldots, p_n\}$, and its respective relative linguistic importance degrees $\{I(p_1), \ldots, I(p_n)\}$. Let $\{e_1^{m,l}, \ldots, e_T^{m,l}\}$ be the set of different visitors to the Web site Web_l who completed the quality evaluation questionnaire $\{q_1, \ldots, q_9\}$ when they searched for information about the topic $\mathcal{A}_m$. In the quality evaluation scheme each question q_i is associated to its respective linguistic importance degree $I(q_i)$. Let $\{q_1^t, \ldots, q_9^t\}$ be a set of linguistic assessments provided by the visitor $e_t^{m,l}$. We must point out that the assessment q_8^t is achieved from the set of linguistic evaluation judgements $\{e_{t1}^{ml}, \ldots, e_{tn}^{ml}\}$ provided by the visitor $e_t^{m,l}$ regarding the set of elements of DTD, $\{p_1, \ldots, p_n\}$, associated to the XML document accessed d_j. Then, q_8^t is obtained using the LWA operator as follows: $q_8^t = \Phi[(I(p_1), e_{t1}^{ml}), \ldots, (I(p_n), e_{tn}^{ml})] = \phi_{Q_3}(h(I(p_1), e_{t1}^{ml}), \ldots, h(I(p_n), e_{tn}^{ml}))$, being Q_3 the linguistic quantifier used to calculate the weighting vector W. If we assume that Q_3 represents the concept of fuzzy majority then q_8^t is a measure of significance that represents the relevance of d_j with respect to the topic A_l according to Q_3 linguistic evaluation judgements provided by $e_t^{m,l}$ on the meaningful elements of DTD associated with d_j. Then, given a search topic $\mathcal{A}_m$, the generation process of a linguistic recommendation $r_l^m \in S$ for a Web site Web_l is obtained using a LWA-LOWA based evaluation method in the following steps:

1. Calculate for $e_t^{m,l}$ his/her individual recommendation $r_t^{m,l}$ by means of LWA Φ: $r_t^{m,l} = \Phi[(I(q_1), q_1^t), \ldots, (I(q_9), q_9^t)] = \phi_{Q_2}(h(I(q_1), q_1^t), \ldots, h(I(q_9), q_9^t))$. $r_t^{m,l}$ is a measure that represents the informative quality of the Web site Web_l with respect to topic $\mathcal{A}_m$ according to the Q_2 linguistic evaluation judgements provided by the visitor $e_t^{m,l}$.

2. Calculate the global recommendation $r^{m,l}$ by means of an LOWA operator guided by the fuzzy majority concept represented by a linguistic quantifier Q_1 as $r_t^i = \phi_{Q_1}(r_1^{m,l}, \ldots, r_T^{m,l})$. In this case, $r^{m,l}$ is a measure that represents the informative quality of the Web site Web_l with respect to topic $\mathcal{A}_m$ according to the Q_2 evaluation judgements provided by the Q_1 visitors or recommenders. $r^{m,l}$ represents the linguistic informative category of Web_l with respect to the topic $\mathcal{A}_m$.

3. Store the recommendation $r^{m,l}$ in order to assist user future search processes.

5 Conclusions

The analysis of the quality of Web sites focusing on the quality of information that they provide has rarely been studied. In this paper, we have shown that this problem can be studied using an information quality framework defined for information systems [7]. We have presented an approach to evaluate the informative quality of Web sites by means of fuzzy linguistic techniques. We consider Web sites that provide information structured in XML documents. This approach is proposed to generate linguistic recommendations on such Web sites that can help other users in their future search processes. In this approach we have defined an evaluation scheme and an evaluation method to measure the informative quality of Web sites. This approach is a user oriented approach because it considers only the visitors' evaluation judgements to generate the recommendations. Considerable use is made of fuzzy set technology to provide the ability to describe the information in a way, using linguistic labels, that is particularly user friendly.

In the future, we propose to continue this research approach by designing other evaluation tools based on fuzzy linguistic techniques for other kinds of Web sites, e.g., commercial Web sites.

References

1. Goldfarb, C., Prescod, P.: *The XML handbook.* Oxford: Prentice Hall. (1998).
2. Herrera, F., Herrera-Viedma, E.: Aggregation operators for linguistic weighted information. IEEE Trans. on Sys. Man and Cyb. Part. A. **27** (1997) 646–656.
3. Herrera, F., Herrera-Viedma, E., Verdegay, J. L.: Direct Approach Processes in Group Decision Making Using Linguistic OWA Operators. Fuzzy Sets and Sys. **79** (1996) 175–190.
4. Herrera-Viedma, E.: Modeling the retrieval process for an information retrieval system using an ordinal fuzzy linguistic approach. J. of the Ame. Soc. for Inf. Sci. and Tech. **52**(6) (2001) 460–475.
5. Herrera-Viedma, E.: An information retrieval system with ordinal linguistic weighted queries based on two weighting elements. Int. J. of Uncertainty, Fuzziness and Knowledge-Based Sys. **9** (2001) 77–88.
6. Herrera-Viedma, E., Peis, E.: Evaluating the informative quality of documents in SGML format from judgements by means of fuzzy linguistic techniques based on computing with words. Inf. Proces. & Manag. **39**(2) (2003) 233–249.
7. Huang, K., Lee, Y.W., Wang, R.Y.: *Quality information and knowledge.* Upper Saddle River, NJ: Prentice Hall, (1999).
8. Katerattanakul, P., Siau, K.: Measuring information quality of Web sites: Development of an instrument. Proc. of 20th Int. Conf. on Inf. Sys. Charlotte, NC, (1999) 279–285.
9. Kobayashi, M., Takeda, K.: Information retrieval on the web. ACM Computing Surveys. **32**(2) (2000) 144–173.
10. Lawrence, S., Giles, C.: Searching the web: General and scientific information access. IEEE Comm. Mag. **37**(1) (1998) 116–122.
11. Lee, Y.W., Strong, D.M., Kahn, B.K., Wang, R.Y.: AIMQ: A methodology for information quality assessment. Inf. & Manag. **40**(2) (2002) 133–146.
12. Rieh, S.Y.: Judgment of information quality and cognitive authority in the Web. J. of the Amer. Soc. for Inf. Sci. and Tech. **53**(2) (2002) 145–161.
13. Reisnick, P. & Varian, H. R. (1997). Recommender systems. Special issue of Comm. of the ACM. **40**(3).

14. Strong, D.M., Lee, Y.W., Wang, R.Y.: Data quality in context. Comm. of the ACM. **40**(5) (1997) 103–110.
15. Wang, R.Y., Strong, D.M.: Beyond accuracy: What data quality means to data consumers. J. of Manag. Inf. Sys. **12**(4) (1996) 5–34.
16. Yager, R.R.: On ordered weighted averaging aggregation operators in multicriteria decision making. IEEE Trans. on Syst., Man, and Cyb. **18** (1988) 183–190.
17. Zadeh, L.A.: The concept of a linguistic variable and its applications to approximate reasoning. Part I. Inf. Sci. **8** (1975) 199–249. Part II. Inf. Sci. **8** (1975) 301–357. Part III. Inf. Sci. **9** (1975) 43–80.
18. Zadeh, L.A.: A computational approach to fuzzy quantifiers in natural languages. Computers and Mathematics with Applications. 9 (1983) 149–184.

Mining Association Rules Using Fuzzy Inference on Web Data

Mariluz Martínez[1], Gelver Vargas[1], Andrés Dorado[2], and Marta Millán[1]

[1] Escuela de Ingeniería de Sistemas y Computación
Universidad del Valle, Cali-Colombia
{mariluz,gelvervb}@libertad.univalle.edu.co
millan@eisc.univalle.edu.co
[2] Carrera de Ingeniería de Sistemas y Computación
Pontificia Universidad Javeriana, Cali-Colombia
adorado@puj.edu.co

Abstract. The association rules model is one of most widely used models in data mining. An association rule is an implication of the form $X \rightarrow Y$, where X and Y are a set of items that satisfy two constraints, given by the user, called minimum support (*minsup*) and minimum confidence (*minconf*). Normally, the values of *minsup* and *minconf* are crisp. In this paper, we analyze how association rules mining is affected when these values are treated as fuzzy.

In order to calculate frequent itemsets and to generate association rules, an algorithm based on fuzzy sets is proposed. Using the fuzzy inference system, FUZZYC, the algorithm offers to user an intuitive way for defining and tuning the *minconf* and *minsup* parameters.

Keywords: frequent pattern mining, association rules, data mining, fuzzy inference systems

1 Introduction

One of the most important tasks in data mining is the one known as the Association Rules task[1]. An association rule is an implication of the form $X \rightarrow Y$, where X and Y are a set of items that satisfy two constraints given by the user called minimum support (*minsup*) and minimum confidence (*minconf*). Intuitively, a rule $X \rightarrow Y$ means that transactions which contain X tend to contain Y.

A common application domain of association rules is sales data, known as *basket data*. In this domain, a transaction consists of general information (e.g. id number and date) and bought items' information. This kind of rules is called *boolean association rules*. Many algorithms (e.g. Apriori, AprioriTID, Apriori-Hybrid, FP-Tree, DIC) have been proposed in order to find association rules [1, 2,3,4,5].

Association rules can also be generated from relational data sets, in which attributes values can take quantitative and categorical values. Quantitative association rules where domain attributes are partitioned into intervals were proposed

E. Menasalvas et al. (Eds.): AWIC 2003, LNAI 2663, pp. 73–82, 2003.

in [2]. According to [7] this approach is used to solve infinite domain problem but in doing so, it brings up another problem known as the sharp boundary problem. In [7], the fuzzy set concept is better than the partition method because fuzzy sets provide a smooth transition between membership and non-membership of an element to the set. They also propose an algorithm for mining fuzzy association rules considering elements near the boundaries in the mining process.

An algorithm to calculate fuzzy sets and their membership functions applying clustering techniques into data is proposed in [8]. Gyenesei et al[9] introduce a new fuzzy association rule definition with categorical and quantitative attributes.

Data mining techniques can also be applied to web data. Web mining has been one of the most important research areas. Web mining categories are defined in [12,15], based on three areas of interest depending on the part of the web to be mined: web content/data/documents, link structure of the Web and web user behavior called respectively Web Content Mining, Web Structure Mining and Web Usage Mining.

When the association rules task [1] is applied to web log files, the goal is to identify sets of pages accessed together with a given support parameter[19]. User's access behavior can be represented in these association rules.

Many systems and approaches [13,14,16] applied to web data include the association rule task. A collaborative recommendation technique based on association rules is presented in [18]. A new and efficient algorithm to obtain these rules is proposed in which only one target user or article at a time is considered in which away that only rules with the target user in the head rule are needed.

On the other hand, considering that in the real-world data there are few rules with both high support and confidence, Pei et al. [17] propose an extended Apriori algorithm called FT-Apriori in order to find approximate and more general patterns called fault-tolerant patterns. According to authors fault-tolerant pattern mining allows to obtain many kinds of novel, interesting and practically useful knowledge.

A fuzzy association rule technique integrated with a case based reasoning approach is proposed in [20]. Fuzzy rules are generated from the case base in which duration of page view is considered as a fuzzy attribute for association rule mining. Rules can be used for prediction and recommendation.

In this paper, a method based on fuzzy inference to select frequent itemsets and to generate association rules is proposed. In contrast with traditional techniques, the proposed method takes into account rules near the threshold of acceptance. In addition, this approach helps the user to set up the *minsup* and *minconf* parameters.

The rest of this paper is organized in sections. In Sect. 2, association rules and fuzzy systems are presented. In Sect. 3, a method based on fuzzy inference for mining association rules is described. Section 4 shows some experimental results. Finally, in Sect. 5 some conclusions are presented.

2   Preliminaries

2.1   Association Rules

The goal of association discovery is to find items that imply the presence of other items. An association rule is formally described as follows:

Let $I = \{i_1, i_2 \ldots, i_n\}$ be a set of literals called items and let D be a set of transactions where each transaction T is a set of items such that $T \subset I$.

An association rule is an implication of the form $X \to Y$ where $X \subset I$ and $Y \subset I$ and $X \cap Y = \emptyset$. The rule $X \to Y$ holds in the transaction set D with confidence c if $c\%$ of transactions in D that contain X also contain Y. The rule $X \to Y$ holds in the transaction set D with support s if $s\%$ of transactions in D contain $X \cup Y$.

Given D a set of transactions, the problem of mining association rules is to generate all association rules having support and confidence greater than a minimum user-specified support (*minsup*) and a minimum user-specified confidence (*minconf*) respectively.

In order to derive the association rules two steps are required: (1) Find the largest itemsets for the given *minsup* and (2) Compute rules for the given *minconf* based on the itemsets obtained in the previous step.

The *Apriori* algorithm for finding all large itemsets makes multiple passes over the database. In the first pass, the algorithm counts item occurrences to determine the large 1-itemsets. The remainder passes (say pass k), consist of two steps: (1) the large itemsets L_{k-1} found in the $(k-1)$th pass are used to generate the candidate itemsets C_k, (2) all itemsets having some $k-1$ subset that is not in L_{k-1} are deleted, yielding C_k. Once the largest itemsets are obtained, rules of the form $a \to (l - a)$ are computed, where $a \subset l$ and l is a large itemset.

2.2   Fuzzy Reasoning

Fuzzy Sets. The use of linguistic terms involving vagueness is very common in daily life. For instance, somebody talking about weather says: "The day is cold" or "the room is warm" rather than "the temperature of the day is $8°C$" or "the temperature of the room is $18°C$". The linguistic term "cold" is relative to the observer and can be numerically defined with a range of temperatures that are "around" $10°C$.

The possible values associated to a linguistic term correspond to the *Universe of Discourse* known as *Fuzzy Set*. The meaning of the linguistic term, characterized by a membership function, is intuitively assigned by the person who uses the term. The membership function maps numeric values into linguistic terms.

Fuzzy Inference Systems. In contrast with classic logic that deals with propositions both true and false, fuzzy logic proposes a formalization of rough reasoning modes. *Fuzzy logic* emerged from the fuzzy sets theory which extends the traditional sets theory to solve problems where the classification in "all or nothing" is not appropriate. Traditionally, a logic expression is either totally true or

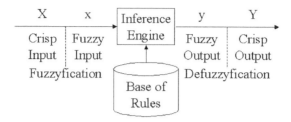

Fig. 1. An overview of a fuzzy inference system

totally false. However, in the fuzzy universe, the values are from 0% to 100% true or false. In other words, all fuzzy propositions have some degree of truth at the interval (0,1].

Systems based on fuzzy logic as well as expert systems take advantage of human experience and knowledge to define its variables and rules. In these systems, variables are compounded by a group of fuzzy sets. A fuzzy inference system involves three primary stages: *fuzzyfication*, *fuzzy inference* and *defuzzyfication*. Figure 1 depicts an overview of a fuzzy inference system.

The input of the *fuzzyfication* stage is a real number or *crisp value* corresponding to an instance of an input variable of the system.The truth degree of membership to each fuzzy set is calculated using membership functions. The output of this stage is a fuzzy value.

The *fuzzy inference* stage uses rules of the form

IF ⟨*Situation*⟩ THEN ⟨*Action*⟩

Inference rules are not a free form of natural language[6]. They are limited to a set of linguistic terms and a strict syntax. Each antecedent (situation or condition associated to the IF-part) of a rule corresponds to a specific value of a fuzzy input. This input value is a result of the fuzzyfication stage. Each consequent (action or conclusion associated to the THEN-part) of a rule corresponds to a fuzzy output.

In addition, this kind of rules has two representative characteristics: they are qualitative rather than quantitative and each "situation" is related to an appropriate "action". The importance of these rules lay on the possibility of representing human knowledge by a hierarchical model of them. Besides, these rules are relatively simple and they are consistent with the human reasoning modes, that are approximate rather than exact.

The fuzzy inference stage calculates the output fuzzy values for the corresponding variables. It uses the relationship among input and output variables from the base of linguistic rules provide by the expert. At this point, a number of rules can be true in different degrees, producing competence among the results.

Using an operator called by some authors[10] *Aggregation's Operator* the instances of the antecedents are combined to determine the value of the rule. This value is applied to the consequents of the rule. This procedure is followed for all rules participating in the inference stage.

It is possible that an output fuzzy variable has a fuzzy set as consequent in several rules. To determine the value for this fuzzy set, an operator called *Composition's Operator* is used.

The *defuzzyfication* stage combines the fuzzy values to each output variable obtaining a real number or crisp value for each one. In the former fuzzy systems, the maximum value was assigned. Currently, this method is considered very poor, due to the fact that ignores the contribution of all the rules. There are, however, alternatives to calculate the output values. In this paper, a method called *Center of Area* which combines fuzzy values using a weighted average to obtain the crisp value is used.

3   Method Based on Fuzzy Inference for Mining Association Rules

Fuzzy inference systems as well as other systems require a model of the process. There are three fundamental aspects for implementing an inference system based on fuzzy logic: (1) knowledge representation (How to define a structure of linguistic rules of the form IF ... THEN with numerical meaning?), (2) reasoning strategy (How to get suitable actions for the identified situations?) and (3) knowledge acquisition (How to define a set of inference rules?).

The proposed method for mining association rules is based on a fuzzy inference system called *FUZZYC* [11]. In Fig. 2 a scheme of the method is shown.

Frequent itemsets are calculated using a variant of the Apriori algorithm. In this case, the method uses FUZZYC to determine, based on acceptance conditions established by the user, when an itemset is or is not frequent. The variant can be summarized as follows:

- The minimum user-specified support is mapped from the real domain into a fuzzy domain
- The support of the itemsets is mapped from the real domain into a fuzzy domain
- The itemsets are evaluated using a fuzzy system

In Fig. 3 the minimum support and the output variable defined in a fuzzy domain are shown.

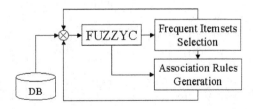

Fig. 2. Scheme of the proposed method

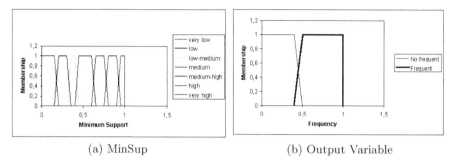

(a) MinSup   (b) Output Variable

Fig. 3. Fuzzy definitions

For instance, a minimum support set to 0.8 is mapped to the fuzzy sets "medium-high" and "high" with membership values of 0.5 and a support calculated of 0.9 is mapped to the fuzzy set "high" with a membership value of 1.0.

From the set of rules depicted in Table 1, the following rules are activated:

- IF minsup IS "high" AND support IS "high"
  THEN itemsets IS "Freq(uent)"
- IF minsup IS "medium-high" AND support IS "high"
  THEN itemsets IS "Freq(uent)"

Once the fuzzy inference stage using these base of rules has been executed, a fuzzy value of 0.5 for the output fuzzy variable is assigned. Association rules are generated from the frequent identified itemsets.

The proposed method can be summarized as follows:

- The minimum user-specified confidence is mapped from the real domain into a fuzzy domain
- The confidence of the candidate rules is mapped from the real domain into a fuzzy domain
- The association rules are generated using a fuzzy system

Table 1. Inference rules to determine frequent itemsets

Support	Minimum Support						
	Very low	Low	Low-Med	Medium	Med-High	High	Very High
Very low	freq	freq	freq	freq	freq	freq	freq
Low	no freq	freq	freq	freq	freq	freq	freq
Low-Medium	no freq	no freq	freq	freq	freq	freq	freq
Medium	no freq	no freq	no freq	freq	freq	freq	freq
Medium-High	no freq	no freq	no freq	no freq	freq	freq	freq
High	no freq	no freq	no freq	no freq	no freq	freq	freq
Very High	no freq	no freq	no freq	no freq	no freq	no freq	freq

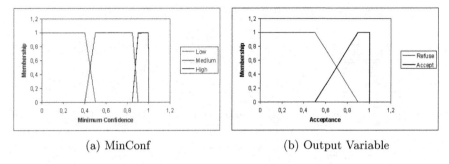

(a) MinConf   (b) Output Variable

Fig. 4. Fuzzy definitions

In Fig. 4 the minimum confidence and the output variable defined in a fuzzy domain are shown.

For instance, a minimum confidence set to 0.87 is mapped to the fuzzy sets "medium" and "high" with membership values of 0.6 and 0.4, respectively. A confidence calculated of 0.9 is mapped to the fuzzy set "high" with a membership value of 1.0.

From the set of rules depicted in Table 2, the following rules are activated:

- IF minconf IS "high" AND confidence IS "high"
  THEN association rule IS "Accept(ed)"
- IF minconf = "medium" AND confidence IS "high"
  THEN association rule IS "Accept(ed)"

Table 2. Inference rules to determine association rules

	Minimum Confidence		
Confidence	Low	Medium	High
Low	Accept	Refuse	Refuse
Medium	Accept	Accept	Refuse
High	Accept	Accept	Accept

Once the fuzzy inference stage using these base of rules has been executed a fuzzy value of 0.6 for the output fuzzy variable is assigned.

4   Experimental Results

Our proposed method, Apriori applying a Fuzzy Inference System called *FIS-Apriori*, was tested using an implementation based on an Apriori version available in ARMINER[21]. The method was applied on web data set from the UCI repository[22].

Table 3. Rules discarded by Apriori

minsup=0.3, minconf=0.6			
Antecedent(s)	Consequent(s)	Support	Confidence
For developer only information	Ms Excel	0.2798	0.5752
Ms Excel	Ms Schedule	0.2907	0.8161
Ms Schedule	Knowledge Base	0.345	0.575

minsup=0.5, minconf=0.4			
Antecedent(s)	Consequent(s)	Support	Confidence
Corporate Desktop evaluation	Fortran	0.7609	0.3716
Ms word news	Window 32 bits developer	0.4550	0.9348
Microsoft TV program information	World wide offices	0.4628	0.4224

minsup=0.6, minconf=0.6			
Antecedent(s)	Consequent(s)	Support	Confidence
Window 32 bits developer	Microsoft TV program information	0.9	0.586
Bookshelf	France	0.5047	0.62
For developer only information	Fortran	0.57	0.46382

minsup=0.8, minconf=0.7			
Antecedent(s)	Consequent(s)	Support	Confidence
Ms Excel	For developer only information	0.77	0.43
For developer only information	Ms Excel	0.77	0.634
Ms Schedule	Microsoft TV program information	0.94	0.48

Some results obtained from comparing Apriori and FIS-Apriori are presented. Table 3 lists groups of rules discarded by Apriori and considered by FIS-Apriori for different settings.

The behavior of the association rules generated by Apriori when the support, the confidence, or both are mapped into a fuzzy domain, is illustrated in Fig. 5.

When support is fuzzy, the amount of generated rules growths with respect to the threshold of the output variable. The bandwidth of threshold is controlled by the slope of the membership function.

A more significant set of rules is obtained including more fuzzy sets, which correspond to "linguistic edges". Analyzing the set of rules, a sensibility of the method to the variations of the support more than the confidence was detected.

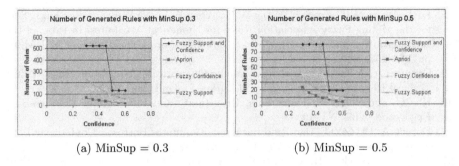

(a) MinSup = 0.3   (b) MinSup = 0.5

Fig. 5. Comparison of generated rules

5 Conclusions

In this paper an extension of the Apriori algorithm was proposed, in which the support and the confidence parameters are treated as fuzzy variables. The proposed method calculates frequent itemsets and association rules based on the fuzzy inference system FUZZYC.

FUZZYC simplifies the test and tuning tasks of the model for mining association rules using fuzzy sets. In addition, the set up of the minsup and minconf is more intuitive for the end-user.

FIS-Apriori (Apriori using a Fuzzy Inference System) could be applied using an Apriori implementation in an iterative process to re-define the minsup and minconf values. However, this option requires expensive computation.

Another alternative can be obtained rounding the support and confidence values. This strategy is less intuitive for the user and the solution achieved by FIS-Apriori is not warranted.

Finally, when FIS-Apriori is used minsup and minconf definition as intervals, the proposed model allows for multiple constraints.

References

1. Agrawal R., Mannila H., Srikant R., Toivonen H., Inkeri A. Fast Discovery of Association Rules, AAAI/MIT Press. Chapter 12, pp. 307–328, 1996.
2. Srikant R., Agrawal R. Mining Quantitive Association Rules in large relational tables. In Proc. ACM SIGMOD, pp. 1–12, 1996
3. Srikant R., Agrawal R. Fast Algorithms for mining Association Rules. In Proc. 20th VLDB Conf., pp. 487–499, 1994
4. Han J., Pei J., Yin Y. Mining Frequent Patterns without Candidate Generation. ACM SIGMOD, 2000.
5. Brin S., Motwani R., Ullman J.D., Tsur S. Dynamic item set counting and implication rules for market basket data. Proc. ACM SIGMOD Conf. 1997
6. Zadeh, L. The calculus of fuzzy if/then rules. AI Expert. 7(3) pp. 23–28. Mar 1992
7. Kuok C.M., Fu A, Wong M.H. Mining Fuzzy Association Rules in large Databases with quantitative attributes. ACM SIGMOD, 27(1), pp. 41–46, 1998

8. Fu A., Wong M.H., Sze S. C.,Wong W.C., Wong W.L., Yu W.K. Finding Fuzzy Sets for the Mining Fuzzy Association Rules for Numerical Attributes. In Proc. of the 1st Intern. Symposium on Intelligent Data Ingeneering and Learning, IDEAL98. pp. 263–268. 1998.

9. Gyenesei A. A Fuzzy Approach for mining Quantitative Association Rules. TUCS Techical Reports N335, University of Turku, Finland, Mar 2000.

10. Klir G. and Folger T. Fuzzy Sets, Uncertainty and Information. Prentice-Hall, Englewood Cliffs, NJ, 1988.

11. Dorado A. FUZZYC: Algoritmo Basado en Conjuntos Borrosos. Conferencia Latinoamericana de Informática CLEI2001. Mérida, Venezuela. Sep 2001.

12. Kosala R., Blockeel H. Web Mining Research: A survey. SIGKDD Explorations 2(1) pp. 1–15, Jun 2000.

13. Mobasher B., Jain N., Han E., Srivastava J. Web Mining: Pattern Discovery from World Wide Web Transactions

14. Han J., Fu Y., Wang K., Koperski K., Zaiane O. Dmql: a data mining query language for relational databases. In SIGMOD'96, Montreal, Canada.

15. Cooley R., Mobaser B., Srivastava J. Web Mining: Information Pattern Discovery on the World Wide Web. In Proc. of the 9th IEEE Intern. Conf. on Tools with Artificial Intelligence, November 1997.

16. Srivastava J., Cooley R., Deshpande M. Tan P. Web Usage Mining: Discovery and Applications of Usage Pattern from Web Data. SIGKDD Explorations 1(2) pp.12–23, 2000.

17. Pei J., Tung A., Han J. Fault-Tolerant frequent Pattern Mining : Problems and Challenges. Workshop Notes, DMKD-2001 pp. 7–13

18. Lin W. Alvarez S., Ruiz C. Efficient Adaptative-Support Association Rules Mining for Recomender Systems, Data Mining and Knowledge Discovery 6(1) pp.83–105, 2002

19. Cooley R. Web Usage Mining: Discovery and Application of Interesting Patterns from Web Data. Ph.D.Thesis. University of Minnesota, 2000.

20. Cody Wong, Simon Shiu and Sankar Pal. Mining fuzzy association rules for web access case adaptation. In Proc. Workshop at the Fourth Intern. Conf. on Case-Based Reasoning 2001. Vancouver, Canada, Jul 2001.

21. Cristofor Dana, Cristofor Laurentiu, Karatihy Abdelmajid, Xiaoyong Kuang, Long-Tsong Li; Arminer. 2000.

22. Blake, C.L. Merz, C.J. UCI Repository of Machine Learning Databases. University of California, Irvine, Dept. of Information and Computer Science. 1998.

The "Who Is It?" Problem Application for Customizable Web Sites

Pierre-Emmanuel Jouve and Nicolas Nicoloyannis

LABORATOIRE ERIC (Equipe de Recherche en Ingénierie des Connaissances)
Université Lumière – Lyon2
Bâtiment L, 5 avenue Pierre Mendès-France
69 676 BRON cedex FRANCE
{Pierre.Jouve, Nicolas.Nicoloyannis}@eric.univ-lyon2.fr
http://eric.univ-lyon2.fr

Abstract. We introduce in this paper a problem only rarely taken under consideration in knowledge engineering: how to acquire the most information with a minimal associated cost. More precisely, the problem that we wish to address is the following: how to obtain the most information concerning an individual by begging him a limited number of questions. We refer to this problem as the "Who is it?" Problem in reference to the famous game of Hasbro for which the objective of the two players is exactly to solve this thorny issue. From a practical point of view, solving this problem may be extremely interesting in several fields and in particular in WWW related fields: customer/user profiling or clustering , web site personalization, creation of efficient questionnaires.

1 Introduction

We introduce in this paper a problem that has been rarely taken under consideration in knowledge engineering: how to acquire the most information with a limited acquisition cost. More precisely, the problem that we wish to investigate is the following: how to obtain the most information concerning an individual by asking him a limited number of questions. Thus, we will call this problem the "Who is it" Problem in reference to the famous game of Hasbro for which the objective of the two protagonists of the game is exactly to solve this thorny question.

From a practical point of view, to solve this problem may be extremely interesting in several fields such as World Wide Web Engineering: it would allow efficient Web sites users profiling.

Actually, let us now consider, the case of a company whose web site should be customizable according to its users' profiles. Obviously, personalization of the web site according to some informations about a user implies to possess those informations and also implies an acquisition step of those informations. We can consider that a phase of questioning preliminary or simultaneous with the visit on the site permits to acquire this knowledge about the visitor. (Some others knowledge acquiring techniques may be used such as Web Log Mining, Web

E. Menasalvas et al. (Eds.): AWIC 2003, LNAI 2663, pp. 83–93, 2003.
© Springer-Verlag Berlin Heidelberg 2003

Navigation Pattern Analysis... but we study a questionnaire like technique in this paper.)

Let us now consider that the number of information which one must dispose of (for the personalization to be really effective) is relatively high and that its acquisition is associated with a questionnaire that the user must fill. Consider moreover that this questionnaire is composed, for instance, of 50 questions. One may then plan to ask these 50 questions to the user before he really does benefit from the personalization of the site, however the high number of questions may imply a refusal of the user to continue its investigations on the site or the obtention of erroneous answers. The problem of the acquisition of knowledge about an individual while limiting the cost associated with this acquisition (by limiting the number of asked questions) is then real.

We propose here a solution for this problem in the form of the development of a questionnaire with a limited number of questions and adaptable according to the answers given to the previously asked questions.

2 The "Who Is It?" Problematic

In the game "Who is it?" two players clash: each player must determine the character of its adversary knowing that this character belongs to a base of several possible characters. In order to find the character of its opponent, each participant asks its adversary questions about the physical aspect of its character, and then, by accumulating information, participants can determine their opponent's character.

The objective being for each player to find the character of its opponent before its adversary, the two protagonists of the game must thus develop a questioning strategy in order to accelerate the process of discovery. The key is here to accelerate the process of collection of information: to ask the less possible questions in order to be able (according to these informations) to determine the opponent's character (e.g. to ask the less possible questions in order to have the more information about the physical aspect of the opponent's character). Moreover, we should note that when the character is determined, the whole set of answers to any question concerning the physical aspect of the character is known.

This stands for the problem we study in this paper and that we name "Who Is it?" Problem . In a more formal way we define this problem as follows:

- $O = \{x_r, r = 1..n\}$ a set of n individuals
- $x_r = \{x_{r_i}, i = 1..p\}$ an individual of O described by p characteristics (the answers this individual would give to p questions, if it was begged those questions)
- $M : x_r \rightarrow (Q(x_r), \tilde{x}_r)$ a questionnaire with p questions, for each individual M associates certain questions to ask and according to the answers for theses questions it infers answers to the non-asked questions.

- $Q : x_r \rightarrow [\delta_{x_{r_1}} ..., \delta_{x_{r_p}}]$ a vector of binary values,

$$\delta_{x_{r_i}} = \begin{cases} 1 \text{ if the question } i \text{ of } M \text{ was asked to individual } x_r \\ 0 \text{ if the question } i \text{ of } M \text{ was not asked to individual } x_r \end{cases}$$

- $\tilde{x}_r = \{\tilde{x}_{r_i}, i = 1..p\}$ the set made up of the answers to the questions asked of and the inferred answers to the non-asked questions.
- $R : (x_r, \tilde{x}_r) \rightarrow [\beta(x_{r_1}, \tilde{x}_{r_1})..., \beta(x_{r_p}, \tilde{x}_{r_p})]$ a vector of binary values,

$$\beta(x_{r_i}, \tilde{x}_{r_i}) = \begin{cases} 1 \text{ if } x_{r_i} = \tilde{x}_{r_i} \\ 0 \text{ otherwise} \end{cases}$$

- $MNQ = \frac{1}{n} \sum_{r=1}^{n} Q(x_r) Q(x_r)^T$ the average number of asked questions per individual
- $MNE = \frac{1}{N} \sum_{r=1}^{n} R(x_r) R(x_r)^T$ the mean number of differences between x_r and $\tilde{x}_r$ per individual, e.g. the mean number of difference between real characteristics of individual x_r and inferred characteristics of this individual

The problem is thus the following:
To find M such as MNQ is minimized knowing that $MNE \leq \alpha$, that is to say to find the questionnaire implying the weakest average number of questions per individual knowing that the average number of errors for inferred profiles must be lower or equal to α.

If we come back to the Web Site Questionnaire problem, we can see that solving the "Who is it?" Problem corresponds to determine the questionnaire that implies the less questions per user and that allows a good level of correction for the inferred profile of users. We can, not only, see the resolution of this problem as one optimization problem but also as a nonconventional learning problem for which one regards each question as a categorical attribute having as many modalities as possible answers to the question. Indeed, the endogenous attribute is not unique and moreover what must be learned can also be used for learning. In fact there is no differentiation between endogenous and exogenous attributes: all endogenous attributes are also exogenous and the reciprocal is true.

3   Solving the "Who Is It?" Problem

As far as we know, the "Who is it?" problem was never really dealt with, however one could fancy to use certain paradigms of Knowledge Discovery in Databases (K.D.D.) to solve it:

- clustering (for categorical data) [2], [6], [7] associated with supervised learning:
  - First determine clusters of individuals relatively homogeneous and well separated from each other.
  - Then, associate with each clusters a profile of answers.

- • Then determine which answers for which questions allow to determine
  the membership of one individual to one of the clusters in order to infer
  the whole set of answers to non-asked questions by referring to the profile
  of the selected cluster.
- – association rules [1], [4], [5] in order to discover possible associations between
  answers to questions and thus determine the questions that are really useful
  to ask and in which order they should be asked by the mean of logical
  deduction.

We briefly explain by the mean of an example those two methodologies:
Let us consider the dataset presented in Table 1., it represents the answers of
12 individuals to 6 questions, to solve the "Who is it" problem would mean
to determine a questioning strategy such that we can minimize the average
number of questions MNQ to ask to an individual so that MNE is lower than
a given value α. For this example, we fix α at 0.05=5%, thus at the end of
the questioning one must perfectly know at least 95% of the answers which the
individuals brought to the questions of the questionnaire.

Table 1.

Q	Q1	Q2	Q3	Q4	Q5	Q6
1	A	A	A	A	A	A
2	A	A	A	B	B	B
3	B	B	A	B	B	C
4	B	B	B	B	B	A
5	C	C	B	B	B	B
6	C	C	A	B	B	C
7	A	A	A	A	A	B
8	A	A	A	B	B	A
9	B	B	B	B	C	C
10	B	B	B	B	B	B
11	C	C	B	B	B	B
12	C	C	A	B	B	A

Here are the two outlines of methods for the resolution of this problem via
the use of K.D.D. methodologies:

- – clustering associated with supervised learning:
  - • this method consists in its first step to the development of a clustering
    which is such that if one associates each individual with the profile of
    the cluster it belongs to (e.g. if one associates each individual with the
    standard answers of the individuals of its cluster) then MNE is lower
    than $\alpha = 0.05 = 5\%$. For this example $MNE = 4,166\%$ (see Fig. 1.).
    Then the second phase consists in learning the concept implied by this
    clustering by the mean of induction tree, this tree therefore constitutes
    the questionnaire (see Fig. 2.). Using this questionnaire further allows to

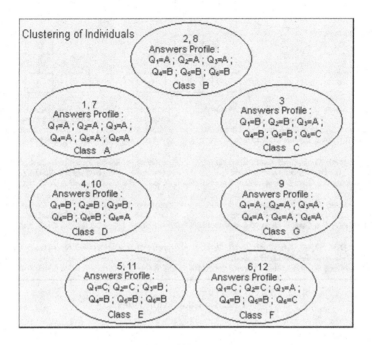

Fig. 1. Clustering

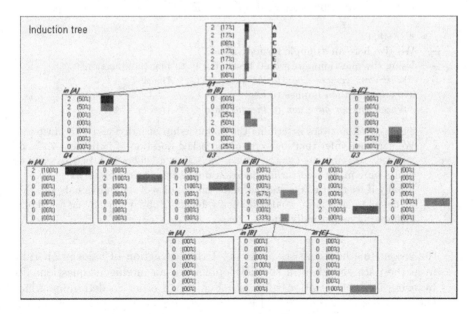

Fig. 2. Induction tree

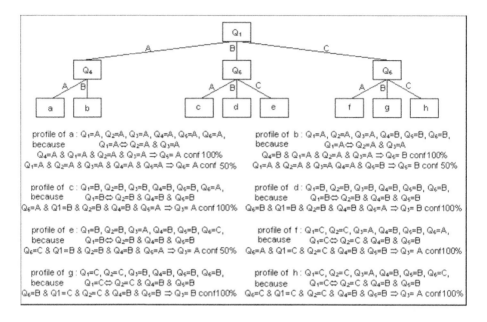

Fig. 3. Association rules

infer answers to non asked questions for each individuals by associating for each individual standard answers of the cluster it belongs to.

- EXAMPLE:
  We give here an example for individual 7:
  Using the questionnaire would firstly imply to beg the question:
  "Which answer gave you to the question Q1? Answer: "A"
  This answer then implies to beg:
  "Which answer gave you to the question Q4? Answer: "A"

  These given answers determine the membership of individual 7 to cluster A. We can then infer that answers to non asked question of individual 7 should strongly resemble to $Q2="A"$ $Q3="A"$ $Q5="A"$ $Q6="A"$. In this case we would only make an error for question 6 (the right answer was "B"). Finally if we use this questionnaire for the totality of the individuals and that we calculate MNE we would obtain a value of 4,166% while having asked only 2.25 questions per individual.

- the second method consists as for it of the extraction of association rules from the data set, then in the development of an intelligent questionnaire by using these association rules (see Fig. 3.) in order to determine which questions have to be asked and in which order they must be asked via logical deductions. The use of this questionnaire is identical to the use of the questionnaire developed for the previously described method. In this case $MNE = 4,166\%$ and 2.25 questions are asked per individual.

These methods are interesting but imply some problems:

- the first method requires several treatments (a clustering process and a learning process), moreover the coupled use of a clustering method and of a learning method does not guarantee a real attempt to minimize the number of questions, finally to determine the parameters of the clustering method such as the condition on MNE is respected may be difficult
- as for the second method, the effective use and development of an intelligent system allowing to determine automatically the questionnaire starting from the association rules is an extremely difficult problem.

We have thus developed a third solution relatively close to the first proposal, but which does not present its disadvantages. It consists of the use of a clustering method for categorical data presented in [7]. This method is based on the New Condorcet Criterion [10] and on an induction tree type approach for discovering clusters. Our matter is not here a complete description of this method but we can say that those two aspects allow to unify the two processes (clustering and supervised learning) of the first presented solution: it allows to discover a clustering with the creation of a questionnaire that permits to determine the membership of an individual to one of the clusters of the clustering. Concerning the discovery of a clustering that respect the condition fixed on MNE, it is made easier thanks to the unique parameter of this method which is called granularity factor. Using this clustering method on the previously used example would lead (thanks to a single process) to the same questionnaire as the one developed for the first method.

We present now an experimental evaluation of the efficiency of this approach for building an effective questionnaire. We used the mushrooms data [9] which is a standard data set for knowledge engineering community. This data set is composed of 8124 objects (mushrooms), each one described by 23 attributes, each attribute may possess 2 or more modalities. We thus consider the following mapping: each object corresponds to an individual and each attribute to an information that one must dispose in order to personalize a web site. We present on Fig. 4. results for different questionnaires according to the average number of questions per individual it would impose to ask (in fact we present the percentage of total information corresponding to the asked questions), and the percentage of the total information it would allow to infer correctly. The questionnaires were created using only 50% of objects of the data set, and shown results correspond to the utilization of the created questionnaires on the remaining 50% of objects. Results are attractive since they show that questionnaires with few questions may permit the obtention of high quality informations (for instance the questionnaire involving only an average of 4.6 questions per individual (e.g. 20% of the total information) permit to correctly infer nearly 90% of the information).

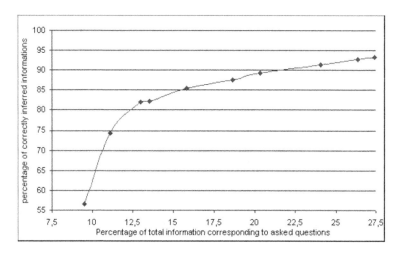

Fig. 4. Experimental evaluation on mushrooms data

4   The "Who Is It?" Problem and Customization of Web Sites

The objective of the personalization of a Web site [8,11] is to propose this site to the user in a form such:

- that it is of a greater interest for him (for example an appropriate form of presentation of information)
- that it is of an interest for the owner of the site (a commercial Web site can possibly plan to personalize its site so as to increase the probability of purchase of the user)

Any personalization of a Web site however requires to have information on the user of the site. Sometimes the number of information necessary may be relatively high and their acquisition may have a relatively high cost. This is problematic insofar as it may lead to a waste of time, a refusal of the user to provide information, the acquisition of erroneous information... In the best case this too high cost will involve a non-optimal use of the personalization, in the worst case the frequentation of the site may strongly decrease. Thus to reduce this acquisition cost of constitutes a significant problem.

Many solutions were proposed to solve this problem, we may quote:

- in [15,3] authors presented a collaborative filtering approach to recommendation, based on users rating specific web pages. Naives Bayes is here used as the prediction tool.
- In [13] fuzzy rules are constructed from user profiles, and used to modify queries in information retrieval. This work was mostly based on ratings of

web pages whose contents are used to build a user interest profile, and later extended to usage profiles by Kraft and Chen.
- in [12] use pre-discovered association rules to provide recommendations based on usage or web navigation patterns.
- Unsupervised robust multi-resolution clustering techniques [14] can reliably discover most of the Web user profiles/interest groups, because they benefit from the multi-resolution mechanism to discover even the less pronounced user profiles, and they benefit from robustness to avoid the noisy/spurious profiles that are common with low support thresholds.

As for us, we situate our work in the particular framework of "Who is it?" Problem (which induce a viewing of the problem from a different perspective), we propose the following general methodology to minimize the acquisition cost of information (however, this methodology may be linked to previous personalization/recommendation methods via collaboration filtering by K- Nearest neighbor or by clustering or by association rules/frequent itemset based prediction techniques):

- Initially draw up the questionnaire allowing to obtain information necessary to the personalization of the Web site.
- Use this questionnaire on a sample of users, the answers of these users then allow the development of the M questionnaire
- Use then the M questionnaire for each new user in order to collect a certain number of informations and infer remaining necessary informations.
- Then automatically adapt the Web site according to those informations.

This process is exposed below (Fig. 5).

5   Current and Future Work

We have just introduced the "Who is it?" Problem, as well as a set of potential solutions to this problem and finally showed its interest within the framework of the personalization of Web sites.

We currently proceed to a set of experiments allowing the validation of the methodology suggested by using the third approach for the resolution of the learning problem. Our first results exhibit a good capacity of the method to significantly reduce the number of questions to ask while ensuring a good level of generalization for the individuals not having been used for the establishment of the questionnaire. Our next work will thus consist of the completion of these tests and a real implementation of this system.

Acknowledgements. We would like to thank the anonymous reviewers for their useful comments and suggestions.

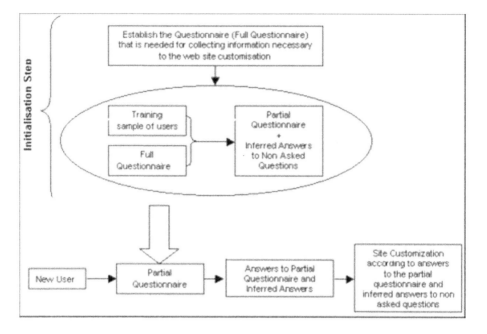

Fig. 5. Customization process

References

1. Agrawal, R., Srikant, R.: Fast Algorithms for Mining Association Rules. in Proc. 20th Int. Conf. Very Large Data Base. (1994) 487–499
2. Berkhin, P.: Survey Of Clustering Data Mining Techniques. in Accrue Softwre Technical Report. (2001)
3. Billsus, D., Pazzani, M.: Revising User Profiles: The Search for Interesting Web Sites. In Proceedings of the Third International Workshop on Multistrategy Learning, AAAI Press. (1996)
4. Cooley, R., Mobasher B., Srivastava, J.: Data Preparation for Mining World Wide Web Browsing Patterns. in Knowledge and Information Systems. vol.1. (1999) 5–32
5. Cooley, R.: Web Usage Mining: Discovery and Application of Interesting Patterns from Web Data. Ph.D. Thesis. University of Minnesota. (2000)
6. Huang Z.: A Fast Clustering Algorithm to Cluster Very Large Categorical Data Sets in Data Mining. in Research Issues on Data Mining and Knowledge Discovery. (1997)
7. Jouve, P.E., Nicoloyannis N.: KEROUAC: an Algorithm for Clustering Categorical Data Sets with Practical Advantages. To appear in PAKDD, International Workshop on Data Mining for Actionable Knowledge. (2003)
8. Kappel, G., Retschitzegger W., Schwinger W.: Modeling Customizable Web Applications. in Kyoto International Conference on Digital Libraries. (2000)
9. Merz, C., Murphy, P.: UCI repository of machine learning databases. http://www.ics.uci.edu/#mlearn/mlrepository.html. (1996)
10. Michaud, P.: Clustering techniques. in Future Generation Computer Systems, Vol. 13 (1997) 135–147

11. Mobasher, B., Cooley, R., Srivastava J.: Automatic personalization based on Web usage mining. in Communications of the ACM. vol.43. (2000) 142–151
12. Mobasher, B., Dai, H., Luo, T., Nakagawa, M.: Effective personalization based on association rule discovery from web usage data. in Web Information and Data Management. (2000) 9–15
13. Martin-Bautista, M.J., Vila, M.A., Kraft, D.H., Chen, J.: User Profiles in Web Retrieval. in FLINT'2001, Berkeley. (2001)
14. Nasraoui, O., Krishnapuram, R.: A New Evolutionary Approach to Web Usage and Context Sensitive Associations Mining. in International Journal on Computational Intelligence and Applications - Special Issue on Internet Intelligent Systems. Vol. 2. No. 3. (2002) 339–348
15. Pazzani, M., Billsus, D.: Learning and Revising User Profiles: The Identification of Interesting Web Sites. In Machine Learning, Arlington. vol.27. (1997) 313–331

Using Case-Based Reasoning to Improve Information Retrieval in Knowledge Management Systems

Norbert Gronau[1] and Frank Laskowski[2]

[1]Universität Oldenburg, Department of Business Information Systems, Germany
gronau@wi-ol.de
[2]OFFIS e.V., Oldenburg, Germany
frank.Laskowski@offis.de

Abstract. Complementary to hypertext navigation, classic information retrieval is broadly used to find information on the World Wide Web and on Web-based systems. Among these there are most knowledge management systems, that typically integrate information accessible on the intranet of an organization or company, and present this information to support users with their knowledge-oriented tasks. In this paper we describe a Case-Based Reasoning component extending information retrieval in the context of KM systems. Our basic assumption is, that a user composing a search query simultaneously is describing a problem he or she seeks to solve. Hence our case-based reasoning component handles an information retrieval request as a description of a problem being part of a case. We will explain how this approach enables various benefits for intelligent query processing and a vast potential for synergies of the case based reasoning component and the embedding knowledge management system.

Keywords. case-based reasoning, information retrieval, knowledge management, software architecture

1 Introduction

As part of the TO_KNOW project a case-based reasoning (CBR) component is being designed for integration into typical knowledge management (KM) systems. ([1]) While there are conceivably various possible applications of case-based reasoning in the context of knowledge management, our approach invokes the CBR algorithm on Information Retrieval (IR) requests.

Our basic assumption is, that a user composing a search query at the same time is describing a problem he or she seeks to solve. Hence our CBR component handles the IR request as a description of a problem being part of a case. Thinking straightforward a good solution for such a case would be a good search result, i.e. a set of links to relevant information with respect to the search query. We propose to include an alternative way of describing a solution: Given a search query that does not result in the optimal set of available information, a good solution is an "improved" query, i.e. performing this query would deliver better support for solving the given problem.

E. Menasalvas et al. (Eds.): AWIC 2003, LNAI 2663, pp. 94–102, 2003.

In the following sections we explain how various benefits for intelligent query processing can be achieved by exchanging context information between the CBR component and the embedding KM system. We outline our approach to design the cases, the case base and the CBR algorithm accordingly.

The ideas presented here are linked for WWW environment for two reasons: Conceptually, the Web (and especially the emerging Semantic Web) delivers a good platform to design knowledge management systems, i.e. the software supporting knowledge management, e.g. [2], [3]. Practically, utilizing means such as artificial intelligence (AI) components to improve information retrieval makes sense for systems that provide access to a vast amount of text documents, mostly web-based systems or at least systems accessible via the Web.

2 Merging CBR into IR: The TO_KNOW Approach

In this section we describe the core part of our approach: conceptually plugging CBR into the processing of IR search queries. This extension facilitates improvements of precision, configuration and the user interface of search applications. Section 3 explains how this CBR-supported IR core integrates with the larger framework of a knowledge management system.

2.1 CBR and IR as Problem-Solving Methods

Case-based reasoning is well established as problem solving method (e.g. [4]). It is based on the concept of the "case" consisting of a description of a problem and its solution. A new problem is solved by retrieving and reusing similar experiences from the "case base". If revision indicates that a substantially new solution has to be provided for the new problem, both are retained as new case, i.e. added to the case base for future retrieval and reuse.

Information retrieval is a classic area of information and computer science (e.g. [5]). With the Web emerging and Web-technology establishing in organizations' and companies' intranets, document retrieval has become an omnipresent application, familiar to the everyday user like text processing. An information retrieval process starts with a user's need of information that is translated to a search query. This query is compared to descriptions of what information can be found in each of the accessible documents (or other kinds of entities). The result of the retrieval process is a set of references to those documents whose descriptors correspond to the query, and by this should be relevant to the user's request.

IR is often explained contrasting the "exactness" of data retrieval. But it can also be looked upon as a *method to support problem solving*: Especially when a problem needs a solution that is considerably new to the user an according search query can be interpreted as describing the users problem rather than describing the information the user is looking for. The search engine delivers references to those contents addressing his or her problem, ideally enabling the user to solve it.

2.2 The Part of CBR in Query Processing

CBR usually is applied to a field of interest, providing solutions or help to find solutions for problems arising in that field, e.g. when deploying Neural Networks to optimize industrial production. The other way around CBR utilizes other techniques for retrieving, reusing, revising or retaining cases, e.g. TO_KNOW uses IR technology for retrieval of cases from the case base.

As already pointed out in the first section, form a user's perspective we deploy CBR and IR on the same level, i.e. both techniques are combined and applied to the same problems. Especially CBR is not used to support a strictly encircled part of the IR process, e.g. pre-translation of "natural language" queries, and on the other hand, it is not used to solve meta problems about IR's "how-tos". However TO_KNOW's CBR component is operating on a meta level in so far as it does not take the documents accessible to IR as cases, although they cover information about problems and their solutions. Instead the *application of information retrieval is recognized as a case*.

Hence the CBR algorithm accompanies the IR process, gathering experiences about it in it's own case base, and interfering with it by proposing alternative solutions to the user. To enable this amalgamation, the CBR component is invoked before and after the search engines operates on a single query. Thus the CBR component can examine and manipulate queries and results of the IR process. This includes changes to the user interface and access to the session data eventually bundling a sequence of several requests as one IR process. Both enable interactive revision of the solutions presented to the users.

Figure 1 illustrates the relationship described above.

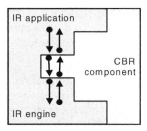

Fig. 1. CBR component plugging into the IR process

2.3 Basic Implications for Case Model and CBR Algorithm

The core of the case model is designed accordingly:

- The *problem description* may include various data (this will be outlined in the following section), but it is centered on the users problem description as it is effectively at hand as search query in an IR application.

- As well, in its central part the *description of the solution* is directly taken from the IR application: At first sight this could be a possibly large set of references to documents that change or even disappear over time and that represent information eventually outdated, especially regarding topics like business statistics or IT tools. As an alternative, we decided to focus on a query, the result of which meets the user's expectations better than the one initially describing the problem. (Remember that a case is made up from a problem that couldn't be handled "as ususal", i.e. where using the search engine did not deliver the desired information.)

The case model does not ban the use of document references. But these point to data while search queries are coded on the level of information, i.e. categories and indices in terms of IR and the problem domain, as well.

Implications for the CBR algorithm that is usually split up into four phases: "retrieve", "reuse", "revise" and "retain", mainly affect the inner two phases, "reuse" and "revise".

The reuse phase has to adopt or recombine existing solutions making them applicable to new problems. This phase might deploy various AI techniques and has to utilize the "domain model", i.e. knowledge about IR, and especially about manipulation of search queries. This might include drawing conclusions from "query refinement histories", or involving the document descriptors from satisfactory result sets to construct improved queries. Work on this task is in progress in the TO_KNOW project, but results are not expected to affect the shape of the integration aspects described in this paper.

The reuse phase ends, either transparently manipulating the IR process, or presenting a choice of one or more alternative solutions, i.e. queries, to the user. (Think about "google" [6], presenting links to related index pages and a spell-checked version of a query, if applicable.) Right away, the revise phase begins.

The revise phase is decisive for retaining cases, i.e. building up the case base, which is the backbone of the CBR components added value.

Ideally the CBR component has means to automatically revise the quality of a solution. Unfortunately, if a search result fails to satisfy the user's needs and automatic revision on average is able to detect this failure, the CBR component would clearly outrival the IR engine regarding core IR capabilities. We suppose this is not likely to happen, assuming that a typical IR engine already makes use of the most important possibilities of how to automatically figure out, what information is contained in documents, respectively search queries. Nonetheless, automatic revision is useful, starting form examination of the size of the result set.

By choosing an alternative query presented after the reuse phase finished, or by ignoring this option, the user manually revises the proposed solutions. Complementary the user can be asked how valuable he regards the result set that is currently displayed.

One logical revise phase might invoke retrieval and reuse of cases for several times, going along with the user refining his or her request. Typically the user interface of a search application should not be essentially altered to preserve usability. Hence some algorithm has to decide which queries belong logically together.

A new case is retained, if a logical revise phase requires more than one reuse phase or substantial manual refinement, to lead to a satisfactory result. The new case at least contains the initial query (as spontaneous description of the user's problem) and the query that the revise phase ended with.

Finally, after repeated positive revision of the same case, it can be marked for transparent application, i.e. the reuse phase will overwrite an initial query before it is forwarded to the IR engine, if the query matches the case. This is the most direct improvement to the IR application possible. Status of transparent applicability can be revoked anytime as response to negative revision.

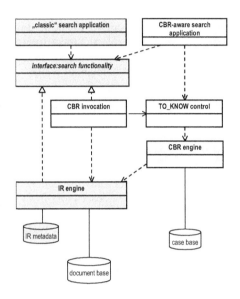

Fig. 2. Architecture of CBR-supported IR application

In [1] we presented several choices for *efficiently implementing and running* a combined system as described above. An outline of the architecture is shown in Fig. 2.

3   Integrating the CBR Component into a KM System

TO_KNOW's main focus is the area of knowledge management systems. In this section, we explain how the CBR component discussed above enables a search application to adapt to the information context provided by an embedding KM system.

3.1   A Practical Definition of KM Systems

In the scope of this paper, we define a KM system as *a set of software* and the data accessed by this software, *deployed* in an organization or a company *to implement knowledge management strategies*.

KM systems range form a Web-Server, providing a single point of access to important document collections, to fully fledged systems integrating many tools, and covering almost all building blocks from the reference architecture shown in figure 3. ([7])

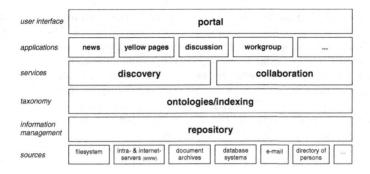

user interface	portal					
applications	news	yellow pages	discussion	workgroup	...	
services	discovery			collaboration		
taxonomy	ontologies/indexing					
information management	repository					
sources	filesystem	intra- & internet-servers (www)	document archives	database systems	e-mail	directory of persons	...

Fig. 3. Reference architecture of a KM system

The third layer in Fig. 3 provides collaboration and discovery services. Document retrieval is the basic application built on the discovery services, and hence a kind of IR engine should be present in any non-trivial KM system.

As a consequence, improving IR quality by itself already leads to an advanced utilization of the knowledge base.

(We are aware that some definitions intentionally avoid focusing on IT support. We do not suggest to ignore these definitions. However, the issues discussed here regard basic parts of electronic support, and should not be affected by preferring or rejecting any of those technically abstract definitions.)

3.2 Adapting to the System Context

A fully fledged KM system might hold many different kinds of metadata, which potentially could be of use to the CBR component described in section 2. Neither the TO_KNOW CBR component, nor any service, application or component that is being added to a reasonably complex KM system can individually adopt to each of the subsystems from which such metadata originates. Hence components rely on the KM system's information management and/or taxonomy layer to provide a kind of centralized and homogenous access to its metadata.

For the CBR component, the KM system can be a source of information about the *context in which a problem is embedded*: On one hand information can be provided about the search queries, on the other hand about the users. As a consequence, on invocation the CBR component first retrieves the according information from the KM system, extending the problem's context.

Basic elements of a search query are significant terms. As the context of a term we define the most associated terms, according to the KM system's taxonomy. When the CBR component is embedded into a KM system, an appropriate adaptor has to be implemented delivering the system-specific context of a term on request. This context information can be exploited if the organization's taxonomy (e.g. administered by a knowledge engineer) diverges from the taxonomy of the IR engine (e.g. a general taxonomy for the language of the organization's country). Taking the system-specific context of a term into account has potential to improve the recall for retrieval of cases and documents.

The context of a user is defined as a simplified user's profile, containing a list name/value-pairs and a list of groups, which the user belongs to. The context of a user group is defined analogous. To retrieve the according information from the KM system, a second context adaptor has to be implemented. Importing user profiles improves all parts of the CBR component that perform collaborative filtering. The utilization of user context generally offers the potential to improve the precision.

Figure 4 updates Fig. 3 including the modules needed for integration of the CBR/IR component with the KM system. ([1] describes other associations and components technically facilitating the integration.)

3.3 Benefits for the KM System

The improvements outlined in the preceding section lead to a better utilization of the knowledge base as already mentioned. In addition, "feedback" from the IR/CBR component to the KM system is possible, as the following examples show:

- Queries that cannot be answered satisfactory (neither by the IR engine nor by the CBR system) are stored as negatively revises cases. This kind of cases indicates "information deficiencies" in the knowledge base. A report can help a knowledge engineer to obtain the needed information and add it to the knowledge base.

- Data from the case base can suggest checking whether terminology in the KM system matches users' conventions. E.g., a check is indicated when often cases are applied, that "translate" a term from the initial search query into another term from the "official company's list of keywords".

- A knowledge engineer can manually revise cases. E.g., cases, which are often applied, can be simplified and hence further optimized for application. Or such cases can be given "titles" or informal descriptions that are displayed like "FAQs" when the solution of the case is proposed to a user.

- The search log of the IR engine might be evaluated for automatic profile generation in the KM system. Additionally logging user interaction from the revise phase provides information that cannot (at least not easily) be extracted from a "classical" search-log.

4   Conclusions and Future Work

In this paper we described an approach to use case based reasoning to improve quality and integration of a standard information retrieval engine in a knowledge management system, presenting intermediate results from the TO_KNOW project.

The first part of the paper shows how the IR process can be enhanced by the CBR method, outlining the case model and the adoption of the CBR algorithm. The second part presents the basics of the integration, achieved by exchange of metadata between the CBR component and the KM system. A central concept is to transform the potentially heterogeneous metadata from the KM system to context information, which can be utilized by the CBR component to further improve its ability to support the IR engine, and to deliver rich feedback about the use of the knowledge base.

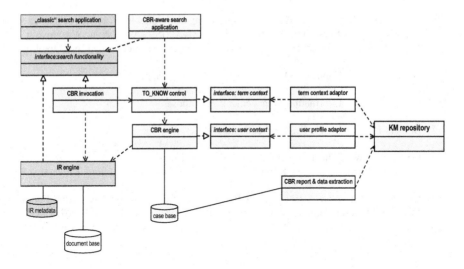

Fig. 4. CBR/IR component integration into KM system

A prototype of the CBR component described here is currently developed as part of the TO_KNOW project. Actually running the component will enable us to configure and optimize the basic combination of IR and CBR, and to learn more about the potential of different context information. Designing a component (instead of a stand-alone system) raised the question whether a framework could be designed that enables efficient integration of a variety of basic and advanced components alike, and finally lead us to plan the project K_SERVICES ([8]).

References

[1] Gronau, N.; Laskowski, F.: An architecture for integrating CBR components into KM systems. In: Mirjam Minor, Steffen Staab (Hrsg.): Proceedings of the 1st German Workshop on Experience Management. Bonner Köllen Verlag, 2002, S. 92–97

[2] http://www.hyperwave.com/

[3] http://www.opentext.com/livelink/

[4] Aamodt, A., Plaza, E.: Case-Based Reasoning: Foundational Issues, Methodological Variations and System Approaches. AI communications 7 (1994), 1, S. 35–39

[5] van Rijsbergen, C.J.: Information Retrieval. Second Edition, Butterworths, London, 1979

[6] http://www.google.com

[7] Gronau, N.: A Procedure Model for Evaluating Knowledge Management Systems. In: Arabnia, H.R.; Youngsong, M.; Prasad, B. (Hrsg.): Proceedings of the International Conference on Information and Knowledge Engineering 2002. CSREA Press, Athens, Georgia, S. 78–83

[8] Gronau, N.; Laskowski, F.: K_SERVICES: From State-of-the-Art Components to Next Generation Distributed KM Systems. IRMA'03 accepted paper, Philadelphia 18.5.– 21.5.2003

[9]   Aha, D.W.; Muñoz-Avila, H. (Hrsg.): Exploring Synergies of Knowledge Management and Case-Based Reasoning: Papers from the AAAI 1999 Workshop. Washington, DC: Naval Research Laboratory, Navy Center for Applied Research in Artificial Intelligence, 1999

[10]   Berners-Lee, T., Connolly, D.: Hypertext Markup Language - 2.0.
       `http://www.rfc-editor.org/rfc/rfc1866.txt`

[11]   Berners-Lee, T.: Information Management: A Proposal.
       `http://www.w3.org/History/1989/proposal.html`

[12]   Berners-Lee, T.; Swick, R.: The Semantic Web.
       `http://www.w3.org/2000/Talks/0516-sweb-tbl/all`

[13]   Choo,Chun wei: The Knowing Organization – How Organizations Use Information to Construct Meaning, Create Knowledge, and Make Decisions. Oxford University Press, 1998

[14]   Rissland, E.L.; Daniels, J.J.: Using CBR to Drive IR. In Proceedings of the Fourteenth International Joint Conference on Artificial Intelligence (IJCAI-95), 400–407, 1995

[15]   Wilson, D.; Bradshaw, S.: CBR Textuality. In Proceedings of the Fourth UK Case-Based Reasoning Workshop, 1999

Web Page Classification: A Soft Computing Approach

Angela Ribeiro[1], Víctor Fresno[2], María C. Garcia-Alegre[1], and Domingo Guinea[1]

[1] Industrial Automation Institute. Spanish Council for Scientific Research.
28500 Arganda del Rey, Madrid, Spain.
{angela,maria,domingo}@iai.csic.es
[2] Escuela Superior de Ciencia y Tecnología
Universidad Rey Juan Carlos
v.fresno@escet.urjc.es

Abstract. The Internet makes it possible to share and manipulate a vast quantity of information efficiently and effectively, but the rapid and chaotic growth experienced by the Net has generated a poorly organized environment that hinders the sharing and mining of useful data. The need for meaningful web-page classification techniques is therefore becoming an urgent issue. This paper describes a novel approach to web-page classification based on a fuzzy representation of web pages. A doublet representation that associates a weight with each of the most representative words of the web document so as to characterize its relevance in the document. This weight is derived by taking advantage of the characteristics of HTML language. Then a fuzzy-rule-based classifier is generated from a supervised learning process that uses a genetic algorithm to search for the minimum fuzzy-rule set that best covers the training examples. The proposed system has been demonstrated with two significantly different classes of web pages.

1 Introduction

The Web has grown by leaps and bounds, making it increasingly difficult to locate useful information. Moreover, Internet users numbered 30% more at the end of 2002 than at the end of 2001 [1]. Under these circumstances the need for tools that adequately extract information from the Web is becoming a major fact.

Classic information retrieval (IR) techniques are normally used to obtain information from the Internet [2], but problems frequently appear when IR techniques are applied. These problems may be due to either the enormous number of pages online or the continuous changes that happen in those pages, but they may also occur because Internet users are significantly different from IR techniques' traditional user groups. In the Web, there is no standard or style rule, and page content is created by a set of heterogeneous, autonomous users. Moreover inherited IR technology has not progressed rapidly enough to take into account the Web's needs. As a consequence, search engines retrieve only a small fraction of the total number of available documents, and only a part of what is retrieved is significant. In fact, when a user places a search request, most known web-search services deliver a ranked list of web pages wherein different topics or aspects of a topic are jumbled together. As stated by Chen and Dumais [3], users often prefer a search result organized as a category-based view

E. Menasalvas et al. (Eds.): AWIC 2003, LNAI 2663, pp. 103–112, 2003.
© Springer-Verlag Berlin Heidelberg 2003

of retrieved documents, to enable them to pick out the most relevant information in the shortest time.

From a general point of view, the first step in tasks such as automatic summarization, text classification, information retrieval, information extraction and text mining for any type of document is to obtain an adequate data structure to represent the text and ease digital processing. However, it is difficult to gain access to text information, since in texts the relationship between structure (usually a sequence of characters) and meaning is not as straightforward as it is in numeric data. Thus, the data structure that represents a web page is essential, since the success of the analysis is strongly dependent on the correctness of the text representation, which selects a document's most relevant aspects. Without a proper set of features, a classifier will not be able to discriminate categories accurately. Text and unstructured documents have traditionally been represented in a vector-space model [4] [5]. The vector representation or bag words takes single words extracted from the training corpus as features. This representation ignores the sequence in which the words occur and is based only on the statistics of single independent words. A feature may be either Boolean or frequency based. Variations on feature selection include removing infrequent words and stop words. In all the descriptions of vector space, the location of the words in the document is lost, and vectors usually have a high dimensionality (of 10^4 to 10^7 components) that prevents the use of knowledge-extraction algorithms [7]. A quite complete relation of web content mining methods for both unstructured and semi-structured documents is presented in [6].

For hyperlink texts, several techniques have been proposed for classifying a web page. Some are based on web content (the intra-document structure), and others, on the structure of the hyperlinks in the web itself (inter-document structure). Here researchers are inspired by the study of social networks and citation analysis [8]. Furthermore, in order to extract rich, predictive features from both sources some researchers combine hyperlinks and textual information. The major point is to be aware that in real-world cases an inspection out of the document can disturb classification performance. Even when there are no hyperlink regularities, no benefit can be expected from using hyperlinks, and in this case the best course is to use standard text classifiers on the text of the document itself. In [9] a study is shown of approaches for hypertext categorization exploring different hypotheses about the structure of the hypertext. This paper's approach was motivated by relevant conclusions of study [9], such as: a) The identification of hypertext regularities in the data and the selection of appropriate representations for hypertext are crucial for an optimal design of a classification system; b) The recognition of useful HTML fields in hypertext pages to be jointly considered with the text contained in the web page improves classification performance.

This paper proposes a supervised learning process based on a genetic algorithm to obtain a classifier. The classifier is expressed in terms of a fuzzy-knowledge-based system, and it is obtained from input web-page examples expressed as feature vectors. The vector contains the web page's most representative words, associated with a value that characterizes each word's degree of relevance in the hyperlink text.

The rest of the paper is organized as follows: Section 2 presents some basic ideas of the web-page representation technique proposed herein [10]. Section 3 is devoted to the description of the learning process that generates the fuzzy classifier. Section 4 presents some classifier performance data, and lastly, Section 5 outlines some conclusions.

2   A Fuzzy Approach to Web-Page Representation

A two-dimensional vector, namely a feature vector composed of features with an associated weight, has been used to represent a web page. Features are words extracted from the page content, and weights are numeric values that evaluate the appropriateness of the word to represent the web page's text. The word-relevance estimate takes into account a combination of traditional text-representation methods and some specific characteristics of HTML language. Web documents are built as a combination of HTML tags and text information that web browsers recognize and visualize. The textual tags are used to assign special properties to the text. Therefore if fragments of the text emerge between two tags (for instance <b> and </b>), the portion of the included text assumes such tags. Textual tags are the core of the web-page representation method proposed in this paper. Some textual tags, such as those that indicate the page title (<title>...</title>) or those that emphasize parts of the text (<b>...</b>, <u>...</u>, <em>...</em>, <i>...</i>, and <strong>... </strong>), are selected to compute the relevance of each word in a web page. In addition to the criteria derived from the tags above, there are other "classical" attributes that could be considered to compute word relevance, such as *word position* and *word frequency* in the text. Other attributes such as *meta* tags are not considered, as they are not widespread [11].   On the other hand, statistical analyses [12] have proved the difficulty of finding an optimal analytical function that adequately combines all the variables extracted variables.

The fundamental cue is that often a variable evaluates the importance of a word only when it appears combined with another variable. For example, it has been demonstrated that the title does not always describe page content, as in many cases it is the result of an automatic process. The opposite happens with emphasis, since emphasis is an operation consciously performed by the user when designing the web page. Therefore, a word visible in the title will really be relevant when it also appears emphasized or with a high appearance frequency in the text [12].

2.1   Definition of Criteria and Variables

The definition of the selected variables follows from the above-mentioned criteria is shown in Table 1.

Table 1. Definitions of the variables taken into account in word relevance

Frequency of a Word in the Page	Frequency of a Word in the Title	Word Emphasis Frequency
$c_f(i) = n_f(i) / N_{max}^{page}$.	$c_t(i) = n_f(i) / N_{max}^{title}$.	$c_e(i) = n_e(i) / N_{max}^{emph}$.

Where N_{max}^{page} is the occurrence of the most frequent word in the page, N_{max}^{title} the occurrence of the most frequent word in the title, and N_{max}^{emph} the occurrence of the most emphasized word. Notice that all these variables are normalized and both title and emphasis frequencies take their values in the [0,1] interval, whereas word frequency in a document never has a 0 value, so its universe of discourse is defined in the (0,1] interval. The membership-function definitions of the linguistic labels of the variables considered as fuzzy sets can be found in [10]. In addition to these variables, a word-position criterion is always considered. Therefore, in order to compute the relevance of a word from the position variable, the web page is split into four parts to characterize the fact that often users structure the text so that the first and the last lines are more relevant than those in the middle. This fact becomes more significant the longer the text is. The position variable for a word is calculated from the contribution of each word position in the page. The contribution of an occurrence o of a word i in a text line l can be expressed as follows:

$$c_p(i,o) = n_p(i,o) / N_{tol} . \tag{1}$$

Where $n_p(i,o)$ is the line number of occurrence o of word i and N_{tol} is the total number of text lines in the page. Another fuzzy-rule-based system has been defined to calculate the global position of a word throughout the whole page, and expression (1) is calculated for each occurrence o of a word i. Through a fuzzification process, linguistic labels such as INTRODUCTION, BODY and CONCLUSION are assigned at each occurrence o of the word i [10]. This procedure captures the gradual behavior exhibited at the transition points of the proposed page partition to be captured. The output of the fuzzy system (the set of IF-THEN rules is described in [10]) is two linguistic labels, STANDARD and PREFERENTIAL, that represent whether or not a word i belongs, in overall terms, to the favored parts of the text.

2.2 The Output of the Fuzzy Knowledge Based System: The Relevance of a Word

The output variable of the fuzzy system formulated to derive the relevance of a word in a hyperlink text has been defined by means of five linguistic labels (see membership functions in Fig. 1). The set of all linguistic labels covers the whole range of possible values for a fuzzy variable and has been selected by a human expert scoring each text word by its degree of relevance in the text. The fuzzy IF-THEN rule based system allows for the fusion of the fuzzy variables. These variables have been defined from a knowledge extraction process that accounts for both a previous statistical study [12] and human common sense in the manual performance of the classification tasks. On the other hand, the following premises were considered to design the fuzzy rule based system [10] that derives the word relevance:
a)   The lack of a word in the title indicates either that the page has no title or that the title has no meaning.
b)   Position variable is defined from a criterion to get higher values the longer the page is.
c)   A word with a high frequency means that the word is a "joker," in the sense that its meaning is not discriminated and thus it can be used in several contexts with different meanings. Notice that the stop-word elimination process does not remove all words whose meaning is unclear.
d)   A word can be non-emphasized simply because no words are emphasized in the whole web page.

Fuzzification of variables, inference and defuzzification processes are performed by means of a tool previously developed at the IAI-CSIC, namely FuzzyShell[1] [13]. The inference engine is defined by means of a center-of-mass (COM) algorithm that weights the output of each rule in the knowledge base with the truth degree of its antecedent. In the approach discussed herein, the output is a linguistic label with an associated value related to the specific word's relevance in the page.

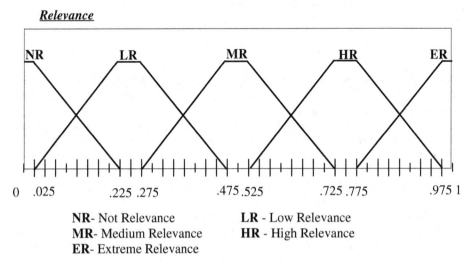

Relevance

NR- Not Relevance   LR - Low Relevance
MR- Medium Relevance   HR - High Relevance
ER- Extreme Relevance

Fig. 1. Membership functions of the output variable *relevance*

3 The Supervised Learning Process

In the approach proposed herein, it is assumed that a web-page class is described by a set of fuzzy rules obtained through a supervised learning process. In addition, it shall be accepted herein from this point on that a feature vector, i.e. a two-dimensional vector wherein the first components store the words of the page and second components store the relevance of each word, represents a web page. The first stage in the learning process involves the generation of the corpus, that is, a vector that holds all words contained in all feature vectors of the training set. The relevance for each of these words is the attributes under the conditions of the fuzzy classification rules . Consequently, the fuzzy-rule base is composed of a set of rules such that:

IF Relev_word$_1$ is V$_1$ **AND** Relev_word$_2$ is V$_2$ **AND...AND** Relev_word$_m$ is V$_m$ **THEN** Class$_1$

Where V$_1$, V$_2$,... and V$_m$ are one of the following linguistic values NR, LR, MR, HR, and ER) defined by trapezoidal membership functions (Fig. 1). The learning process has been demonstrated in the descriptor extraction of two classes, *Medicine-Pharmacology* and *Aerospace-Technology*. The classes were previously analyzed [10]

---

[1] FUZZYSHELL is a CSIC registered trademark 1643983.

and this enables to contrast the performance of the proposed approach with the former analytical method. The *Medicine-Pharmacology* class is composed of 77 web pages, and the *Aerospace-Technology* class has 101 web pages. The two sets were manually obtained from an expert decision.

Finally, the development of a Genetic Algorithm (GA) for rule discovery involves a number of nontrivial design decisions, such as individual representation, operators, population initialization, selection methods and fitness function. All these decisions are fully described in the paragraphs below.

3.1 Individual Representation: Encoding the Fuzzy-Rule Antecedent

In the approach proposed herein, each individual of the GA population represents a set of classification rules, i.e. an entire candidate solution. In the GA context, this rule-inference approach is known as the Pittsburgh approach [14]. The selected codification of an individual involves a fixed-length binary string where bits are grouped in as many five-bit groups as there are words in the corpus. The encoding of an individual is illustrated in Table 2. An individual is encoded as a set of *m* conditions where *m* is the number of classification attributes, and since each attribute represents the relevance of a word in the corpus, *m* is the number of corpus elements. Note that this model implicitly assumes a positional encoding of attributes. In other words, in each individual the first condition refers to the first classification attribute, the second condition refers to the second attribute, and so on. Given this positional convention, the attribute name (in the current case, the word), need not be encoded. In addition, there is an implicit logical AND operator connecting the conditions encoded into the genotype, which is explicitly shown in the decoded rule antecedent. Lastly, each value for each attribute (NR, LR, MR, HR and ER; see Fig. 1) is encoded in a single bit; thus, for each bit of the attribute *relevance_word$_i$* , if the bit is set at "1," the corresponding attribute value would be included in the rule condition, and otherwise it would not. Therefore, keeping in mind the five linguistic labels defined for relevance, the example displayed in Table 2 can be decoded as the antecedent: (Relev_word$_1$ is NR *OR* HR *OR* ER) *AND* (Relev_word$_3$ is HR *OR* ER) *AND...AND* (Relev_word$_m$ is MR). Now then, when two or more linguistic labels are activated in a condition, the antecedent can be split in two or more rules, hence avoiding the definition of the OR operator, as follows:

(Relev_word$_1$ is NR) *AND* (Relev_word$_3$ is HR) *AND...AND* (Relev_word$_m$ is MR)
(Relev_word$_1$ is NR) *AND* (Relev_word$_3$ is ER) *AND...AND* (Relev_word$_{im}$is MR)
(Relev_word$_1$ is HR) *AND* (Relev_word$_3$ is HR) *AND...AND* (Relev_word$_m$ is MR)
(Relev_word$_1$ is HR) *AND* (Relev_word$_3$ is ER) *AND...AND* (Relev_word$_m$ is MR)
(Relev_word$_1$ is ER) *AND* (Relev_word$_3$ is HR) *AND...AND* (Relev_word$_{im}$is MR)
(Relev_word$_1$ is ER) *AND* (Relev_word$_3$ is ER) *AND...AND* (Relev_word$_m$ is MR)

Table 2. Encoding the antecedent of a rule

Condition 1	Condition 2	Condition 3...	Condition i ...	Condition m
Relev_word$_1$	Relev_word$_2$	Relev_word$_3$	Relev_word$_i$	Relev_word$_m$
1 0 0 1 1	1 1 1 1 1	0 0 0 1 1	0 0 0 0 0	0 0 1 0 0

Whenever all bits of an attribute are simultaneously set at 1, the corresponding rule condition is not included in the rule antecedent, since the value of the corresponding attribute is irrelevant to determining whether or not a data instance satisfies the rule antecedent. The learning of each class is accomplished in sequence; in other words, in step one the classifier of the *Medicine-Pharmacology* class is achieved, and then the fuzzy-rule set for the *Aerospace-Technology* training examples is built in a similar way. The consequent therefore need not be encoded in the genotype.

3.2 Selection Method and Operators

The initial population was randomly generated. Selection is not a problem for the Pittsburgh approach, since in this approach an individual corresponds to a rule set. Hence, a conventional selection method such as a proportional selection (roulette-wheel selection) [14] was used. Interestingly, the positional convention adopted herein simplifies the action of generic operators such as crossovers. By choosing the same crossover points in both parents, the corresponding genetic material can be swapped directly between two individuals without any risk of producing invalid offspring of any sort, such as an individual (rule antecedent) with a duplicate attribute. The two-point crossover was selected and applied with a probability of 0.5. For the mutation operator, a bit-by-bit mutation was used with a probability equal to 0.01.

3.3 Fitness Function

In addition to selecting a good representation, it is important to define a good payoff function. Moreover, a classification-rule set's performance in terms of predictive accuracy can be summarized by a contingency matrix [15]. In the current case, this can be accomplished with the 2x2 contingency matrix shown in Fig. 2. The labels in each quadrant of the matrix have the following meaning:

TP = Summarization of the degree of membership in the antecedent for all instances that have class c;
FP = Summarization of the degree of membership in the antecedent for all instances that do not have class c;
FN = Summarization of the degree of membership in (not (the antecedent)) for all instances that have class c;
TN = Summarization of the degree of membership in (not (the antecedent)) for all instances that do not have class c.

Actual Class

		c	not c
Predicted Class	c	TP	FP
	not c	FN	TN

Fig. 2. Contingency matrix for a classification-rule set

Note that one could work with a crisp confusion matrix by defuzzifying a rule when the fitness is computed [16]. In the current case, once the degree of matching between the rule antecedent and a data instance is computed, there are two possibilities: (a) If this degree is greater than or equal to 0.5, then the instance satisfies the rule antecedent in a crisp sense; that is, the instance will contribute a value of 1 for either the TP or the FP cell of the confusion matrix, depending on the instance class. (b) If the rule antecedent is not satisfied in a crisp sense, the instances will contribute a value of 1 for either the FN or the TN cell of the confusion matrix, depending on the instance class.

Therefore the fitness function that evaluates the quality of the rule set with respect to predictive accuracy is defined as follows:

$$\text{Fitness} = \text{true\_positive\_rate} \times \text{true\_negative\_rate} = \frac{TP}{(TP + FN)} \times \frac{TN}{(TN + FP)}. \tag{2}$$

4 Results

The number of words in the corpus is a function of the number of examples examined ("Ex." in Table 3) to build the corpus and the length of the feature vector. The size of the corpus thus generated has been analyzed from three points of view (see Table 3): 1) all feature-vector components (Ct), 2) ten components only (C10) and 3) five components. It is important to mention that corpus size decreases considerably with feature-vector size without losing practically any high-relevance words. In fact, for the *Medicine-Pharmacology* class, some words that appear in the corpus generated from 36 examples and the first five components of the feature vector are: "psychiatric," "pharmacology," "preclinical," "clinical," "drug," "medication," "therapy," "pharmacy," "medical," "pharmacotherapy" and "toxic." In the case of the *Aerospace-Technology* class, some words that appear in the corpus generated from 50 examples and the first five components of the feature vectors are: "space," "tool," "aeronautics," "aerospace," "aerodynamics," "flight," "mechanisms," "spacecraft," "mechanics," "engineering," "shuttle," "fluid," "dynamics," "laboratory" and "technology."

Table 3. Corpus size according to the number of feature-vector components selected

Medicine-Pharmacology				Aerospace-Technology			
Ex.	Ct	C10	C5	Ex.	Ct	C10	C5
77	5546	448	259	101	8255	666	356
38	3285	292	155	50	5456	365	200

Finally, the learning process was performed using 40 examples for each class as input data. Training examples were randomly selected. Next a classification process was carried out for the rest of the examples in order to test the performance of the fuzzy-rule base obtained in the learning step. Some important preliminary results of the comparative study of the proposed fuzzy system versus previous work [10] using a Naive Bayes classifier are shown in Table 4.

Table 4. . Main results of the comparative study of the Fuzzy vs. the Naive Bayes classifier

Relevance/ Classifier	Medicine-Pharmacology (%)		Aerospace-Technology (%)		Mean Values (%)	
	Successes	Failures	Successes	Failures	Succes.	Failures
FUZZY / Naive Bayes	84.21	15.79	89.47	10.53	86.84	13.16
FUZZY/ FUZZY	75.05	24.95	72.33	27.67	73.69	26.31

5 Conclusion

This paper presents a novel approach to web-page classification. The proposed method offers two major issues. The first is a two-dimensional vector where the first component is words extracted from the textual component of the page and the second component is numeric values that evaluate each word's relevance in the web page's text. To calculate word relevance, a fuzzy model is proposed that takes into account some characteristics of HTML language and other more "classic" attributes often used in information retrieval.

The second issue is the use of two web-page sets that exemplify two specific classes to describe a supervised learning method that enables a set of fuzzy rules to be generated to explain the input data sets. Preliminary experiments show that the approach proposed herein is suitable for handling the ambiguity inherent in web-page classification, although wider experimentation is necessary in order to profit from the capacities of a GA search. In the near future improvements should be considered such as a better population-initialization method and a fitness function that accounts for the size of the rule set and penalizes longer rule sets.

References

1. UNCTAD E-Commerce and development report 2002. Report of the United Nations Conference on Trade and Development. United Nations, New York and Geneva (2002).
2. Gudivada, V.N., Raghavan, V.V., Grosky, W.I., and Kasanagottu, R.: Information retrieval on the World Wide Web. IEEE Internet Computing. September-October (1997) 58–68.
3. Chen, H. and Dumais, S.T.: Bringing order to the Web: automatically categorizing search results. Proceedings of the CHI'00, Human Factor in Computing Systems, Den Haag, New York, US. ACM Press (2000) 145–152.
4. Salton, G., Wong, A., and Yang, C.S.: A vector space model for information retrieval. Communications of the ACM. 18-11 (1975) 613–620.
5. Baeza-Yates, R. and Ribeiro-Neto, B..:Modern information retrieval. ACM Press Books, Addison-Wesley (1999).
6. Kosala, R. and Blockeel H.: Web mining research: a survey. ACM SIGKDD Explorations. 2-1 (2000) 1–15.
7. Koller, D. and Sahami, M.: Toward Optimal feature selection. Proceedings of the Thirteenth International Conference on Machine Learning. Morgan Kaufmann, San Francisco, CA (1996) 284–292.
8. Henzinger, M.: Link analysis in web information retrieval. Bulletin of the Technical Committee on Data Engineering. 23-3 (2000) 3–8.
9. Yang, Y.: A study of approach to hypertext categorization. Journal of Intelligent Information Systems. 18-2/3 (2002) 219–241.
10. Ribeiro, A., Fresno, V., García-Alegre, M.C., and Guinea, D.: A fuzzy system for the web representation. Intelligent Exploration of the Web. Studies in Fuzziness and Soft Computing. Szczepaniak, P.S., Segovia, J., Kacprzyk, J., and Zadeh, L.A. Editors. Physica-Verlag, Berlin Heidelberg New York (2003) 19–37.
11. Pierre, J.M.: On the automated classification of web sites. Linköping Electronic Articles in Computer and Information Science. Linköping University Electronic Press Linköping, Sweden. 6 (2001).
12. Fresno V. and Ribeiro.: A.feature selection and dimensionality reduction in web pages representation. Proceedings of the International Congress on Computational Intelligence: Methods & Applications. Bangor, Wales, U.K. (2001) 416–421.
13. Gasós J., Fernandéz P.D., García-Alegre M.C., Garcia Rosa R.: Environment for the development of fuzzy controllers. Proceedings of the International Conference. on AI: Applications & N.N. (1990) 121–124.
14. Michalewicz Z.: Genetic Algorithms + Data Structures = Evolution Programs. 3rd edn. Springer-Verlag, Berlin Heidelberg New York (1996).
15. Freitas, A.A.: Data mining and knowledge discovery with evolutionary algorithms. Natural Computing Series. Springer-Verlag, Berlin Heidelberg New York (2002).
16. Dasgupta, D. and Gonzales, F.A.: Evolving complex fuzzy classifier rules using a linear tree genetic representation. Proceedings of the Genetic and Evolutionary Computation Conference (GECCO'2001). Morgan Kaufmann (2001) 299–305.

Content-Based Methodology for Anomaly Detection on the Web

Mark Last[1], Bracha Shapira[1], Yuval Elovici[1], Omer Zaafrany[1], and
Abraham Kandel[2]

[1]Department of Information Systems Engineering, Ben-Gurion University of the Negev
Beer-Sheva 84105, Israel
{mlast,bshapira,zaafrany}@bgumail.bgu.ac.il
elovici@inter.net.il
[2]Department of Computer Science and Engineering, University of South Florida
4202 E. Fowler Ave. ENB 118
Tampa, FL, 33620, USA
kandel@csee.usf.edu

Abstract. As became apparent after the tragic events of September 11, 2001, terrorist organizations and other criminal groups are increasingly using the legitimate ways of Internet access to conduct their malicious activities. Such actions cannot be detected by existing intrusion detection systems that are generally aimed at protecting computer systems and networks from some kind of "cyber attacks". Preparation of an attack against the human society itself can only be detected through analysis of the *content* accessed by the users. The proposed study aims at developing an innovative methodology for abnormal activity detection, which uses web content as the audit information provided to the detection system. The new behavior-based detection method learns the normal behavior by applying an unsupervised clustering algorithm to the contents of publicly available web pages viewed by a group of similar users. In this paper, we represent page content by the well-known vector space model. The content models of normal behavior are used in real-time to reveal deviation from normal behavior at a specific location on the net. The detection algorithm sensitivity is controlled by a threshold parameter. The method is evaluated by the trade-off between the detection rate (TP) and the false positive rate (FP).

Keywords. information retrieval, unsupervised clustering, user modeling, web security, anomaly detection, activity monitoring.

1 Introduction

Even though *Intrusion Detection Systems* (IDS's) possess a variety of means to protect computer systems from unauthorized users, the question of the authorized and legitimate users who abuse their privileges by being involved in criminal (such as terrorist) activities remains unsolved. Existing IDS would detect those users only in case of abnormal behavior at the command level. However, in case of normal but non-legitimate behavior these systems will fail to issue an alarm. For example, they will not detect an employee who is using the web in his regular working hours to read instructions on bomb-making. The main goal of our research is to develop a new method for identification of authorized users with abnormal access patterns to pub-

E. Menasalvas et al. (Eds.): AWIC 2003, LNAI 2663, pp. 113–123, 2003.
© Springer-Verlag Berlin Heidelberg 2003

licly available information on the web. Using IDS terminology, we consider those users as intruders as well, though their activity may not be an "intrusion" in the traditional sense.

This research integrates issues from the research fields of computer security, information retrieval, and cluster analysis. The following sub-sections include a brief
overview of these topics.

1.1   Intrusion Detection Systems

An intrusion detection system constantly monitors actions taken in a given environment, and decides whether these actions are suspected to be an attack or are part of a
legitimate use of the environment [1]. The environment may be a computer, several
computers connected to a network or the network itself. An IDS analyzes various
kinds of action information coming from the environment to evaluate the probability
that these actions are symptoms of intrusions. Such information includes for example,
configuration information about the current state of the system, audit information describing the events that occur in the system (e.g., event log in Windows NT) or network traffic.

In [1] Debar at. al. present the following characteristics of intrusion detection systems: the *Detection method (behavior-based IDS*, or *anomaly detection systems,* vs.
knowledge-based IDS), *Behavior on detection* (*active IDS* vs. *passive IDS*), *Audit
source location* (*Host-based* IDS [1, 6] vs. *Network-based* IDS), and *Usage frequency*
(*real-time* monitoring vs. IDSs that are run *periodically* [1, 6]).

Several measures to evaluate an IDS are suggested in the literature [1, 5, 6, 7].
These include accuracy, completeness, performance, efficiency, fault tolerance, timeliness, and adaptivity. The most widely used measures are percentage of intrusive actions that are detected by the system (True Positives), percentage of normal actions
that the system incorrectly identifies as intrusive (False Positives), and percentage of
alarms that are found to represent abnormal behavior out of the total number of
alarms (Accuracy).

1.2   Content Representation Models

One major issue in this research is the representation of web pages content. More specifically, how to represent the normal content vs. the content of currently accessed
document, in order to efficiently compute the similarity between them. Our study will
apply the vector-space model that is commonly used in Information Retrieval applications [30]. In the vector space model, a document d is represented by an n-
dimensional vector $d = (w_1, w_2, ..., w_n)$, where w_i represents the frequency-based weight
of term i in document d. To indicate if two data items represented as vectors are related, a similarity between them may be computed by using one of the known vector
distance measuring methods, such as Euclidian distance or Cosine [21,23]. This can
apply to predicting whether a new document belongs to an existing cluster provided
that the document and the cluster centroid are both represented as vectors.

1.3 Cluster Analysis

Cluster analysis or *clustering* is the process of partitioning data objects (records, documents, etc.) into meaningful groups or *clusters* so that objects within a cluster have similar characteristics, but are very dissimilar to objects in other clusters [33]. Clustering can be viewed as *unsupervised classification* of unlabelled patterns (observations, data items, or feature vectors), since no pre-defined category labels are associated with the objects in the training set. Applications of clustering include data mining, document retrieval, image segmentation, and pattern classification [28]. Thus, clustering of web documents browsed by Internet users can reveal collections of documents belonging to the same topic. As shown in [34], clustering is also an efficient tool for anomaly detection: normality of a new object can be evaluated by its distance from the most similar cluster under the assumption that all clusters are based on "normal" data only.

1.4 Paper Organization

This paper is organized as follows. In Section 2, we present our methodology for content-based anomaly detection. Section 3 describes an initial case study designed to test the feasibility of the proposed approach. Finally, in Section 4 we outline directions for the next stages of our research.

2 Content-Based Methodology for Anomaly Detection

2.1 System Architecture

We suggest a new type of behavior-based anomaly detection system that uses the content of web pages browsed by a specific group of users as an input for detecting abnormal activity. In this study, we refer to the *textual* content of web pages only excluding images, music, video clips, and other complex data types. We assume that content normally viewed by the group users represent their information needs and can be used as input data for learning the users' normal behavior and for detecting an abnormal user. We define user abnormal behavior as an access to information that is not expected to be viewed by a normal member of the group. The general architecture of the proposed system is described in Figure 1. Each user is identified by a "user's computer" having a unique IP address rather than by his or her name. In case of a real-time alarm, the detected IP can be used to locate the computer and hopefully the abnormal user himself who may still be logged on to the same computer.

The suggested methodology has two modes of operation:

1. Learning normal behavior – in this mode, the web traffic of a group of users (content of publicly available web pages) is recorded and represented as a set of vectors. The collected data is used to derive and represent the normal behavior of the group's users by applying techniques of unsupervised clustering.

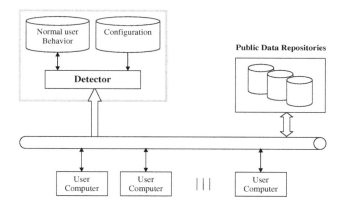

Fig. 1. Suggested IDS architecture and environment

The suggested methodology has two modes of operation:

2. Monitoring network users – This mode is aimed at detecting abnormal users by representing the content of information accessed by a monitored user as an *access vector*. Abnormal behavior is detected when similarity between the access vector and information interests of the group's users is below a pre-defined threshold.

In the following sub-sections, we describe in details the normal user behavior learning and the abnormal behavior detection algorithm.

2.2   Learning the Normal User Behavior

The "learning normal behavior" part of the method defines and represents the normal behavior of a group of users based on the content of their web activity. Figure 2 describes the learning mode. We assume that it is possible to access all public traffic of a group of users by eavesdropping on the communication or by direct access to a proxy that is being used by the entire group (Sniffer module). The page content is sent by the Sniffer to the Filter module. The Filter excludes transactions that do not include enough meaningful textual information. For the included transactions, images and all the tags related to the content format are removed (for example, the tags of an HTML document are filtered out). The filtered pages are sent to the Vector- Generator module. This module converts the content of each page into a vector of terms. The vectors are stored for future processing.

The Clustering module (Fig. 2) accesses the vectors that were collected during a specific period of time (for example, one week) and performs clustering that results in n clusters representing the normal content viewed by the group members. For each cluster, the Group-Representer module computes one centroid vector (denoted by Cv_i) which represents a topic normally accessed by the users.

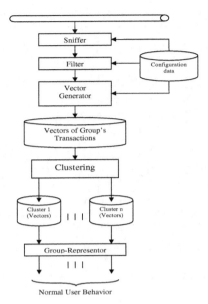

Fig. 2. Learning the normal user behavior

2.3 Detecting Abnormal Behavior

In the monitoring mode of the system, the content of transactions of the group members is collected (Figure 3). The first three modules (Sniffer, Filter, and Vector - Generator) have the same pre-processing functionality as in the learning part. The Vector-Generator module converts the user transactions content into vector representation (*access vector av*). The Detector uses access vector and the "normal user behavior" and tries to determine whether the access vector is similar to one of the centroid vectors of the "normal user behavior". This resembles the approach used in collaborative filtering [38] where relevancy of a document to a user is predicted by comparing the vector representing his or her interests to the vectors of all other users and finding the most similar user. In our application study, we used the cosine measure to find the similarity. The detector issues the alarm when the similarity between the access vector and the nearest centroid is lower than the threshold denoted by *tr*:

$$Min\left(\frac{\sum_{i=1}^{m}\left(tCv_{i1}\cdot tAv_i\right)}{\sqrt{\sum_{i=1}^{m}tCv_{i1}^2\cdot\sum_{i=1}^{m}tAv_i^2}},\ldots,\frac{\sum_{i=1}^{m}\left(tCv_{in}\cdot tAv_i\right)}{\sqrt{\sum_{i=1}^{m}tCv_{in}^2\cdot\sum_{i=1}^{m}tAv_i^2}}\right) < tr$$

where Cv_i is the ith centroid vector, Av - the access vector, tCv_{i1} - the ith term in the vector Cv_i, tAv_i - the ith term in the vector Av, and m - the number of unique terms in each vector.

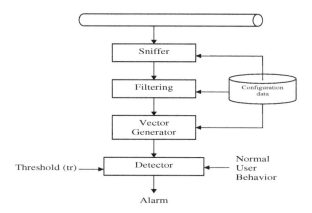

Fig. 3. Detecting sbnormal user behavior

3 Application Study

3.1 Application Study Environment

We have conducted an initial evaluation of the proposed content-based anomaly detection methodology through a prototype system. The experimental environment includes a small network of 11 computers where each computer has a constant IP address and a proxy server through which all the computers access the web. Ten students belonging to the Department of Information Systems Engineering were instructed to access web sites related to general computer programming subjects (the students represented a homogenous group of users). During the experiment the ten users, generated about 1000 transactions (page views). In order to simulate an "intruder" one student was instructed to explore a different domain (tourism). The Sniffer, Filter, Vector Generator, Clustering and Detector modules described above were implemented and installed inside the server. We have used the *vcluster* program from the Cluto Clustering Tool [37] to implement the Clustering module where the clustering algorithm was "k-way" and the similarity between the objects was cosine.

3.2 Evaluation Measures

To evaluate the system performance we derived the following performance measures (based on [34]):

1. *True Positive Rate (Detection Rate or Completeness)*: percentage of OTHER (abnormal) internet access pages that receives a rating below the *tr* threshold. In our experiments, an "abnormal" page will be obtained from the 11th user that is not a member of the homogenous group.
2. *False Positive Rate:* percentage of SELF (normal) internet access pages that the system incorrectly determines to be abnormal, i.e., the percentage of SELF pages that receive a rating below the *tr* threshold .

3. *Accuracy* – percentage of alarms that are found to represent OTHER (abnormal) behavior out of the total number of alarms.

Since no benchmark data on content-based anomaly detection is currently available, our results are compared to the best results achieved with user command-level data [34].

3.3 Initial Results

In the initial study, we had 1000 vectors representing pages accessed by normal users and 100 vectors representing pages accessed by an abnormal user. The experiment included the following steps:

1. Set an initial value of the threshold parameter *tr*.
2. Randomly select 100 vectors from the normal set of vectors as a validation set. These vectors will be used for testing the system ability to ignore normal users.
3. Train the system (learning phase) using the remaining 900 vectors representing pages accessed by normal users.
4. Use the 100 vectors representing pages accessed by normal users as an input to the detector and find how many vectors mistakenly raised an alarm (false positive rate measure).
5. Use the 100 vectors representing pages accessed by an abnormal user as an input to the detector and find how many vectors did raise an alarm (true positive rate measure).
6. Repeat steps 2-5 for different values of the threshold.

The ROC (Receiver-Operator Characteristic) graphs in Fig. 4 describe the entire evaluation process for 11 clusters and for 20 clusters. Every point at the ROC graphs represents an average result of ten cross-validation runs where in each run different 100 vectors were selected at random from the 1000 vectors accessed by normal users. We have not observed a significant improvement in system performance as a result of almost doubling the number of clusters.

The graph in Fig 5. describes the accuracy as a function of the threshold parameter. The results suggest that the threshold values should be between 0.05 and 0.2 in order to achieve the highest accuracy level.

Based on the performance measures demonstrated in Figs. 4 and 5, the user of the system may choose an optimal threshold value. This decision is affected by the utility function of the user. It is clear from our initial application study that our model is feasible and it can reliably detect an abnormal user based on the content of monitored web traffic. The prototype system based on our methodology achieved TP=0.7 and FP=0.008 compared to TP=0.7 and FP=0.15 of ADMIT system [34], which utilized user command-level data.

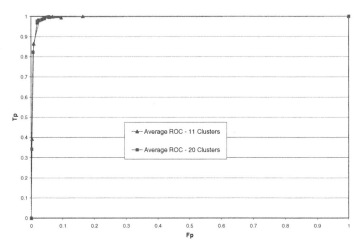

Fig. 4. True positive and false positive rate for 11 and 20 clusters

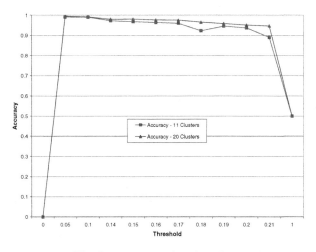

Fig. 5. Accuracy as function of threshold

4   Conclusions

In this paper, we have presented an innovative, content-based methodology for anomaly detection on the web. The results of an initial case study indicate that the method can be useful for detecting authorized users that perform non-legitimate access to publicly available information. These types of activities are completely ignored by standard Intrusion Detection Systems.

The suggested methodology can be implemented by government agencies in one of the following ways:

1)   ISPs awareness and cooperation - the proposed anomaly detection system can be installed inside the ISP infrastructure to monitor users' activities. When needed, the ISPs are able to provide the exact identity of a suspicious user detected by the system.

2)   Without ISPs cooperation or awareness – in this case the system can be installed at communication lines connecting the ISPs to the Internet backbone. By eavesdropping on this line and detecting abnormal activities, it is possible to detect the IP address which is the source of the activity. The exact identity of the user remains unknown. However, this alternative does not require ISP cooperation and protects the privacy of the ISP subscribers.

The ongoing research includes the following two main issues:

- *Document Representation.* We are planning to perform a comparison between the common vector-space model and a novel graph-based model [29] that can capture relationships between terms in a textual document.

- *Detection Methodology.* We expect to obtain more accurate results in a real-world environment by detecting *anomalous sequences* of page views rather than raising an alarm after every abnormal page. Identifying pages related to specific topics (such as bomb-making) in a stream of legitimate information is another important challenge.

References

1.   H. Debar, M. Dacier, A. Wespi, "Towards a taxonomy of intrusion-detection systems", Computer Networks, 1999, Vol. 31, pp. 805–822.
2.   W. Lee, S.J. Stolfo, P. K. Chan, E. Eskin, W. Fan, M. Miller, S. Hershkop, J. Zhang, "Real Time Data Mining-based Intrusion Detection", Proceedings of DISCEX II, 2001.
3.   W. Lee, S.J. Stolfo, "A Framework for Constructing Features and Models for Intrusion Detection Systems", ACM Transactions on Information and System Security, 2000, Vol. 3, No. 4.
4.   W. Lee, S.J. Stolfo, "Data Mining Approaches for Intrusion Detection ", In Proceedings of the Seventh USENIX Security Symposium, San Antonio, TX, 1998.
5.   K. Richards, "Network Based Intrusion Detection: A Review of Technologies", Computers & Security, 1999, Vol. 18, pp. 671–682.
6.   E.H. Spafford, D. Zamboni, "Intrusion detection using autonomous agents", Computer Networks, 2000, Vol. 34, pp. 547–570.
7.   J.S. Balasubramaniyan, J.O. Garcia-Fernandez, D Isacoff, E. Spafford, D. Zamboni, "An architecture for intrusion detection using autonomous agents", Proceedings 14th Annual Computer Security Applications Conference, IEEE Comput. Soc, Los Alamitos, CA, USA, 1998, xiii+365, pp. 13–24.
8.   J. Cannady, "Next Generation Intrusion Detection: Autonomous Reinforcement Learning of Network Attacks", Proceedings of the 23rd National Information Systems Security Conference, 2000.
9.   J. Cannady, "Neural Networks for Misuse Detection: Initial Results", Proceedings of the Recent Advances in Intrusion Detection '98 Conference, 1998, pp. 31–47.
10. B. Balajinath, S. Raghavan, "Intrusion detection through learning behavior model", International Journal Of Computer Communications, 2001, Vol. 24, No. 12, pp. 1202–1212.
11. G. White, V. Pooch, "Cooperating Security Managers: distribute intrusion detection systems", Computers & Security, 1996, Vol. 15, No. 5, pp. 441–450.

12. M. Y. Huang, R.J. Jasper, T.M. Wicks, "A large scale distributed intrusion detection framework based on attack strategy analysis", Computer Networks,1999, Vol. 31, pp. 2465–2475.
13. P. Ning, X.S. Wang, S. Jajodia, "Modeling requests among cooperating intrusion detection systems", Computer Communications, 2000, Vol. 23, pp. 1702–1715.
14. J. Cannady, "Applying CMAC-based on-line learning to intrusion detection", In Proceedings of the International Joint Conference on Neural Networks, Italy, 2000, Vol. 5, pp. 405–410.
15. V. Paxson, "Bro: a system for detecting network intruders in real-time", Computer Networks, 1999, Vol. 31, pp. 2435–2463.
16. B.C. Rhodes, J.A. Mahaffey, J.D. Cannady, "Multiple Self-Organizing Maps for Intrusion Detection", 23rd National Information Systems Security Conference, 2000.
17. E. Eskin, A. Arnold, M. Prerau, L. Portnoy, S. Stolfo, "A Geometric Framework for Unsupervised Anomaly Detection: Detecting Intrusions in Unlabeled Data", Data Mining in Security Applications, Kluwer Academic Publishers, 2002.
18. R.P. Lippmann, R.K. Cunningham, "Improving intrusion detection performance using keyword selection and neural networks", Computer Networks, 2000, Vol. 34, pp. 597–603.
19. J.A. Marin, D. Ragsdale, J. Surdu, "A hybrid approach to the profile creation and intrusion detection", Proceedings DARPA Information Survivability Conference and Exposition II, IEEE Comput. Soc, CA, USA, 2001, Vol. 1, pp. 69–76.
20. T. Fawcett, F. Provost, "Activity Monitoring: Noticing interesting changes in behavior", Proceedings on the Fifth ACM SIGKDD International Conference on Knowledge Discovery and Data Mining, 1999.
21. Z. Boger, T. Kuflik, P. Shoval, B. Shapira, "Automatic keyword identification by artificial neural networks compared to manual identification by users of filtering systems", Information Processing and Management, 2001, Vol. 37, pp. 187–198.
22. E. Bloedorn, I. Mani, "Using NLP for Machine Learning of User Profiles", Intelligent Data Analysis, 1998, Vol. 2, pp. 3–18.
23. S. Pierrea, C. Kacanb, W. Probstc, "An agent-based approach for integrating user profile into a knowledge management process", 2000, Knowledge-Based Systems, Vol. 13, pp. 307–314.
24. B. Shapira, P. Shoval, U. Hanani, "Stereotypes in Information Filtering Systems", Information Processing & Management, 1997, Vol. 33, No. 3, pp.273–287.
25. B. Shapira, P. Shoval, U. Hanani, " Experimentation with an information filtering system that combines cognitive and sociological filtering integrated with user stereotypes", Decision Support Systems, 1999, Vol. 27, pp. 5–24.
26. D. Hand, H. Mannila, P. Smyth, "Principles of Data Mining", MIt Press, England, 2001.
27. U. Fayyad, G.Piatetsky-Shapiro, P. Smyth, "From Data Mining to Knowledge Discovery in Databases", AI Magazine, 1996, Vol. 17, No. 3, pp. 37–54.
28. A.K. Jain, M.N. Murty, P.J. Flynn, "Data Clustering: A Review", ACM Computing Surveys, 1999, Vol. 31, No. 3, pp. 264–323.
29. A. Schenker, M. Last, H. Bunke, and A. Kandel, " Clustering of Web Documents using a Graph Model", to appear in "Web Document Analysis: Challenges and Opportunities", Apostolos Antonacopoulos and Jianying Hu (Editors), World Scientific, 2003.
30. G. Salton, Automatic Text Processing: the Transformation, Analysis, and Retrieval of Information by Computer (Addison-Wesley, Reading, 1989).
31. S. Russell and P. Norvig, Artificial Intelligence: A Modern Approach (Prentice-Hall, Upper Saddle River, 1995).
32. X. Lu, Document retrieval: a structural approach, Information Processing and Management 26, 2 (1990) 209–218.
33. Han, J. and Kamber, M., "Data Mining: Concepts and Techniques", Morgan Kaufmann, 2001.
34. K. Sequeira and M. Zaki, "ADMIT: Anomaly-based Data Mining for Intrusions", Proceeding of SIGKDD 02, pp. 386–395, ACM, 2002.

35. Salton, G., Wong, A., and Yang C.S.A.: *Vector Space Model for Automatic Indexing.* Communications of the ACM 18, 613-620, 1975
36. R. Lemos, "What are the real risks of cyberterrorism?", ZDNet, August 26, 2002, URL: `http://zdnet.com.com/2100-1105-955293.html`.
37. George Karypis, CLUTO - A Clustering Toolkit, Release 2.0, University of Minnesota, 2002 [`http://www-users.cs.umn.edu/~karypis/cluto/download.html`].
38. U. Hanani, B. Shapira and P. Shoval , "Information Filtering: Overview of Issues, Research and Systems", User Modeling and User-Adapted Interaction (UMUAI), Vol. 11(3), 203-259, 2001.

Designing Reliable Web Security Systems Using Rule-Based Systems Approach*

Grzegorz J. Nalepa and Antoni Ligęza

Institute of Automatics
University of Mining and Metallurgy
Al. Mickiewicza 30, 30-059 Kraków, Poland
gjn@agh.edu.pl,ligeza@agh.edu.pl

Abstract. This paper shows that rule-based web security systems, such as firewalls, can be largely improved by using formal design and verification techniques. The principal idea consists of an integrated design and verification methodology, supported by an integrated graphical environment for rule-based systems development. System structure is described in a XML-based meta-level knowledge representation language. System domain knowledge and semantics is represented in RDF and Ontologies-based description. Formal properties of the system can be verified on-line by an integrated Prolog-based inference engine.

1 Introduction

One of the main concerns in modern web and network-based systems is security. Nowdays network traffic control is achieved by using devices known as *firewalls*. A firewall is a special case of a *control system*. Its task is real-time filtering of network traffic. Using built-in *knowledge* it makes *decision* about route of the packets in the network.

Designing a reliable firewall mainly consists in designing its knowledge-base, known as a *security policy*. Almost all firewalls share the same knowledge representation method of knowledge-base, so it is possible to design a security policy suitable for multiple firewall products. The knowledge representation method used above is based on simple *rules*.

Network security systems such as firewalls use knowledge representation which is one of most sucessfull artificial intelligence (AI) technique. In the field of AI *Rule-Based Systems* (RBS) have been carefully studied. The intention of this paper is to show that results of these studies may be applied to the process of design and verification of network security systems. In Sect. 2 main notions of AI rule-based systems theory are presented. Furthermore, in Sect. 3 problems of verification of rule-based systems qualitative properties are discussed. Section 4 includes a proposal of application of RBS theory to design of network firewalls.

The paper extends some of the ideas presented in [9,10], discussing graphical design concepts exercised in the field of RBS. In [9] a prototype graphical-algebraic generic CAD/CASE tool supporting the design of rule-based systems

---

* Research supported from a KBN Research Project No.: 4 T11C 027 24

E. Menasalvas et al. (Eds.): AWIC 2003, LNAI 2663, pp. 124–133, 2003.

and providing verification possibilities was presented. Basing on the experience with that tool a new proposal of an integrated tool for design and on-line verification of RBS using a meta-level knowledge representation format and wide range of verified characteristics is discussed. The paper presents possible aplications of the new tool for the design of firewall systems which constitute one of the key elements in web-based systems security.

2   Background of the Research in Rule-Based Systems

A rule-based system consists of a number of rules (the so-called rule-base or knowledge-base) and an inference engine allowing for inference control. A more complete presentation of the current state-of-the art of the rule-based systems approach can be found in [7].

Implementation of rule-based systems encounters two main problems. The first one is known as the *knowledge acquisition bottleneck* and it consists in the well known difficulties with obtaining precise knowledge specification. The second one concerns verification and validation of the knowledge. It consists in checking certain characteristics and correctness of the system built.

Several methodologies for building knowledge-based systems have been studied and proposed as conceptual tools for simplifying the design of such systems [6], with KADS and CommonKADS appearing as some best known examples. Such methodologies support mainly subsequent stages of the *conceptual design* in case of large systems, while direct technical support of the logical design and during the implementation phase is mostly limited to providing a context-sensitive, syntax checking editors. In order to assure safe, reliable and efficient performance, analysis and verification of selected qualitative properties should be carried out [1,2,5]. Those properties, discussed in the following sections, include features such as, completeness, subsumption and determinism. However, their verification *after the design* of a rule-based system is both costly and late. This is why a new approach is discussed in Sect. 6.2.

3   Verification of Qualitative Properties

In case of rule-based systems there are some important qualitative properties, which can be verified to assure reliable system performance. These properties are presented below; they were discussed in [9].

3.1   Subsumption

We consider the most general case of subsumption; some particular definitions are considered in [1]. A rule subsumes another if the following conditions hold:

- the precondition part of the first rule is *weaker* (more general) than the precondition of the subsumed rule,
- the conclusion part of the first rule is *stronger* (more specific) than the conclusion of the subsumed rule.

3.2   Determinism

A set of rules is *deterministic* iff no two different rules can succeed for the same input state. A set of rules which is not deterministic is also referred to as *ambivalent*. The idea of having a deterministic system consists in *a priori* elimination of rules which operate on a common situation.

3.3   Completeness

For intuition, a RBS is considered to be *complete* if there exists at least one rule succeeding for any possible input situation [1].

4   Rule-Based Systems in the Field of Network Security

It was asserted in Sec. 1 that rule-based systems theory can be applied to network firewalls. We shall now proceed in demonstrating that this is a case by analyzing an example firewall structure.

4.1   An Example Firewall Structure

Let us consider an example firewall implementation in the GNU/Linux environment. Version 2.4 of the Linux Kernel uses the so-called NetFilter statefull firewall implementation. The firewall's engine security policy can be controlled by *IPTables* tool. It consists of three default rule-sets, called "chains" (or "tables"), controlling the input, output and forwarding policy applied to IP (*Internet Protocol*) packets. It is worth noting, that most of other both commercial and open firewall implementations have a very similar structure.

All IPTables rules-sets (policies) share common structure. They consist of rules matching selected properties of IP packets, such as source and destination addresses, TCP ports, or network protocols such as TCP, UDP, ICMP. Each rule includes number of conditions and conclusion (called "target"), eg.:

```
iptables -A OUTPUT -s 192.168.1.0/24 -d 10.1.0.0/16 -j ACCEPT
```

It reads as follows: if a packet comes to the "OUTPUT" chain and if it comes from 192.168.1.0/24 network and is addressed to 10.1.0.0/16 network it will be accepted ("ACCEPT"). A simple example is given below:

```
Chain OUTPUT (policy ACCEPT)
target  prot  source            destination
ACCEPT  all   192.168.1.0/24    10.1.0.0/16
LOG     icmp  192.168.2.0/24    0.0.0.0/0
REJECT  udp   192.168.2.0/24    0.0.0.0/0
DROP    all   0.0.0.0/0         10.2.0.0/16
ACCEPT  tcp   0.0.0.0/0         0.0.0.0/0      tcp dpt:80
HTTPS   tcp   0.0.0.0/0         0.0.0.0/0      tcp dpt:443
Chain HTTPS (1 references)
target  prot  source            destination
ACCEPT  all   149.156.0.0/16    0.0.0.0/0
DROP    all   0.0.0.0/0         0.0.0.0/0
```

Table 1. RBS NetFilter firewall description

Attribute	Description	Domain description	Domain
pr	protocol	a set of values	ip,icmp,tcp,udp
sa	source address	IP address range	$0 - 2^{32}$
da	destination address	IP address range	$0 - 2^{32}$
sp	source port	TCP port range	$0 - 2^{16}$
dp	destination port	TCP port range	$0 - 2^{16}$
st	state of TCP connection	a set of values	INVALID, ESTABLISHED, NEW, RELATED
j	routing decision	a set of values	ACCEPT, REJECT, DROP, other_chain

Every default chain has the so-called default policy, a default rule. Rules in every chain are analyzed from the first one to the last one. When first rule matching the packet fires, all remaining rules are ignored.

The firewall rule-base can be modularized with introduction of additional chains linked to the default ones. The example presented above shows how all port 443 (default HTTP over SSL port) connections can be directed to a separate chain called "HTTPS".

4.2 Rule-Based System Model of Firewall Security Policy

We can describe a simplified NetFilter-based firewall in terms of RBS as having attributes presented in Table 1. Rules are ordered in chains. They are analyzed from the first one to the last one. When a first matching rule is found the routing decision is made. This strategy allows to avoid problems with contradicting rules or non-deterministic cases.

It will be demonstrated in the following sections how this structure can be graphically represented during the design process.

4.3 Formal Properties Interpretation

We can now give a terse interpretation of rule-based system formal properties in case of a firewall system.

Subsumption. If a rule subsumption occurs it means that the security policy is not optimal. Some firewall rules can be safely removed, which may possibly lead to increased performance.

Determinism. A deterministic firewall policy assures certain level of system reliability. In this case firewall will always make the same routing decision every time it receives packet with given properties. In the NetFilter case determinism is assured by the rule analyzing strategy. Even if there is more then one rule matching the packet, only the first one found will fire.

Completeness. Completeness of the firewall policy implies, that the system is able to make a routing decision for every packet it can possibly receive. In the NetFilter case completeness is assured by the default policy rule.

On-Line Validation. A validating design environment can verify properties described above, and help in optimizing and improving reliability of a firewall system designed.

4.4 Other Applications of Rule-Based Systems Approach

In Sec. 4.1 an example firewall implementation has been discussed. Linux 2.4 NetFilter is one of many firewall systems available. There are other *free software* implementations such as FreeBSD's *IPFW* and OpenBSD *PF*. There are also commercial firewall products such as *Checkpoint Firewall-1*. Applications of rule-based approach in the field of network security are not limited to firewalls. An important class of modern security systems are *Intrusion Detection Systems* (IDS), such as *SNORT*([13]). They often offer more powerful network monitoring methods than firewalls. They are another example of complex real-time network security systems which use rule-based knowledge representation. Another interesting example of rule-based security system is *Rule Set Based Access Control for Linux*([14]), a set of kernel level and user space tools for hardening Linux-based system security.

The rule-based systems approach presented in this article is a generic one. It may be applied not just to Linux's firewall implementation, but to many others. It is possible since they all share common *knowledge base structure*, even though they employ different syntax in order to describe it. It may also be applied to IDS systems design. An integrated environment providing different plugins translating the same *structure* to different *syntaxes* will be proposed in Sec. 6.

5 Selected Knowledge Representation Concepts

There are several approaches for knowledge representation and extraction, which is needed in the stage of rule-based system design. Some most commonly used ones are:

Production Rules and Logic. This classic method relies on *if-then-else* construct. It is well known form procedural programming languages.
Decision Tables. Decision tables are an engineering way of representing production rules. Conditions are formed into a table which also holds appropriate actions. Classical decision tables use binary logic extended with "not important" mark to express states of conditions and actions to be performed.
Decision Trees. Tree-like representations are readable, easy to use and understand. The root of the tree is an entry node, under any node there are some branching links. The selection of a link is carried out with respect to a conditional statement assigned to the node. Evaluation of this condition determines the selection of the link. The tree is traversed top-down, and at the leaves final decisions are defined.

These approaches have some advantages and disadvantages depending on the purpose they were created for. This means there is an opportunity to formulate a new approach offering clear and efficient way to represent logical structures during the design stage. It is called the tree-table (or Tab-Tree) representation and it is given below along with some other methods.

5.1   The Tab-Tree Representation

This new approach was presented in [9,10]. It aims at combining some of knowledge-representation methods presented above in order to create a method which is more suitable for graphical design and representation of RBS.

The main idea is to build a hierarchy of OATs [3]. This hierarchy is based on the ψ-tree structure. Each row of a OAV table is right connected to the other OAV table. Such a connection implies logical AND relation in between. (OAV stands for Object-Attribute-Value, OAT –Object-Attribute-value-Table)

OAV tables used in Tab-Tree representation are divided into two kinds: attribute tables and action tables. Attribute tables are the attribute part of a classical OAT, action tables are the action part. It is worth noting that the tree-table representation is similar to Relational-Data-Base (RDB) data representation scheme.

The main features of the Tab-Tree representation are: simplicity, hierarchical, tree-like representation, highly efficient way of visualization with high data density, power of the decision table representation, analogies to the RDB data representation scheme.

5.2   Tab-Tree-Based CAD/CASE Tool Example

Tab-tree-based design concepts were used in building an integrated design environment for Kheops system[1]. Two different software tools were developed [9]: *gKheops, Osiris*.

The gKheops system is a graphical user interface to Kheops expert system. It simplifies the development of expert systems in the Kheops environment by providing a coherent graphical interface to Kheops itself.

Osiris aims at supporting both graphical design and some formal verification of rule-based systems. It is a multi-module system, consisting of a graphical environment for computer-aided development of rules, a code generator for Kheops system, a validator, which provides completeness checking and a run-time environment for created rules. For visualization the Tab-Tree representation was chosen (see Sect. 5.1).

5.3   Tab-Tree Firewall Representation

We can give a graphical, tab-tree-based representation of the NetFilter policy example given in Sect. 4.1. It is presented in Fig. 1. One should note, that firewall

---

[1] The Kheops system was used as one of the principal components in the TIGER project, a large scale, real-domain application in knowledge-based monitoring, supervision, and diagnosis.

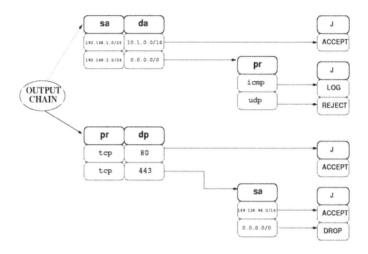

Fig. 1. Tab-tree firewall representation

chains don't have to map exactly to tables in a tab-tree. Tab-trees represent logical structure of the rule-base, while chains are used to optionally group rules sharing one condition.

6   Towards an Integrated Process of Design and Implementation of Reliable Rule-Based Systems

6.1   Conclusions Drawn from Designing Environment for Kheops

In the case discussed in Sect. 5.2, for research and development of rule-based systems Kheops has been chosen because of its generic character. Currently there are few software tools supporting design and implementation of rule-based systems. Developing gKheops and Osiris revealed serious limitations of Kheops as a development platform. Some of these limitations also apply to other tools that are available, eg.: support for limited class of systems only, no formal verification of system properties, lack of integrated development process from design to implementation phase.

6.2   New Approach to Integrated Design

A new integrated environment for design and on-line verification of rule-based systems using a meta-level knowledge representation format and wide range of verified characteristics is proposed. The principal idea is to include the *verification* stage into the *design* process, as well as to support the design with flexible graphical environment of the CAD/CASE type. Those ideas were proposed first in [3] and have been further developed in [9,10,8]. The design process is supported with a graphical tool which is used to display the structure of a tabular system. In order to present the structure in a transparent way tabular-trees are used. Prototypes forming different classes of rule-based can be generated and tested.

A central part of the new tool is a meta-language which allows for creation of a unified description of rule-based systems. Such a description would contain both specification of system domain and formal structure of the system – a set of rules. In creating this meta-language some existing XML-based solutions will be evaluated. One of these is RuleML ([12]), a XML-based language for describing rules in XML-based format. W3C's RDF language shall be used for system domain knowledge description. Ontologies are another technology that could improve the knowledge-base formulation, however at this stage of design it is not entirely clear whether they are suitable for this task.

Domain information is needed for automatic generation and testing of system prototype. It will be possible to create system rules with graphical design methods which would allow for on-line system structure verification during the design phase. Online verification will be achieved by combining graphical user interface with Prolog-based verification procedures. Some modern Prolog implementations have been evaluated such as SWI-Prolog compiler. Visualization of system structure will be conducted by tab-trees representation.

Architecture of the new system, consisting of several layers, is presented in Fig. 2. In presentation layers different export plugins (such as NetFilter or Kheops) and visualizations plugins (such as Tab-Trees) can be used. In knowledge base layer different validation plugins can be programmed (eg. completeness, determinism, subsumption plugin). It is hoped that this architecture will allow for design and validation of wide class of rule-based systems, including network firewalls.

6.3   Related Work

Although the principal idea to include the *verification* stage into the *design* process, as well as to support the design with flexible graphical environment of the CAD/CASE type dates back to [3], there exists only few papers devoted to its further development, e.g. [9], [10], [8]. A similar idea was present in [15]. The main differences between the proposed approach and the one of [15] is that his approach is oriented towards application for Prolog-like backward-chaining systems based on simple attributive language and Horn-like clauses. Further, its verification capabilities are limited mostly to local properties of the so-called decision units. Moreover, the set and definitions of the formal properties are a bit different with respect to forward-chaining systems as considered here.

7   Concluding Remarks

This paper presents results of ongoing research on graphical design environment for rule-based systems. Basing on the experience with designed systems developed for Kheops, a new proposal of an integrated environment for design and

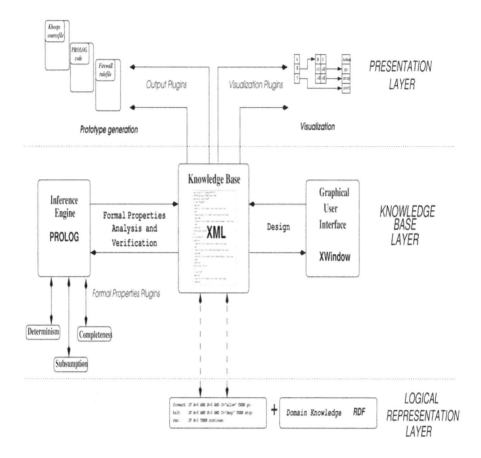

Fig. 2. Architecture of new integrated design tool

on-line verification of rule-based systems using a meta-level knowledge representation format and wide range of verified characteristics was discussed. Web-based systems relies on reliable firewall systems. Network firewalls and IDS constitute a particular case of systems which that could benefit from the use of the new integrated design environment.

A modular, multi-level architecture of new environment combines tabular-trees-based graphical design methods with on-line verification procedures in Prolog. Architecture of the environment will allow for design and validation of wide class of rule-based systems. The environment will simplify rule-based system design process, and improve its reliability by allowing formal properties verification during the design phase.

References

1. Andert, E.P.: Integrated knowledge-based system design and validation for solving problems in uncertain environments. *Int. J. of Man-Machine Studies*, 36, 1992, 357–373.
2. Coenen, F.: Validation and verification of knowledge based systems: Report on EUROVAV'99. *Knowledge Engineering Review*, 15:2, 2000, 187–196.
3. Ligęza, A.: Logical support for design of rule-based systems. Reliability and quality issues, *ECAI-96 Workshop on Validation, Verification and Refinement of Knowledge-based Systems*, ECAI'96, 1996, Budapest, 28–34.
4. Ligęza, A.: Intelligent data and knowledge analysis and verification; towards a taxonomy of specific problems. In [5], 1999, 313–325.
5. Vermesan, A. and F. Coenen (Eds.): Validation and Verification of Knowledge Based Systems – Theory, Tools and Practice. Kluwer Academic Publishers, Boston, 1999.
6. de Hoog, R.: Methodologies for Building Knowledge-Based Systems: Achievements and Prospectus. A Chapter in [7].
7. Liebowitz, J.: *The Handbook of Applied Expert Systems*. CRC Press, Boca Raton, 1998.
8. Ligęza, A.: Toward logical analysis of tabular rule-based systems. *International Journal of Intelligent Systems*, Vol. 16, 333–360, 2001.
9. Ligęza A, Wojnicki I., Nalepa G.J., *Tab-Trees: a CASE tool for the design of extended tabular systems* Database and expert systems applications: 12th International Conference, DEXA 2001: Munich, September 3–5, 2001,: proceedings / eds. Heinrich C. Mayr [et al.]. – Berlin: Springer, 2001. – (Lecture Notes in Computer Science; 2113).
10. Nalepa G.J., Ligęza A, *Graphical CASE tools for integrated design and verification of rule-based systems*, Symposium on Methods of Artificial Intelligence: proceedings/ eds. Burczynski T. [et al.], Silesian University of Technology, Polish Association for Computational Mechanics, Gliwice, 2001.
11. Wielinga B. J., Schreiber A. Th. Breuker J. A.: *KADS: A modeling approach to knowledge engineering*. Readings in Knowledge Acquisition and Learning, Morgan Kaufmann 1992, Los Altos, CA.
12. Lee K. J., Boley H., Tabet S.: *Issues in Semantic Web-based E-Commerce and Rule Markup Languages*, ICEC 2001, Workshop on Semantic Web-based E-Commerce and Rules Markup Languages, November 2nd, 2001, Vienna, Austria.
13. Roesch M., Green C.,: *Snort Users Manual Snort Release: 1.9.1*, http://www.snort.org – The Open Source Network Intrusion Detection System, 2002.
14. Ott A., Fischer-Hubner S.: *The Rule Set Based Access Control (RSBAC) Framework for Linux*, Karlstad University Studies, 2001, (http://www.rsbac.org).
15. Siminski R.: *Knowledge-base verification based on the decision unit concept*, Proceedings of Knowledge Engineering and Expert Systems, Z. Bubnicki and A. Grzech (Eds.), Wroclaw, 2000, Vol. II, 73–80 (in Polish).

Secure Intelligent Agents Based on Formal Description Techniques[1]

L. Mengual and C. de la Puente

Dpto. de Lenguajes y Sistemas Informáticos e Ingeniería de Software
Facultad de Informática (UPM), 28660 Boadilla del Monte, Madrid
lmengual@fi.upm.es, cpuenteg@yahoo.com
Tel: 913367397 Fax: 913367393

Abstract. This paper describes a practical solution for the incorporation of *security services* in *agents*. From a set of basic user requirements, the *agents* will be able to find out the best way to implement a *security policy* to accomplish the communication. A tipical scenario could be the following: one user wants to provide his communications with *security*, but he only knows a set of basic user requirements, and he has not any knowledge about *cryptography*, *security protocols*, *security keys*, etc. Configuring the *agent* correctly, this would be able to find out the optimal *security protocol* which best fit with those requirements. Once the best *protocol* is found, our *agents* will interpret it dynamically, for which formal description techniques will be used. The main aim of this work consists of finding out this *security protocol*. To do it, a global optimization method will be used, in particular, *genetic algorithms*. These *algorithms* are capable of finding out the optimal value in a function, within a domain. Our domain will be the *security protocols* which could be optimal, and the function to optimize would be a function capable of evaluating those *protocols*, and the optimal value will be the protocol that best fit with the security requirements. In short, our *agents* will be capable of finding out and interpreting dynamically the *ad-hoc security protocol* from a set of basic user requirements.

1 Introduction

Nowadays, is a fact that *data networks* are evolving and growing in terms of number of users, as long as number of services and applications offered. This involves that security issues have to evolve at the same time in order to provide the demanded *security services*. Depending on the several issues, different networks need different *security services*. For instance, a particular *application* running on a *server* provides contents *non-sensible*, but *clients* must be sure that they are connected to that *server* indeed; on the other hand, we could have another *server* providing very *sensitive* information, but *clients* are sure about the identity of the *server*, because are in the same *intranet* and can guarantee the authenticity by the *IP address*. In first example, is critical the *authentication* service from the *server* to the *client*, and the *confidentiall-*

[1] This work is supported by *Science and Technology Ministry* of *Spain* under the proyect *"A Multi-Agent System Architecture for the automatic and dynamic implementation of security protocols (TIC2001-3376)."*

E. Menasalvas et al. (Eds.): AWIC 2003, LNAI 2663, pp. 134–141, 2003.

ity is indifferent, but in the second example occurs exactly the contrary. It is evident that we should build different *security protocols* in both cases, each one made *ad-hoc*.

There are several solutions based in *multi-agent systems* to detect complex coordinated attacks ([1–3]), in which the user can configure the kind of attack that wants to prevent. However, none of these can offer ad-hoc *security protocols*. To do this, we need to model the *security protocols*, for which we use *formal specifications* ([4,5]), which are based on formal description techniques. In [6], we illustrate how we can interpret dynamically a *formal specification*.

In this work, we are going to use a three-*agent* system: *client* agent, *server agent* and *CA agent* (*Certification Authority* agent). From a basic set of user requirements, the system could be capable of finding out the *security protocol* which best fulfills those requirements. This process will be done by one *agent*, the *main agent*, and once the best protocol in found out, will be distributed to the rest of the *agents* and will be interpreted. The process is decomposed in three steps:

1. *Requirements-preprocessing stage*. At first time, the basic user requirements provided by the user must be preprocessed, in order to get a new set of requirements which we will denominate *evaluable requirements*. A basic *rules* production system will be enough.
2. *Global optimization stage*. Once we have got the evaluable requirements, we could fix a function whose optimal element is the *security protocol* that we are looking for. Due to the function to optimize is very complex, we will use an stochastic method as global optimization method, in particular, *genetic algorithms* are thought to be the most suitable.
3. *Dynamic interpretation stage*. At this point, the main *agent* will distribute the protocol obtained (in the form of a *formal specification*) and then the *agents* will interpret it dynamically.

2 Requirements – Preprocessing Stage

The solution proposed for this stage consists of a *rules production system*, capable of getting a set of evaluable requirements form the initial set of user requirements. The production system is composed of the following elements:

1. *Variables and Values*. It will be possible to configure the different variables used in the production system, as long as its values. It will also be possible to configure different sets of variables and values.
2. *Rules Base*. It will also be possible to configure the *rules* of a *rule base*, using the variables and values previously configured. We can have several *rule bases*.
3. *Inference Engine*. From a initial facts base, the inference engine will iterate through a defined *rule base*, until to reach to a final facts base. This final facts base should contain the evaluable requirements. The evaluable requirements which not be in the final facts base, will be considered as irrelevant, and will be updated to "*0*".

3   Global Optimization Stage

In this stage we are going to use an *genetic algorithm* to get the optimal *security protocol*. It is necessary to characterize each component of the *algorithm*.

3.1   Evolving Population

The elements which are going to evolve are the *formal specifications*. From a set A composed by the whole *formal specifications*, we say that our feasible set (*formal specifications* which are candidate to be optimal) F is a subset of A. The population p_i at the iteration number i is always a subset of F, and will evolve until to reach the optimal value.

$$p_0 \rightarrow p_1 \rightarrow p_2 \rightarrow \dots \rightarrow p_i \rightarrow \dots \rightarrow p_n \qquad p_i \subseteq F \subseteq A, \qquad i = 1..n$$

The initial population p_0 is a randomly chosen subset of F. The population size and the stop criteria, are configurable.

3.2   Codification

Each *formal specification*, must have asigned a number greater than zero, named *PID* (*protocol id*). The codificacion used consists of binary strings, representing each *PID*. The length of the strings must be fixed, and long enough to be able to codify any element of the feasible set, but regarding that if is too long, it will be more likely to choose a element from outside of the feasible region, therefore will have to be discarded at runtime, which makes it inefficient.

3.3   Fitness Function and *Evaluators*

The fitness function to optimize by the *algorithm* is as follows:

$$f: F \rightarrow R$$

$$f(x) = \sum_{i=0}^{n-1} \alpha_i r_i \qquad where \quad r_i = e_i(x), \qquad x \in F \qquad \alpha_i, r_i \in [0, 1]$$

Being:

- n the number of evaluable requirements
- x a *formal specification* from the feasible set F.
- each α_i is a weight, and indicates the importance of the requirement i. Each α_i is obtained from the final facts base resulted after executing the requirements-preprocessing stage.
- r_i is the result obtained after applying to x the *evaluator* e_i of the evaluable requirement i.

We must have one evaluator for each evaluable requirement, and is applied to the *formal specifications*. For a given evaluable requirement, its evaluator gives an estimation about how well certain *formal specification* fulfills this requirement. Three *evaluators* have been developed:

1. *Confidentiality evaluator*, for the evaluable requirement *confidentiality*.
2. *Authentication evaluator*, for the evaluable requirement *authentication*. This can be of six types: *authentication* of *client* against *server*, *authentication* of *server* against *client*, *authentication* of *client* against CA, etc.
3. *Efficiency evaluator*, for the evaluable requirement *efficiency*.

The system has been developed so that to add new *evaluators* be a simple task. Each *evaluator* can be more or less complex, and its efficiency is essential to get a good performance of the whole process. Although the idea was to have independent *evaluators*, it will depend on the nature of the requirement evaluated by the *evaluator*. For instance, to evaluate the confidentiality, we need to distribute a session key, for what we need some kind of *authentication* first, therefore it means that the confidentiality depends on the *authentication*. However, it does not matter if no cycles raise and we apply the *evaluators* in the correct order. Details about how the evaluators work fall outside of the scope of this article, because each evaluator has a very complex performance and can be treated as a different problem.

3.4 Genetic Operators

The genetic operators used by the *algorithm* are the standard operators [7]: reproduction, crossover, mutation. It is important to prove that each new element created belongs to the feasible region, otherwise, it has to be discarded.

3.5 Convergence and Performance

Holland (*The schema theorem* [8,9]) provides the conditions which should fulfill a *genetic algorithm* in order to guarantee the convergence. The process is very simplified if binary strings codification is used. Performance is limited by the nature of the *algorithm*. It will depend on several issues, such as the number of iterations and the efficiency of the fitness function, which depends basically on the efficiency of the *evaluators*.

4 Dynamic Interpretation Stage

Once the *formal specification* has been generated, we need it to be interpreted dynamically each time we want to have a secure communication. This interpretation engine has been successfully developed in [6].

In general, to find the optimal *formal specification* can be a very slow process, and is not a good idea to generate them on-line. What we are going to do is to generate the optimal *formal specification* for a set of user requirements by one agent, which we name as the *active agent*. This *agent* use to be the *client agent*, and stores in a data base the *PID* of the *formal specification* obtained, and associates it to the set of user requirements. Therefore, we have a cache which associates a set of user requirements with the *PID* of the optimal *formal specification* which best fulfill those user requirements.

At this moment, we can *interpret* dynamically the formal especificaction, as is described in [6]. In short, it starts with the Initial Communication Protocol, where the *client agent* sends to the *CA agent* the *PID* of the *formal specification* desired. The *CA agent* has access to the data base which associates each *PID* with its *formal specification*. Once the *CA agent* receives the *PID* from the *client agent*, retrieves the *formal specification* associated with the *PID* received and sends this *formal specification* to the rest of the *agents*. All these messages are sent in a secure way. At this point, all *agents* have the *formal specification*, and the Initial Communication Protocol ends. Now each *agent* will interpret the *formal specification*, each one assuming its own *rol* within the *protocol*.

5   Performance Example

We are going to explain how the system works with an example. Suppose that we have a network where everybody is trusted, thanks to a very robust access controls. Therefore we can guarantee that we are not going to have *authentication* problems, since all users are supposed to be trusted.

Thus, we could have a user with two requisites, described as: *efficiency = high*, *confidentiality = high*.

The feasible set *F* is composed only by two *formal specifications*:

```
FORMAL SPECIFICATION 0          FORMAL SPECIFICATION 1
MESSAGES                        MESSAGES
1:A->B:KPA;                     1:A->C:KPA;
2:B->A:encrypt(KPA,KS).         2:B->C:KPB;
·RELATIONS                      3:C->A:encrypt(KPA,KS);
1:public_key(A,KPA:A);          4:C->B:encrypt(KPB,KS).
2:session_key(KS:B).            RELATIONS
                                1:public_key(A,KPA:A);
                                2:public_key(B,KPB:B);
                                3:session_key(KS:C).
```

In a real case, we could have a very huge feasible set, so that the *genetic algorithm* make his search to find the best population. In this example, the population size is of the two elements, having the whole feasible set.

With this elements, the active *agent* will start the execution. The first stage is the requirement preprocessing stage. Within the *rule base*, we have the two following ones:

Ri: *efficiency = high* → *efficiency = 1*
Rj: *confidentiality = high* → *confidentiality = 1*

After executing, we will obtain the value of the evaluable requirements between 0 and 1, having *efficiency = 1, confidentiality = 1, authentication = 0*.

The second stage is the optimization stage. The *genetic algorithm* will iterate over the search space. The codification used will be strings of two bits length. The codification for the first *formal specification* will be the string *00*, and for the second, the string *01*. Other combinations are not allowed, and will be discarded. Lets begin the *algorithm* with the initial population, composed by the two *formal specifications* of the feasible set. The *algorithm* will calculate the value of the fitness functions for each element of the population. In this implementation, we have three evaluable requirements, so the fitness function would be:

$$f(x) = \alpha_e e_e(x) + \alpha_c e_c(x) + \alpha_a e_a(x), \qquad x \in F \qquad \alpha_i \in [0, 1]$$

Being:

- α_e the weight for the evaluable requirement *efficiency*, obtained in the requirements preprocessing stage with the value 1.
- α_c the weight for the evaluable requirement *confidentiality*, obtained in the requirements preprocessing stage with the value 1.
- α_a the weight for the evaluable requirement *authentication*, obtained in the requirements preprocessing stage with the value 0.
- $e_e(x)$ the result obtained after applying the *evaluator* of *efficiency* to the *formal specification x*.
- $e_c(x)$ the result obtained after applying the *evaluator* of *confidentiality* to the *formal specification x*.
- $e_a(x)$ the result obtained after applying the *evaluator* of *authentication* to the *formal specification x*.

Thus, the fitness function will be:

$$f(x) = e_e(x) + e_c(x), \qquad x \in F$$

For the first element of the population, the string 00, the function will return:

$$f(00) = e_e(00) + e_c(00) = 0.8 + 1 = 1.8$$

and for the second one:

$$f(01) = e_e(01) + e_c(01) = 0.55 + 1 = 1.55$$

So the best element is 00, corresponding to the *formal specification* with *PID* 0. This *formal specification* is which best fulfills the user requirements specified. In the following iterations of the *algorithm*, the elements of the population created after applying the genetic operators, only could be 00, 01, 10, 11, the two later will be always discarded since they fall outside the feasible set. So the population will have always the same elements, and the *algorithm* will stop.

How each *evaluator* works is a different problem. For example, the efficiency *evaluator* takes into account the number of messages interchanged in the *formal specification*, the amount of data encrypted and the *algorithms* used to encrypt, and the size of the messages. Obviously, the first *formal specification* is more efficient. The confidentiality *evaluator* mainly search patterns to ensure that a session key has been distributed in a secure way (and the key length is long enough for the *algorithm*, etc) , and in both cases is true. Details about how the evaluators work fall outside of the scope of this article, as we explained before.

The last stage is the dynamic interpretation of the *protocol* obtained. The *formal specification* will be distributed to all the *agents* and will be interpreted dynamically, as is described in [6].

6 Conclusions

A multi-*agent* system has been developed, and is capable of offering to the user an ad-hoc *security protocol*, from a basic set of user requirements.

It is very important to configure properly the *rule base* used in the requirements-preprocessing stage, in order to get a good value for the evaluable requirements.

Due to the modular design of the architecture, the system has a very good scalability, and is very easy to add new evaluable requirements, since the only thing we should do is to add its *evaluator* (a class that implements an interface which defines the *evaluators*).

Other alternatives of implementation could be analyzed in detail, as the following ones:

- To probe with another stochastic *algorithms* of global optimization, such as Tabu Search or Simulated Annealing.

- When the feasible set is very small, to use simpler algorithms, as systematic exhaustive search is bound to be more effective.

- To probe with different fitness functions, adding another types of parameters or weights.

- To research about the possibility of using a generic *evaluator*, using some clustering technique, such as Neural Networks. At first sight, it seems quite complicated, since we should make discrete the results of the *evaluators*.

- It would be a good idea to refine the result of the *genetic algorithm*, using a local optimization technique, starting at the result of the *genetic algorithm* as initial point.

References

1. Boudaoud, K.; McCathieNevile, C. "An intelligent agent-based model for security management". *Seventh International Symposium on Computers and Communications, 2002*. Proceedings. ISCC 2002. Taormina, Italy. Page(s): 877–882.
2. Gorodetski, V.; Kotenko, I. "The multi-agent systems for computer network security assurance: frameworks and case studies". *IEEE International Conference on Artificial Intelligence Systems, 2002*. (ICAIS 2002), Divnomorskoe, Russia. Page(s): 297–302.
3. Borselius, N.; Hur, N.; Kaprynski, M.; Mitchell, C.J. "A security architecture for agent-based mobile systems". *Third International Conference on 3G Mobile Communication Technologies,* 2002 (Conf. Publ. No. 489), London, UK. Page(s): 312–318.
4. Mengual, L., Barcia, N., Menasalvas, E., Jiménez, E., Setién, J., Yágüez J. "Automatic Implementation System Of *Security protocols* Based On Formal Description Techniques". *Proceedings of the Seventh IEEE Symposium on Computers and Comunications (ISCC'02).*Taormina, Italy. 2002. Pags. 355–360.

5. Mengual, L., Barcia, N., Bobadilla, J., Jiménez, E., Setién, J., Yágüez J. "Infraestructura de Sistema Multi-Agente para la Implementación Automática de Protocolos de Seguridad". *I Simposio Español de Negocio Electrónico*. Málaga. 2001.
6. Puente C. de la.: Incorporación de mecanismos de seguridad en un sistema de implementación automática de protocolos. Dpto. de Lenguajes y sistemas Informáticos e Ingeniería del Software, Facultad de Informática (UPM), 28660 Boadilla del Monte, Madrid (2002). Trabajo fin de carrera. 2000.
7. De Goldberg. *"Genetic algorithms in search, optimisation and machine learning"*. Addison Wesley. 1989.
8. Darrell Whitley. "A Genetic Algorithm Tutorial". Computer Science Department, Colorado State University, Fort Collins, CO 80523. 1994.
9. D. Whitley, S. Rana and R. Heckendorn. *"Genetic algorithms and Evolution Strategies in Engineering and Computer Science"*. John Wiley. 1997.

A Natural Language Interface for Information Retrieval on Semantic Web Documents

Paulo Quaresma and Irene Pimenta Rodrigues

Departamento de Informática
Universidade de Évora
Portugal
{pq,ipr}@di.uevora.pt

Abstract. We present a dialogue system that enables the access in natural language to a web information retrieval system. We use a Web Semantic Language to model the knowledge conveyed by the texts. In this way we are able to obtain the associated knowledge necessary to perform the different analysis stages of natural language sentences.

In the context of information retrieval, we aim to develop a system that, by increasing the interaction management capabilities, is able to achieve a better degree of cooperativeness and to reduce the average number of interactions needed to retrieve the intended set of documents.

The documents in the IR system considered here are composed by the set of documents produced by the Portuguese Attorney General since 1940. These documents were analyzed and an ontology describing their structure and content was defined. Then, they were automatically parsed and a (partial) semantic structure was created. The ontology and the semantic content was represented in the OWL language.

An example of a user interaction session is presented and explained in detail.

Keywords: agents, knowledge based systems, web semantics, information retrieval, natural language dialogues.

1 Introduction

As the size and complexity of documents bases increase, users develop new desires leading to information retrieval systems that should be able to act as rational, autonomous, and cooperative agents, helping them in their searches.

Actually, we claim that in order to improve the search results, information retrieval systems should be able to represent and to use the knowledge conveyed by the texts, using web semantic languages to model the knowledge.

In fact, in the last years, much work has been done trying to satisfy some of these goals creating what is sometimes called third generation knowledge based systems [YS99].

Our IR system aims to achieve some of these goals and it has an architecture with two layers:

E. Menasalvas et al. (Eds.): AWIC 2003, LNAI 2663, pp. 142–154, 2003.

- The information retrieval layer – This layer integrates the text search engine with natural language processing techniques;
- The interaction layer – This layer is the responsible for handling the interaction between users and the information retrieval modules.

These two layers are implemented as autonomous agents, which are able to communicate between them and with other agents. Communication is achieved through the interpretation of the received actions in the context of the agents' mental state. Each agent models its mental state, namely its beliefs, intentions and goals, and plans its own actions trying to be as much cooperative as possible.

Cooperation is achieved through the inference of the other agents' intentions from their actions. The inferred agents' intentions are the input of a abductive planning procedure, which selects the actions needed to satisfy the agents goals.

In the context of information retrieval, one of the main goals of our work is to show the need for interaction management capabilities and to develop a system that is able to achieve a better degree of cooperativeness and to reduce the average number of interactions needed to retrieve the intended set of documents.

Namely, we would like our agents to be able: To model their mental state (beliefs, intentions, goals); To record all the interactions (other agents questions and their own answers) [CL99,CCC98]; To infer the new agents attitudes from their mental state, the interaction history, and the agents actions. In fact, agents queries may not directly state their final goals [Loc98,Pol90]; And to plan their actions, using the inferred agents attitudes and their cooperative rules of behavior.

The integration of specific information retrieval agents with dialogue management agents in a general information retrieval system is a quite new approach and it allows us to model the system's behavior (cooperative, pro-active) and to modularize the solution, specializing the agents, and being able to handle future extensions of the system (through the use of new agents or the extension of the existent ones).

Some of the components of our system can be compared with other existent IR systems. For instance, our IR agent is based on SINO [GMK97] and it was changed in a way that has many similarities with the work described in [BvWM+99], namely, allowing the extraction of textual information using localization, inference, and controlled vocabulary. As in [OS99], we are also able to use concepts and a concept taxonomy in order to retrieve sets of documents. On the other hand, in the dialogue management domain, the use of speech acts to recognize plans has many similarities with the work of Carberry [CL99] and Litman [LA87] and the representation of plans as mental attitudes was also the approach followed by Pollack [Pol90] in her work.

The different analysis stages of a natural language sentence requires specific domain knowledge. Namely, to obtain the sentence pragmatic interpretation we need to have a large knowledge base describing the sentence entities and its relations to other entities. This problem is overcame by using Web semantic Languages to describe an ontology representing our world (documents domain) main classes of the objects, their properties and their relations. The semantic content of our database documents can then be represented using the defined ontology in the Web semantic language allowing the system to retrieve the information conveyed by the user sentences. The extraction of the semantic content of our documents is done by using specific tools that perform a robust natural language analysis in order to extract and represent some of the document entities and relations.

By now, it is only possible to partially represent the documents semantic content because there is a need for more complete ontologies and more powerful natural language analyzers.

As basic semantic language we are using the Web Ontology Language (OWL) - [www00]) language, which is defined using the RDF (Resource Description Framework - [LS99,BG99]) language and it has a XML version.

Using OWL it was possible to represent the documents structure and some of its semantic content. Moreover, the user natural language queries can be semantically analyzed accordingly with the base ontology.

Using this approach, the dialogue system that we propose is able to supply adequate answers to the Portuguese Attorney General's Office documents database (PGR). For instance, in the context of an user interrogation searching for information on injuries in service, the following question could be posed:

Who has service injuries?

The user is expecting to have as an answer some characteristics of the individuals that have been injured at work. He does not intend to have a list of those individuals or the documents that refer to the act of asserting that the injury was in service. In order to obtain the adequate answer our system must collect all individuals referred in the documents database that have a service injury and then it must supply the common characteristics to the user in a dialogue.

As it was referred, our system must have an adequate representation of injuries and individuals in a semantic web ontology and all documents must have the adequate labels in the semantic web language representing the knowledge on 'Injuries' and 'Individuals' and 'Service' conveyed by the document[1].

The answer to the above question could be: 'Individuals that were agents of an injury and of a subaction of working that occurred in a overlapping time interval and the cause of the injury is not exclusively responsibility from the agent'

This information can be obtained by extracting what properties those individuals have in common or by manually representing parts of the Portuguese law. The possibility of extracting what are the common characteristics of a set of objects is a powerful tool for presenting the answers to our users. This behavior can be achieved by choosing an adequate ontology to represent the objects including events present at the documents.

The dialogue system obtains the knowledge necessary for the interpretation of natural language sentences from the Semantic Web description of the documents databases. The vocabulary and the rules for the semantic pragmatic

---

[1] By now this has be done manually.

interpretation are automatically generated using the existent ontology (this will be explained in more detail in the next sections).

The dialogue module is built with a logic programming language for describing actions and events, EVOLP [ABLP02], which allows the system to make inferences about the user intentions and beliefs and to be able to have cooperative dialogues with the users.

The remainder of this article is structured as follows: in Sect. 2, a brief introduction to the OWL Semantic Web language is presented. In Sect. 3, the EVOLP language is briefly described. In Sect. 4 the overall structure of the system is presented; Sect. 5 deal with the semantic/ pragmatic interpretation. In Sect. 7 a more extensive example is presented and, finally, in Sect. 8 we discuss some current limitations of the system and lay out possible lines of future work.

2   Web Semantics

The documents domain knowledge was partially represented using a semantic web language. The first step was to define an ontology adequate for the domain. We have selected a domain of the Portuguese Attorney General documents – injury in service (asserted or retracted) – and, in this domain, we have selected smaller sub-domains, such as, injuries for firemen, or militaries, or civilians; injuries at the traject from home to work or vice-versa, injuries at work place, injuries at labor time.

The ontology was represented using the OWL (Ontology Web Language) language, which is based on the DAML+OIL (Darpa Agent Markup Language - [www00]) language, and it is defined using RDF (Resource Description Framework - [LS99,BG99]). As an example, the *Individual* class is presented below (only some of the class attributes are shown):

```
<owl:Class rdf:ID="Individual">
     <owl:label>Individual</owl:label>
</owl:Class>
<owl:DatatypeProperty rdf:ID="individualCode">
        <owl:domain rdf:resource="#Individual"/>
        <owl:type rdf:resource="&owl;FuncionalProperty"/>
        <owl:range rdf:resource="&xsd;integer"/>
</owl:DatatypeProperty>
<owl:DatatypeProperty rdf:ID="individualName">
        <owl:domain rdf:resource="#Individual"/>
        <owl:type rdf:resource="&owl;FuncionalProperty"/>
        <owl:range rdf:resource="&xsd;String"/>
</owl:DatatypeProperty>
<owl:ObjectProperty rdf:ID="individualProfession">
        <owl:domain rdf:resource="#Individual"/>
        <owl:range rdf:resource="#Profession"/>
</owl:ObjectProperty>
```

After defining an ontology, the documents need to be analyzed and their semantic content should be represented in OWL. However, this is a very complex open problem and we have decided to manually represent subsets of the document content for the chosen sub-domains.

These two steps (ontology + document semantic representation) are the basis of the proposed system and allow the implementation of other steps, such as, the semantic/pragmatic interpretation and the dialogue management.

3   EVOLP

As referred, there is also a need for a declarative language to represent actions and to model the evolution of the knowledge.

In [APP+99] it was introduced a declarative, high-level language for knowledge updates called *LUPS* ("Language of UPdateS") that describes transitions between consecutive knowledge states. Recently, a new language, EVOLP [ABLP02], was proposed having a simpler and more general formulation of logic program updates. In this section a brief description of the EVOLP language will be given, but the interested reader should refer to the cited article for a detailed description of the language and of its formalization.

EVOLP allows the specification of a program's evolution, through the existence of rules which indicate assertions to the program. EVOLP programs are sets of generalized logic program rules defined over an extended propositional language L_{assert}, defined over any propositional language L in the following way [ABLP02]:

- All propositional atoms in L are propositional atoms in L_{assert}
- If each of $L_0, \ldots, L_n$ is a literal in L_{assert}, then $L_0 \leftarrow L_1, \ldots, L_n$ is a generalized logic program rule over L_{assert}.
- If R is a rule over L_{assert} then $assert(R)$ is a propositional atom of L_{assert}.
- Nothing else is a propositional atom in L_{assert}.

The formal definition of the semantics of EVOLP is presented at the referred article, but the general idea is the following: whenever the atom $assert(R)$ belongs to an interpretation, i.e. belongs to a model according to the stable model semantics of the current program, then R must belong to the program in the next state. For instance, the following rule form:

$$assert(b \leftarrow a) \leftarrow c \tag{1}$$

means that if c is true in a state, then the next state must have rule $b \leftarrow a$.

EVOLP has also the notion of external events, i.e. assertions that do not persist by inertia. This notion is fundamental to model interaction between agents and to represent actions. For instance, it is important to be able to represent actions and its effects and pre-conditions:

$$assert(Effect) \leftarrow Action, PreConditions \tag{2}$$

If, in a specific state, there is the event *Action* and if *PreConditions* hold, then the next state will have *Effect*.

4   Natural Language Dialogue System

As was already stated the main goal of this work was to build a system that could get a Portuguese natural language sentence sent by a user through a web interface and respond accordingly. To answer the question/sentence the system has to pass it from a web-based interface to a specialized process; the process must analyze the sentence accessing the documents database(s); and finally when acquiring all needed information, it has to build a comprehensive answer and pass it to the web-based interface.

The analysis of a natural language sentence is split in four subprocesses: Syntax, Semantics, Pragmatics, Dialogue manager.

The user asks the question, which is redirected to an active process that already has information about all the documents semantic structure (the ontology). A specialized natura language processing agent manages the conversion of the sentence to declarative logic programming predicates. These predicates allow the access to the documents through the information retrieval system. After analyzing the sentence received, the process has to generate an adequate answer, which will be shown to the user through the web interface.

Syntax Analysis: Our syntactic interpreter was built using *Chart Parsers*[GM89]. This is one of many techniques to build syntactic interpreters. The decision of developing the interpreter using this technique was mainly because chart parsers can parse incomplete sentences. The user can place complete or incomplete questions and the system must be able to answer them accordingly, so the need to parse incomplete sentences is essential. The chart parser uses a set of syntactic rules that identify the Portuguese sentence structures and tries to match these rules with the input sentence(s). As an example, the following sentence:

"Who has a injury in service?"

Has the following structure:

```
phrase([np([det(who,_+_+_), n('individual',_+s+m)]),
       vp(v('have',3+p+_)),
           args_v([np([det(a,_+s+_), n('injury',_+s+_),
           pp(in,np([n('service',_+s+m)]))])])]).
```

Semantic Interpretation: Each syntactic structure is rewritten into a First-Order Logic expression. The technique used for this analysis is based on DRS's (Discourse Representation Structures [KR93]). This technique identifies triggering syntactic configurations on the global sentence structure, which activates the rewriting rules. We always rewrite the pp's by the relation 'rel(A,B)' postponing its interpretation to the semantic pragmatic module. The semantic representation of sentence is a DRS build with two lists, one with the new sentence rewritten and the other with the sentence discourse referents. For instance, the semantic representation of the sentence above is the following expression:

individual(A), injury(B), service(C), rel(B,C), have(A,B).

and the following discourse referents list:

[ref(A,p+_+_,what),ref(B,s+_+_,undef),ref(C,p+_+_,undef)]

5   Semantic/Pragmatic Interpretation

The semantic/pragmatic module receives the sentence rewritten (into a First Order Logic form) and tries to interpret it in the context of the document database
information (ontology). In order to achieve this behavior the system tries to find
the best explanations for the sentence logic form to be true in the knowledge
base for the semantic/pragmatic interpretation. This strategy for interpretation is known as "interpretation as abduction" [HSAM90]. The knowledge base
for the semantic/pragmatic interpretation is built from the Semantic Web description of the document database. The inference in this knowledge base uses
abduction, restrictions (GNU Prolog Finite Domain (FD) constraint solver) and
accesses the document databases through an Information Retrieval Agent. The
knowledge base rules contain the information for each term interpretation in the
sentence logic form as logic programming terms. The KB rules are generated
from the Semantic Web databases descriptions. This process was described in
detail in [QRA01]. From the description of the class *injury*, the KB has rules
for the interpretation of the predicates: *injury(A)* and *rel(A,B)*. Suppose there
exists the following description of the class $Injury$ and of two subclasses[2]:

```
<owl:Class rdf:ID="Injury">
    <owl:label>Injury</owl:label>
</owl:Class>
<owl:DatatypeProperty rdf:ID="injuryCode">
    <owl:domain rdf:resource="#Injury"/>
    <owl:type rdf:resource="&owl;FuncionalProperty"/>
    <owl:range rdf:resource="&xsd;integer"/>
</owl:DatatypeProperty>
<owl:ObjectProperty rdf:ID="individual">
    <owl:domain rdf:resource="#Injury"/>
    <owl:type rdf:resource="&owl;FuncionalProperty"/>
    <owl:range rdf:resource="#Individual"/>
</owl:ObjectProperty>
<owl:ObjectProperty rdf:ID="event">
    <owl:domain rdf:resource="#Injury"/>
    <owl:range rdf:resource="#Event"/>
</owl:ObjectProperty>
<owl:ObjectProperty rdf:ID="supportDocuments">
    <owl:domain rdf:resource="#Injury"/>
    <owl:range rdf:resource="#DocumentList"/>
</owl:ObjectProperty>

<owl:Class rdf:ID="Injury_in_service">
    <owl:label>Injury in Service</owl:label>
    <rdfs:subClassOf rdf:resource="#Injury"/>
</owl:Class>
<owl:Class rdf:ID="Injury_not_in_service">
```

---

[2] Due to its complexity, in this paper we only present a small subset of the complete
ontology.

```
            <owl:label>Injury not in service</owl:label>
            <rdfs:subClassOf rdf:resource="#Injury"/>
</owl:Class>
```

This description means that "injury" is a class which has some properties: the individual that gets the injury, an event describing the action supporting the injury, and a list of supporting documents. Moreover, "injury" has two subclasses: injury in service and injury not on service. Using the ontology, a set of rules was automatically produced enabling the semantic/pragmatic interpretation of a sentence like "injury" as the Predicate Logic expression $injury(A,\_,\_,\_,\_)$. This description will also give rise to rules allowing for the interpretation of noun phrases such as "injury in service".

```
rel(A,B) <-
    injury(A),
    service(B),
    abduct(injury_in_service(A,_,_,_,_)).
```

From the previous description of the class Individual (in Sect. 2) the KB has rules that will allow the interpretation of the noun "Person" and of noun phrases such as: "Individual name", "Individual Profession". One of the generated rules is:

```
rel(B,A) <-
    individual(B),
    profession(A)
    abduct(individual(B,_,A,_)).
```

This rule enables us to obtain the expression $individual(B,\_, A,\_)$ as the interpretation of the noun phrase "profession of individual".

During the semantic/pragmatic interpretation the evaluation of a predicate like "Individual(A)" is done by an access to the Semantic Web documents. The result of such an evaluation is the constraint of variable A to database identifiers of objects from class individual. The interpretation of nouns (eg. injury(A)) is done by accessing the documents database in order to collect in (constraint) A all entities identifiers that have in their name the word 'injury'. The result of interpreting the sentence represented by[3]:

individual(A),injury(B),services(C),rel(B,C),rel(A,B)
[ref(A,s+_+_,what),ref(B,s+_+_,undef),ref(C,s+_+_,undef)]

is the following expression:

$injury\_in\_service(B, A, \_, \_, \_), individual(A, \_, \_, \_).$

Where:

- $B =_{\#}$ (1046..1049 : 1345 : 1456..1457) – B constrained to all injuries in service.
- $A =_{\#}$ (7001...7852) – A is constraint to individuals

---

[3] The interpretation of A *have* B is the same of B *of* A, so $have(A, B)$ is equivalent to $rel(A, B)$

The above LP expression contain the possible interpretations of the sentence in the context of our documents database. The dialogue manager is responsible to interact with the user by supplying him an answer or by posing him pertinent questions.

6   Dialogue Manager

The Dialogue Manager must recognize the speech act associated with the sentence (in this domain it can be an *inform*, a *request*, or a *askif* speech act), to model the user attitudes (intentions and beliefs), and to represent and make inferences over the dialogue domain. In order to achieve this goal the system needs to model the speech acts, the user attitudes (intentions and beliefs) and the connection between attitudes and actions. This task is also achieved through the use of the EVOLP language (see [QR01,QL95] for a more detailed description of these rules). For instance, the rules which describe the effect of an inform, a request, and a ask-if speech act from the point of view of the receptor are:

$$assert(bel(A, bel(B, P))) \leftarrow inform(B, A, P). \tag{3}$$

$$assert(bel(A, int(B, Action))) \leftarrow request(B, A, Action). \tag{4}$$

$$assert(bel(A, int(B, inform\_if(A, B, P)))) \leftarrow ask\_if(B, A, P) \tag{5}$$

In order to represent collaborative behavior it is necessary to model how information is transferred between the different agents:

$$assert(bel(A, P)) \leftarrow bel(A, bel(B, P)). \tag{6}$$

$$assert(int(A, Action)) \leftarrow bel(A, int(B, Action)). \tag{7}$$

These two rules allow beliefs and intentions to be transferred between agents if they are not inconsistent with their previous mental state. There is also the need for rules that link the system intentions and the accesses to the databases:

$$assert(yes(P)) \leftarrow query(P), one\_sol(P), int(A, inform(A, B, P)). \tag{8}$$

$$assert(no(P)) \leftarrow query(P), no\_sol(P), int(A, inform(A, B, P)). \tag{9}$$

$$assert(clarif(P)) \leftarrow query(P), n\_sol(P), int(A, inform(A, B, P)). \tag{10}$$

These three rules update the system's mental state with the result of accessing the databases: yes, if there is only one solution; no, if there are no solutions; and clarification, if there are many solutions (the predicates that determine the cardinality of the solution are not presented here due to space problems). After accessing the databases, the system should answer the user:

$$assert(confirm(A, B, P)) \leftarrow yes, int(A, inform(A, B, P)). \tag{11}$$

$$assert(notint(A, inform\_if(A, B, P))) \leftarrow yes, int(A, inform(A, B, P)). \tag{12}$$

$$assert(reject(A, B, P)) \leftarrow no, int(A, inform(A, B, P)). \tag{13}$$

$$assert(notint(A, inform\_if(A, B, P))) \leftarrow yes, int(A, inform(A, B, P)). \tag{14}$$

$$assert(ask(A, B, C)) \leftarrow cluster(P, C), clarif(P), int(A, inform(A, B, P)). \tag{15}$$

The first two rules define that, after a unique solution query, the system confirms the answer and terminates the intention to answer the user. The next two rules define that, after a no solution query, the system rejects the question and terminates the intention to answer the user. The last rule defines that, after a multiple solution query, the system starts a clarification answer, asking the user to select one of the possible solutions. In order to collaborate with the user we have defined a cluster predicate that tries to aggregate the solutions into coherent sets. The strategy behind this predicate is to aggregate the solutions accordingly with the range of property values of the selected objects. For instance, in the presented example the selected individuals might be clustered by their profession, or by their support documents, or by the events in which they are actors. In the next section, this strategy will be described in more detail.

7   Example

Considering the already presented question:

Who has an injury in service?

The dialogue manager receives this sentence semantic/pragmatic interpretation, as we presented in the previous sections it will be the following expression:

```
injury_in_service(B,A,_,_,_), individual(A,_,_,_).
```

with the following restrictions:

- $B =_{\#} (1046..1049 : 1345 : 1456..1457)$ – B is constraint to all injuries in service.
- $A =_{\#} (7001...7852)$ – A is constraint to individuals
- $[ref(A, p + \_ + \_, what), ref(B, s + \_ + \_, undef), ref(C, p + \_ + \_, undef)]$

After having the sentence re-written into its semantic representation form, the speech act is recognized and we'll have:

```
request(user, system, inform(user, system,
        [injury_in_service(injuryCode=B,individual=A)]))
```

Using the "request" and the EVOLP transference of intentions rules we'll have:

```
int(system,inform(system, user,
        [injury_in_service(injuryCode=B,individual=A)]))
```

Now, using the rules presented in the previous section, the system accesses the databases (via the *query* predicate). Suppose there are several possible solutions. We'll have A and B constrained to related individuals and injuries in service:

- $B =_{\#} (1046..1049 : 1345 : 1456..1457)$
- $A =_{\#} (7030...7842 : 7850)$ – A is constrained to individuals that have an injury in service.

As a consequence of having several solutions, predicate *clarif* will hold and the system launches the *cluster* predicate to aggregate the obtained solutions (accordingly with the rule presented in the previous section).

```
cluster([injury_in_service(injuryCode=B,individual=A)],C).
```

The *cluster*(P, C) rule identifies the variable which is the focus of the query (obtained in the syntactical analysis) and aggregates the property values for the associated objects. For instance, in this example it will detect that the query is about individuals (variable A) and it tries to cluster its constrained values accordingly with their professions, events, and documents relation. After having clustered the property values, the system uses an heuristic to choose the property that better divides the objects (by better we mean that the cardinality of the obtained sets has the same magnitude order) and it performs the *ask_select* action.

In this example the answer might be: 'Individuals that are firemen, or militaries or civilians'.

Or, using another property (event list): 'Individuals that were agents of an action getting injuries and of an action that is a subaction of working that occurred in a overlapping time interval and the cause of the injury is not exclusively responsibility from the agent'

8   Conclusions and Future Work

The dialogue system described in this paper is quite complex and some of its modules still require a manual intervention. Namely, it is not possible to have a complete automatic semantic interpretation and representation of the documents.

However, we have developed a small prototype, which is being tested and, in the future, it will be made available to all users in the context of the Portuguese Attorney General's web information retrieval system (http://www.pgr.pt).

Regarding future work, it is clear that all modules have aspects that may be improved: the syntactical coverage of the Portuguese grammar; the coverage of the semantic analyzer (plurals, quantifiers, ...); the ontology coverage; the semantic representation of the documents content; and the capability of the dialogue manager to take into account previous interactions and the user models.

As we have a modular approach to the systems' architecture, there is a complete separation of all the processing phases. This separation will enable us, for instance, to use grammars already developed in other formalisms such as the project described in [Bic00] (in fact, this is an actual project ongoing task).

As a final conclusion, we believe that this system represents a relevant step in the transformation of "traditional" information retrieval systems into semantic-aware IR systems.

References

[ABLP02]   J. Alferes, A. Brogi, J. Leite, and L. Pereira. Evolving logic programs. In S. Flesca, S. Greco, N. Leone, and G. Ianni, editors, *JELIA'02 – Proceedings of the 8th European Conference on Logics and Artificial Intelligence*, pages 50–61. Springer-Verlag LNCS 2424, 2002.

[APP⁺99]   J. J. Alferes, L. M. Pereira, H. Przymusinska, T. C. Przymusinski, and
           P. Quaresma. Preliminary exploration on actions as updates. In M. C.
           Meo and M. Vilares-Ferro, editors, *Procs. of the 1999 Joint Conference
           on Declarative Programming (AGP'99)*, pages 259–271, L'Aquila, Italy,
           September 1999.

[BG99]   D. Brickley and R. Guha. *Resource Description Framework (RDF) -
           Schema Specification*. W3C, 1999.

[Bic00]   Eckhard Bick. *The Parsing System PALAVRAS: Automatic Grammat-
           ical Analysis of Portuguese in a Constraint Grammar Framework*. PhD
           thesis, Århus University, Århus, 2000.

[BvWM⁺99] Tania Bueno, Christiane von Wangenheim, Eduardo Mattos, Hugo
           Hoeschl, and Ricardo Barcia. Jurisconsulto: Retrieval in jurisprudencial
           text bases using juridical terminology. In *Proceedings of the ICAIL'99
           – 7th International Conference on Artificial Intelligence and Law*, pages
           147–155. ACM, June 1999.

[CCC98]   J. Chu-Carroll and S. Carberry. Response generation in planning dia-
           logues. *Computational Linguistics*, 24(3), 1998.

[CL99]   Sandra Carberry and Lynn Lambert. A process model for recognizing
           communicative acts and modeling negotiation subdialogs. *Computa-
           tional Linguistics*, 25(1), 1999.

[GM89]   Gerald Gazdar and Chris Mellish. *Natural Language Processing in PRO-
           LOG*. Addison-Wesley, 1989.

[GMK97]   G. Greenleaf, A. Mowbray, and G. King. Law on the net via austlii -
           14 m hypertext links can't be right? In *In Information Online and On
           Disk'97 Conference, Sydney*, 1997.

[HSAM90]   Jerry Hobbs, Mark Stickel, Douglas Appelt, and Paul Martin. Inter-
           pretation as abduction. Technical Report SRI Technical Note 499, 333
           Ravenswood Ave., Menlo Park, CA 94025, 1990.

[KR93]   H. Kamp and U. Reyle. *From Discourse to Logic*. Kluwer, Dordrecht,
           1993.

[LA87]   Diane Litman and James Allen. A plan recognition model for subdia-
           logues in conversation. *Cognitive Science*, 11(1), 1987.

[Loc98]   Karen E. Lochbaum. A collaborative planning model of intentional
           structure. *Computational Linguistics*, 24(4), 1998.

[LS99]   O. Lassila and R. Swick. *Resource Description Framework (RDF) -
           Model and Syntax Specification*. W3C, 1999.

[OS99]   James Osborn and Leon Sterling. A judicial search tool using intelligent
           concept extraction. In *Proceedings of the ICAIL'99 – 7th International
           Conference on Artificial Intelligence and Law*, pages 173–181. ACM,
           June 1999.

[Pol90]   Martha Pollack. Plans as complex mental attitudes. In Philip Cohen,
           Jerry Morgan, and Martha Pollack, editors, *Intentions in Communica-
           tions*. MIT Press Cambridge, 1990.

[QL95]   P. Quaresma and J. G. Lopes. Unified logic programming approach to
           the abduction of plans and intentions in information-seeking dialogues.
           Journal of Logic Programming, 54, 1995.

[QR01]   Paulo Quaresma and Irene Rodrigues. Using logic programming to
           model multi-agent web legal systems – an application report. In *Proceed-
           ings of the ICAIL'01 - International Conference on Artificial Intelligence
           and Law*, St. Louis, USA, May 2001. ACM.

[QRA01]   Luis Quintano, Irene Rodrigues, and Salvador Abreu. Relational infor-
           mation retrieval through natural lanaguage analysis. In *Proceedings of
           INAP'01*, Tokyo, Japan, October 2001. INAP.
[www00]   www.daml.org. *DAML+OIL – DARPA Agent Markup Language*, 2000.
[YS99]   John Yearwood and Andrew Stranieri. The integration of retrieval, rea-
           soning and drafting for refugee law: a third generation legal knowledge
           based system. In *Proceedings of the ICAIL'99 – 7th International Con-
           ference on Artificial Intelligence and Law*, pages 117–125. ACM, June
           1999.

Conceptual User Tracking

Daniel Oberle[1], Bettina Berendt[2], Andreas Hotho[1], and Jorge Gonzalez[1]

[1] Institute of Applied Informatics and Formal Description Methods AIFB
University of Karlsruhe
D–76128 Karlsruhe, Germany
{oberle,hotho,gonzalez}@aifb.uni-karlsruhe.de
[2] Institute of Information Systems
Humboldt University Berlin
D–10178 Berlin, Germany
berendt@wiwi.hu-berlin.de

Abstract. Web usage mining applies data mining techniques to records of
Web site visits. To better understand patterns of usage, analysis should take
the semantics of visited URLs into account. This paper presents a framework
for enhancing Web usage records with formal semantics based on an ontology
underlying the site. Besides, it elicits automated methods of mapping URLs to
application events. Using the ontology's taxonomy, we describe user actions
at different levels of abstractions. Using the ontology's concepts and relations,
we capture the multitude of user interests expressed by a visit to one page.
We employ our ideas in an application of SEAL, a framework for semantic
portals that uses Semantic Web technologies to support communities of interest.
Different realizations of semantically enriched user tracking are discussed and
related to other approaches. We describe first results from a prototypical system,
and discuss benefits of Conceptual User Tracking for Web usage mining.

Keywords. web (usage) mining, user tracking, semantic portal, ontology

1 Introduction

Web usage mining applies data mining techniques to the usage of Web resources, as
recorded in Web server logs or other logs of requested URLs (plus, possibly, further
parameters) [24].

Web logs were initially designed to help site administrators identify traffic and possible bandwidth problems, broken links, etc., and analyzed using simple statistics like hit
and pageview counts. More and more, their value for understanding site users' behavior
is also being recognized, and techniques like association rule mining, clustering, or sequential pattern discovery are being used to identify co-occurring items in browsing and
shopping histories, different user segments, navigation strategies, etc. This knowledge
can be exploited to improve site design and navigation opportunities [5,7,12], to develop
marketing strategies including recommender systems [18,15], etc.

However, because the primary focus of this kind of usage recording is technical, an
interpretation of URLs in terms of user behavior, interests, and intentions, is not always
straightforward. For example, the site owners of an online bookstore will not be interested

E. Menasalvas et al. (Eds.): AWIC 2003, LNAI 2663, pp. 155–164, 2003.

in an association rule like "If `http://www.the_shop.com/show.html?item=123`, then `http://www.the_shop.com/show.html?item=456`, support = 0.05, confidence = 0.4", but in a statement like "Users who bought *Hamlet* also tended to buy *How to stop worrying and start living*.". In other words, Web usage analysis is not interested in *patterns of URLs*, but rather in *patterns of application events*, where application events are usually described by actions (such as "buying") or content (such as "(showing interest in) *Hamlet*").

So in order to obtain meaningful results, Web usage mining must exploit the semantics of the pages visited along user paths. In this process, meaningful application events have to be identified, URLs have to be mapped to application events, and different levels of abstraction (taxonomical knowledge) have to be taken into account.

A number of recent studies have shown the usefulness of exploiting semantics for mining. After the preprocessing steps in which access data have been mapped into taxonomies, different approaches are taken in subsequent mining steps. Particularly interesting are mining algorithms that can deal flexibly with taxonomical knowledge (a simple form of ontological knowledge). Srikant and Agrawal [23] search for associations in given taxonomies, using support and confidence thresholds to guide the choice of level of abstraction. Dai and Mobasher [8] present a scheme for aggregating towards more general concepts when an explicit taxonomy is missing. They apply clustering to sets of sessions; this clustering identifies related concepts at different levels of abstraction. They are thus able to identify common interests of users at a more abstract level than that of the invidividual pages (e.g., that they all liked films in which a certain actor played an important role), which allows them to circumvent the "new item problem" in a recommender system.

However, for all these mining techniques to work, the semantics of the pages have to be extracted first in order to perform the mapping from requested URLs to requested contents/services. Also, an ontology has to be defined (we use the term "ontology" in the sense of [10]).

In this paper, we describe a novel scheme for providing semantics. After an introduction to the underlying Semantic Web technology and community portals as an important application area (Sects. 2.1 and 2.2), we present a framework for the semantic enrichment of Web logs (Sect. 2.3). We show how our approach, described in Sects. 2.4 and 2.5, extends current proposals (Sect. 2.4). In Sect. 3, we briefly describe a case study that shows the kinds of knowledge that can be discovered using Conceptual User Tracking. Section 4 concludes our study.

2   Semantic Enrichment of Web Logs

2.1   SEmantic portAL

A Web portal is the center of the information needs of a certain interest group in the WWW. On the conceptual, knowledge sharing level it was found that "people can't share knowledge if they don't speak a common language" is utterly crucial for the case of community Web portals. Besides people, the knowledge has to be shared between machines, too. This approach, called SEmantic portAL [16], demands a conceptual structuring for the representation of information. This is achieved by an ontology, agreed upon by the community and used as the portal's backbone.

Such portals benefit from the Semantic Web, one of today's hot topics which brings "[...] structure to the meaningful content of Web pages." [6]. To build the Semantic Web, pages are supplemented with semi-structured meta-data that provide the formal semantics for Web content by referring to ontologies. In the case of SEAL, an ontology would not only be used to structure the portal itself, but also for annotating the portal's resources with meta-data. The technological basis for representing data in the Semantic Web is RDF [14], a semi-structured data format that resembles directed labelled graphs. Ontologies are represented in RDF Schema (RDFS) which defines primitives similar to object-oriented data models. Web pages are equipped with such meta-data by XML-serializations of RDF.

2.2   The KA^2-Portal

For demonstration purposes, we use the so-called KA^2 Portal [1] (Knowledge Annotation Initiative of the Knowledge Acquisition Community, http://ka2portal.aifb.uni-karlsruhe.de) as a particular application of SEAL. The KA^2 initiative was conceived for obtaining knowledge out of annotated resources belonging to the Knowledge Acquisition Community. The ontology was created in international collaboration; it describes a universe of relevant concepts for research, as shown in Fig. 1.

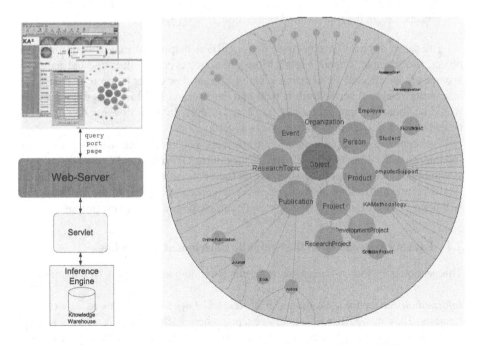

Fig. 1. KA^2 Portal architecture and its ontology (visualized by the Hyperbolic View Applet)

Ontobroker [9], an inference engine based on F-Logic, hosts the ontology and allows the generation of dynamic pages as discussed below. It is important to note that all of the static pages are annotated with RDF meta-data according to the same ontology. As shown in Fig. 1, the interface between the portal and Ontobroker is implemented via a servlet carrying out queries to the inference engine. The servlet is referenced with the parameters query, page and port. The first one contains the query in F-Logic syntax, which is routed to the inference engine listening on port. Finally, the results are written in an HTML template specified via page. Explicit queries can be stated by HTML and JavaScript templates as well as the so-called Hyperbolic View Applet (cf. Fig. 1). Besides, queries are implicitly issued while navigating through the portal.

2.3   A General Framework for the Semantic Enrichment of Web Logs

In this section, we propose a formal framework that investigates how a request to a portal and its associated semantics are represented. We use this framework to analyze existing methods, and to introduce our new method. Any kind of semantic Web usage mining consists of three steps:

1. **description of raw data**: the description of the transaction, which is generally a user visit/session, as a set or sequence T of URLs u: $T = \{u_i\}$ or $T = [u_i]$,
2. **mapping**: the mapping of URLs to objects that are meaningful within the application domain (e.g., concepts from an ontology), with $m(u) = O$ describing the mapping of URL u to a set of objects O, and
3. **mining**: the identification of patterns in the set or sequence of these meaningful objects, i.e., in the transformed transaction $T' = \{\bigcup_i O(u_i)\}$ or $T' = [O(u_i)]$.

The set of application objects O that a URL is mapped to may contain only one object, for example, *"home page"*. More often, however, the multi-faceted nature of Web pages is reflected by O being a set of objects. For example, on a given page, a researcher R may describe both herself and her projects *PR*, so in this case that page would be about the application objects $O = \{R, PR\}$. In the following, $O(u_i)$ will be described by $\{o_{ij}\}$ to emphasize that it is a set.

Two central assumptions underly this process: (a) "requesting the URL u" signals "an interest in the object(s) $m(u)$", and (b) the mining algorithm neither destroys existing structure nor creates a spurious structure on the transaction T.

Different realizations of the three steps have been proposed. In the following, we will describe two existing procedures, and contrast them with our new proposal.

2.4   Existing Approaches to the Semantic Enrichment of Web Logs

This section describes two existing proposals for adding semantics to Web log files.

Information Extraction.   Mobasher et al. (e.g., [19,8]) treat sessions as sets of URL requests. They map URLs to sets of concepts, where each concept is a term extracted from a Web page's text. This allows them to represent each page as a feature vector, with (in the simplest case) the jth component being "1" if the jth term is present, and "0" otherwise. A session is defined as a feature vector with the jth component being "1" if the jth term was present in any of the pages visited in that session, and "0" otherwise. Vectors with non-binary weights express the relative importance of a term in a page or session. The authors then apply clustering algorithms (e.g., k-means) on these vectors of term weights to identify similar sessions. These algorithms as well as other methods used for further processing rely on the assumption that the set-based interpretation of both sessions and pages is applicable.

This assumption appears to be justified for the analysis of a number of sites, e.g. information sites like the fictitious movie site or the real-estate site analyzed in [8]. Another good example are portal sites that contain lists of topics and pointers to them. A disadvantage of this approach is that the essentially syntactic method of keyword extraction has some inherent problems in achieving a truly semantic mapping of URLs.

Information Dimensions. Berendt and Spiliopoulou [5,3] treat sessions as sequences of URL requests. They map URLs to sets of concepts, with each concept being one value along one information dimension. For example, a listing of objects from a database may be both an *Events* page (because it is a listing of event names) and an *Entities-in-Germany* page (because it shows only the names of events taking place in Germany). These two values are values along the information dimensions "kind of entity" and "location of entity". Depending on the question of the analysis, one information dimension is then chosen, which means that each visited page is mapped to only one concept. So mining is performed on $T' = [o_{ij}]$, with some j identifying the dimension. This approach identifies each URL with one elementary action, and subsequent mining aims at identifying browsing strategies in this sequential choice of concepts. The analysis in [5,3] shows that some actions can only be understood if sequence is considered. For example, a search for events with a user-specified topic (mapped to the concept "events-by-topic"), followed by a search for events with a user-specified topic and a user-specified project (mapped to the concept "events-by-topic-and-project"), signals a *refinement* of search.

This approach is particularly suited to the analysis of strategic behavior, or more generally decision processes, in a Web site, where a user can be assumed to "bundle" his current interests and intentions into the request for the next page. For example, the approach has been successfully applied to information search and online shopping behavior [5,2,22,17]. A disadvantage of this approach is that the restriction to an analysis dimension may cause the oversight of unexpected structure in user visits.

The classification of URLs themselves, using the URL stem and the query string, is particularly interesting for dynamically generated pages. Dynamically generated pages do not exist before they are requested, so their semantics cannot be fully contained in existing HTML text or annotations.

However, the query string that leads to the generation of a page, together with a possibly existing page template, determines the contents and thus the semantics of a page. An additional determinant is the current content of the database / knowledge base being queried. When focusing on user *interests*, we can ignore this: The query shows what a user *wanted and expected* to see. So query strings are particularly suited for understanding user interests.

The kind of mapping introduced in the previous paragraphs can be said to *aggregate* the query string. In contrast to this, our new approach *decomposes* query strings. This can be regarded as a combination of the *information extraction* approach described above with the *information dimensions approach*.

2.5   Conceptual User Tracking: Semantic Log Files Created by Meta-Data and Ontology-Based Query Decomposition

Within our exemplary KA[2] portal, we exploit the RDF annotations of static sites to map a URL into the set of ontological entities, i.e. concepts, attributes and/or relations, it deals with. This has the advantage that the semantics are decoupled from URL technicalities, and that the mapping is likely to remain correct across updates because the annotations are within the Web pages and are updated together with them. RDF annotations also ensure a better mapping to a page's semantics than syntax-based methods like keyword extraction.

Dynamically generated pages are mapped to semantics by analyzing their query strings[1]. The advantage of the KA[2] architecture is that it provides independent logging of the full query strings which are expressions in F-logic [13] and thus refer only to concepts and relations in the ontology. For details see [21].

In a first approach, we have treated static and dynamic pages as a set, i.e. $m(u) = \{o_{ij}\}$. In the following, this set will be represented as a feature vector, which contains "1" or a weight if a feature o_{ij} is present in the page, and "0" otherwise. The Semantic Log File thus produced contains, for each request, the time stamp, the URL or query-string, and a feature vector. In addition, a user ID may be contained for non-anonymous sessions. In subsequent mining, we could then use sets or sequences. It would also be possible to restrict the mapping of URLs to a subset of the concepts contained in them, analogously to the information dimensions approach.

The next question to ask is what information the feature vector should contain. In the simplest case, the feature vector only contains the extracted concepts. For example, assume that user 4711 asks for a list of all *Publications*, querying the inference engine with "FORALL x,y,z <- x:Person[name->>y] AND z:Publication[author->>x]". Then, the entry in the Semantic Log File would look like this[2]:

```
Authenticated UserID Timestamp Querystring Feature Vector
                                           Person,Publication...
   YES      4711    ...         FORALL ...   1,      1,      ...
```

The advantage of this option is its great simplicity, and the ease of transformations. For example, the above notation, which shows requests as vectors of concepts, can easily be transformed into a representation that shows concepts as vectors of requests. This allows the analyst to compute the total number of times a concept has been referred to, and a grouping by users. Using the timestamp information, we could in addition analyze users' sequential and temporal navigation behavior.

---

[1] Query strings can be recorded in a number of ways; e.g., in the standard Web server log when they are sent in GET requests, or in additional logs when they are sent in POST requests or when – as in our case – a servlet handles the queries.

[2] All other feature vector components contain 0.

However, this method ignores attributes and relations in general. This can lead to imprecise results, particularly when queries address complex concepts with many attributes and relations.

Hence, another alternative would be to extract concepts, attributes, and relations from the query string into a feature vector. The resulting Semantic Log File entry can again contain one line per request. Alternatively, further processing can aggregate this by time intervals, in which the references made to each of the C concepts, the A attributes, and the R relations during that interval are recorded. As before, the references can be coded in binary form (whether the ontological entity was referenced or not) or using weights (for example, the number of occurrences of that entity in the user's requests). References are collected for all U users and for all T time intervals. All requests from anonymous users can be aggregated into one pseudo-user u_{anon}. The resulting matrix can be directly input to several mining algorithms such as clustering:

UserID	Time Int.	Person	Publication	...	name	...	author	...
4711	$t_{4711,1}$	1	1	...	1	...	1	...
4711	$t_{4711,2}$	1	0	...	1	...	0	...
0815	$t_{0815,1}$	0	1	...	0	...	1	...
...								
u_{anon}	t_{anon}	1	1	...	1	...	1	...

2.6   Semantic Analysis and Enrichment of Preprocessing

The simplest way to analyze user behavior is to use the Semantic Log File described in the previous section. To achieve even better results, we can take the concept hierarchy into account, or we can use query subsumption to generalize queries. This can be used either for instant analysis or for further transformation of the feature vector enriching the input for the mining step.

Consideration of the Concept Hierarchy. Taking the preprocessed logging matrix as a basis, generalizations and specializations of the inherent taxonomy can be taken into account. The following example serves as a motivation. Assume that a user issues the query "FORALL x, y <- x:AcademicStaff[name->>y]." resulting in all the staff's names. According to the concept hierarchy in the KA^2 ontology (cf. Fig. 1), the user isn't only interested in *AcademicStaff*, but also in its super-concepts *Employee* and *Person*. By such generalizations, the feature vector will have additional entries that could result in better mining results (see [23,8] for examples of the use of subconcepts and superconcepts to derive more meaningful mining results).

Query Lattice. Finally, the most powerful method is the use of a query lattice. Consider the following example, where Q_1 yields all existent projects and Q_2 only those dealing with Data Mining. Q_2 is more general than Q_1 according to the ϑ-subsumption known from Inductive Logic Programming [20], as its output features an additional attribute. The most general query would be the one retrieving *Project*s with all their attributes and relations.

```
Q1 = FORALL x,y   <- x:Project[title->>y].
Q2 = FORALL x,y,z <- x:Project[title->>y] AND
                     x:Project[subject->>"Data Mining"].
```

It is obvious that the log file will contain many different queries which have to be generalized to detect a certain interest. Thus, the advantage of this approach is that queries as a whole can be generalized. So far, we only considered the concepts, attributes and relations disjointly. With this method, we are able to grasp the user's interest in its most concise semantical way.

3   Using Conceptual User Tracking for Web Usage Mining

In order to use advanced mining schemes like those of Dai and Mobasher [8], we need both a reliable identification of ontological entities and a reliable mapping from URLs to ontological entities. Our approach is advantageous because it ensures that we retain the full information on each user request, and that this information is already described in semantic terms. Thus, both information loss due to incomplete logging, and the possible errors when extracting semantics from syntax are avoided. In addition, an ontology-based site usually provides a cleaner mapping from URLs to semantics because this problem is addressed *during site design*, rather than *during later analysis*.

We expect that these features of Conceptual User Tracking will help improve mining results. It can be utilized across the whole range of mining techniques applied to Web usage logs.

As mentioned above, we implemented our ideas in the KA^2 Portal (cf. Sect. 2.2), and we used the Semantic Log File for a first clustering analysis. The log file ranged from 04-25-2001 to 09-25-2002 and contained 140394 entries. We converted it into the well known arff format from the WEKA system [25], counting 1098 sessions along 22 concepts from the KA^2 ontology. After the transformation of the data with $log(x + 1)$ to achieve a distribution more similar to the normal distribution, we applied the EM clustering algorithm and found 4 clusters (containing 88, 529, 246, and 197 sessions, respectively) with the following characteristics.

For each cluster we investigated the number of accesses and the number of accesses to the different concepts and relations of our ontology. We found that cluster 1 contains the visitors with few clicks and cluster 0 the heavy users. Visitors grouped into cluster 2 are interested in *Person* and its specializations. Our preprocessing made use of concept generalization, i.e. if the visitor queried for *Researcher* or other sub-concepts of *Person*, interest in *Person* is automatically added to the feature vector. Visitors grouped into cluster 3 showed particular interest in *Project*s and *Publication*s. We were thus able to identify two specific groups of user interests. This knowledge could be used to improve the navigational structure of the portal.

Besides the EM clustering algorithm, we also applied association rules which resulted in trivial rules only. Most queries within the portal are hidden behind HTML forms and always have the same form. A query like "FORALL x,y,z <- x:Person[name ->>y] AND z:Publication [author->>x]" would associate *Person* with *Publication* for example. We are currently exploring the effects of such "artificial" associations on mining results, and investigating which ways of mapping query strings to ontological entities are most appropriate for deriving valid results.

Nevertheless, the mining results are promising and we are working on the implementation of our logging system into larger Web sites. We are also working on the integration of a component like [11] which allows a better understanding of the clustering and browsing. We expect that usage records from a larger portal will help us show the benefits of our approach in more detail.

4   Conclusion and Outlook

We have discussed earlier work related to the semantic enrichment of Web log files and outlined some problems encountered by these approaches. We have then given an overview of a prototypical system. Besides, the paper described a case study that applies Conceptual User Tracking to the Semantic Log File of the KA^2 Portal.

The KA^2 Portal is only a prototype with a small number of hits per day. Therefore, we intend to widen our analysis to larger portals with higher traffic in order to fully assess and measure the benefits of our approach. In the future, the Semantic Log File could also be leveraged to provide recommendation and personalization functionalities within SEmantic portALs. Another area of future work is the combination of the methods described here (which rely heavily on manual and thus costly ontology definition and page markup) with (semi-)automatic methods of information extraction (cf. [4]).

Acknowledgements. We would like to thank York Sure, Alexander Maedche, Steffen Staab and Gerd Stumme for their supervision as well as their insightful ideas and comments, and two anonymous reviewers for valuable comments and questions .

References

1. R. Benjamins, D. Fensel, and S. Decker. KA^2: Building ontologies for the internet: A midterm report. *International Journal of Human Computer Studies*, 51(3):687, 1999.
2. B. Berendt. Detail and context in web usage mining: Coarsening and visualizing sequences. In R. Kohavi, B. Masand, M. Spiliopoulou, and J. Srivastava, editors, *WEBKDD 2001 – Mining Web Log Data Across All Customer Touch Points*, pages 1–24. Springer-Verlag, Berlin Heidelberg, 2002.
3. B. Berendt. Using site semantics to analyze, visualize and support navigation. *Data Mining and Knowledge Discovery*, 6:37–59, 2002.
4. B. Berendt, A. Hotho, and G. Stumme. Towards semantic web mining. In *I. Horrocks and J. Hendler (Eds.), The Semantic Web - ISWC 2002. (Proceedings of the 1st International Semantic Web Conference, June 9-12th, 2002, Sardinia, Italy)*, pages 264–278. LNCS, Heidelberg, Germany: Springer, 2002.
5. B. Berendt and M. Spiliopoulou. Analysing navigation behaviour in web sites integrating multiple information systems. *The VLDB Journal*, 9(1):56–75, 2000.
6. T. Berners-Lee. XML 2000 - Semantic Web Talk, December 2000. http://www.w3.org/2000/Talks/1206-xml2k-tbl/Overview.html.
7. R. Cooley. *Web Usage Mining: Discovery and Application of Interesting Patterns from Web Data*. PhD thesis, University of Minnesota, Faculty of the Graduate School, 2000.

8. H. Dai and B. Mobasher. Using ontologies to discover domain-level web usage profiles. In *Proceedings of the Second Semantic Web Mining Workshop at PKDD 2001, Helsinki, Finland, August 20, 2002*, 2002.

9. S. Decker, M. Erdmann, D. Fensel, and R. Studer. Ontobroker: Ontology Based Access to Distributed and Semi-Structured Information. In R. Meersman et al., editors, *Database Semantics*, pages 351–369. Kluwer Academic Publisher, 1999.

10. T. R. Gruber. Towards Principles for the Design of Ontologies Used for Knowledge Sharing. In N. Guarino and R. Poli, editors, *Formal Ontology in Conceptual Analysis and Knowledge Representation*, Deventer, The Netherlands, 1993. Kluwer Academic Publishers.

11. A. Hotho and G. Stumme. Conceptual clustering of text clusters. In *Proceedings of FGML Workshop*, pages 37–45. Special Interest Group of German Informatics Society (FGML — Fachgruppe Maschinelles Lernen der GI e.V.), 2002.

12. H. Kato, T. Nakayama, and Y. Yamane. Navigation analysis tool based on the correlation between contents distribution and access patterns. In *WebKDD Workshop on Web Mining for E-Commerce at the 6th ACM SIGKDD*, pages 95–104, Boston, MA, 2000.

13. M. Kifer and G. Lausen. F-logic: A higher-order language for reasoning about objects, inheritance, and scheme. In J. Clifford, B. G. Lindsay, and D. Maier, editors, *Proceedings of the 1989 ACM SIGMOD International Conference on Management of Data, Portland, Oregon, May 31 - June 2, 1989*, pages 134–146. ACM Press, 1989.

14. O. Lassila and R. Swick. Resource description framework (RDF) model and syntax specification. Technical report, W3C, 1999. `http://www.w3.org/TR/REC-rdf-syntax`.

15. W. Lin, S. Alvarez, and C. Ruiz. Efficient adaptive-support association rule mining for recommender systems. *Data Mining and Knowledge Discovery*, 6:83–105, 2002.

16. A. Maedche, S. Staab, R. Studer, Y. Sure, and R. Volz. SEAL – Tying up information integration and web site management by ontologies. *IEEE-CS Data Engineering Bulletin, Special Issue on Organizing and Discovering the Semantic Web*, March 2002.

17. A. Maedche and V. Zacharias. Clustering ontology-based metadata in the semantic web. In *Proc. of the Joint Conferences ECML and PKDD, Finland, Helsinki*, LNAI. Springer, 2002.

18. B. Mobasher, R. Cooley, and J. Srivastava. Automatic personalization based on web usage mining. *Communications of the ACM*, 43(8):142–151, 2000.

19. B. Mobasher, H. Dai, T. Luo, Y. Sun, and J. Zhu. Integrating web usage and content mining for more effective personalization. In *Proc. of ECWeb*, pages 165–176, Greenwich, UK, 2000.

20. S. Muggleton and L. de Raedt. Inductive logic programming: Theory and methods. *Journal of Logic Programming*, 19(20):629–679, 1994.

21. D. Oberle. Semantic community web portals - personalization. Technical Report 424, University of Karlsruhe, Institute AIFB, 2 2003.

22. M. Spiliopoulou, C. Pohle, and M. Teltzrow. Modelling and mining web site usage strategies. In *Proc. of the Multi-Konferenz Wirtschaftsinformatik, Nürnberg, Germany, Sept. 9-11*, 2002.

23. R. Srikant and R. Agrawal. Mining generalized association rules. In *Proc. 21st VLDB, Zurich, Switzerland, September 1995*, pages 407–419, 1995.

24. J. Srivastava, R. Cooley, M. Deshpande, and P.-N. Tan. Web usage mining: discovery and application of usage patterns from web data. *SIGKDD Explorations*, 1(2):12–23, 2000.

25. I. H. Witten and E. Frank. *Data Mining: Practical Machine Learning Tools and Techniques with Java Implementations*. Morgan Kaufmann, 1999.

Coping with Web Knowledge*

J.L. Arjona, R. Corchuelo, J. Peña, and D. Ruiz

The Distributed Group
Avda. de la Reina Mercedes, s/n, Sevilla (Spain)
{arjona,corchuelo,joaquinp, druiz}@lsi.us.es

Abstract. The web seems to be the biggest existing information repository. The extraction of information from this repository has attracted the interest of many researchers, who have developed intelligent algorithms (wrappers) able to extract structured syntactic information automatically.
In this article, we formalise a new solution in order to extract knowledge from today's non-semantic web. It is novel in that it associates semantics with the information extracted, which improves agent interoperability; furthermore, it achieves to delegate the knowledge extraction procedure to specialist agents, easing software development and promoting software reuse and maintainability.

Keywords: knowledge extraction, wrappers, web agents and ontologies

1 Introduction

In recent years, the web has consolidated as one of the most important knowledge repositories. Furthermore, the technology has evolved to a point in which sophisticated new generation web agents proliferate. A major challenge for them has become sifting through an unwieldy amount of data to extract meaningful information. This process is difficult because the information on the web is mostly available in human-readable forms that lack formalised semantics that would help agents use it.

The Semantic Web is *"an extension to the current web in which information is given well–defined meaning, better enabling computers and people to work in cooperation"* [3], which implies a transition from today's web to a web in which machine reasoning will be ubiquitous and devastatingly powerful. This transition is achieved by annotating web pages with meta–data that describe the concepts that define the semantics associated with the information in which we are interested. Ontologies play an important role in this task, and there are many ontological languages that aim at solving this problem, e.g., DAML+OIL [13], SHOE [17] or RDF-Schema [5]. The Semantic Web shall simplify and improve

* The work reported in this article was supported by the Spanish Interministerial Commission on Science and Technology under grants TIC2000-1106-C02-01 and FIT-150100-2001-78.

E. Menasalvas et al. (Eds.): AWIC 2003, LNAI 2663, pp. 165–178, 2003.

the accuracy of current information extraction techniques tremendously. Nevertheless, this extension requires a great deal of effort to annotate current web pages with semantics, which suggests that it is not likely to be adopted in the immediate future [9].

Several authors have worked on techniques for extracting information from today's non-semantic web, and inductive wrappers are amongst the most popular ones [6,14,15,16,19]. They are components that use automated learning techniques to extract information from similar pages automatically. Although induction wrappers are suited to extract information from the web, they do not associate semantics with the data extracted, this being their major drawback. Furthermore, adding these algorithms to logic that a web agent encapsulates, can produce tangled code and does not achieve a clear separation of concerns.

In this article, we present a new solution in order to extract semantically-meaningful information from today's non-semantic web. It is novel in that it associates semantics with the information extracted, which improves agent interoperability, and it delegates the knowledge extraction procedure to specialist agents, easing software development and promoting software reuse and maintainability.

We address these issues by developing *knowledge channels*, or KCs for short. They are agents [21] that allow to separate the extraction of knowledge from the logic of an agent, and they are able to react to knowledge inquiries (reactivity) from other agents (social ability), and act in the background (autonomy) to maintain a local knowledge base (KB) with knowledge extracted from a web site (proactivity). In order to allow for semantic interoperability, the knowledge they manage references a number of concepts in a given application domain that are described by means of ontologies. KCs extract knowledge from the web using *semantic wrappers*, which are a natural extension to current inductive wrappers to deal with knowledge on the web. Thus, we take advantage of the work made by researchers in the syntactic wrappers arena.

The rest of the paper is organised as follows: Next section glances at other proposals and motivates the need for solutions to solve the problems behind knowledge extraction; Section 3 presents the case study used to illustrate our proposal and some initial concepts related to knowledge representation; Section 4 gives the reader an insight into our proposal; finally, Section 5 summarises our main conclusions.

2   Related Work

Wrappers [8] are one of the the most popular mechanisms for extracting information from the web. Generally, a wrapper is an algorithm that translates the information represented in model M_1 to model M_2. In information extraction, they are able to translate the information in a web page to a data structure that can be used by software applications.

In the beginning, these algorithms were codified manually, using some properties of a web page, normally looking for strings that delimit the data that we need to extract. But hand-coded wrappers are error–prone, tedious, costly and time–consuming to build and maintain. An important contribution to this field was provided by Kushmerick [15]. He introduced induction techniques to define a new class of wrappers called inductive wrappers. These inductive algorithms are components that use a number of extraction rules generated by means of automated learning techniques such as inductive logic programming, statistical methods, and inductive grammars. These rules set up a generic algorithm to extract information from similar pages automatically. Boosted techniques [10] are proposed to improve the performance of the machine learning algorithm by repeatedly applying it to a training set with different example weightings.

Although induction wrappers are suited to extract information from the web, they do not associate semantics with the data extracted, this being their major drawback [2]. Thus, we call current inductive wrappers syntactic because they extract syntactic information devoid of semantic formalisation that expresses its meaning.

Our solution builds on the best of current inductive wrappers, and extends them with techniques that allow us to deal with web knowledge. Using inductive wrappers allows us take advantage of all the work developed in this arena, as boosted techniques or verification algorithms [15,19] that detect if there are changes in the layout of a web page that invalidate the wrapper.

3   Preliminaries

3.1   A Case Study

We illustrate the problem to solve by means of a simple, real example in which we are interested in extracting information about the score of golfers in a PGA Championship. This information was given at `http://www.golfweb.com`. Figure 1 shows a web page from this site.

Note that the implied meaning of the terms that appear in this page can be easily interpreted by humans, but there is not a reference to the concepts that describe them precisely, which complicates communication and interoperability amongst software applications [3,4].

3.2   Dealing with Knowledge

There are many formalisms to dealt with knowledge, namely: semantic networks [20], frames systems [18], logic, decision trees, and so on. Their aim is to represent ontologies, which are specifications of concepts and relationships amongst them in a concrete domain. Ontologies [7] allows us to specify the meaning of the concepts about which we are extracting information. Some authors [11,12] have specified a formal model for ontologies; our formalisation builds on the work by Heflin in his PhD dissertation [12].

Definition 1. *Let $\mathcal{L}$ be a logical language; an **ontology** is a tuple (P, A), where P is a subset of the vocabulary of predicate symbols of $\mathcal{L}$ and A is a subset of*

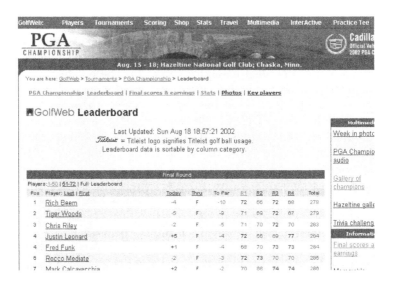

Fig. 1. A web page with information about scores in a golf championship.

well–formed formula in $\mathcal{L}$ (axioms). Thus, an ontology is a subset of $\mathcal{L}$ in which concepts are specified by predicates and relationships amongst then are specified as a set of axioms.

First–order languages (FOL) offer us the power and flexibility needed to describe knowledge. Many knowledge representation languages and structures can be formulated in first–order logic [12]. Then, we are able to use a wide range of knowledge representation formalisms; we only need to define a mechanism to translate from some formalism to FOL and vice versa.

In Appendix A, we specify[1] some concepts related to logical languages that establish the basis of our model. In our proposal, a logical language ($\mathcal{L}$) is characterized by a vocabulary of constant identifiers ($Ident_c$), a vocabulary of variable identifiers ($Ident_v$), a vocabulary of function identifiers ($Ident_f$), a vocabulary of predicate identifiers ($Ident_p$) and a (in)finite set of well–formed formulae (Wff), which is a subset of the formulae derived from $\mathcal{L}$. For the sake of simplicity, we assume that $Ident_f = \varnothing$.

Next schema specifies an ontology. Three constrains are imposed: the former states that P and A are non–empty subsets of the set of predicate symbols and well–formed formulae of $\mathcal{L}$, respectively; the second, asserts that axioms are defined using the predicate symbols in P^2; the latter asserts that the set of axioms is consistent. Predicate $\vdash$ references a theorem prover; let be $F : \mathbb{P}\ Wff$, and $f : Wff$ then $F \vdash f$ is satisfied if f is formally provable or derivable from F,

---

[1] In this paper we use notation Z as a formal specification language because it is an ISO standard [1], and an extremely expressive language.

[2] Function $PredSyms$ is specified in Appendix A. It returns the set of predicate symbols in a formula.

thus f belongs to the set of all well–formed formulae that we can obtain from F (theory of F).

Ontology

$P : \mathbb{P}\, Ident_p$
$A : \mathbb{P}\, Wff$

$P \neq \varnothing \wedge A \neq \varnothing$
$\forall f : A \bullet PredSyms(f) \subseteq P$
$\neg \exists g : Wff \bullet A \vdash g \wedge A \vdash \neg g$

Definition 2. *An **instance** of a concept, specified in an ontology, is an interpretation of this concept over some domain. In information extraction, this domain is established by the information to be extracted.*

We model instances as ground predicate atoms. Thus, they are well–formed formula. We specify the set of all instances that we can derive from an ontology by the function *GroundPredicateAtoms*:

$GroundPredicateAtoms : Ontology \rightarrow \mathbb{P}\, Wff$

$\forall o : Ontology \bullet GroundPredicateAtoms(o) =$
$\quad \{f : Wff;\ ip : Ident_p;\ sc : seq_1\, Term;\ ic : Ident_c\ |$
$\quad\quad (f = atom(pred(ip, sc))) \wedge$
$\quad\quad \forall c : Term \mid c \in sc \bullet c = const(ic) \wedge$
$\quad\quad PredSyms(f) \subseteq o.P) \bullet f\}$

Definition 3. *A **Knowledge Base** (KB) is a tuple (O, K), where O is an ontology and K a set of instances of concepts specified in O.*

A KB is specified as follows:

KB

$O : Ontology$
$K : \mathbb{P}\, Wff$

$\forall f : K \bullet PredSyms(f) \subseteq O.P$
$K \in GroundPredicateAtoms(O)$

The constrains imposed assert that the instances are formed with predicates defined in the ontology and they are ground predicate atoms.

Example 1. The following object defines a KB in the domain of a golf championship in which we were interested in modelling knowledge about the position and score of golfers in a PGA championship (for the sake of readability, we do not use the abstract syntax in Appendix A. The mapping between this syntax and the usual logic symbols is straightforward):

$$KB_0 = \langle\!\langle\ O \rightsquigarrow\ \langle\!\langle\ P \rightsquigarrow \{Person, Golfer, Score, Position\},$$
$$A \rightsquigarrow \{\forall\, x \bullet Golfer(x) \Rightarrow Person(x),$$
$$\forall\, x \bullet \exists\, y \bullet Golfer(x) \Rightarrow Score(x,y),$$
$$\forall\, x \bullet \exists\, y \bullet Golfer(x) \Rightarrow Position(x,y)\}\ \rangle\!\rangle,$$
$$K \rightsquigarrow \{Golfer(\text{Rich\_Beem}), Score(\text{Rich\_Beem}, 278),$$
$$Position(\text{Rich\_Beem}, 1)\}\ \rangle\!\rangle$$

The ontology has four predicate symbols called *Person*, *Golfer*, *Score* and *Position*; the first axiom asserts that every *Golfer* is a *Person*; the second one states that every *Golfer* has a *Score*, where y represents the total number of points obtained; the last one asserts that every *Golfer* has a *Position* y in the championship. The instances in KB_0 can be interpreted using the ontology, and they asserts that *Rich Beem* is a golfer, and he is the first in the ranking with 278 points.

4 Our Proposal

Our proposal is a framework agent developers can use to extract information with semantics from non–annotated web pages, so that this procedure can be clearly separated from the rest in an attempt to reduce development costs and improve maintainability. This frameworks gives the mechanisms to develop core web agents called knowledge channels. Figure 2 illustrate this idea.

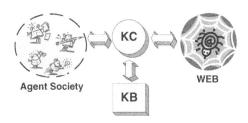

Fig. 2. Knowledge Channels.

A KC is responsible for managing a local knowledge base (KB). This knowledge is extracted from a web site using *semantic wrappers*. KCs answer also inquiries from other agents that need some knowledge to accomplish their goals.

4.1 Knowledge Extraction

A semantic wrapper is an extension to current syntactic wrappers, as shown in Figure 3. Thus, we first need to define such wrappers formally.

Definition 4. *A **syntactic wrapper** is a function that takes a web page as input, and returns structured information.*

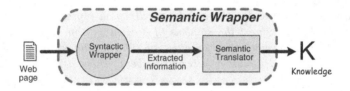

Fig. 3. A semantic wrapper.

Next schema specifies a syntactic wrapper:

$[String, WebPage]$
$Datum == \mathbb{P}\, String$
$Data == \mathrm{seq}\, Datum$
$Information == \mathbb{P}\, Data$

$Wrapper : WebPage \nrightarrow Information$

$\mathrm{dom}\; Wrapper \neq \varnothing$

A syntactic wrapper is modelled as a partial function because its domain is a subset of web pages. This subset defines the scope of the wrapper, and it references the web pages in which the wrapper can be used. The output is modelled as data type *Information*, which is a set of data type *Data*. *Data* is sequence of *Datum*, it allows us to have a structured vision of the data to be extracted and to set a location for each datum. Data type *Datum* represents facts, and it is specified as a set of strings; this allows us to deal with multi–valuated attributes (attributes that can have 0 or more values).

Example 2. If we were interested in extracting information about the position and score of golfers in a PGA championship, a syntactic wrapper would output the following *Information* from the web page in Figure 1:

$\{\langle\{\text{Rich\_Beem}\}, \{278\}, \{1\}\rangle, \langle\{\text{Tiger\_Woods}\}, \{279\}, \{2\}\rangle,$
$\quad \langle\{\text{Chris\_Riley}\}, \{283\}, \{3\}\rangle, \ldots\}$

Definition 5. *A **semantic wrapper** is a function that takes a web page as input, and returns a set of instances of concepts defined in an ontology that represents the information of interest.*

A semantic wrapper is composed of a syntactic wrapper and a semantic translator. In order to extract knowledge from the web, it is necessary to feed the semantic wrapper with the web page that contains the information. The syntactic wrapper extracts the structured information from that web page, and the semantic translator assigns then meaning to it by means of an ontology.

$SemanticWrapper : WebPage \nrightarrow \mathbb{P}\, Wff$

$\forall\, p : WebPage \mid p \in \mathrm{dom}\; Wrapper \bullet SemanticWrapper(p) =$
$\quad\quad SemanticTranslator(Wrapper(p))$

The semantic translator needs the user to specify a *semantic description* that relates the information to be extracted with the predicates defined in the ontology to perform this task.

Definition 6. *A **semantic description** (SD) is a representation of the relationships that hold amongst the symbols of predicates from an ontology and the positions that their arguments occupy in an Information structure. Thus, each predicate P is associated with n natural numbers, where n is the arity of P.*

An SD is modelled using the following schema, which is composed of three elements: an ontology (O), a set of predicate symbols ($S_p{}^3$) and a function (Pos) that maps predicate symbols onto the location of *Datum* in *Data* belonging to the *Information* structure. This scheme also asserts that S_p is a subset of the set of predicates symbols in O, and the domain of Pos is a subset of the symbols in S_p.

$$
\begin{array}{l}
\underline{\quad SemanticDescription \quad} \\
O : Ontology \\
S_p : \mathbb{P}\ Ident_p \\
Pos : Ident_p \twoheadrightarrow \mathrm{seq}_1\ \mathbb{N} \\
\hline
S_p \subseteq O.P \wedge \mathrm{dom}\ Pos = S_p
\end{array}
$$

Example 3. In our study case, we can define the following semantic description:

$$
\langle\!\langle\ O \rightsquigarrow o_0, S_p \rightsquigarrow \{Golfer, Score, Position\}, \\
Pos \rightsquigarrow \{Golfer \mapsto \langle 1 \rangle, Score \mapsto \langle 1, 2 \rangle, Position \mapsto \langle 1, 3 \rangle\}\ \rangle\!\rangle
$$

In this SD, predicate *Golfer* takes constant values from location $Pos(Golfer)$ of each *Data* (sequence) in an *Information* structure, In this case, the first position of the sequence. Predicate *Score* takes its values from $Pos(Score) = \langle 1, 2 \rangle^4$, and so on. Thus, it is possible to generate automatically well-formed formula that express the meaning of the information for all the *Data* elements in an *Information* structure extracted.

Definition 7. *A **semantic translator** is a function that receives the Information structure obtained using a syntactic wrapper as input and uses a semantic description specified by the user, and outputs a set of instances.*

$$
\begin{array}{l}
SemanticTranslator : Information \twoheadrightarrow \mathbb{P}\ Wff \\
sd : SemanticDescription \\
\hline
\forall\, i : Information \mid i \in \mathrm{ran}\ Wrapper \bullet \\
\quad SemanticTranslator(i) = \bigcup\{d : Data \mid d \in i \bullet buildWffs(d)\}
\end{array}
$$

---

[3] We might not need to use all the predicate defined in the ontology to give meaning to the information extracted.

[4] The arguments in a predicate follows a strict order. Using a sequence allows us to get arguments orderly. For instance, If $Pos(Score)$ were $\langle 2, 1 \rangle$, the result would be erroneous: $Score(278, Tiger\_Woods)$ states that the score of 278 is Tiger_Woods.

Function *buildWffs* returns the set of well formed formula for each *data* in an *Information* structure. It is defined as follows[5]:

$$buildWffs : Data \nrightarrow \mathbb{P}\ Wff$$

$$\forall\, e : Data;\ t : \mathbb{P}\,(Ident_p \times Data) \mid e \in \bigcup ran\,Wrapper \wedge$$
$$t = \{x : sd.S_p \bullet (x, e \upharpoonright \{n : ran\,Pos(x) \bullet e(n)\})\} \bullet$$
$$buildWffs(e) = \bigcup\{k : t \bullet BuildPredicates(k)\}$$

The function *BuildPredicates* is specified as follows:

$$BuildPredicates : Ident_p \times seq\,\mathbb{P}\,Ident_c \rightarrow \mathbb{P}\ Wff$$

$$\forall\, ip : Ident_p;\ ssc : seq\,\mathbb{P}\,Ident_c \bullet$$
$$BuildPredicates(ip, ssc) = \{si : seq\,Ident_c;\ n : \mathbb{N} \mid$$
$$n \in 1..\#ssc \wedge si(n) \in ssc(n) \bullet atom(pred(ip, si))\}$$

It takes a pair composed of an identifier of predicate and a sequence of strings sets from an *Information* structure, and returns a set of predicates. The predicates are composed using the identifier of predicate and each element of the sequence.

Example 4. The following instances represent the knowledge extracted by a semantic wrapper from the web page in Figure 1:

$\{atom(pred(Golfer, \langle const(\text{Rich\_Beem})\rangle)),$
$atom(pred(Score, \langle const(\text{Rich\_Beem}), const(278)\rangle)),$
$atom(pred(Position, \langle const(\text{Rich\_Beem}), const(1)\rangle)),$
$atom(pred(Golfer, \langle const(\text{Tiger\_Woods})\rangle)),$
$atom(pred(Score, \langle const(\text{Tiger\_Woods}), const(279)\rangle)),$
$atom(pred(Position, \langle const(\text{Tiger\_Woods}), const(2)\rangle)),$
$atom(pred(Golfer, \langle const(\text{Chris\_Riley})\rangle)),$
$atom(pred(Score, \langle const(\text{Chris\_Riley}), const(283)\rangle)),$
$atom(pred(Position, \langle const(\text{Chris\_Riley}), const(3)\rangle)), \ldots\}$

4.2   A Model for KCs

The schema bellow formalises a KC. It has a declarative part containing two variables; the former (SW) references the semantic wrapper to be used, and the latter (SV) the semantic verifier.

KnowledgeChannel
$SW : Semantic\,Wrapper$
$SV : Semantic\,Verificator$

---

[5] The filtering operator ($\upharpoonright$) takes from a sequence the elements in a set. For instance:

$$\langle jun, nov, feb, jul\rangle \upharpoonright \{sep, oct, nov, dec, jan, feb, mar, apr\} = \langle nov, feb\rangle$$

Next schema defines the overall state of our system. It is composed of a knowledge channel, a local KB and its environment. The environment (the perceivable features of the KC agent) is specified as set of web pages, and we constraint that the semantic wrapper must be defined for these web pages.

```
┌─ KnowledgeChannelState ─────────────────────────────────────
│ KC : KnowledgeChannel
│ KB : KnowledgeBase
│ Environment : ℙ WebPage
├─────────────────────────────────────────────────────────────
│ Environment ⊆ dom KC.SW
└─────────────────────────────────────────────────────────────
```

The motivation of the knowledge channel is to synchronize the knowledge that resides in web documents with the one in the knowledge base (KB). This motivation allows us define a KC as an autonomous piece of software. Next schema specifies an agent's motivation. Δ means that the system's state can change and the imposed constrains indicates that all knowledge on environment must be on local KB, and vice versa.

```
┌─ KnowledgeChannelMotivation ────────────────────────────────
│ ΔKnowledgeChannelState
├─────────────────────────────────────────────────────────────
│ ∀ p : Environment • KB.K ⊆ KC.SW(p)
│ ∀ f : Wff | f ∈ KB.K • ∃ p : Environment • f ∈ SW(p)
└─────────────────────────────────────────────────────────────
```

The KC server requests from agents, thus they show social ability. Delegating the task of knowledge extraction to KCs allows agent developers to achieve a complete separation between the knowledge extraction procedure and the logic or base functionality an agent encapsulates. Any agent can send messages to a KC in order to extract knowledge. Knowledge requests are expressed as predicate symbols. The reply from the KC are ground predicate atoms that satisfies the predicates in query.

```
┌─ KnowledgeChannelQuery ─────────────────────────────────────
│ ΞKnowledgeChannelState
│ Q? : ℙ Ident_p
│ R! : ℙ Wff
├─────────────────────────────────────────────────────────────
│ Q ≠ ∅
│ R = {f : KB.K; ip : Ident_p; sc : seq₁ Term; | f = atom(pred(ip, sc) • f}
└─────────────────────────────────────────────────────────────
```

Example 5. If we launch the query $Q = \{Golfer\}$ the KC would reply with $R = \{Golfer(\text{Rich\_Beem}), Golfer(\text{Tiger \_Woods}), Golfer(\text{Chris\_Riley}), \ldots\}$. This knowledge can be used to infer new knowledge. It also makes it possible to reuse knowledge. For instance, an agent using the golfer ontology can infer that the golfers *Rich Beem* and *Tiger Woods* are people, according to the axiom $\forall x • Golfer(x) \Rightarrow Person(x)$, these knowledge can be shared by applications in order to collaborate to accomplish a task.

5   Conclusions

The current web is mostly user–oriented. The semantic web shall help extract information with well–defined semantics, regardless of the way it is rendered, but it does not seem it is going to be adopted in the immediate future, which argues for another solution to the problem in the meanwhile.

In this article, we have presented a new approach to knowledge extraction from web sites based on semantic wrappers. In this article, we have presented a framework that is based on specialised knowledge channels agents that extract information from the web. It improves on other proposals in that it associates semantics with the extracted information. Furthermore, our proposal achieves a separation of the knowledge extraction procedure from the base logic that web agents encapsulate, thus easing both development and maintenance.

References

1. ISO/IEC 13568:2002. Information technology—Z formal specification notation—syntax, type system and semantics. International Standard.
2. J. L. Arjona, R. Corchuelo, A. Ruiz, and M. Toro. A practical agent-based method to extract semantic information from the web. In *Advanced Information Systems Engineering, 14th International Conference, CAiSE 2002*, volume 2348 of *Lecture Notes in Computer Science*, pages 697–700. Springer, 2002.
3. T. Berners-Lee, J. Hendler, and O. Lassila. The semantic Web. *Scientific American*, 284(5):34–43, May 2001.
4. T.J. Berners-Lee, R. Cailliau, and J.-F. Groff. The World-Wide Web. *Computer Networks and ISDN Systems*, 25(4–5):454–459, November 1992.
5. D. Brickley and R.V. Guha. Resource description framework schema specification 1.0. Technical Report http://www.w3.org/TR/2000/CR-rdf-schema-20000327, W3C Consortium, March 2000.
6. W.W. Cohen and L.S. Jensen. A structured wrapper induction system for extracting information from semi-structured documents. In *Proceedings of the Workshop on Adaptive Text Extraction and Mining (IJCAI'01)*, 2001.
7. O. Corcho and A. Gómez-Pérez. A road map on ontology specification languages. In *Proceedings of the Workshop on Applications of Ontologies and Problem Solving Methods. 14th European Conference on Artificial Intelligence (ECAI'00)*, pages 80–96, 2000.
8. L. Eikvil. Information extraction from world wide web - a survey. Technical Report 945, Norweigan Computing Center, 1999.
9. D. Fensel, editor. *Spinning the Semantic Web: Bringing the World Wide Web to Its Full Potential*. The MIT Press, 2002.
10. Dayne Freitag and Nicholas Kushmerick. Boosted wrapper induction. In *AAAI/IAAI*, pages 577–583, 2000.
11. N. Guarino. Formal ontology and information systems. In N. Guarino, editor, *Proceedings of the 1st International Conference on Formal Ontologies in Information Systems, FOIS'98, Trento, Italy*, pages 3–15. IOS Press, June 1998.
12. J. Heflin. *Towards the Semantic Web: Knowledge Representation in a Dynamic, Distributed Environment*. PhD thesis, University of Maryland, College Park, 2001.

13. I. Horrocks, P.F. Patel-Schneider, and F. van Harmelen. Reviewing the design of DAML+OIL: An ontology language for the semantic web. Technical Report http://www.daml.org, Defense Advanced Research Projects Agency, 2002.

14. C.A. Knoblock, K. Lerman, S. Minton, and I. Muslea. Accurately and reliably extracting data from the web: A machine learning approach. *IEEE Data Engineering Bulletin*, 23(4):33–41, 2000.

15. N. Kushmerick. Wrapper verification. *World Wide Web Journal*, 3(2):79–94, 2000.

16. Ling Liu, Calton Pu, and Wei Han. XWRAP: An XML-enabled wrapper construction system for web information sources. In *ICDE*, pages 611–621, 2000.

17. S. Luke, L. Spector, D. Rager, and J. Hendler. Ontology-based web agents. In W.L. Johnson and B. Hayes-Roth, editors, *Proceedings of the First International Conference on Autonomous Agents (Agents'97)*, pages 59–68, Marina del Rey, CA, USA, 1997. ACM Press.

18. M. Minsky. *A framework for representing knowledge*. McGraw-Hill, New York, 1975.

19. I. Muslea, S. Minton, and C. Knoblock. STALKER: Learning extraction rules for semistructured, web–based information sources. In *Proceedings of the AAAI-98 Workshop on AI and Information Integration*, 1998.

20. M. R. Quillian. Word concepts: A theory and simulation of some basic semantic capabilities. *Behavioral Science*, 12:410–430, 1967.

21. M.J. Wooldridge and M.R. Jennings. Intelligent agents: Theory and practice. *The Knowledge Engineering Review*, 10(2):115–152, 1995.

A   Well-Formed Formula

Let $Ident_c$, $Ident_v$, $Ident_f$, $Ident_p$ be the sets of identifiers of constants, variables, functions and predicates, respectively, in a first–order logical language. Then the complete language can be specified as the $\mathcal{Z}$ free type *Formula* in the following way:

$$
\begin{array}{lll}
[Ident_c, Ident_v, Ident_f, Ident_p] \\
Term & ::= & const\langle\!\langle Ident_c \rangle\!\rangle \\
& & \mid\ var\langle\!\langle Ident_v \rangle\!\rangle \\
& & \mid\ func\langle\!\langle Ident_f \times \mathrm{seq}_1\ Term \rangle\!\rangle \\
Atom & ::= & pred\langle\!\langle Ident_p \times \mathrm{seq}_1\ Term \rangle\!\rangle \\
& & \mid\ not\langle\!\langle Atom \rangle\!\rangle \\
& & \mid\ and\langle\!\langle Atom \times Atom \rangle\!\rangle \\
& & \mid\ or\langle\!\langle Atom \times Atom \rangle\!\rangle \\
& & \mid\ implies\langle\!\langle Atom \times Atom \rangle\!\rangle \\
& & \mid\ iff\langle\!\langle Atom \times Atom \rangle\!\rangle \\
Formula & ::= & atom\langle\!\langle Atom \rangle\!\rangle \\
& & \mid\ forall\langle\!\langle Ident_v \times Formula \rangle\!\rangle \\
& & \mid\ exists\langle\!\langle Ident_v \times Formula \rangle\!\rangle
\end{array}
$$

This states that a *Formula* is either an *atom* or an universal quantifier over a formula or an existencial quantifier over a formula. An *atom* is either an n-ary predicate or the negation of an atom or the conjunction of two atoms or the disjunction of two atoms or the implication formed from two atoms or the bi–implication formed from two atoms. A term is an identifier of constant or an identifier of variable or a n-ary function. To illustrate the use of this free type, formula $\forall P(x) \Rightarrow Q(x)$ is represented by the following term:

$$forall(x, atom(implies(pred(P, \langle var(x) \rangle), pred(Q, \langle var(x) \rangle))))$$

A well–formed formula (Wff) is a formula that does not contain any *free* variables, that is, its variables are *bounded* by universal or existencial quantifiers. In order to define the set of the well–formed formula in a logical language, we need to specify axiomatically a recursive function called *Free Vars*. It obtains the free variables in a formula or atom or term.

$FormulaAtomTerm ::= Formula \mid Atom \mid Term$

$FreeVars : FormulaAtomTerm \rightarrow \mathbb{P}\ Ident_v$

$\forall f : Formula;\ a, a1, a2 : Atom;\ iv : Ident_v;\ ip : Ident_p;\ if : Ident_f \bullet$
  $FreeVars(atom(a)) = FreeVars(a) \wedge$
  $FreeVars(forall(iv, f)) = FreeVars(f) \setminus \{iv\} \wedge$
  $FreeVars(exists(iv, f)) = FreeVars(f) \setminus \{iv\} \wedge$
  $FreeVars(not(a)) = FreeVars(a) \wedge$
  $FreeVars(and(a1, a2)) = FreeVars(a1) \cup FreeVars(a2) \wedge$
  $FreeVars(or(a1, a2)) = FreeVars(a1) \cup FreeVars(a2) \wedge$
  $FreeVars(implies(a1, a2)) = FreeVars(a1) \cup FreeVars(a2) \wedge$
  $FreeVars(iff(a1, a2)) = FreeVars(a1) \cup FreeVars(a2) \wedge$
  $FreeVars(pred(ip, st)) = \bigcup\{t : Term \mid t \in st \bullet FreeVars(t)\} \wedge$
  $FreeVars(var(iv)) = \{iv\} \wedge$
  $FreeVars(const(c)) = \varnothing \wedge$
  $FreeVars(func(if, st)) = \bigcup\{t : Term \mid t \in st \bullet FreeVars(t)\}$

Set *Wff* is specified as the set of logical formula that does not have any free variables.

$Wff : \mathbb{P}\ Formula$

$\forall f : Formula \bullet f \in Wff \Leftrightarrow Freevar(f) = \varnothing$

We can also obtain the set of predicate symbols in a formula:

$FormulaAtom ::= Formula \mid Atom$

$PredSyms : FormulaAtom \rightarrow \mathbb{P}\ Ident_p$

$\forall f : Formula;\ a, a1, a2 : Atom;\ iv : Ident_v;\ ip : Ident_p \bullet$
  $PredSyms(formula(a)) = PredSyms(a) \wedge$
  $PredSyms(forall(iv, f)) = PredSyms(f) \wedge$
  $PredSyms(exists(iv, f)) = PredSyms(f) \wedge$
  $PredSyms(not(a)) = PredSyms(a) \wedge$
  $PredSyms(and(a1, a2)) = PredSyms(a1) \cup PredSyms(a2) \wedge$
  $PredSyms(or(a1, a2)) = PredSyms(a1) \cup PredSyms(a2) \wedge$
  $PredSyms(implies(a1, a2)) = PredSyms(a1) \cup PredSyms(a2) \wedge$
  $PredSyms(iff(a1, a2)) = PredSyms(a1) \cup PredSyms(a2) \wedge$
  $PredSyms(pred(ip, st)) = \{ip\}$

Formalization of Web Design Patterns Using Ontologies

Susana Montero, Paloma Díaz, and Ignacio Aedo

Laboratorio DEI. Dpto. de Informática
Universidad Carlos III de Madrid
Avda. de la Universidad 30. 28911 Leganés, Spain
smontero@inf.uc3m.es, pdp@inf.uc3m.es, aedo@ia.uc3m.es
http://www.dei.inf.uc3m.es

Abstract. Design patterns have been enthusiastically embraced in the software engineering community as well as in the web community since they capture knowledge about how and when to apply a specific solution to a recurring problem in software systems. However, web design involves both cognitive and aesthetic aspects, for that there are several design patterns that describe the same problem but from different points of view and with different vocabulary, so it is more difficult to understand and to reuse that knowledge.

To achieve a common vocabulary and improve reusability we propose to formalize web design patterns by means of ontologies. At the same time the ontology would allow us to express web design patterns in a formal way, that can be understood by a computer. So a design pattern knowledge base can be integrated in a software tool for web application modeling in order to suggest web design patterns that better suit some design requirements. Moreover, changes and alterations needed for applying design patterns to the design can be proposed.

This paper describe the core ontology using DAML+OIL and show how web design patterns can be described by our ontology.

Keywords: web applications, design patterns, ontologies, hypermedia

1 Introduction and Motivation

Web applications[1] have been extremely demanded in different areas like e-commerce, tele-education, health, and libraries, both to provide a web interface for existing information systems and to create new applications. Even though most developers skip the conceptual design phase and directly go to the implementation stage using authoring tools like DreamWeaver or NetObjects' Fusion because they allow for setting up a website in a very short period of time, there are tools based on hypermedia design methods that perform a conceptual design [13].

Conceptual modeling allows for describing the general features of an application in an abstract and implementation independent way, producing applications of better quality, usability and maintainability. However, there is little guidance on how to match models to implementations.

---

[1] We use the term hypermedia application as a synonym for web application since the later is a particular case of hypermedia application

E. Menasalvas et al. (Eds.): AWIC 2003, LNAI 2663, pp. 179–188, 2003.

In order to mitigate this gap between conceptual modeling and application implementation design patterns have been enthusiastically embraced both in the software engineering community [6] and later in the web community [14] as a effective mean for reusing good design solutions. A design pattern *captures knowledge of how and when to apply the solution to a recurring problem, besides providing a shared vocabulary for expressing and communicating such a knowledge.* Moreover, the use of design patterns for web applications can increase the quality of their design and decrease the time and cost of design and implementation [7].

Although the spirit of design patterns is to capture design experience in a form which can be used effectively, we find a twofold problem. On the one hand, using patterns is not a trivial process. The designer or developer has to have a high knowledge of the design process and high level of abstraction. On the other hand, analysing web design patterns there is a large number of them published and some of which describe the same problem but from different points of view. Consequently, reuse is hindered by the absence of a common language and a catalog of patterns in such a way that designer could be assisted.

In order to face up these problems we propose to conceptualize the web design pattern knowledge using an ontology, since both design patterns and ontologies have as main motivation *share and reuse knowledge bodies* [16].

The aim of this paper is to introduce an ontology in order to have a formal representation of expert knowledge captured in web design patterns and to facilitate their application in computational form. Not only web design patterns could be described by means of a common vocabulary in order to be shared and reused by the web community, for example by means of repositories, one of the main pending issues in this area [7,9], but incorporated in software tools of some hypermedia design methods to help designers in their practical application.

To conceptualize the domain, we identify two different areas: hypermedia models and design patterns. On the one hand, most hypermedia design methods [13] are based on hypermedia models. They define the components describing any hypermedia and web application. On the other side, design patterns are described by means of a format like the one used in [6].

The rest of the paper is organized as follows: next section presents those meaningful concepts identified from our domain knowledge. Section 3 defines the ontology to specify web design patterns and how a concrete web design pattern can be formalized with the ontology encoded in DAML+OIL. Section 4 presents some related works. Finally, some conclusions and future works are drawn.

2   Domain Description: Hypermedia and Design Patterns

In ontological engineering, the knowledge is investigated in terms of its origin and elements from which knowledge is produced [12]. Web design patterns are described by a number of particular terms (e.g. nodes, links, etc.) and have a fixed format (e.g. name, problem, etc.). Thus, in a first approach, we need to combine knowledge from two different areas: *hypermedia models* and *design patterns*. The formers provide a vocabulary of terms and concepts to describe the general features of a hypermedia application in a conceptual way. The latters describe a specific problem and propose solutions for them using a specific format.

2.1 Hypermedia Models

Web applications are based on the hypertext paradigm: associative navigation through a heterogeneous information space. Therefore they are considered as a particular hypermedia application.

Hypermedia models, such as the Dexter [11], HDM [8] or Labyrith [3], propose a number of elements and constructs for describing the structure and behaviour of any hypermedia application. Thus, a basic vocabulary of terms and concepts about the web domain may be defined from them. Taking into account only the elements related to their structure, all hypermedia models include:

- **Node** is an information holder able to contain a number of contents. Examples of nodes are a web page, a frame or a pop-up window.
- **Content**, is a piece of information of any type like text, audio, graphics, animations or programs.
- **Link** is a connection among two or more nodes or contents. A link is defined between two set of anchors.
- **Anchor** is source or target of a link, and determines a reference locus into a node and/or content.

An example of a web application marking their different elements is illustrated in Fig. 1. Each web page is a node where several text and image contents are placed. Some contents have anchors that set up the links offered to the users.

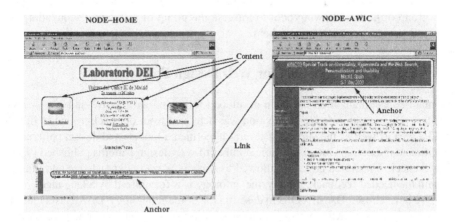

Fig. 1. Example of the elements of a web application

Depending on models we can find more complex elements such as composite nodes or contents and virtual or dangling links to describe hypermedia applications. However, the above elements are crucial to represent the knowledge of the hypermedia domain.

2.2 Design Patterns

Design patterns usually are expressed in natural language. Our aim is not to conceptualize the semantic underlying natural language, but to make them understandable from a computational point of view. Thus, we focus on the way they are described. They usually contain certain essential elements that describe the context where problem occurs, the statement of the problem, a description of the relevant forces and how to generate the solution. In our case, we take into account the following parts of a design pattern according to the format specified in [6]:

- **Name** is used to unambiguously identify the pattern itself. For instance, in [7] we find a pattern called *Index Navigation*.
- **Category** is used for classifying the pattern according to several criteria such as its purpose or scope. Web design patterns are usually organized by design activity and the level of abstraction where they are applied. For example, the *Index Navigation* pattern belongs to the *navigational category* because its design activity is concerned with organizing the navigation through the hypermedia application. Moreover, the pattern is described in a detailed way regardless of the implementation.
- **Problem** describes the scenario in which the pattern can be applied. For example, the *Index Navigation* pattern is applied to provide *fast access* to a *group of elements* with the possibility of choosing one of them.
- **Solution** describes how to obtain the desired outcome. For example, in order to apply the *Index Navigation* pattern, *links* should be defined from the entry point to each *node*, and from each node to the entry point.
- **Related-patterns** relates a pattern with others if they address similar or complementary problems or solutions. Thus, another pattern related with the *Index Navigation* pattern is *Hybrid Collection*. This pattern provides an easy-to-use access to a small group of nodes, allowing both to traverse the group of nodes in a sequential way and to access specific one of them.

3   Modeling an Ontology for Web Design Patterns

Domain conceptualization has been developed following an iterative and incremental process. Domain knowledge acquisition was achieved from our background in hypermedia area as well as the survey of several hypermedia models and design patterns, as mentioned in Sect. 2. Due to the large number of web design patterns published [9] we could check if acquired concepts allowed to conceptualize the knowledge and thus, to obtain the needed feedback. Finally, the ontology was formalized by a language.

We have chosen DAML+OIL to describe the domain ontology. DAML is a markup language based on XML and is built on top of Resource Description Framework (RDF) and its schema (RDFS) [2] which is compatible with emerging web standards. OIL combines frame-like syntax with the power and flexibility of a description logic (DL) which facilitates reasoning services. The OilEd editor[3] has been used for the definition and description of classes, slots, individuals and axioms of the ontology.

---

[2] http://www.w3c.org/RDF/
[3] http://oiled.man.ac.uk/index.shtml

3.1 Domain Ontology

Our ontology is defined in three different layers. The first layer is represented by pattern components and hypermedia elements. Each of them can be reused in other ontologies because they have been defined in an independent way regardless of hypermedia design patterns. This layer is the basis to represent the second layer, hypermedia design patterns. Concrete instances of this second layer are considered the third layer.

Figure 2 shows the whole class hierarchy for the first and second layer. The knowledge of design patterns is represented by subclasses of the class PatternComponent. The subclasses of the class HypermediaElement represent elements of a web application. Finally, the class HypermediaPattern gathers the format of a design pattern with hypermedia elements that take part in the problem and solution of the pattern. The only new concept is the class Actor which represents the state of elements that take part both in the problem and in the solution of a design pattern. This allows to express design patterns independently of their domain.

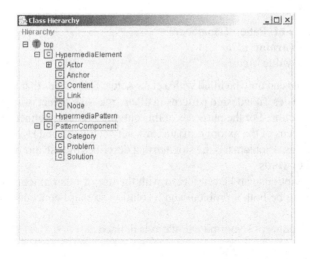

Fig. 2. Hierarchy derived from the ontology

Next, the subclasses of PatternComponent and HypermediaPattern with their slots are briefly described. The subclasses of HypermediaElement are the same concepts mentioned in Sect. 2, so they do not need further explanation.

Regarding design patterns, only three of their components are represented as a class: Category, Problem and Solution. The rest of the elements are slots of the class HypermediaPattern.

The class Category classifies a pattern according to the values of *scope* and *level*. The former represents the design activity where a pattern can be applied such as navigation or presentation. The latter defines the level of abstraction, such as conceptual, detailed or implementation.

class-def Category
    subclass-of PatternComponent
    slot-constraint *scope*
       value-type string
    slot-constraint *level*
       value-type string

Both the class Problem and the class Solution are described by means of the specific state of Actors that participate in the scenario in which a pattern is applied and its desired outcome respectively.

class-def Problem
    subclass-of PatternComponent
    slot-constraint *aim*
       value-type string
    slot-constraint *state*
       has-value Actor

class-def Solution
    subclass-of PatternComponent
    slot-constraint *state*
       has-value Actor

The slot *state* can only be filled with a class Actor. This means that these components can be reused to describe design patterns in other areas like object orientation or human computer interaction. For the purposes of this ontology Actor is defined as a HypermediaElement by means of the axiom `equivalent` between Actor and HypermediaElement. Moreover the class Problem has the slot *aim* that describes the use motivation of a pattern by means of keywords.

These descriptions can be reinforced with the use of other axioms. For instance, it is not possible to be both a problem and a solution so these concepts are described as disjoint.

Finally, the concept HypermediaPattern is defined as:

class-def HypermediaPattern
    slot-constraint *name*
       value-type string
    slot-constraint *hasCategory*
       has-value Category
    slot-constraint *hasProblem*
       has-value Problem
    slot-constraint *hasSolution*
       has-value Solution
    slot-constraint *relatedTo*
       has-value HypermediaPattern

The slots describe that a hypermedia design pattern must have a name, a category, a problem, a solution and related patterns. From the definition of this last concept web design patterns can be described by its individuals.

3.2   Describing a Web Design Pattern

The classes described above belong to the first and second layer of our ontology. In the third layer concrete web design patterns are instanced from those levels. Next we show an example of how to make these instances.

In [7] some web design patterns can be found. One of these is the Index Navigation pattern that was already explained in Sect. 2.2. Since our approach is based on the idea of viewing a design pattern as a set of actors that play two different roles: the problem and the solution state, the design pattern must first be projected onto two states.

Below it is described as an instance of the class HypermediaPattern with DAML+OIL.

```
<rdf:Description rdf:about="#IndexNavigation">
      <rdf:type>
          <daml:Class  rdf:about="#HypermediaPattern"/>
      </rdf:type>
   <ns1:name>
          <xsd:string xsd:value="Index Navigation"/>
      </ns1:name>
      <ns0:hasCategory rdf:resource="#CategoryNC"/>
      <ns0:hasSolution rdf:resource="#solutionIndexNavigation"/>
      <ns0:hasProblem rdf:resource="#problemIndexNavigation"/>
      <ns0:relatedTo rdf:resource="#HybridCollection"/>
   </rdf:Description>
   <rdf:Description rdf:about="#CategoryNC">
      <rdf:type>
          <daml:#Category"/>
      </rdf:type>
      <ns0:level>
          <xsd:string xsd:value="Conceptual"/>
      </ns0:level>
      <ns0:scope>
          <xsd:string xsd:value="Navigation"/>
      </ns0:scope>
   </rdf:Description>
   <rdf:Description rdf:about="#problemIndexNavigation">
      <rdf:type>
          <daml:Class rdf:about="#Problem"/>
      </rdf:type>
      <ns1:aim>
          <xsd:string xsd:value="fast access"/>
      </ns1:aim>
      <ns0:state rdf:resource="#aNode"/>
   </rdf:Description>
   <rdf:Description rdf:about="#solutionIndexNavigation">
```

```
        <rdf:type>
            <daml:Class rdf:about="#Solution"/>
        </rdf:type>
        <ns0:state rdf:resource="#aNode"/>
        <ns0:state rdf:resource="#aNodeIndex"/>
        <ns0:state rdf:resource="#aLink"/>
    </rdf:Description>
</rdf:RDF>
```

In order to make this instance the following slots have been filled as:

- *name* is Index Navigation
- *hasCategory* is an instance of the class Category whose slots *level* and *scope* have the values conceptual and navigation respectively.
- *hasProblem* is an instance of the class Problem. The slot *aim* has the value fast access and the slot *state* has an instance of the class Node. That means that we should apply this pattern to provide fast access to a group of nodes.
- *hasSolution* is an instance of the class Solution whose slot *state* has three values. The value aNode represents the group of nodes on which this design pattern is applied. The value aNodeIndex hold the set of the entry points to aNode. Finally, the value aLink represents links from the node aNodeIndex to each member of aNode and vice versa.
- *relatedTo* is a instance of the class HypermediaPattern whose value is HybridCollection, that is the other pattern which is related to.

This example represents the *Index Navigation* pattern in a formal way and is expressed in a understandable computational language, DAML+OIL. Therefore it is can be shared with the rest of the web community and integrated in a software development environments for web applications.

A knowledge base with web design patterns formalized with this ontology is being built.

4   Related Work

There are two approaches to consider for the formalization of design patterns for their automatic processing. One of them employs formal methods to represent design patterns. For example, Cornils and Hedin [2] model design patterns using reference attributed grammars with syntactic and context-sensitive rules. Eden et al. [4] define LePlus (LanguagE for Patterns Uniform Specification) to represent design pattens as logic formulas which consist of participants (i.e. classes, functions or hierarchies) and relations imposed amongst. Smith and Stotts [15] use an extension of sigma calculus which defines relationships between the elements of object oriented language for expressing design patterns. Although, these approaches provide rigorous reasoning, it is hard to understand the structure and relationship to represent a design pattern and even more to provide design guidelines to the practitioners.

The second approach implements solutions for the automatic processing of design patterns. These solutions are too much dependent of software tools in order to be used directly as a formalization, although some ideas can be taken into account. For example, Gomes et al. [10] describe a design pattern as a set of participants with their properties that specify when the design pattern is applicable and an operator which defines how to apply the design pattern. Abin-Amiot et al. [1] define a meta-model to describe the structural and behavioural aspects of the design pattens. It is made up of a set of meta-entities which represent participants and each entity contains a collection of elements, representing relationships among entities. Florijn et al. [5] represent design patterns as a collection of fragments where each of them is a design element (i.e class, method, pattern, etc.) with particular information and roles that contain references to other fragments.

All of these approaches, including the our one, are based on the representation of design patterns as a set participants and their relationships among them. However our approach has two distinguishing points. On the one hand, the specification of design patterns is made with the same elements as the design methods to describe applications. Moreover, design patterns are applied during design process, so they are independent of programming languages. On the other hand, the use of ontologies for the formalization of design patterns provide us not only the same aspects as the formal approaches such as elements, relations, rules and reasoning (e.g. description logic) but enabling communication and knowledge reuse between different systems and/or people.

5   Conclusions and Future Work

This paper deals with a problem of knowledge sharing and reuse, the web design pattern knowledge. It presents a domain ontology that describes the concepts and properties of an application area from the elements that are required for expressing web design patterns in a formal way.

Our ontology has been defined from the primitives of several well-known hypermedia models as well as from the generic format of a design pattern, both of them in an independent way. This approach allows designers to exchange and share knowledge of web design patterns among different hypermedia methods as well as to integrate web design patterns into the design process.

Moreover, parts of the ontology can be reused and extended. On the one hand, the knowledge of design patterns can be used to build the others in other domains. On the other hand, the knowledge domain of hypermedia elements can be used as a hypermedia model itself.

Since our ontology was intended for automatic application purposes we are currently working on describing tasks needed to detect and apply web design patterns that better suit different design views and its later integration into a hypermedia design tool.

Acknowledgements. This work is supported by The Ariadne project funded by "Dirección General de Investigación del Ministerio de Ciencia y Tecnología" (TIC2000-0402)."

References

1. H. Albin-Amiot and Y. Guéhéneuc. Meta-modeling design patterns: Application to pattern detection and code synthesis. In *Proceedings of the ECOOP Workshop on Automating Object-Oriented Software Development Methods*, pages 57–64, June 2001.

2. A. Cornils and G. Hedin. Tool support for design patterns based on reference attribute grammars. In *Proc. of WAGA'00, Ponte de Lima, Portugal*, 2000.

3. P. Díaz, I. Aedo, and F. Panetsos. Labyrinth, an abstract model for hypermedia applications. description of its static components. *Information Systems*, 22(8):447–464, 1997.

4. A. H. Eden, A. Yehudai, and J. Gil. Precise specification and automatic application of design patterns. In *Proc. of International Conference on Automated Software Engineering (ASE '97)*, pages 143–152, Lake Tahoe, CA, USA, 1997.

5. G. Florijn, M. Meijers, and P. van Winsen. Tool support for object-oriented patterns. In *Proceedings of ECOOP'97*, Finland, 1997.

6. E. Gamma, R. Helm, R. Johnson, and J. Vlissides. *Design Patterns, Elements of Reusable Object-Oriented Software*. Addison-Wesley, 1995.

7. F. Garzotto, P. Paolini, D. Bolchini, and S. Valenti. Modeling-by-Patterns of web applications. In *Advances in Conceptual Modeling: ER '99 Workshops on Evolution and Change in Data Management, Reverse Engineering in Information Systems, and the World Wide Web and Conceptual Modeling*, pages 293–306, Paris, France, 1999.

8. F. Garzotto, P. Paolini, and D. Schwbe. HDM- a model-based approach to hypertext application design. *ACM Transactions on Information Systems*, 11(1):1–26, 1993.

9. D. German and D. Cowan. Towards a unified catalog of hypermedia design patterns. In *Proceedings of 33rd Hawaii International Conference on System Sciences*, Maui, Hawaii, 2000.

10. P. Gomes, F. Pereira, P. Paiva, N. Seco, P. Carreiro, J.L. Ferreira, and C. Bento. Using CBR for automation of software design pattern. In *Proceedings of the European Conference Case-Based Reasoning (ECCBR'02)*, pages 534–548, 2002.

11. F. G. Halasz and M. Schwartz. The dexter hypertext reference model. In *Proc. of World Conference of Hypertext*, pages 95–133, 1990.

12. R. Mizoguchi, T. Sano, and Y. Kitamura. An ontology-based human friendly message generation in a multiagent human media system for oil refinery plant operation. In *Proc. of the IEEE SMC99, IEEE Systems, Man and Cybernetics Society*, 1999.

13. S. Montero, P. Díaz, and I. Aedo. Requirements for hypermedia development methods: A survey of outstanding method. In *Proc. of Advanced Information Systems Engineering, 14th International Conference, CAiSE*, pages 747–751, 2002.

14. G. Rossi, A. Garrido, and S. Carvalho. *Design Patterns for Object-Oriented Hypermedia Applications. Pattern Languages of Programs II*. Addison-Wesley, 1996.

15. J. Smith and D. Stotts. Elemental design patterns: A link between architecture and object semantics. Technical Report Technical Report TR02-011, Univ. of North Carolina at Chapel Hill, March 2002.

16. R. Studer, V. R. Benjamins, and D. Fensel. Knowledge engineering: Principles and methods. *Data Knowledge Engineering*, 25(1-2):161–197, 1998.

A Multi-agent System for Web Document Authoring

**M. Pérez-Coutiño, A. López-López, M. Montes-y-Gómez,
and L. Villaseñor-Pineda**

Instituto Nacional de Astrofísica, Óptica y Electrónica (INAOE)
Luís Enrique Erro No. 1, Sta Ma Tonantzintla, 72840, Puebla, Pue, México.
{mapco,allopez,mmontesg,villasen}@inaoep.mx

Abstract. Current efforts on the semantic web are mainly focused on the creation of recommendations and standards for adding semantic descriptions to web resources. This situation represents a huge challenge to content creators that have to construct manually such descriptions, implying high costs in material and human resources. This paper presents a multi-agent system that automates partially this task, i.e. the authoring of web documents, reducing content creators labor. This system automatically extracts descriptive information from a set of documents in Spanish language, and constructs two output (web) document collections from them. The first collection is a set of meta-information descriptions based on the Dublin Core specifications. The second output is a collection of XHTML documents for human visualizing and browsing. In order to build the two output collections, the proposed multi-agent system applies several intelligent text processing approaches. This paper describes these approaches, as well as, the methodology used to encode the extracted metadata. It also reports results from processing three document collections of about 45 MB of text, including their associated resources – descriptions and hypertext – generated by the system.

Keywords: Semantic web, web document authoring, metadata extraction, automatic link generation, multi-agent system.

1 Introduction

The Internet has become the preferred media for interchange of both information and knowledge. However, nowadays, this information is mainly designed for human usage and not for the computers (Berners-Lee et al., 2001). Several problems arise as a result of the unstructured nature of the web information. For instance, the information retrieval engines are incapable of getting appropriate results, with acceptable levels of both recall and precision (Kobayashi and Takeda, 2000); and automated approaches such as information software agents cannot reach their goals (Berners-Lee et al., 2001).

In order to improve and extend the automated usage of the web, its information must be enriched. A common way to enrich this information is to include *meta-information*, i.e. information about the resource itself describing its content and its relations to other resources, in a meaningful way to machines. Currently, humans, with expertise in a specific domain, construct the meta-information descriptions.

E. Menasalvas et al. (Eds.): AWIC 2003, LNAI 2663, pp. 189–198, 2003.

There are several initiatives focused on creating standard schemas to capture semantics of many domains (Egnor and Lord, 2000). For instance, the World Wide Web Consortium (W3C) promotes the *semantic web* initiative with the aim of extending the current web to facilitate web automation and universally accessible content, and the Dublin Core Metadata Initiative (DCMI) considers the development of interoperable online metadata standards that support a broad range of purposes and business models.

Despite of these standardization efforts, it is clear that the consolidation of the semantic web requires the creation of automatic methods for both, authoring and retrieval tasks.

This paper focuses on *information authoring*. It proposes a multi-agent system for automatically extracting descriptive information from Spanish documents, and constructing their meta-information descriptions based on the Dublin Core element set. Additionally, this system generates a collection of XHTML documents allowing effortless visualization of the extracted information.

The proposed authoring system is expected to be of impact since the extracted meta-information can be used to improve web processing by search engines and web agents.

The rest of the paper is organized as follows. Section 2 reviews previous work on metadata creation. Section 3 presents an overview of our multi-agent system. Section 4 shows some experimental results obtained from the processing of three document collections of about 45 MB of text. Finally, section 5 discusses the main contributions and further improvements.

2   Related Work

The efforts on the creation of *metadata schemes* for the web are lead by the World Wide Web Consortium (W3C) through its semantic web initiative[1]. They define the semantic web as an abstract representation of data on the web, mainly based on the RDF standard (SemanticWeb, 2001).

Other domain specific communities, such as the *Dublin Core Metadata Initiative*[2] (DCMI), also use RDF/XML for publishing data on the web. Additionally, there are several metadata initiatives for encoding bibliographic resources and literary and linguistic texts. Two popular examples are the Machine Readable Cataloging Record (MARC), and the Text Encoding Initiative (TEI).

Our work is based on the DCMI because of its simplicity, semantic interoperability, international consensus and extensibility. The entire DCMI considers 15 elements grouped in 3 categories: content, intellectual property and instantiation. The proposed system considers all three categories, but it mainly focuses on the extraction of the subject and relation elements.

The task of *subject extraction* is typical for information retrieval systems (Baeza-Yates and Ribeiro-Neto, 1999). Traditional systems use statistical methods to select the set of words that best represents the content of the documents. On the contrary,

---

[1] http://www.w3.org/2001/sw/
[2] http://www.dublincore.org

recent approaches tend to apply simple natural language methods to obtain representative phrases as document descriptions (Strzalkowski et al., 1997; Buckley et al., 1995).

Our system represents document content as a list of topics, i.e. sequences of words indicating a unique entity. Currently, we extract these topics based on simple heuristics for Spanish language; however we are developing a Mexican-Spanish POS tagger for a further richer analysis[3].

Most work on relation extraction, also known as *automatic link generation*, considers applications not necessarily working on Internet or the Web. For instance, Allan (1996) automatically generates links for a set of documents based on their similarity measure; Golovchinsky (1999) presents the system VOIR capable of identifying candidate links based on some user-specified topics; and Kaindl and Kramer (1999) propose a semiautomatic glossary link generator allowing the interaction with the users.

Our system is based on Allan's work, but employs improved document representation (the list of topics); produces metadata in the RDF/XML format in accordance with the DCMI and semantic web guidelines; and generates a XHTML output collection that becomes a hypertext volume for human reading and navigation.

3   The Multi-agent System

As we mentioned, the main goal of our multi-agent system (MAS) is to automate the authoring of metadata and hypertext for large collections of electronic Spanish documents. In order to reach its goal, the MAS carry out two main tasks:

- *Input processing*, consisting of the identification of language, subject, and other attributes for each document, as well as the inter-document relations.
- *Output generation*, considering the creation of a set of metadata in the RDF/XML format suited for machine processing, and a collection of XHTML documents for human reading and browsing.

The general architecture of our MAS is shown in the figure 1. It consists of two layers of agents: the input processing and the output generation agents. These agents are heterogeneous and extensible, i.e., each agent has a specific plan, and its behavior is separated from its functionality. This design allows easily implementing and modifying the agent algorithms.

The MAS was developed based on the Jack Intelligent Agent Framework (Busetta et al., 1999). This framework provides a set of Java components for developing multi-agent systems in accordance with the Belief-Desire-Intention model. The communication among the agents is based on the contract net protocol.

The subsequent sections describe the goals and functionality of the four main agents: the subject extractor, the relation finder, the metadata generator and the XHTML generator.

---

[3] "Etiquetador de Partes de la Oración para el Español de México", Project CONACYT R31886-A, 1999-2002.

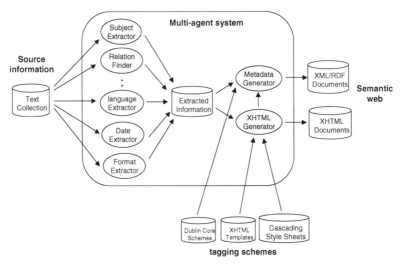

Fig. 1. General architecture of the multi-agent system

3.1 Subject Extractor

The subject extractor agent has two main tasks: to identify the candidate topics for each document of a given collection, and to build a formal representation of their content.

In order to identify the set of topics of a document, this agent uses a method similar to that proposed by Gay and Croft (1990), where the topics are related to noun strings. Basically, this agent applies a set of heuristic rules specific for Spanish, based on the proximity of words, that allows identifying and extracting key phrases. These rules are driven by the occurrence of articles and the preposition *de* ('of') along with nouns or proper names. Some morphological inflection patterns (typical endings of nouns and verbs) are also taken into account. For instance, given the following paragraph, the subject extractor agent selects the underlined words as the candidate topics:

"*Góngora Pimentel* aseguró que estas *demandas* se resolverán en un *plazo* no mayor de 30 días y que sin duda la *demanda interpuesta* por el *PRD* ante la *Suprema Corte de Justicia* se anexará a la que presentó el *Partido Acción Nacional*".[4]

Then, based on the candidate topics, this agent builds an enriched representation of the documents. This representation is expressed as a weighted vector of topics in a given n-dimensional vector space. That is, for a given collection of documents $D = \{d_i\}$, with a corresponding set of topics $\{t_1, ..., t_n\}$, the new document representation is formally expressed as follows:

---

[4] '*Góngora Pimentel* confirmed that these *demands* will be satisfied in a *period* not longer than 30 days and that without any doubt the *demand introduced* by the *PRD* to the *Justice Supreme Court* will be added to that presented by the *National Action Party*.'

$$d_i \rightarrow \bar{d}_i = \left(w_i(t_1), w_i(t_2), \ldots, w_i(t_n) \right), \text{ where :}$$

$$w_i(t_j) = \frac{f_{ij}}{\sum_{k=1}^{n} f_{ik}}$$

In these formulas, $w_i(t_j)$ is the normalized weight of the topic j in the document i; f_{ij} is the number of occurrences of the topic j in the document i; and n is the number of topics in the whole collection.

3.2 Relation Finder

The goal of the relation finder agent is to identify the most significant inter-document relations. Basically, this agent finds the set of thematically related documents for each item of the given source collection.

In order to accomplish its goal, the relation finder agent computes the similarity for every pair of documents in the source collection, and then determines the most important connections.

The similarity measure used is based on the Dice coefficient:

$$s(d_i, d_j) = s_{ij} = \frac{1}{2} \sum_{\forall t \in d_i \cap d_j} w_i(t) + w_j(t)$$

Here, the topic $t \in d_i \cap d_j$ is a common topic of both documents d_i and d_j, and $w_k(t)$ indicates the weight of the topic t in the document d_k.

The criteria used to determine the set of related items associated to the document d_i, after computing the similarities is the following:

$$R_i = \left\{ d_j \,\middle|\, s_{ij} \geq s_\mu, \, j \neq i \right\} \text{ where :}$$

$$s_\mu = \frac{2}{N(N-1)} \sum_{i=1}^{N} \sum_{\substack{j=i+1 \\ s_{ij}>0}}^{N} s_{ij}$$

Here, R_i is the set of thematically related documents for the document d_i, s_{ij} is the similarity measure of documents d_i and d_j, and N is the number of documents in the whole collection. Basing this criterion on the average similarity among documents allows producing the associated set of items independent of how homogeneous is the collection. That is, even in highly heterogeneous collection (a very diverse set of topics), we can obtain existing relations.

3.3 Metadata Generator

This agent gathers the extracted metadata information (i.e., the subject and the relation elements) along with other information coming from the documents, such as last modification date, the language, and the format. Then, it encodes these elements based on the recommendations for generating Dublin Core metadata in RDF/XML (Becket and Miller, 2002). The resulting metadata set serves as machine-readable information, allowing their automatic processing by software agents and search engines.

In order to generate the metadata in the Dublin Core format, this agent uses the template detailed below. In this template, the bold-font elements are automatically generated by our system, while the rest of them are pre-configured or post-produced by the user. For instance, in our private experimills the system fills the creator element with the system signature and the publisher element with the data from our laboratory.

```
<?xml version="1.0"?>
<!DOCTYPE rdf:RDF SYSTEM "http://dublincore.org/2000/12/01-
dcmes-xml-dtd.dtd">
<rdf:RDF xmlns:rdf="http://www.w3.org/ 1999/02/22-rdf-syntax-
ns#" xmlns:dc="http://purl.org/dc/elements/1.1/">
<rdf:Description>
  <dc:creator>cre</dc:creator>
  <dc:contributor>con</dc:contributor>
  <dc:publisher>pub</dc:publisher>
  <dc:subject>sub</dc:subject>
  <dc:description>des</dc:description>
  <dc:identifier>ide</dc:identifier>
  <dc:relation>rel</dc:relation>
  <dc:source>sou</dc:source>
  <dc:rights>rig</dc:rights>
  <dc:format>for</dc:format>
  <dc:type>typ</dc:type>
  <dc:title>tit</dc:title>
  <dc:date>dat</dc:date>
  <dc:coverage>cov</dc:coverage>
  <dc:language>lan</dc:language>
</rdf:Description>
</rdf:RDF>
```

The metadata in RDF/XML format corresponding to an example document is showed in the section 4.

3.4   XHTML Generator

As we mentioned in the section 2, our system generates two different outputs for a given document source collection. One is a set of XML/RDF documents corresponding to the semantic description of the input documents (as described in section 3.3). The other output is a collection of XHTML documents. The main purpose of this collection is to become a *hypertext volume* for human reading and browsing. The output collection is based on a template that fulfills the standard XHTML 1.0 proposed by the World Wide Web Consortium (W3C), and includes the following set of metadata: title, creator, publisher, date, subject and relation. It also contains the source document and a pointer to the Dublin Core document representation instrumented by the tag: *<link rel="meta" href="SomeURL/xml/file.shtml.rdf">*.

The XHTML output corresponding to the example text is showed in the Sect. 4.

4   Experimental Results

4.1   The Test Collections

In order to prove the functionality of the proposed MAS, we analyzed three document collections: *News94*, *ExcelNews* and *Nexos90s*. These collections are all in raw text format (i.e. ASCII). They differ from each other in their topics and in the document average size.

Next, we describe the main characteristics of the three test collections. More details are in Table 1.

Collection News94

News94 is a set of 94 news documents. The average size per document is 3.44 Kb, and the biggest document size is 18 Kb. This collection is a subset of the ExcelNews data set.

Collection ExcelNews

This collection consists of 1,357 documents. These documents contain national and international news from 1998 to 2000 as well as cultural notes about literature, science and technology. The document average size is 3.52 Kb, and the biggest document size is 28 Kb.

An important characteristic of the ExcelNews collection is the variety of writing styles and lexical forms of its documents, causing a large distribution of terms in the vocabulary.

Collection Nexos90s

This collection contains the articles that appeared in the issues of the 1990`s from the Mexican magazine "Nexos". It includes 120 documents –one per month– with an average size of 344 Kb (i.e., approximately 100 pages). Their content is mainly political, but some other topics, such as literature, art and culture, are also treated.

Table 1. Main data of test collections

Collection	Size (Mb)	Number of documents	Average document size	Average number of pages	Number of lexical forms	Number of terms
News94	372 Kb	94	3.44 Kb	124	11,562	29,611
ExcelNews	4.81	1357	3.52 Kb	1,642	41,717	391,003
Nexos90s	41.10	120	344 Kb	14,029	133,742	3,433,654

4.2   Results

Table 2 summarizes the results obtained from the analysis of the test collections. These results consider three main aspects: (1) the topic distribution of the test collections, (2) the required time for their analysis, and (3) the connectivity level of the resulting hypertext document sets.

Table 2. Main results from the collection analysis

Collection	Topics	Instances of topics	Indexing time	Searching time	Connected documents	Relations	Average of related documents
News94	2,571	4,874	0''.26	0''.55	90	459	5
ExcelNews	24,298	72,983	3''.56	3'50''.59	1350	47,486	35
Nexos90s	145,813	1,096,421	5'14''.72	580'26''.7	118	3,803	32

Next, there is an example of the metadata set gathered from a given input document. Then, Fig. 2 shows the resulting XHTML document.

```
<?xml version="1.0"?>
<!DOCTYPE rdf:RDF SYSTEM "http://dublincore.org/2000/12/01-
dcmes-xml-dtd.dtd">
<rdf:RDF xmlns:rdf="http://www.w3.org/1999/02/22-rdf-syntax-ns#"
xmlns:dc="http://purl.org/dc/elements/1.1/">
<rdf:Description>
<dc:creator>AcreS, Multi-Agent System for web document authoring
</dc:creator>
<dc:publisher>Language Technologies Lab, Csc, Inaoe
</dc:publisher>
<dc:subject>Presidente Ortiz Rubio, selección de candidato, PRI,
Partido Socialista Fronterizo, PNR, Poncho Martínez Domínguez,
fuerza caciquil, Supuso Madrazo, Polo Sánchez Celis, Javier
Romero, derrota automática, Madrazo, partido callista, PPS de
Lombardo, desaparición de poder, entrega final, venia central,
Portes Gil, candidato, poca política
</dc:subject>
<dc:identifier>010698-1Lunes</dc:identifier>
<dc:relation>http://ccc.inaoep.mx/~mapco/acres/n94/020598Sabado.
xhtml </dc:relation>
<dc:relation>http://ccc.inaoep.mx/~mapco/acres/n94/050698-
1Viernes.xhtml </dc:relation>
<dc:relation>http://ccc.inaoep.mx/~mapco/acres/n94/150598-
1Viernes.xhtml </dc:relation>
<dc:relation>http://ccc.inaoep.mx/~mapco/acres/n94/180698-
1Jueves.xhtml </dc:relation>
<dc:relation>http://ccc.inaoep.mx/~mapco/acres/n94/200698Sabado.
xhtml </dc:relation>
<dc:relation>http://ccc.inaoep.mx/~mapco/acres/n4/280698Domingo.
xhtml </dc:relation>
<dc:relation>http://ccc.inaoep.mx/~mapco/acres/n94/300598-
1Sabado.xhtml </dc:relation>
<dc:relation>http://ccc.inaoep.mx/~mapco/acres/news94/300698Mart
es.xhtml </dc:relation>
<dc:format>xhtml</dc:format>
```

```
<dc:date>06-01-1998</dc:date>
<dc:language>es</dc:language>
</rdf:Description> </rdf:RDF>
```

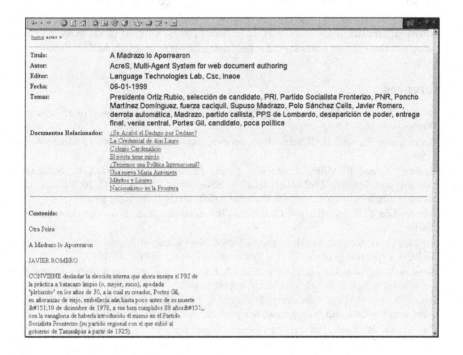

Fig. 2. A sample page generated by the MAS

5   Conclusions and Future Work

We have proposed a multi-agent system that partially automates the generation of semantic descriptions for web resources, considering the identification of language, subject, date and the inter-document relations, as well as the generation of two kind of outputs, one suited for machine processing, and other for human reading and browsing.

We performed experiments with collections of different sizes and characteristics. Among the conclusions obtained from these experiments are the following:

- Representing the documents by a set of topics instead of a set of keywords speeds up document processing, reduces the number of relations among documents, and improves semantics of subject and relation metadata.
- Applying a topic weight scheme that considers their inverse frequency causes the identification of several relations with no semantic meaning since favours terms in relatively few documents, reducing considerably the influence of central topics.
- In contrast, using a criterion based on the average similarity for identifying relations among documents allows processing both homogeneous and heterogeneous document collections.

As future work we plan to: (1) apply shallow NLP techniques such as POS tagging to improve document topics identification, (2) propose an extension to the Dublin Core template in order to capture the semantics of the inter-document relations, and (3) explore some other criteria for establishing inter-document relations.

Acknowledgements. This work was done under partial support of CONACYT, SNI-Mexico, and the Human Language Technologies Laboratory of INAOE.

References

1. Allan J. Automatic Hypertext Link Typing. *Proc. of ACM Conference of Hypertext 96*, Washington, D.C, 1996.
2. Baeza-Yates R., and B. Ribeiro-Neto. *Modern Information Retrieval*, Addison-Wesley, 1999.
3. Beckett D., and E. Miller. *Expressing Simple Dublin Core in RDF/XML*, Institute for Learning and Research Technology (ILRT) University of Bristol; W3C, 2002-07-31. URL: http://dublincore.org/documents/2002/07/31/dcmes-xml.
4. Berners-Lee T., J. Hendler and O. Lassila. The Semantic Web, *Scientific American*, May 2001.
5. Buckley C., A. Singhal, M. Mitra and G. Salton. New Retrieval Approaches using SMART: TREC 4. *Proceedings of the 3rd Text Retrieval Conference (TREC-4)*, 1995.
6. Busseta P., R. Rönnquist, A. Hodgson, and A. Lucas. *Jack Intelligent Agents – Components for Intelligent Agents in Java*, Technical Report 1, 1999.
7. Egnor D., and R. Lord. Structured Information Retrieval using XML, *ACM SIGIR 2000 Workshop On XML and Information Retrieval*, Athens, Greece, July 2000.
8. Gay L., and W. Croft. Interpreting Nominal Compounds for Information Retrieval. *Information Processing and Management* 26(1): 21–38, 1990.
9. Golovchinsky G. What the Query Told the Link: The Integration of Hypertext and Information Retrieval. *Proc. 8th ACM Conference on Hypertext*, 1997.
10. Kaindl H., and S. Kramer. Semiautomatic Generation of Glossary Links: A practical solution. *Proceedings of the tenth ACM Conference on Hypertext and Hypermedia*, Darmstadt, Germany, 1999.
11. Kobayashi M., and K. Takeda. Information Retrieval on the Web. *ACM Computing Surveys*, Vol. 32, No. 2, p. 144–173, June 2000.
12. Strzalkowski T., F. Lin, J. Perez-Carballo and J. Wang. Building Effective Queries in Natural language Information Retrieval. *Proceedings of the 5th Applied Natural Language Conference ANLP-97*, Washington D.C., USA, 1997.

On the Vague Modelling of Web Page Characteristics Regarding Usability

Elena García Barriocanal[1], Miguel A. Sicilia Urbán[2], and J. Antonio Gutiérrez[1]

[1] Computer Science Department. Polytechnic School
University of Alcalá. Ctra. Barcelona km. 33.6
28871. Alcalá de Henares, Madrid. Spain
{elena.garciab,jantonio.gutierrez}@uah.es

[2] Computer Science Department. Polytechnic School
Carlos III University. Avd. de la Universidad, 30
28911. Leganés, Madrid. Spain
msicilia@inf.uc3m.es

Abstract. Vagueness is an inherent property of man-machine systems associated with some perceptual and cognitive characteristics of human information processing, as pointed out by Karwowski and other researchers. More concretely, some perceivable characteristics of interface designs, including sizes and quantities, are usually perceived by humans as vague categories that result in imprecise guidelines for interface usability. In this paper, we describe how such categories – in the specific case of the Web – can be modelled as fuzzy sets by using conventional membership function elicitation procedures, using Web page length and number of links as case studies. The resulting fuzzy sets can then be used for automated usability analysis processes using fuzzy rules to formalize vague guidelines.

Keywords: fuzzy sets, automated usability analysis, membership function elicitation

1 Introduction

Usability is a multi-faceted concept that encompasses several attributes of human interaction with software systems, in many cases summarized in three interdependent aspects named efficiency, effectiveness and satisfaction [8]. In consequence, human cognitive and perceptual abilities are relevant to interface design [24]. As described in [14], fuzziness is an inherent characteristic of human-machine systems and can not be overlooked in human information processing models and applications. Fuzzy set theory and related imperfect information handling mathematical frameworks [13] have already been applied to the field of human computer interaction [14]. Concrete applications include the fuzzy modelling of GOMS selection rules [15], the use of fuzzy set to model usability scores in usability evaluation [5], the extraction of personality indicators from textual contents and images [23] and the use of fuzzy aggregation operators in the aggregation of heuristic usability evaluation questionnaires [9].

E. Menasalvas et al. (Eds.): AWIC 2003, LNAI 2663, pp. 199–207, 2003.

In the specific context of usability evaluation [6], guidelines and patterns often refer to the *structure* of the design of the software system, i.e. to the perceivable features of the interface. Examples – for the specific case of Web systems [21]– are *sizes* (of sections, headers, navigation bars and the like), *quantities* (of links, images) and *navigational patterns* (depth of hierarchies, frames). Many of these kinds of guidelines, when formulated by humans, are vague and intended to be approximate orientations. For example, in [3], it is said that "headers should not take more than 25% of a letter size page" or "pages should not be overcrowded with links". The first guideline is clearly an arbitrary selection of a limit for a blurred size-relation, and the second one makes reference to a vague amount of links per page. The question that follows from the just described observations is: how can we make machines work with these vague categories?. The solution for the representation of many of these guidelines is that of characterizing the concepts that underlie them mathematically, and fuzzy set theory is a candidate for that purpose.

In this paper, an approach based on fuzzy sets for *automated usability analysis* (according to the definition in [12]) of Web sites is illustrated by focusing on two quantitative attributes of Web pages: page length and number of links, which are known to affect design quality and usability [11]. Concretely, it is described how existing membership function elicitation techniques [16] can be applied to the fuzzy characterization of these attributes, and how the resulting fuzzy sets, combined with fuzzy rules, can be used to develop automated usability analyzers.

The rest of this paper is structured as follows. In Sect. 2, the experimental design, procedure and results of the membership function elicitation is described. Section 3 briefly describes the design of a Web page analyzer based on vague page attribute characterizations. Finally, conclusions and future research directions are provided in Sect. 4.

2   Membership Function Elicitation

A variety of methods for the elicitation of membership functions have been described in the literature [16]. The focus of our study are two highly specific psychological categories with blurred edges, that must be characterized by data analysis on subjective perceptions. The selection of the elicitation technique was driven by a first phase of examination of the problem, which allowed for the establishment of the objectives and assumptions about the interpretation of membership values:

- The expected result was the obtention of a number of fuzzy sets representing granulated page lengths (short pages, medium pages, long pages and the like) and granulated quantities of links per page (few # of links, excessive # of links and the like).
- The presence of interpersonal disagreements in assessing what is a long page and what is a link overcrowded leaded us to assume that fuzziness in these constructions is *subjective* and determined in part by device limitations.

As a consequence, we have adopted a *similarity* interpretation of membership (opposed to other views like *likelihood* or *random set* as described in [2]). In this view, the membership value $\mu_A(x)$ represents "the distance of x from a prototypical element y which fully belonging to A $(\mu_A(y) = 1)$". Thus, users rate the belonging of a page into a concrete set by estimating a "distance" from an ideal, imagined prototypical instance which would be classified as crisply belonging to the given set. Although we have not selected concrete prototypes for the attributes being measured, they are easily determined by Web users (e.g. specific clearly "long" and "link overcrowded" pages are easily determined by them).

From the available techniques, we have selected two that are coherent with the interpretation adopted:

- First, the membership functions are directly determined by *membership exemplification* [2].
- And second, a variant of the *polling* technique [10] was used to validate the results obtained by membership function exemplification.

The details of the case building, the measurement procedure and its results are described in the rest of this section. It should be noted that the aim of the study was not that of achieving statistical significance, but to demonstrate the feasibility of an empirical approach.

2.1   Experiment Design

The experiment required a first step for the obtention of an appropriate Web page database, and after that, the procedure for the obtention of vague measures was defined, as described in this subsection.

Obtention of Page Sample Database. As a matter of fact, the majority of common Web users today use Microsoft Internet Explorer (IE) to navigate the Web[1], and common screen resolutions are over 800x600 pixels. Due to these statistical measures, we have limited our study to the latest stable version of IE on that resolution[2].

Two Web page URL sets were built, containing 50 pages each. They were obtained automatically from `Google`[3] by a program in the `Java` language, and stored in a Microsoft `Access` database. Pages were selected randomly from the most relevant results obtained from taking a random sample of query strings from the most used in the year 2002[4]. An approximately distribution of number

---

[1] According to OneStat.com metrics published December 2002, its share was about 95% of the market share

[2] Nonetheless, the experiments could be extended in the future to other kinds of configurations according to more detailed browser and screen data.

[3] One of the most used search engines, which provides programmable interfaces: [http://www.google.com/apis/]

[4] Available at [http://www.google.com/press/zeitgeist2002.html]

of links an page length was obtained by manually filtering the larger set of pages obtained from `Google`.

After that, the size in pixels and number of links of the pages were obtained. The number of links was estimated by simply counting `href` tags [5]. Page length required a more elaborate procedure, since the actual length is dependant of the rendering of the page in the browser. Due to this fact, we developed a Windows program using the `WebBrowser` control in `VisualBasic.NET` – contained in the `SHDOCVW.DLL` library– which provides the same rendering engine than the one used directly by IE. The program load the collected locators, and measure its size on a default IE configuration in pixels. Technically, this is accomplished by using the `IHTMLElement2` interface in the `MSHTML.DLL` library to address the body of the document and asking for the property `scrollHeight`.

Procedure. The experiment take place on a Internet connected computer with the configuration mentioned above. Participants were given two list of clickable URLs to visit the corresponding pages. The first one was sorted in ascending order by length, and the second was sorted by number of links in the page. They were asked to put a grade in the $[0..100]$ interval (the same scale used by Zysno in [25]) to the compatibility of each page with the linguistic labels in the label sets:

$$LS_{page-length} = \{very - short, short, medium, long, very - long\} \quad (1)$$

$$LS_{\#-links}\{very - few, few, acceptable, excessive, crowded\} \quad (2)$$

Both label sets are considered to be ordered and to cover the whole semantic domain of the concept being measured. The usability-related interpretation of the terms was formulated by questions of the form "do you think this page is X?" and "do you think that there are X links in this page?". The number of labels suffices the purposes of the study, since guidelines and texts on usability rarely use linguistic hedges related to the concepts under study.

The evaluator observed them in the process of membership grade exemplification, taking notes on significant behavior. In our experimental design we have also taken into account Rosch observation about the speed of processing [22], according to which humans categorize faster the objects that are more prototypical, i.e. those perceived more clearly as typical cases of the category. Concretely, pairs [page, fuzzy set] that were found difficult to exemplify by participants were recorded.

2.2 Results and Discussion

The procedure was carried out with ten adult subjects. Only experienced Web users were included. The mean of the membership grade examples obtained was used to build discrete fuzzy sets with the pages ranked as domain. From

---

[5] Although this method is not completely accurate, due to "hidden" dynamically estimated links, it suffices for the purposes of this study.

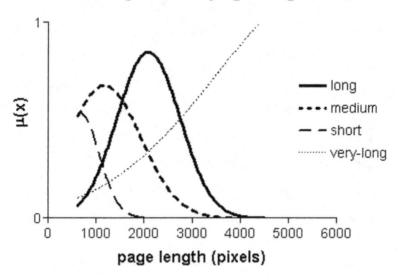

Fig. 1. Non-normalizing membership functions to describe page length.

them, a function for the final, continuous fuzzy sets were estimated by nonlinear regression.

Figure 1 shows the (non-normalized) resulting membership functions that describe page length.

The "very-short" label was fitted to a polinomial function. It has been omitted from the analysis since it resulted in a very sharp function around the minimum page lengths that can be found, of about 600 pixels, which makes it seldom useful for usability analysis. The rest of the labels were fitted using a Gaussian model. It should be noted that pages begin to be considered as rather "long" for values above two thousands pixels length, which in practice corresponds to more than three 800x600 areas. Since most pages used for the study were home pages, this result is mainly consistent with existing approximate guidelines like [17]. For example, if we take the following guideline: "short pages, those containing *one or two* screens of text, work well for the home page and menu pages when users are scanning for link choices"[6]. Then, our observations would extend the number of "tolerable" screens at least to three. Another interesting fact is the large degree of overlap between long and very long pages, reflecting diverse user's preferences.

---

[6] [http://usability.gov/guidelines/page_length.html]

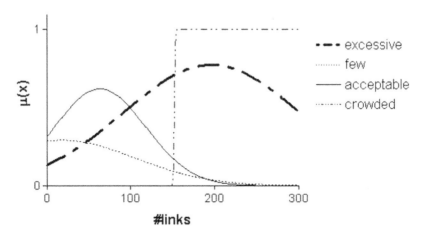

Fig. 2. Non-normalizing membership functions to describe quantity of links.

Figure 2 shows the non-normalized resulting membership functions that describe quantities of links. The "very-few" label has been omitted since its number of non-zero points was non significant.

A sigmoid function was used to model the "crowded" concept, showing a sharp boundary around the one hundred and a half amount of links. The observations of the experiments leaded us to conclude that this function is not appropriate to model the concept due to two main reasons: users took longer to make their assessments about this category, and many comments about its dependency on page-length were raised. Future studies should take the links–page length ratio as the underlying measure instead.

3 Use of the Vague Concepts in Automated Usability Analysis

Once the fuzzy sets that represent the measures are determined, they can be used to develop software that automatically diagnoses usability problems associated with them. To do so, rules encoding specific uses of usability *heuristics* [19] are combined with the fuzzy sets describing the vague measures. We have used the *Fuzzy Java Toolkit*[7] to implement some of them in a simple usability analysis prototype.

For example, a (hypothetical) rule about page length can be stated as follows:

---

[7] [http://www.iit.nrc.ca/IR_public/fuzzy/fuzzyJToolkit.html]

```
if page is long and page is homepage then
                      reading-efficiency is low
```

```
if page is link-crowded then
                 reading-efficiency is very low
```

These kinds of rules can be subsequently used to fire other rules that relate the concrete measures with more abstract and generic usability attributes [24]. For example, reading-efficiency contributes to the general efficiency attribute, which can be used to report or suggest corrective actions.

```
if reading-efficiency is low then
                      efficiency is low
if efficiency is low then
        <<take the appropriate corrective or reporting action>>
```

Of course, the knowledge encoded in the formulation of the rules must come from usability experts or other empirical sources like [11].

4   Conclusions and Future Work

Existing membership elicitation techniques can be used for the measurement of linguistic values for Web page characteristics that are known to have influence in the usability of interfaces. As a case study, we have carried out an experiment to determine a number of fuzzy sets regarding Web page length and amount of links per page. It has been also described how these sets can be combined with fuzzy rules to come up with automated usability analysis tools.

Future studies should address a more rich repertory of usability-related quantifiable Web site attributes [11], and also more ambitious elicitation studies for membership functions. In addition, *diachronic* studies are worth being carried out, since some evidence has been found about the evolution of the user's attitudes, like willingness to scroll [20], which affects page length guidelines.

The experimental design followed provides a overall estimation of the studied parameters, but further stratification of the population would be desirable due to the highly heterogeneous nature of Web users. Particularly, age (due to the different needs of elderly or disabled people, see, for example [7,18]) and navigation expertise (see, for example [1]) are good candidates for future studies. In addition, the *reverse rating* elicitation method could be used as an alternative method or for the sake of verifying results obtained with other techniques [4], if only experienced Web users are considered. This method consists essentially in asking subjects to identify known Web pages that have a specific degree of membership in the concept being determined, so that expert users would be able to remember prototypical cases easily. In addition, the type of the pages should also be considered, since guidelines differ depending on it, e.g. home pages are "allowed" to be longer than normal reading pages [17], and the interaction between attributes should also be considered, for example, the #-links–page length ratio.

References

1. Benyon, D.: Adaptive systems: a solution to usability problems. User Modeling and User-Adapted Interaction 3 (1993):65–87
2. Bilgiç, T. and Türksen, T.: Measurement of Membership Functions: Theoretical and Empirical Work. In: D. Dubois and H. Prade (eds.) Handbook of Fuzzy Sets and Systems Vol. 1, Chapter+3, Fundamentals of Fuzzy Sets, Kluwer (1999):195–232
3. Borges, J.A., Morales, I. and Rodríguez, N.J.: Guidelines for designing usable World Wide Web pages. In: Proceedings of the ACM Conference on Human factors in computing systems (1996):277–278
4. Chameau, J.L. and Santamarina, J.C.: Membership Functions I: Comparing Methods of Measurement, International Journal of Approximate Reasoning 1 (1987):287–301
5. Chang, E., Dillon, T.S., Cook, D.: Measurement of Usability of Software Using a Fuzzy Systems Approach. In: Proceedings of the 8th International Conference on Software Engineering and Knowledge Engineering, SEKE '96 (1996): 69–76
6. Dumas, J S. and Redish, J C.: A practical guide to usability testing. Intellect (2000)
7. Ellis, R. D. and Kurniawan, S. H.: Increasing the usability of Online information for older users: A case study in participatory design. International Journal of Human-Computer Interaction, 12(2) (2000):263–276
8. Frøkjær, E., Hertzum, M. and Hornbæk, K.: Measuring Usability: are effectiveness, efficiency and satisfaction really correlated?. In: Proc. of Human Factors in Computing Systems (2000):345–352
9. García, E., Sicilia, M.A., Hilera, J.R., Gutierrez, J.A.: Computer-Aided Usability Evaluation: A Questionnaire Case Study. In: Advances in Human Computer Interaction. Typorama (2001) 85–91
10. Hersh, H.M. and Caramazza, A.: A fuzzy set approach to modifiers and vagueness in natural language. Journal Experimental Psychology, 105(3) (1976):254–276
11. Ivory, M.Y. and Hearst, M.A.: Improving Web Site Design. IEEE Internet Computing, Special Issue on Usability and the World Wide Web 6(2), March/April (2002): 56–63
12. Ivory, M.Y. and Hearst, M.A.: The State of the Art in Automated Usability Evaluation of User Interfaces. ACM Computing Surveys, 33(4) (2001):1–47
13. Klir, G.J. and Wiermann, M.J.: Uncertainty-Based Information. Elements of Generalized Information Theory. Physica-Verlag, Heidelberg (1998)
14. Karwowski, W. and Mital, A. (editors): Applications of Fuzzy Set Theory in Human Factors, Elsevier Science Publishers, Amsterdam (1986)
15. Karwowski, W., Kosiba, E., Benabdallah, S. and Salvendy, G.: A framework for development of fuzzy GOMS model for human-computer interaction. International Journal of Human-Computer Interaction 2(4) (1990):287–305
16. Krishnapuram, R.: Membership Function Elicitation. In: E. Ruspini, P. Bonissone and W. Pedrycz (editors): Handbook of Fuzzy Computation, Institute of Physics Publishing (1998):B3.2:1–11
17. Lynch, P.J. and Horton, S.: Web Style Guide: Basic Design Principles for creating Web Sites, Yale University Press (1999)
18. Meyer, B., Sit, R.A., Spaulding, V.A., Mead, S.E., Walker, N.: Age Group Differences in World Wide Web Navigation. In: Proceedings of the ACM Conference on Human Factors in Computing Systems (1997)

19. Nielsen, J.: Heuristic evaluation. In Nielsen, J., and Mack, R.L. (eds.): Usability Inspection Methods, John Wiley and Sons, New York (1994):25–61
20. Nielsen, J.: Changes in Web Usability Since 1994. Alertbox for December 1 (1997), available at http://www.useit.com/alertbox/9712a.html
21. Nielsen, J.: Designing Web Usability: The Practice of Simplicity. New Riders (1999)
22. Rosch, E.: Principles of categorization. In Rosch, E. and Lloyd, B. (Eds.) Cognition and Categorization. Hillsdale, NJ, Lawrence Erlbaum Associates (1978)
23. Sanchez, E. and Santini, J.A.: Fuzzy Logic and the Internet: a Fuzzy Web Site Evaluator. In: Proceedings of the North American Fuzzy Information Processing Society (NAFIPS'02) (2002):344–347
24. Van Welie, M., van der Veer, G.C. and Eliëns, A. (1999), Breaking down usability. In: Proc. of Interact'99 (1999):613–620
25. Zysno, P.: Modeling membership functions. In Rieger (ed.): Empirical Semantics I, Vol. 1 of Quantitative Semantics, vol. 12, Studienverlag Brockmeyer, Bochum (1981): 350-375

Semantic Interoperability Based on Ontology Mapping in Distributed Collaborative Design Environment

Jingyi Zhang[1], Shensheng Zhang[1], Chun Chen[1], and Bo Wang[1]

[1] Department of Computer Science and Engineering, Shanghai Jiaotong University
Shanghai 200030,China
zhang-jy@cs.situ.edu.cn

Abstract. With the increasing of global competition, it is important to make the product design process as fast and efficient as possible. One way to achieve improvements in efficiency and innovation is through better collaboration of designers working on a common design task and interacting in the design process, so that unnecessary backtracking and delays are avoided. In an integrated and concurrent design environment, designers interact and reach agreement by sharing common information. But it is not an easy task due to the heterogeneity of information resources. We have to solve semantic interoperability first in order to implement "cooperation" between different information systems. There are many legacy systems based on conflicting ontologies which hinder the communications among them and become the obstacle of software reuse and system interoperability. By analyzing relations between agents and ontologies, a semantic interoperability algorithm based on ontology mapping is proposed in the paper. And the DCDP framework presented here provides a software architecture for synchronous groupware applications to deal with heterogeneity. The framework's main characteristic is data centricity. The users collaborate on and exchange data, and the data is dynamically transformed to adapt to the particular computing platform.

Keywords: Interoperability; heterogeneous application; Collaborative design; Information exchange; Ontology;

1 Introduction

With the increasing of global competition, it is important to make the product design process as fast and efficient as possible. One way to achieve improvements in efficiency and innovation is through better collaboration of designers working on a common design task and interacting in the design process, so that unnecessary backtracking and delays are avoided. In an integrated and concurrent design environment, designers interact and reach agreement by sharing common information [1]. In addition, information system technology has long expectation to provide communication channel that seamlessly enable members of a team to exchange data and information across physical and temporal boundaries. As the networks (i.e., Internet and Intranet)

E. Menasalvas et al. (Eds.): AWIC 2003, LNAI 2663, pp. 208–217, 2003.

proliferate all over the world, it is inevitable to move some product data information and design activities into the shared space to support cooperative design in distributed and heterogeneous computing environments. It is important to obtain the agility for improving the competitiveness of firms.

However, product data have complex semantics and thus are not properly exchanged by different application programs [2]. The obstacle is the fact that data is tightly bound to the applications that create/use the data, which means that moving data between applications requires a conversion or translation process. Even though some neutral formats of product data have been developed by standard organizations, translating them among various application programs still needs the comprehensive understanding of the complex semantics. Recently, it is widely recognized that capturing more knowledge is the next step to overcome the current difficulties on sharing product data [3], especially in the collaborative environment.

In the collaborative design environment, the knowledge we consider is different from that used by most conventional knowledge-based systems that operate based on if-then rules and inference engines [4]. DCDP (Distributed Collaborative Design Platform) is a replicated system that realized on a C/S architecture based on operation information sharing. Since the participants in the collaborative design environment come from different places and research fields, so it is possible that they use different CAD design tools (CAD software). After the collaboration begins, users or application programs will exchange and access the enormous amount of heterogeneous information issued by one of participants. So, it becomes essential to have proper expression and management mechanism to deal with the information. This requirement has brought about active research on various new types of knowledge representation, some of which includes ontology, metadata, and agents [5–7]. On the base of research work mentioned above, we present a semantic interoperability algorithm based on ontology mapping to facilitate seamless sharing of product data among various application programs in DCDP.

The organization of this paper is as follows. Section 2 reviews previous work on knowledge representation and conversion. Section 3 introduces the architecture of the collaborative design platform-DCDP. Section 4 analyzes the relationship between agents and their ontologies, then the algorithm is presented to solve the reusage and communication among heterogeneous applications. Finally, Sect. 5 concludes the paper and discusses some future work.

2 Related Work

An important aspect of heterogeneity is interoperability between different groupware systems. Dewan and Sharma [8] focus on interoperating group systems with different policies (concurrency control, coupling) and architectures (centralized vs. replicated), but do not consider semantic consistency issues due to computing platform heterogeneities.

A recent approach to collaboration in heterogeneous computing environments is the CMU Pebbles project [9]. Pebbles is focused on single-display groupware, with the team being in a single meeting room. Multiple handheld personal digital assistants (PDAs) provide simultaneous input (mouse, keyboard) to a single workstation. PDAs are not treated as equal partners in the collaboration, which belies the need for heterogeneous data representation.

In addition, the integration of disparate and heterogeneous information systems has been pursued since the recognition that two different systems are using some of the same information in order to share data and save time [10]. Approaches that have been developed include the following [11–13].

- Point-to-point translators that convert data bound to one system into the data format of a target system.
- A shared database that is used by multiple applications.
- Product Data Exchange (PDE) standards that specify a neutral, application-independent data structure used to convey data between applications (and translators written to/from the PDE standard).
- Product Data Management (PDM) and Enterprise Resource Planning (ERP) applications that "throw a net" over the applications within an enterprise and route, control, and constrain data that moves between individuals and/or applications.
- The ubiquity of the Internet breaks spatial and temporal barriers and provides the opportunity for users to access data anywhere, anytime. Furthermore, the rapid rise in popularity of the Extensible Markup Language (XML) provides a platform independent and web-friendly data structuring syntax for the representation and exchange of data [14].

However, these methods cannot provide ideal scheme for collaborative design due to three reasons follows:

(1) The complexity of application interoperability coupled with the huge variety of platform and implementation.

(2) The exchange of bits does not equate to the exchange of meaning.

(3) The ever-changing requirements on system use make point solution brittle and short-lived.

Since we want to do our best to reach the goal that all of the participants with different specialized background can communicate and exchange their intention and knowledge freely in our heterogeneous design environment, so how to represent and exchange varieties of data is a crucial problem.

3   The Architecture of the Collaborative Design Platform

DCDP is a medium rather than an application-an important goal of this work is to enable easy sharing of third-party single-user CAD applications, since the majority of applications continue to be developed for a single user. DCDP is a CSCD (Computer Supported Cooperative Design) platform based on operation information sharing. It extends an exiting single-location CAD system to a multi-location CAD application so that multiple geographically dispersed designers can work together on three-dimensional CAD-geometry coediting and CAD-related tasks collaboratively and dynamically. Each user runs a copy of the collaboration client, and each client contains a copy of the CAD application that is to be collaborated upon. All copies of replicated application are kept in synchrony and activities occurring on any one of them are reflected on the other copies. Sharing data and collaborative information is located on server; CAD application and local configuration information is located on client. By using this structure, the system will not only take advantage of free configuration, but also make the data sharing and translating easy. The architecture is shown as Fig. 1.

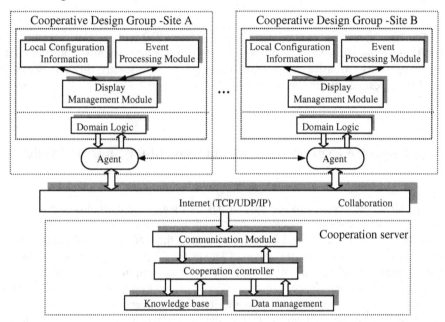

Fig. 1. The architecture of DCDP

The DCDP is organized into a three-layer architecture, which comprises *Display* layer, *Application* or *Domain Logic* layer, and *Storage* layer. The Display layer is virtually free of application logic and deals with visualizing the domain data and accepting user inputs. The Domain layer deals with the semantics of tasks and rules. The Display layer and Domain layer belong to CAD application seemingly, but the events from Display layer have been intercepted and translated before they get executed in the Domain to support event ordering, floor control, and concurrency control algorithms. The key user activity in graphical user interfaces is direct manipulation of screen object. According to the *Domain Logic*, the corresponding agent will be generated to encapsulate these manipulations in the form of CommandEvents, which are the targets other clients interact with the collaboration bus (shown in Fig. 2). After the *Cooperation Server* monitors that there are events on the bus, it picks them off and starts up the translation mechanism based on supporting of the *Knowledge base* and *Data management*, which is called Storage layer.

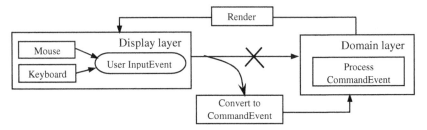

Fig. 2. Event interception in DCDP

The key for interoperability and adaptation in DCDP is data-centric approach to application sharing, where conferees share the same or semantically equivalent data. The data can be transformed and/or visualized in significantly different ways, as needed or desired, but the users should still be able to collaborate in a meaningful fashion.

4   Knowledge Expression and Management for Sharing Product Data

As we all know, every software system has its own concept architecture named as ontology, which consists of objects, their relations and the description of transaction processing. In information technology, ontology is the working model of entities and interactions in some particular domain of knowledge or practices. We use ontology as the meaning and relationship of domain knowledge to improve the semantic conversion capability among heterogeneous systems. Different domain agents may communicate with the help of services provided by special agents such as "mediator" or "facilitator". But the difficulties are that the conversion is not based on one-to-one mechanism and legacy systems (CAD systems) usually do not show their concept structure clearly, so this make the "mediator" does not know what content he can translate.

In this section, we first analyze the relationship between agents and their ontology, and then a software structure based on conversion between them is presented to realize the communication and reusage of legacy systems. In this structure, we express the ontology definitely and introduce a set of conversion rules to solve the semantic conflict among multi-ontologies. At last a semantic interoperability algorithm based on ontology mapping among heterogeneous applications is presented.

4.1   Ontology and Field Knowledge

A distributed heterogeneous software system may include many agents, and each agent can be divided into ontology, domain knowledge and knowledge exertion. Ontology is the base of the domain knowledge representation. All of the knowledge about the intension, the truth, the ability and the rules, et al, of the agent should obey its ontology. The information communication between the agent and the outside world will also be described by its ontology. Most of the software system will not declare its ontology definitely (the ontology always hide in the program), and some object-oriented systems only declare part of its ontology. To abstract the ontology from the agent's domain knowledge is an important step to realize the semantic exchange among different agents [15].

The communication between two agents should obey certain communication language ontology. This kind of ontology can provide basic conversation behavior, and establish channels to express the domain sentence. From the perspective of agent communication, agent ontology can be divided into three layers, that is *Domain ontology, Knowledge description language ontology,* and *Knowledge query language ontology.* The first contains domain objects, relations and corresponding vocabulary, the second specifies how to describe the propositions and their combination, such as KIF, and the third specifies the basic query conversation behavior, such as KQML. Agent Communication Language (ACL) is just constituted based on this structure.

4. 2   Framework of Software Communication Based on Multi-ontology

In order to realize the communication among legacy systems (CAD systems), the first problem we should solve is that the conversion among legacy system's ontologies. Therefore, the ontology hide in the legacy system should be expressed first.

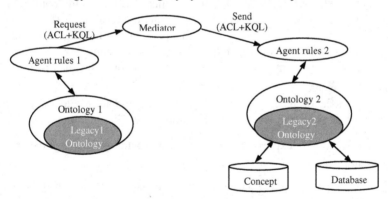

Fig. 3. The architecture of the ontology conversion mechanism

The agent ontology includes the object classes, the class attributes and constraints, the class methods and the relationships, et al. The class methods are related with the legacy system functions, and the function parameters are corresponding with the object classes, the class attributes and inter-class relationships. When the function is executed, corresponding operations can be gotten according to the relationship between the legacy system and the classes and attributes in the ontology. The logic architecture based on mediator layer has shown in Fig.3.

The mediator layer, which includes the **mediator agent**, the **directory service agent** and the **ontology conversion agent**, performs such works as inter-ontologies conversion, sending request, and choosing appropriate information agents according to the request from the client. Moreover, the mediator agent takes charge of the generation, execution and ceasing of the client process. The directory service agent registers the capability of every information service agent and look for the address according to the request. The ontology conversion performs the translation between agent ontology and public ontology. The architecture of our ontology conversion mechanism has shown in Fig. 4.

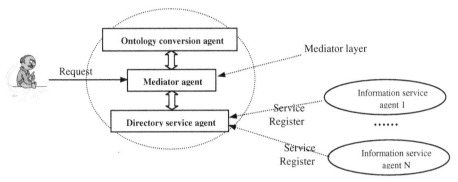

Fig. 4. The function view of Mediator layer

In our system, we use the first order predicate to express the information (request and result, et al.) passed among different agents, and realize the conversion among ontologies through the conversion rules based on predicate logic. The semantic interoperability algorithm based on ontology mapping among heterogeneous applications is given below, which follows the request execution procedure.

(1) Client A defines its request R_1 according to its ontology, and then sends R_1 to the mediator agent.

(2) The mediator agent generates a process P automatically to record the state of R_1, and sends R_1 to the ontology conversion agent. The ontology conversion agent translates R_1 into R_1' expressed with the mediator ontology language then returns it to the mediator agent.

(3) The mediator agent sends the translated request R_1' to the directory service agent. The latter locates the information service agents by matching the register information to the request content, then returns the agents' names and addresses to the mediator agent.

(4) The mediator agent records the names and addresses in the process P, and decomposes the mediator ontology request R_1' into $R_{11}', R_{12}' \dots R_{1m}'$ expressed by the ontology languages of the information service agents, then sends them to these agents respectively.

(5) After receives the request, the information service agents will find the solution automatically, then returns the result to the mediator agent.

(6) The mediator agent passes the result to the ontology conversion agent. After being translated, the result is sent by the mediator agent to the client A, then the process P terminates.

The content passed among agents to communicate is a sentence contains a kind of semantic meanings. Since the structure and granularity differences exist among the ontologies, the semantic conversion often is not based on one-to-one mechanism. That is, one semantic sentence used in an ontology may equal to several sentences in another ontology. Sometimes, the translation from an ontology to another is not based on one-to-one relationship, so the request can be widened or narrowed by adding or subtracting conjunction form and disjunction form respectively.

4.3 Heterogeneity Representation Using XML

In addition, we use XML to express sentences for interoperability the heterogeneous domains.

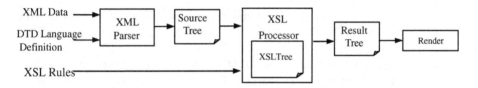

Fig. 5. A typical XML document rendering process using a DOM parser

Figure 5 illustrates the processing of the XML/XSL messages. The source is the representation of the parsed XML source document. All XML documents can be represented as trees. The XSL processor starts with the source tree and processes it by finding the template in the style sheet that describes how that element should be mapped. The pattern that most closely matches this particular source node is applied and that rule is used to generate a new result node. The tree that is created in this process is called the result tree. The result tree is in a format readily understood by the displaying application. The XSL document maps elements in the XML document (source tree) to nodes in the result tree such that the Render knows how to render them. Parsing the common XML file and the local XSL file generates the ideal result at a particular user's machine.

We define the format for the message as ASCII text using XML notation. This allows structured definition of the events, which in turn yields the following:

- The change notification is more meaningful, as the change information includes the type of change taking place as well as the data being manipulated.
- The XSL rules can be used to transform the CommandEvent so that it applied to the remote domain.

The events are communicated over the DCDP collaboration bus to the peers as XML fragments.

```
<COMMAND_EVENT USER_ID="John"
TYPE="set Property" TARGET_ID="Part03">
      NAME="Length" VALUE="30"
</COMMAND_EVENT>
```

5 Conclusions

The proliferation of network and collaboration commerce raises the need for applications that are adaptable to heterogeneous computing and communication environments and the contexts in which they are used. To realize information sharing and interoperability between heterogeneous applications, the first problem to be solved is the conversion between their ontologies. In order reach this goal, we need:

(1) Abstract the ontology hidden in the legacy system, and express it definitely;
(2) Constitute effective mediator ontology according to domain knowledge;
(3) A set of conversion rules to solve the semantic conflict among multi-ontologies.

The semantic interoperability algorithm based on ontology mapping presented in this paper provides an effective way to realize reusage and integration of legacy systems.

We have developed a framework (DCDP) based on this working mechanism to help users or application systems sharing information via network in a collaborative design environment that designers locate in distributed places. The DCDP framework solves the problem of information transformation to maintain a semantically consistent state across the shared applications. XML is used for information representation suitable for generic cross-domain transformations. This allows the interoperation of different application through translation, updates to the corresponding local model components and communicating the other parties in the session-hence heterogeneous collaboration.

References

1. N. Senin, N. Borland, David R. Wallace, "Distributed modeling of product design problems in a collaborative design environment", Technical Report. CAD Lab., Department of Mechanical Engineering, MIT. 1998.
2. M. Hardwick, D. Spooner, T. Rando, K.C. Morris, Sharing manufacturing information in virtual enterprises, Communications of the ACM 39(2)(1996) 46–54.
3. J. Liebowitz, Knowledge Management Handbook, CRC Press, NewYork, 1999.
4. Y. Chen, C. Liao, B. Prasad, A systematic approach of virtual enterprising through knowledge management techniques, Concurrent Engineering: Research and Applications, 6(3)(1998) 225–244.
5. N. Matta, O. Corby, B. Prasad, A generic library of knowledge components to manage conflicts in CE tasks, Concurrent Engineering: Research and Applications, 6 (4) (1998) 274–287.

6. D.E. O'Leary, Using AI in knowledge management: Knowledge bases and ontologies, IEEE Intelligent Systems,13 (3) (1998) 34–39.
7. O. Lassila, R. Swick, Resource Description Framework (RDF) model and syntax specification (W3C Recommendation),Available in
    `http://www.w3.org/TR/REC-rdfsyntax/`, 1999.
8. Dewan, P. ,and Sharma, An experiment in interoperating heterogeneous collaborative systems. *Proc. 6th European Conf. On Computer Supported Cooperative Work (ECSCW'99)* (Copenhagen, Denmark, Sep. 1999), Kluwer Acad. Publ. 371–390.
9. Myers, B. A., Stiel, H., and Gargiulo, R. Collaboration using multiple PDAs connected to a PC. *Proc. Conf. Computer-Supported Cooperative Work (CSCW'98)* (Seattle, WA, November 1998), ACM Press, 285–294
10. Renner, S.A., A.S. Rosenthal, and J.G. Scarano. Data Interoperability:Standardization or Mediation,. The MITRE organisation:
    `http://www.nml.org/resources/misc/metadata/proceedings/metadata/renner/.`
11. Mike Uschold & Michael Gruninger. Ontologies : Principles, Methods and Applications. Knowledge Engineering Review. Volume 11 Number 2, June 1996
12. Thomas R. Gruber. The role of common on tology in achieving sharable, reusable knowledge bases. In J. A. Allen, R. Fikes, and E. Sandewall, editors, Principles of Knowle dge Representation and Reasoning: Proceedings of the Second International Conference , pages 601–602, Cambridge, MA, 1991. Morgan Kaufmann.
13. Gio Wiederhold. Mediators in the architecture of future information systems. IEEE Computer. March 1992. v20: 38–49.
14. Bray T, Paoli J, Sperberg-McQueen CM. Extensible Markup Language (XML) 1.0 W3C Recommendation 10 February 1998.
15. Visser, P.R.S., D.M. Jones,T.J.M. Bench-Capon and M.J.R. Shave. An Analysis of Ontology Mismatches; Heterogeneity versus Interoperability. AAAI 1997 Spring Symposium on Ontological Engineering, Stanford University, California USA, pp 164–172.

The Use of Data Mining Techniques to Classify Styles and Types of Web-Based Information: Generation of Style Sheets Using Data Mining

Kathryn E.B. Thornton and Mark Carrington

Data Mining Group, Department of Computer Science
Durham University, Science Park, Durham City, Durham, UK
Tel: + 44 191 374 7017 Fax: + 44 191 374 7002

Abstract. In this paper we describe a tool, based upon Data Mining techniques, which can be used to classify information contained on web pages and hence generate style sheets (or XML and XSL)[1] for use in web page/site creation .

We show that by considering the information contained on a web page in terms of its position, nature, and type it was possible to classify the web sites investigated into ten classes. We also describe how, as a by-product of this work, we have produced a set of style sheets which can be used as a basis for web page/site design.

The implications of the use of the style sheets for web page/site design are discussed as well as the potential for the use of our tool in enabling companies and/or individuals to standardize their web site(s).

Keywords: knowledge based system, data mining.

1 Introduction

Since becoming `open to public use` in 1991,The World Wide Web (Web) has become very popular with the current number of documents available on the Web being estimated to be 620 million pages in 2001 with an expected growth of over 1000% by 2004 [1]. Despite the emergence of java[2] the majority of these pages are written HTML [2].

However, HTML does not provide a great deal of insight regarding *structure* of the page [2]. For example, a page might include a list of student's names and chosen courses. The name of the student might be formatted in bold and the rest of the information in the standard font, but by reading the HTML code this structure is not made explicit.

The lack of explicit knowledge regarding the structure results in low *maintainability* of a web page. If the formatting of the page needs to be changed for example the names need to be changed from being in bold to being a different font and colour, this can be a long and laborious task, with a large risk of making errors. A better

---

[1] Description of this is beyond the scope of this paper.
[2] It might be expected that the emergence of java might be mirrored by its use in the creation of web pages.

E. Menasalvas et al. (Eds.): AWIC 2003, LNAI 2663, pp. 218–229, 2003.

means of achieving rapid, and accurate, modifications would be to indicate in the document those sections of the text which contain the name of a student, and then be able to change the formatting of any such sections. This would ensure that the formatting of all names is consistent throughout the document.

This paper describes a tool which has been developed in order to alleviate the problem of web page/site maintainability. The first section of this paper describes possible means by which rapid, accurate, maintainability of the web pages could be obtained – followed by a description of recent tool developments for this purpose. This is followed by a brief introduction to Data Mining and the approach taken. Data Mining algorithms appropriate to the task are described along with a description of the tool and the algorithms which were used in providing the tool's engine. A discussion of the effectiveness of the tool at performing the conversion, conclusions which may be drawn from the work and future avenues for exploration then follow.

2   Potential Technical Solutions

Two possible technologies that appear to be capable of providing the required functionality are *Cascading Style Sheets (CSS)*, and the *eXtensible Markup Language (XML)* in combination with the *eXtensible Style Language (XSL)* [2].

In CSS, a named style can be defined that describes the formatting properties of any text to which it is applied. These can then be referred to from the HTML file by means of the name of the style. The formatting of all the sections to which it is applied can then be altered by changing the single definition of the style. Maintainability can be improved by reducing the amount of code that needs to be changed for a single style change, and by using meaningful names for the styles [3].

In XML, all but the general structure of the information is removed from the HTML file. The XML file then contains only the information content of the HTML file and none of the formatting information. All the formatting information is stored in a separate XSL file that defines a series of transformations which can be recursively applied to the XML document. In this way, the XML file can contain a section of text that is *marked up* as a student name, and the XSL file can contain a template that is applied to all student names and replaces them with all the necessary HTML formatting commands. This improves maintainability because it easy to target maintenance to a specific template to change the formatting, or to a section of the XML file to change the information. Maintainability is also greatly improved by the use of meaningful names for the templates and the tags used in the structure of the XML file [3]. Since XML does not define the semantics of any particular tag, any appropriate names can be used in the XML file to refer to the meaning of the enclosed data. Responsibility for the maintenance of the content, and formatting, of the pages can be effectively distributed within a company, so the most appropriate people can be left in charge of either the content, or the formatting, without interference.

A large problem contributing to the poor maintainability of web pages is that owners of web pages often do not understand the structure of the documents, which is necessary in order to maintain them properly. This often occurs because web pages are commonly written by contractors or students [4]. If documents could be converted to XML, the structure of the documents would become more evident. A *Document*

Type Definition (DTD) for the XML documents helps to document the structure of the XML used, making it more maintainable when the original author is not available. The use of a DTD will also make it possible to ensure that a modified XML document is syntactically correct [5].

The following section describes recent tool advances which have been made in this area.

3 Recent Tool Development

The tool predominantly used for creating styles from a web page is *HTML Tidy*[6]. However, conversion to use style sheets is only part of the tool's functionality - which is primarily orientated to correcting malformed HTML code within the page. The conversion to style sheets is therefore simplistic and the styles it produces are stored within the web page from which they were created. This limits their use to that web page only, removing one of the main reasons for creating styles, i.e. that the styles can be referenced from any number of pages.

Other approaches for improving the maintainability of a web site are available, including storing the information contained in the site in an object-oriented database, then creating views of this database formatted in HTML [7]. This approach has the same benefits of storing the information in XML as it should still be relatively easy to update the information stored for each page, but converting the information into a format suitable for storage is more difficult and the transformation back to HTML does not use approaches as standardised as XSL. An additional benefit of this approach is that it can be used to create personalised views of the data, and store extra information such as security attributes of the data [8].

The general approach described in [9] is very much similar to the approach taken by this work, in that traditional reengineering practises are applied to the web site to find common styles and content in each page and extract these into a style sheet, and leave the remaining content. However, in this approach, the content for each page is stored in a relational database and various other aspects of the pages are altered, including the directory structure of the site. Again, this approach does not use methods for recreating the HTML documents from the database that are as standardised as XSL, and the directory structure changes forced on the site would break any links to the site from external pages. In a business environment, such broken links could lose sales because a customer would not be able to get to information about the company's products.

A number of *document management systems* are available which use XML to store the raw information for each document and can use XSL to transform this as needed to a web page or to other formats and for other purposes, such as for printing. This means that each format of the document will be consistent. However, these systems do not have a facility for creating the XML files from existing web pages, so this conversion must be done by hand. We consider that these tools are complementary to our work because they will produce added customer benefit regarding the usefulness of the files produced by this work.

XML and XSL are relatively new technologies, although tools are becoming available that support their use. In order to view a page stored as XML and XSL, there must be some means of transforming it back to HTML. Currently this can be performed to some extent in the latest versions of Microsoft Internet Explorer, although support is limited to early recommendations of the XSL specification. Greater support is offered by free tools produced in open source projects available at http://xml.apache.org. It is one of these tools, Xalan, which was used in the testing of the transformation of XML and XSL back to HTML – which is described elsewhere [13].

Data Mining appears to have the capability of providing the functionality required to enable the use of file conversion both the manners described above. However, the discussion will be limited to HTML to CSS file conversion – a detailed description may be found in [13]

4 Data Mining

A Data Mining process is a process of finding previously known & unknown relationships in sets of data samples[10]. The process can be divided into seven steps each of which are described below with reference to the task in hand.
1. Goal definition. The goal of this system is to define the style sheets which are used in order to create a web page (or pages) by finding the patterns of *presentational HTML* in the web page, converting these to CSS and hence producing the original web page (or pages).
2. Data selection. The choice of the data being mined can have a large impact on the success of the process. This step does not apply in this case, because the data is pre-selected by the user.
3. Data preparation and transformation. In this step, each section of presentational HTML is converted to a corresponding section of CSS code.
4. Data exploration. During this step, the prepared data is explored to find useful statistics that may be of help during the later steps. This step does not apply because the tool is required to be fully automated and so no user interaction, as required by this step, is to be allowed.
5. Pattern discovery (relationships between variables exiting within the data). The previously unknown relationships in the data are found. In this system, the groups of presentational HTML that give rise to similar sections of CSS code are found. Possible methods for performing this step are described later in this paper.
6. Pattern deployment. The discovered patterns are used to solve some business goal of the work. The sections of CSS code found in the previous step are used to produce a style sheet, while the sections of presentational HTML are replaced with a reference to the name of the related style in the style sheet.
7. Pattern validity monitoring. The pattern validity monitoring step is not applicable as this process is to be run once only.

5 Approach Taken

The approach taken used the underlying assumption that if each section of presentational HTML can be converted directly to a section of CSS code that would produce the same effect. In order to carry out the task the samples of HTML and related CSS code produced need to be grouped together to produce the named styles that can then be applied to the original HTML file.

It also follows that, if two sections of presentational HTML can be converted to similar sections of CSS code, the maintainability of the HTML file can be further improved if both sections of presentational HTML are replaced with a reference to the same named style rather than producing two slightly different named styles and referencing each of these. This requires a measure of uncertainty when mapping the samples of HTML and related CSS code to named styles. This can be achieved through *clustering* [11]. Figure 1 demonstrates how clustering is achieved.

In Fig. 1 each sample in the classifier is marked with a cross indicating the HTML code giving rise to the sample, and the CSS section that was generated from the HTML.[3] Samples that have similar values are given the same classification. Note that, in this figure, it is implied that the HTML and CSS code can be expressed as an absolute numerical value. However, since this is categorical data this is not simple to carry out in practise. The difference between two samples can be found as a numerical value, but the combination of these values may not be able to be represented on a 2D grid. *These diagrams are a simplification for the purposes of explanation.*

Fig. 1. Clustering

In clustering, each CSS section is *classified* in turn. If it is sufficiently similar to other previously classified sections, it is added to the same *classification* (class) as these other sections. In this domain, a classification is equivalent to a named style (or style sheet). If it is not sufficiently similar to another section, a new classification is created.

The most appropriate algorithm for the conversion from HTML to CSS appears to be the K Nearest Neighbours algorithm. The other algorithms are not appropriate because they either require too many samples to work effectively in this application (decision trees, Bayesian classifiers), require numerical data (Fisher's linear discriminants), or require prior knowledge of the classes (K Means). However, K Nearest Neighbours can work effectively with a small number of samples, can work with categorical data given an appropriate function to compare two samples, and does not require any prior knowledge of the number of classes.

The application of *kNN* to a new sample is described in the following section.

---

[3] It is assumed that using this tool clustering of HTML can be achieved by clustering of CSSs and their conversion back to HTML if required.

6 Application of KNN

If a new sample is to be classified, it is most likely that it will have similar attributes to previously classified samples. A reasonable classification for the new sample can therefore be found by finding the K nearest previously classified samples. The classification for the new sample is then set to the most frequent class given to these neighbours [11]. Figure 2 demonstrates *kNN* being used to classify a new sample using the five nearest neighbours. These all lie within the circle centred on the new sample. Since the majority of these neighbours have previously been classified as "Style 2", the new sample is given this same classification.

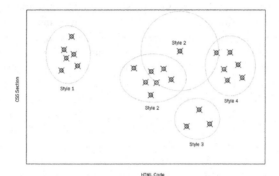

Fig. 2. kNN classifying a new sample

To work effectively, this algorithm needs to be given a reasonably sized training set of previously classified samples and a method of comparing two sections of CSS and HTML code. A training set can be gained by asking the user to classify sections of HTML code and resulting CSS code from one page in a site. These classifications can then be used as a training set for classifying samples gained from other pages in that site.

7 Implementation of KNN

In order to implement the kNN algorithm, some means of finding a numeric difference between two samples of HTML and CSS code is required. This can be carried out by determining the percentage of elements of the code in one sample which is not present in the other sample[4].

Adjacent presentational tags form clusters of tags that can be represented by a single CSS style. The first stage of the algorithm is therefore to find these clusters of

---

[4] It should be noted that this approach ensures that a majority decision is made regarding any borderline classification which could result in such text being misclassified. This is currently under investigation.

tags. This is carried out by first comparing each tag against a list of known presentational tags to check if that tag is presentational. These presentational tags are then compared against each other to check which are found next to each other in the page. These adjacent tags are then placed in a new cluster.

Each cluster of presentational tags is converted to a CSS code sample using a set of rules that are defined in a data file. This can be changed by the user as CSS evolves. Each line is in the format:

Tag-name	CSS-equivalent	Keep-or-remove-tag

The tag names indicate which tags are "presentational". In some cases, the tag by itself may not be presentational but one of the possible attributes for that tag is. In that case, the tag and attribute are listed together. The CSS equivalent provides the actual conversion for this tag or attribute. If the tag is not useful after the conversion to CSS, it can be removed from the final page. In some cases, the tag may have some effect other than that expressed by the CSS, in which case it should be kept in the final page.

Each browser supports a different subset of CSS [11], so that it is important that the only attributes converted are those that are supported by a large range of the most popular browsers. As the support for CSS increases, the data file can be easily changed to accommodate more conversions.

After each cluster is converted to a CSS code sample, the algorithm iterates through each samples and compares it to any which have already been classified. At the start of the loop, none will have been classified. Otherwise, a list of the other classified samples is created and ordered by difference to the new sample. If no sample is within a threshold distance, it is assumed that the new sample is not sufficiently similar to any previous classification, and so the user is prompted for a new classification for this sample. Otherwise, the closest K samples are taken from this list and the new sample is assigned the same classification as the majority of these K samples. An appropriate value of K can be found through trial and error during the implementation.

For the final conversion of the classifications to a style sheet, an arbitrary sample from each classification is used to supply the definition of the style, and the name assigned to the classification is used as the name of the style. As each sample in the class should be very similar, it should not matter which sample is used for the style definition.

An almost identical class containing a slightly different implementation of the kNN algorithm was used in order to create a web page form an existing style sheet. The difference in the algorithm is that a new style is not created if no close match among the previously classified samples is found. The contents of the style sheet are read in and set as the classified samples to provide the classification.

The same approach is used for finding groups of pages with the same style. The major differences in this case are the methods used to represent each page and the differences between them, and the fact that each group does not have a name given by the user – the process is completely unsupervised.

Each page is represented by a set of statistics, including a list of the fonts and images that are used and the number of times each one is used, and the distribution of table tags throughout the page. The combination of these statistics gives a good overall impression of the visual style of the page, as the fonts and images in use will change what the user sees, while the distribution of table tags will change how this is laid out on the screen.

The difference between two sets of these statistics is found by the number of fonts and images that are not present in one set of statistics and is present in another, or those where the font or image is used more than twice as many times in one than in the other. The table distributions are compared using the *chi-squared test*. Each distribution is composed of 100 values, indicating the number of table tags in that 100th of the page. The chi-squared value is calculated as the sum of the squares of the differences of each of these values, as given by the formula:

$$\mathbf{x} \qquad \text{Distribution of table tags in page 1.}$$
$$\mathbf{y} \qquad \text{Distribution of table tags in page 2.}$$

$$\chi^2 = \sum_{i=1}^{100} \frac{(x_i - y_i)^2}{y_i} \tag{12}$$

The sum of these statistics gives an overall value for the difference between the two pages. This can then be directly compared to the value for any other two pages. Again, if the page being classified is not sufficiently similar to any previously classified page, a new classification is created for it.

The following section describes the results of application of the tool to selected test web pages/sites.

8 Results

In order to test the accuracy, and speed[5], of conversion to CSS, and hence CSS based HTML page(s), five sites containing a cross section of styles commonly used in web pages where investigated (Amazon, Google, mutant penguin, Department of Computer Science and University of Durham). Five metrics were used to score the conversion namely:- Time taken to make changes to both the original and modified page, Number of styles produced, Number of sections of HTML still present that could potentially have been converted to CSS and Number of visual differences between the original and modified page.

Tables 1–5 show examples of results of the investigation of these five metrics (respectively).

---

[5] This is inportant if many pages are to be modified.

Table 1. Time to make changes to original pages and pages converted to CSS

Tester	Test	Time to alter original page (Seconds)	Time to alter modified page (Seconds)
1	1	75	60
1	2	70	70
1	3	N/A	120
1	4	80	30
1	5	300	20

Table 2. Number of presentational attributes remaining

Metric	No. of remaining table attributes	No. of remaining font attributes	No. of other remaining attributes	Total
1	235	0	0	235
2	1	0	0	1
3	39	0	0	39
4	170	0	0	170
5	47	0	1	48

Table 3. Number of styles created

Test	Number of styles
1	17
2	3
3	12
4	9
5	5

Table 4 .Visual differences between original pages and pages converted to CSS

Test	No. of incorrect groupings
1	0
2	1
3	1
4	0
5	4
6	3
7	0
8	1
9	0
10	2
11	0
12	0

Table 5. Number of incorrect groupings

Test	No. of incorrect groupings
1	0
2	1
3	1
4	0
5	4
6	3
7	0
8	1
9	0
10	2
11	0
12	0

The investigations showed that the CSS based HTML pages were faster to modify and included over 17 KNN defined styles. However, this was achieved at the expense of errors for table attributes and border styles but that errors in total style grouping were less than 2%.

9   Conclusions

The design of the tool involved a combination of both well-established algorithms (K nearest neighbours) and an entirely new approach based on recent research. This combination was necessary due to the different structures of the problems of producing a CSS style sheet and converting HTML pages to XML and XSL[6].

The tool can be seen to have performed well against these original criteria when being applied to real-world web sites. The converted web sites have been shown to be highly maintainable compared to the original versions of the same web sites.

In general, a reader will not notice any difference between the pages before and after the tool has been used, although in a few cases where CSS style sheets were already being used to some extent, references to the new style definitions replaced references to the original definitions which changed the visual appearance of the pages. This modification would be a useful future development of the system.

10 Future Work

There is great potential for extension to this tool in order to fulfil the needs of the current web community. At present, general knowledge and understanding of XML and XSL is low, and there are no fully mature tools for using XSLT. Although this may change, web designers are more familiar with other imperative scripting languages. One of the most commonly used such language in use in the web is PHP (http://www.php.net). A useful extension to the tool would be to produce a representation of a legacy web site in PHP. In this approach, the data unique to each page could be stored in a relational database rather than in XML files, while the presentational information could be stored in a PHP script rather than in an XSL style sheet. The relevant information could be extracted from the database as needed by the script for displaying in a browser.

In order to make this approach more acceptable for many web designers to use, it would be beneficial if the tool was integrated into a standard web authoring environment so the functionality of the tool was available to web designers who would not otherwise consider moving to an XML representation of their web site. This kind of integration may also spur on development of standards-compatible tools for editing XML documents and performing XSL transformations to produce the web pages from the XML and XSL files.

---

[6] Discussed elsewhere.

References

1. Lawrence, S., Giles, C.L: Searching the World Wide We. Science. **280** (1998) 98–100.
2. Wilde, E.: Wilde's WWW. Techincal foundations of the World Wide Web. Springer-Verlag, London (1999).
3. Sommerville, I.: Software Engineering. Addison-Wesley, Wokingham (1996).
4. Brereton, P., Budgen, D., Hamilton, G.:Hypertext: The Next Maintenance Mountain. Computer Journal. **12** (1998) 49-55.
5. Megginson, D.: Structuring XML documents. Prentice-Hall, New York (1998).
6. Raggett, D.: Clean up your Web pages with HTML Tidy:
    `http://www.w3.org/People/Raggett/tidy/`, January 10th, 2000.
7. Chen, L.: SERFing the web: The Re-Web approach for web re-structuring. World Wide Web. **3** (2000) 95-109.
8. Claypool, K.T., Chen L., Rudensteiner E.A.: Personal Views for Web Catalogs. Data Engineering, **23** (2000) 10-16.
9. Boldyreff, C. , Kewish R.: Reverse Engineering to Achieve Maintainable WWW Sites. Proc.I EEE Working Conference on Reverse Engineering 2001, Stuttgart, Germany.
10. Michie, D., Spiegelhalter, D.J., Taylor, C.C. : Machine learning, neural and statistical classification (eds.) Ellis Horwood, New York (1994).
11. RichInStyle.com. CSS support table.
    `http://www.richinstyle.com/bugs/table.html`, January 20th 2002.
12. Rice, J.A.: Mathematical statistics and data analysis. 2nd ed. Wadsworth, California (1995).
13. Burn-Thornton, K.E., Carrington, M.: A Data Mining Tool for web reuse. manuscript in progress.

Building Topic Profiles Based on Expert Profile Aggregation

Miguel Delgado, María J. Martín-Bautista, Daniel Sánchez, José M. Serrano, and María-Amparo Vila

Dept. of Computer Science and Artificial Intelligence,
University of Granada
C/ Periodista Daniel Saucedo Aranda s/n
18071 Granada, Spain
mdelgado@ugr.es
{mbautis,daniel,jmserrano,vila}@decsai.ugr.es
http://frontdb.ugr.es

Abstract. In this work, we present a method to characterize a given topic on an Information Retrieval System based on expert user profiles. We start from a set of documents from which a set of characteristic terms is extracted. The presence of any term in each document is known and we want to establish the most significant ones in order to select relevant documents about a given topic Π. For that purpose, a group of experts are required to assess the set of documents. The experts can query with the same terms (an unique query) to the system or with different terms (several queries). By aggregating these assessments with the weight associated to the terms, a topic profile can be obtained. An overview of these different situations and an experimental example are also presented.

1 Introduction

In the last decade, research in the field of Information Retrieval has helped users looking for information in Internet. Optimization mechanisms at query and indexing stages, as well as filtering tasks and user profile construction, have contributed to enhance the retrieval process. The problems of surfing through the web include not only the browsing of sites, but also the query in search engines. Besides the amount of information that the user can find in the web, sometimes the user do not know how to query due to the lack of knowledge about the topic, due to a lack of vocabulary in the field or just because the suitable words do not come to user's mind at query moment.

In the literature, some approaches have been presented to solve this problem called in general querying expansion or query refinement (good reviews in the field can be found in (Efthimiadis, 1996) and (Bodner and Song, 1996)). In all of them, the general idea is to obtain a list of additional terms to be added to the original query terms to improve the system answer. The addition of these terms can be made automatically (without the intervention of the user) or semi-automatically (the user sees the list and chooses the most suitable terms for the query).

E. Menasalvas et al. (Eds.): AWIC 2003, LNAI 2663, pp. 230–239, 2003.

In our approach, we suppose that expert users[1] query the system and their profiles are available. Profiles contain terms representing user preferences, and can be used to query the system. These profiles represent queries about a certain topic, and can be used as starting point for other queries coming from non-expert users. In this sense, our approach can be considered automatic, since the information stored in the constructed profile can be used automatically as profile for a novel user looking for information in the same topic. Moreover, a list of terms from this profile could be shown to the user who can select the most interesting terms and learn new vocabulary about the topic. This fact represents an advantage above other approaches in the literature (Harman, 1992), since the user can see the expert profiles and can use the system in automatic way or can select the most appropriated terms in a semi-automatic one.

This approach is inspired in the Collaborative Filtering (Foltz and Dumais, 1992), (Goldberg et al., 1992), where a shared decision-making process is carried out. When users look for information in a data source, the time and knowledge spent in searching can be useful for other users looking for documents in the same field. Collaborative Filtering deals with this problem. A filter process is performed in the search, and the resulting filtered information is shared with other users. The knowledge about user preferences and relevance feedback is stored in user profiles. In a Collaborative Filtering framework, the evaluation of documents from users is utilized to filter retrieved documents when other users query the IRS[2]. In our work, we use not only the document evaluation from users, but also the information stored in the profiles.

The vagueness and uncertainty inherently present in the Information Retrieval tasks, specially in the query construction and user evaluation processes make Fuzzy Logic be one of the best tools to give flexibility and facility when dealing with imprecision (Buell and Kraft, 1981), (Bookstein, 1980), (Bordogna & Pasi, 1993), (Kraft et al., 1997), (Martín-Bautista et al., 2000a), (Martín-Bautista et al., 2000b). Fuzzy logic has also been applied to collaborative filtering based on fuzzy preference relations, as is presented in (Perny and Zucker, 1999). We apply fuzzy logic to profile representation, as well as to the aggregation of expert profiles and opinions to help non-expert users to query an IRS.

In this paper, we start with a presentation of the problem of constructing topic profiles. In Sect. 3, a model for the aggregation of expert profiles to obtain an unique topic profile is exposed. Different cases based on the fact that the experts can make the same or different queries are considered in this section. An experimental example with one of these cases is explained in Sect. 4. Finally, some concluding remarks and future lines of work can be found in Sect. 5.

---

[1] By expert users, we understand users with background knowledge about the topic and its vocabulary. Moreover, an extension of the proposed approach could have different confidence levels for the experts. So the profiles could be weighted based on these knowledge levels.

[2] We use the term IRS referring to a general Information Retrieval System, including the filtering systems, which are sometimes referred as IFS (Information Filtering Systems) in the literature (Belkin and Croft, 1992).

2   Construction of a Topic Profile

Let us suppose a user looks for relevant documents about a certain topic Π on an IRS. When this search is represented by a query, the user try to express her/his needs by a set or terms which are usually not very specific due to the lack of background knowledge of the user about the topic or just because in the moment of the query, the terms do not come to the user's mind. To help the user with the query construction, terms related to the words of a first query may be added to the query. These words are usually extracted from the documents retrieved in the first query (Harman, 1992).

For instance, let us consider a very common situation in any research group: a beginner is asked by a senior researcher to read and comment some papers or works about Machine Learning. If the user formulates a query using the terms "Machine Learning", it is quite possible that she/he fails to obtain certain interesting papers about "sub-symbolic models", that are useful tools in Machine Learning (and thus a term very relevant for this topic), a fact surely unknown for the beginner.

To cope with this situation, we propose a model for a search help tool based on the construction of a profile for the topic Π. We present here a methodology where an aggregation of the opinions of a set of experts is carried out to obtain what we call the "topic-profile". Roughly speaking, this profile may be characterized as a set of terms with an associated weight. This is important both for the characterization of the topic and for constructing efficient queries about it.

Once the expert profiles are constructed, as a result of a filtering process, both the term in profiles and the expert opinions have to be aggregated and combined to obtain a global assessment for each term to take part of the topic profile.

We can deal with two different cases in our model. On the one hand, each expert can query the system with different terms, so a set of documents would be obtained as a response to each expert query. An expert profile is built for each expert. We can aggregate these profiles that represent queries about the topic Π. On the other hand, if experts make an unique query with the same terms, the retrieved set of documents will be the same. However, as the evaluation of the experts over the documents is different, the expert profiles would contain different terms with different evaluations. We can aggregate these profiles to obtain the topic profile.

We combine evaluation of documents from different experts (before the profile construction), or terms in the expert profiles once they have been obtained. The result of this aggregation is a profile that characterizes Π. For this purpose, we need the following elements:

- A given topic Π.
- A set $\{D_1,...,D_m\}$ of documents related to Π. This set of documents could be obtained in a different way based on the framework (information retrieval or filtering one). In our case, we are dealing with a filtering framework.
- A set $T = \{t_1,...t_n\}$ of terms obtained from the abovementioned documents. For each term t_i and document D_j, there exists the "representation of t_i in D_j", i.e. a pair $(t_i, D_j(t_i))$ where $D_j(t_i) = f_{ij}$ assesses, in some way, the weight of t_i in D_j, $i=1,...,n$; $j=1,...,m$. In classical models, f_{ij} is some frequency scheme (generally the relative frequency) measuring the occurrences of t_i in D_j, $i=1,...,n$; $j=1,...,m$, but some other very interesting representations for these weights have been introduced in the

last years, mainly by using fuzzy numbers to obtain a more expressive representation (see (Martín-Bautista, 2000) for details).

- A set of experts $\{E_1,...,E_p\}$, where each of them is asked to evaluate the relevance of any document in relation with Π. Let us suppose that an expert E_k is able to assess the relevance of the document D_j for the topic Π represented by s_{kj}, $k=1, ..., P$; $j=1, ..., M$.

- A set of profiles $Z = \{z_1,...,z_p\}$, where each profile z_k corresponds to the expert E_k.

2.1   Concept of User Profile

In a filtering process, the users can feedback the system by evaluating some of the retrieved documents. This evaluation allows the construction of profiles, where the terms appearing in the most relevant documents, as well as terms presented in non-relevant documents expressing what users do not like (Martín-Bautista et al., 2000a).

A user profile consists of a set of terms and a weight indicating the strength of each term in relation to the topic for that user. Terms in the profiles can be extracted from both previous queries and index terms in relevant documents retrieved in response to those queries for the considered user. In a fuzzy framework, each term in a profile has associated a fuzzy value signifying the strength of user interest in the topic(s) represented by that term (Martín-Bautista et al., 2000b).

We start from a given set of user profiles $Z = \{z_1,...,z_p\}$, with p the number of profiles (we suppose the number of profiles equal to the number of experts), and where $z_i = \{t'_{i1},...,t'_{ia}\}$ $t'_{ij} \in T$, $1 \le i \le p$, $1 \le j \le a$, being a the number of terms in the profile. We can define a function analogous to the indexing function defined in (Buell and Kraft, 1981) for the extended Boolean model, but for user profiles where the representation of the terms is expressed by a fuzzy degree of membership of the term to the profile (Martín-Bautista et al., 2002a):

$$G: ZxT \to [0,1] \ \forall \ z \in Z, \ t \in T \ \ G(z,t) = \mu_z(t) . \tag{1}$$

This presence value of terms in the profiles can be calculated as is suggested in (Martín-Bautista et al., 2000a), and is based in both the presence of the term in a document and in the relevance that the user gives to the document where the term is.

This profile representation differs from other approaches where the evaluation of documents from the user is stored in the profiles, but the evaluation corresponding to each term is not calculated. Therefore, our profiles are in a term level, and not in a document one, although the evaluation of the documents can be also stored in the profiles. The main advantage of representing the profiles at the term level is the use of terms in the profiles as possible queries. This storage of user preferences in the low level, allows us to compare the terms to other terms in documents, queries, user profiles, etc.

Taking into account that users querying a system can be considered 'experts' in different fields, we can obtain a set of expert profiles after the filtering process. The knowledge extracted from these expert profiles can be used to help non-expert users to query an IRS. In this way, the non-expert user can take advantage of the expert awareness about a certain topic, besides of the time spent in the document evaluation.

3   Aggregation of Expert Profiles

When an expert user queries a system, a filtering process can be carried out, and a user profile can be generated. We call this profile *expert profile*. We can assume that expert profiles have some advantageous features. On the one hand, the documents evaluated by the expert about a topic, that can be stored in the profile, have a guarantee, in some way, above documents evaluated by non-expert users in the topic. On the other hand, the terms representative from those documents to be stored in the profiles, can be terms extracted from the query of the expert or from the retrieved documents (title, abstract, keywords, indexing terms, body, etc.). These terms, besides coming from documents evaluated as relevant from expert users in the topic, can be valuable for non-expert users and can suggest query terms that do not come to the non-expert user's mind in a natural way. This is generally due to a lack of knowledge about the technical words, or about translating words into other language related to the queried topic.

When we deal with a group of experts $\{E_1, \ldots, E_p\}$, we can consider two different situations for this model:

- **A Unique Query:** This situation is the simplest because all the experts query the system using the same terms. The set of retrieved documents is the same for all the experts, assuming that the system for all of them has the same document collection. The evaluation of the documents from all the experts can be aggregated for each document. From the overall aggregation of the documents, we can extract the terms to be part of the 'topic profile'. Another possibility is to obtain first the different profiles of the experts by extracting terms from documents on the basis of documents' relevance (according to the expert's evaluation). The topic profile can be obtained from the aggregation of these expert profiles.
- **Several Queries:** In this case, the experts make different queries to the system, which implies to retrieve different sets of documents for each query. As the experts evaluate different sets of retrieved documents, the best way to aggregate this information is to aggregate the corresponding profiles. Therefore, we first construct the profiles for each expert, and then we can aggregate them to obtain the topic profile. Another possibility is to combine previously the document sets obtained by each expert in order to obtain an unique ranked list of documents based on the reliability of each expert.

In the following, we present some ideas to face with the problem when an unique or several queries are performed by the experts. In all the cases, we assume that the expert opinions are numerically expressed. Further considerations and proposals where expert opinions are given by symbolic statements or by pure ordinal opinions can be found in (Delgado et al., 2001).

3.1.1   Expert Profile Aggregation with a Unique Query

Let $q = (t_1 r_1, ..., t_h r_h)$ be the query formulated by the experts $\{E_1, ..., E_p\}$, where $(r_1, ..., r_k)$ are importance weights associated to the terms in the query (Bordogna et al., 1995), which can be given by the experts. An unique document set $\{D_1, ..., D_M\}$ is retrieved as a response to the query q.

Thus, let assume that the expert E_k is able to assess the relevance of the document D_j for the topic Π to be $u_{kj} \in [0,1]$, $k=1, ..., P$; $j=1, ..., M$. Then the experts' opinions may be summarized into the matrix:

$$U = (u_{kj})_{k=1,...,P; j=1,...,M} .$$

(2)

Two different situations arise at this point:

- We can first aggregate experts opinions (the rows in U) into a only global evaluation vector $(u_1, ..., u_M)$ and then, obtain a topic profile as in a filtering problem, where starting from a set of documents and their evaluations by the user, we can obtain the user profile. The topic profile is a set of terms selected from the evaluated documents, and importance weights that can be utilized in future queries by non-expert users. We represent the topic profile by $\Pi = (t_1 w_1, ..., t_n w_n)$.

- We can first construct the profile $z_i = (t_{i1} w_{i1}, ..., t_{ik} w_{ik})$, $1 \leq i \leq p$, $1 \leq k \leq n$ for each expert as the result of the filtering process with the document evaluations of each expert, and then aggregate the weights related to each profile into an unique topic profile $\Pi = (t_1 w_1, ..., t_k w_k)$.

As in the first model, approaches to solve group decision and/or consensus problems can be used (Delgado et al., 1998).

3.1.2 Expert Profile Aggregation with Several Queries

In this case, each expert E_k formulates a query $q_k = (t_1 r_{k1}, ..., t_h r_{kh})$, $1 \leq k \leq P$, $1 \leq h \leq N$, where $(r_1, ..., r_k)$ are again the weights associated to the term queries, that can be different for each term and expert (a simplification of the model would be the consideration of the query without these importance degrees). A set of documents $\{D_{k1}, ..., D_{kM}\}$ is retrieved as a response to each query q_k formulated by the expert E_k. Each expert evaluates the document set, given an evaluation vector $\{U_{k1}, ..., U_{kM}\}$. A profile $z_k = (t_{k1} w_{k1}, ..., t_{kh} w_{kh})$, $1 \leq k \leq p, 1 \leq h \leq N$ defined as a set of terms with associated importance weights related to the topic Π is constructed for each expert. Once all the expert profiles $\{z_1, ..., z_p\}$ have been obtained, an aggregation process is needed in order to obtain an overall topic profile.

4   An Experimental Example

In order to test the proposed model, we have considered a system for constructing user profiles based on previous research, where genetic algorithms are utilized (Martín-Bautista et al., 2002b). In this system, a profile is constructed based on the feedback of the user over a previous set of documents retrieved as a result of a query to an IRS. Initially, the population of the genetic algorithm is initialized with indexing terms from the first set of retrieved documents. With the evaluation given by the user over some of the retrieved documents, the weights of terms in the population are recalculated and the population evolves towards the space of terms that best represents the user's preferences. Each chromosome of the population is a possible query representing the user's preferences. When the profile is an expert one, the queries (chromosomes) in the population can be considered as 'high-quality' possible queries about the topic the expert asked.

In previous experiments, all the population has been considered as user profile, since the profile as a whole is used to initialize the population again when a new query in the same channel is carried out. The size and the chromosome length considered for the population was 80 chromosomes and 10 terms each chromosome, respectively. We have to take into account that a term can appear more than once in a chromosome. The chromosomes represented in Table 4 contain only different terms within each chromosome.

The simulation of the process is made considering the first model where an unique query is formulated for all the experts. A query with the terms "genetic algorithms" is performed using *Google*. The first set of documents retrieved from this query is shown in Table 1. In a second step, the experts see the documents and feedback the system by an interface that allows us to assign a label to each document. The labels are (*very high, high, medium, low, very low*). The feedback of the experts for the top ten documents is detailed in Table 2.

Table 1. Top 10 results of Google to the query 'genetic algorithms'

Document Id.	Document address
D_1	http://www.aic.nrl.navy.mil/galist
D_2	http://gal4.ge.uiuc.edu/illegal.home.html
D_3	http://www.cs.cmu.edu/Groups/AI/html/fqas/ai/genetic/top.html
D_4	http://cs.gmu.edu/research/gag/
D_5	http://www.scs.carleton.ca/~csgs/resources/gaal.html
D_6	http://www.fqas.org/fqas/ai-faq/genetic/
D_7	http://lancet.mit.edu.ga/
D_8	http://www.mat.sbg.ac.at/~uhl/GA.html
D_9	http://www.cs.bgu.ac.il/~omri/NNUGA/
D_{10}	http://www.aridolan.com/ga/gaa/gaa.html

Table 2. Evaluations of experts to the top 10 results of Google to the query 'genetic algorithms'

Document Id	Expert 1	Expert 2	Expert 3	Expert 4
D_1	very high	---	---	high
D_2	---	very high	---	---
D_3	very high	---	---	medium
D_4	High	very high	medium	---
D_5	---	very high	---	Very high
D_6	very high	---	---	medium
D_7	---	---	very high	---
D_8	very high	---	---	medium
D_9	---	Low	---	---
D_{10}	---	---	very high	---

As we have explained above, the experiments have been performed according to the first model explained in Sect. 3.1.1 where all the experts query the system with the same terms and the opinions of the experts are first aggregated and then the profile of the aggregation is generated. Supposing we aggregate using the AND operator, the results of the aggregation over the expert evaluations can be seen in Table 3. If a document is not evaluated by all the experts, the aggregation will be only over the available evaluation given by some of the experts.

The best first chromosomes generated by these aggregated evaluations are shown in Table 4. The complete population can be used as a starting point for a new query. From this population, a list of terms with their weights is extracted to form the topic profile. Any of them may be used as user guide to retrieve information about the topic, with the suggestion of new terms related to the original query ones.

Table 3. Aggregation of expert evaluations

Doc. Id.	D_1	D_2	D_3	D_4	D_5	D_6	D_7	D_8	D_9	D_{10}
Expert Aggreg.	me-dium	very high	me-dium	me-dium	high	me-dium	very high	me-dium	low	very high

Table 4. Chromosomes of the population of the genetic algorithm to construct the topic profile 'genetic algorithms'

Valuation	Chromosome
Very high	(schwefel, org, Pollack, algorithms, illegal, kinds, purpose, traveling, multi)
Very high	(programming, rastrigin, ziv, galib, algorithms, implemented, faq, optimization)
Very high	(witty, modal, nature, laboratory, search, algorithms, omri)
Very high	(neural, org, Pollack, algorithms, Alabama, index, matthew, java, algorithms, page)
Very high	(traveling, unconventional, reference, urbana, technology, nnuga, introductory, web, algorithms)
Very high	(nnuga, algorithms, ackley, related, Alabama, experiments, playground, rastrigin, links)

Table 4. (Continuation)

Valuation	Chromosome
Very high	(evolutionary, unconventional, free, references, rosenbrock, algorithms, Pollack, bibliographies, examples)
High	(tools, online, designed, references, rosenbrock, search, life, final, experiments, algorithms)
High	(faq, sphere, active, algorithms, applied, resources, Pollack, neural, ep)
High	(links, online, experiments, life, diverse, lab, algorithms, griewank, list, programming)

5   Concluding Remarks and Future Work

We have presented a system that allows us to construct a topic profile when expert profiles about queries related to the topic are available. The resulting topic profile can be used in two different ways: on the one hand, a list of terms with associated importance weights can be shown to novel users for suggesting queries that do not come naturally to users' mind. On the other hand, the topic profile in its original form of chromosomes of a genetic algorithm can be used as starting population for future queries of novel users.

Several situations arise based on the way experts query the system (by an unique query or several queries), and the aggregation method: we can aggregate first the experts opinions over the top documents and then obtain a topic profile, or we can first obtain the experts profiles based on their evaluations, and then aggregate them to generate the topic profile.

We have to point out the dynamical aspect of the system. The topic profile may be incrementally constructed by aggregating the opinion of several users, when the users are the experts themselves.

In the future, other aggregation operators that incorporate the existence of weights measuring the importance or reliability assigned to each expert opinion will be considered. Further experiments where each expert asks the system about the same topic but with different queries will be performed as well.

References

Belkin, N.J. and Croft, W.B. (1992). Information Filtering and Information Retrieval: Two Sides of the Same Coin?. Communications of the ACM, Vol. 35, n. 12 , (1992) 29–38

Bodner, R.C. and Song, F. "Knowledge-Based Approaches to Query Expansion in Information Retrieval". In McGalla, G. (Ed.) Advances in Artificial Intelligence. Springer, New York, (1996) 146–158

Bookstein, A. Fuzzy Requests: an Approach to Weighted Boolean Searches. Journal of the American Society for Information Science, Vol. 31, n. 4, (1980) 240–247

Bordogna G., Carrara, P. and Pasi, G. Fuzzy Approaches to Extend Boolean Information Retrieval. In P. Bosc and J. Kacprzyk (Eds.) Fuzziness in Database Management Systems. Germany: Physica-Verlag (1995) 231–274

Bordogna G. and Pasi, G. A Fuzzy Linguistic Approach Generalizing Boolean Information Retrieval: a Model and its Evaluation. Journal of the American Society for Information Science, Vol. 44, n. 2, (1993) 70–82

Buell, D.A. and Kraft, D.H. Performance Measurement in a Fuzzy Retrieval Environment. Proceedings of the Fourth International Conference on Information Storage and Retrieval. ACM/SIGIR Forum, Vol. 16, n. 1, Oakland, CA. (1981) 56–62

Delgado, M., Verdegay, J.L. and Vila, M.A. Linguistic Decision Making Models. International Journal of Intelligent Systems, Vol. 7, (1993a) 479–492

Delgado, M., Verdegay, J.L. and Vila, M.A. On Aggregation Operations of Linguistic Labels. International Journal of Intelligent Systems, Vol. 8, (1993b) 351–370

Delgado, M., Herrera, F., Herrera-Viedma, E. and Martinez, L. Combining Numerical and Linguistic Information in Group Decision Making. Information Sciences, Vol. 107, (1998) 177–194

Delgado, M., Martín-Bautista, M.J., Sánchez, D. and Vila, M.A. Aggregating Opinions in an Information Retrieval Problem. Proc. of EUROFUSE Workshop on Preference Modelling and Applications, Granada, Spain (2001) 169–173

Efthimiadis, R. Query Expansion. Annual Review of Information Systems and Technology, Vol. 31 (1996) 121-187

Foltz, P.W. and Dumais, S.T. Using Collaborative Filtering to Weave an Information Tapestry. Communications of the ACM, Vol. 35, n. 12, (1992) 51–60

Goldberg, D., Nichols, D., Oki, B.M. and Terry, D. Using Collaborative Filtering to Weave an Information Tapestry. Communications of the ACM, Vol. 35, n. 12, (1992) 61–70

Harman, D. Relevance Feedback and Other Query Modification Techniques. In W.B. Frakes and R. Baeza-Yates (Eds.), Information Retrieval: Data Structures and Algorithms. Prentice Hall (1992) 241–263

Kraft, D.H., Petry, F.E., Buckles, B.P. and Sadasivan, T. Genetic Algorithms for Query Optimization in Information Retrieval: Relevance Feedback. In E. Sanchez, T. Shibata, L. Zadeh (Eds.), Advances in Fuzziness. Vol. 7. Singapore: World Scientific (1997) 155–173

Martín-Bautista, M.J. Soft Computing Models for Information Retrieval (in spanish). Ph. Doctoral Thesis. University of Granada, Spain (2000)

Martín-Bautista, M.J., Vila, M.A. and Larsen, H.L. Building Adaptive User Profiles by a Genetic Fuzzy Classifier with Feature Selection. Proceedings of the IEEE Conference on Fuzzy Systems. Vol. 1, San Antonio, Texas (2000a) 308–312

Martín-Bautista, M.J., Sánchez, D., Vila, M.A. and Larsen, H.L. Fuzzy Genes: Improving Effectiveness of Information Retrieval. Proceedings of the IEEE Conference on Evolutionary Computation. Vol. 1. La Jolla, California (2000b) 471–478

Martín-Bautista, M.J., Kraft, D.H., Vila, M.A., Chen, J. and Cruz, J. User Profiles and Fuzzy Logic for Web Retrieval Issues. Soft Computing. Vol.6, n. 5. (2002a) 365-372

Martín-Bautista, M.J., Vila, M.A., Sánchez, D. and Larsen, H.L. Intelligent Filtering with Genetic Algorithms and Fuzzy Logic. In B. Bouchon-Meunier, J. Gutiérrez-Ríos, L. Magdalena, R.R. Yager (eds.) Technologies for Constructing Intelligent Systems Vol. 1. Germany: Physica-Verlag (2002b) 351–362

Perny, P. and J.D. Zucker Collaborative Filtering Methods Based on Fuzzy Preference Relations, EUROFUSE-SIC'99, Budapest (1999) 279–285.

Yager, R. Fusion of Multi-Agent Preference Orderings, Fuzzy Sets and Systems, Vol. 177. (2001) 1–12

Zadeh, L.A. The Concept of a Linguistic Variable and its Applications to Approximate Reasoning. Part I, Information Sciences. Vol. 8. (1975) 199-249; Part II, Information Sciences. Vol. 8. (1975) 301-357; Part III, Information Sciences. Vol. 9. (1975) 43–80

Carrot² and Language Properties in Web Search Results Clustering

Jerzy Stefanowski and Dawid Weiss

Institute of Computing Science, Poznań University of Technology
ul. Piotrowo 3A, 60–965 Poznań, Poland
{Jerzy.Stefanowski,Dawid.Weiss}@cs.put.poznan.pl

Abstract. This paper relates to a technique of improving results visualization in Web search engines known as *search results clustering*. We introduce an open extensible research system for examination and development of search results clustering algorithms – Carrot². We also discuss attempts to measuring quality of discovered clusters and demonstrate results of our experiments with quality assessment when inflectionally rich language (Polish) is clustered using a representative algorithm - Suffix Tree Clustering.

Keywords: information retrieval, web browsing and exploration, web search clustering, suffix tree clustering

1 Introduction

The Internet, not even two decades old, has already changed the world by wiping physical distance limitations, bringing down information access restrictions and causing unprecedented growth of new technologies and services. However, with new possibilities come new boundaries. In particular, as it quickly turned out, easier access to large volumes of data was accompanied by an increasing level of difficulty in its organizing, browsing and understanding. Search engines thus quickly gained popularity and became the most popular tool for locating relevant information on the Web.

The user interface of the most popular modern search engines is based on keyword-based queries and endless lists of matching documents (all of the most popular search engines listed by Nielsen//NetRankings[1] use it). Unfortunately, even when exceptional ranking algorithms are used, relevance sorting inevitably promotes quality based on some notion of popularity of what can be found on the Web. If an overview of the topic, or an in-depth analysis of a certain subject is required, search engines usually fail in delivering such information. It seems natural to expect that search engines should not only return the most popular documents matching a query but also provide another, potentially more comprehensive, overview of the subject it covers. Certain inventions have already been introduced in the commercial world: query expansion suggestions in Teoma

---

[1] (01/2002) http://www.searchenginewatch.com/reports/netratings.html

E. Menasalvas et al. (Eds.): AWIC 2003, LNAI 2663, pp. 240–249, 2003.

or Infonetware, graphical visualization of results in Kartoo, image-based interface in Ditto or Google Images.

One of the most promising approaches, both commercially and research-wise, is to automatically group search results into thematic categories, called *clusters*. Assuming clusters descriptions are informative about the documents they contain, the user spends much less time following irrelevant links. He also gets an excellent overview of subjects present in the search result and thus knows when the query needs to be reformulated. Because the clustering process is performed dynamically for each query, the discovered set of groups is apt to depict the real structure of results, not some predefined categories (to differentiate this process from off-line clustering or classification, we call it *ephemeral* [1], or *on-line clustering* [2]). Our research follows this direction also taking into account certain characteristic properties of the Polish language – rich inflection (words have different suffixes depending on their role in a sentence) and less strict word order in a sentence (compared to English).

In this paper we introduce an open, flexible and free research project for building search results clustering systems – Carrot^2. We hope this framework could facilitate cross-comparison of algorithms and spawn new ideas for visualization of search results. We also discuss the topic of measuring the quality of on-line search results clustering, and demonstrate certain results acquired from application of an entropy-based measure to clustering Polish queries. We tried to analyze the influence of several term conflation algorithms on the quality of clusters acquired from a representative algorithm – *Suffix Tree Clustering*, in order to show differences between clustering two inflectionally different languages (Polish and English). This is an extension of our preliminary experiments presented in [3] – we enlarged the set of queries and included English queries as well as Polish.

2   Related Work

Clustering algorithms have been present in Information Retrieval for a long time, a comprehensive review of classic methods can be found in [4]. One of their common applications was to organize large volumes of semi numerical data into entities of higher abstraction level, easier to perceive by humans. *Agglomerative Hierarchical Clustering* (AHC) and *K-means* algorithms gained widespread popularity when speed was of no such critical importance, because processing was performed off-line and only once in a while. These algorithms, used successfully in many fields were quickly transformed to the domain of search results clustering. However, their computational complexity, difficult tuning of parameters and sensitivity to malicious input data soon raised the need of improvements.

The first proposal for *on-line and dynamic* search results clustering was perhaps presented in the Scatter-Gather system [5], where non-hierarchical, partitioning Fractionation algorithm was used. Undesired and troublesome high dimensionality of term frequency vectors was addressed in [6], where two derivations of graph-partitioning were presented. Simple terms were replaced with "lexical affinities" (pairs of words commonly appearing together in the text) in [1], with a modification of AHC as the clustering algorithm. A different approach to finding similarity measure between documents was introduced in Grouper [2] and MSEEC [7] systems. Both of these discover *phrases* shared by document references in the search results and perform clustering according to this information. The former system introduces novel, very efficient *Suffix Tree Clustering* algorithm (described in Sect. 3), while the latter proposes utilization of LZW compression algorithm to find recurring sequences of terms in the input. STC produces flat, but overlapping clusters, which is usually perceived as an advantage, because documents tend to belong to more than one subject. An extension of STC producing hierarchical structure of clusters was recently proposed in [8].

All of the already mentioned algorithms were designed primarily to work on English texts and take English grammar and inflection into account. According to our knowledge, the only search results clustering technique working on sequences of characters, as opposed to words, was presented in [9].

3   Suffix Tree Clustering Algorithm

In this section, we present a very brief description of the Suffix Tree Clustering algorithm (STC), which we decided to perform our experiment on. An uninitiated Reader may want to refer to [10] for an in-depth overview.

Suffix Tree Clustering algorithm (STC) works under assumption that common topics are usually expressed using identical phrases (ordered sequences of words). For example, if two documents contain a phrase "Ben and Jerry's ice cream", then we may assume these documents are somehow relevant to each other and could be placed in one group. The same process applies to all other phrases shared by at least two documents. In the above example, the ice cream flavors (such as "chunky monkey" or "cherry garcia") would also become candidates for separate groups. One can notice that the discovered clusters could form a hierarchical structure. The original STC, however, produced the results as a set of (possibly overlapping) clusters, without any hierarchy on top of them. Several methods based on STC were successively proposed for this particular area [9,8].

The main advantage of STC over methods utilizing term frequency distribution only (*keywords*) is that phrases are usually more informative than unorganized set of keywords, and can be directly used to label the discovered clusters, which in other clustering algorithms becomes a problem in itself. STC is organized into two phases: discovering sets of documents sharing the same phrase (*base clusters*) and combining them into larger entities (*final clusters*).

Base clusters are discovered by creating a generalized suffix tree for all terms in the search result. The description of this process is fairly complex (we encourage the Reader to refer to [11,10] for details), so we should omit its description here. In the end, the result of this step is a set of phrases shared by at least two documents, with links to all documents they occur in. This part of STC is characterized by (at least theoretically) linear complexity and can be performed incrementally.

Each base cluster a is described by its associated phrase m_a and the set of documents that phrase occurs in d_a. We then calculate a *base cluster score* defined as: $s(a) = |m_a| \times f(|m_a|) \times \sum_{w \in m_a}(tfidf(w))$, where $|m_a|$ is the number of terms in phrase m_a, $f(|m_a|)$ is a function penalizing short-phrases (because we prefer longer, more descriptive sequences of terms), and $\sum_{w \in m_a}(tfidf(w))$ is a sum of standard Salton's *term frequency-inverse document frequency* term ranking factor for all terms in phrase m_a.

Only base clusters with the score higher than a *minimal base cluster score threshold* are promoted for the second step of the algorithm – merging. Merging of two base clusters a and b is performed, when their document sets d_a and d_b overlap more than a predefined *merge threshold*. STC thus way groups documents which relate to a subject expressed by more than one phrase. For example, base clusters "Ben and Jerry's ice cream" and "chocolate fudge" would hopefully express documents relevant to this particular flavor of ice creams.

The merge process is in fact a variation of agglomerative hierarchical clustering algorithm: if α denotes the *merge threshold* and $|x|$ denotes the number of documents in cluster x, the binary merge criterion for the AHC algorithm is defined by: $similarity(a, b) = 1 \Leftrightarrow \left(\frac{|d_a \cap d_b|}{|d_a|} > \alpha \right) \wedge \left(\frac{|d_a \cap d_b|}{|d_b|} > \alpha \right)$.

Eventually, the base cluster score is recalculated for merged clusters and the top-scoring clusters are displayed to the user.

4 Carrot^2 Search Results Clustering Framework

We started asking questions about feasibility of search results clustering in Polish around the time Grouper was available on-line. Unfortunately, we could not proceed with further experiments because that system was never released in source code. We created Carrot then – an open source implementation of STC – where we introduced certain features dedicated to processing of the Polish language: quasi-stemming, simple lemmatization method and a large corpora of Polish texts, from which stop words were extracted. These were our own contribution because morphological analysis of Polish requires significant effort and hence, understandably, out of several existing algorithms, none is available free of charge. Carrot was used to perform initial experiments and user studies, also bringing new questions regarding sensitiveness of STC's thresholds, influence of stemming quality and inflection. Although Carrot was a well designed prototype, its development was very rapid and several design decisions limited further experiments. Having learned from that example, we decided to create a new, open and extensible research framework for experimenting with search results clustering - Carrot^2.

We have observed, that almost every search results clustering system described in literature could be split into reusable and fairly autonomous parts: a data source (usually a search engine wrapper), preprocessing (stemming or lemmatization, identifying sentence boundaries and irrelevant terms), finally clustering and visualization. Many of these remain very similar from system to system and it would be a waste of time and effort to rewrite them. In Carrot^2 we have physically split these functional areas into separate *components*, so that almost any part of the system can be easily reused or replaced with another implementation or algorithm.

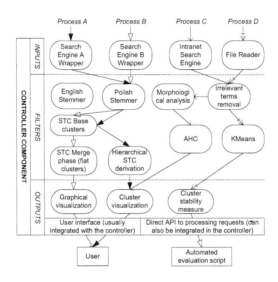

Fig. 1. Sample potential components and their arrangement into four processing chains in Carrot^2 framework. Processes are distinguished with different arrowheads. We show how different algorithms and input components can be reused to achieve different results

We have distinguished the following types of components: *inputs, filters, outputs* and *controllers*. Inputs accept a query and produce an initial list of references to documents. Filters alter the result by pruning, filtering, term conflation or adding additional information like that about clusters or suggested query expansion keywords. Outputs accept the filtered result and produce a response (whether visual output to the user or some other response is up to the component designer). Finally, a special type of component is the *controller*. It is in charge of interacting with the environment, for example, displaying a search interface to the user and displaying whatever the output component returned as a result. It also manages data exchange among other parts of the system when a query is processed according to a certain *processing chain* – ordered sequence of components starting with an input, with filters in between and ending in some output. Components are data-driven, independent programs, which can be perceived as black boxes – only the specification of input and output data format is important, while inside processing is entirely up to the designer. Since the mentioned ease of component programming was our main goal, we decided to refrain from the new wave of technologies like SOAP or XML-RPC, and remain with HTTP POST. This provides great flexibility in adding new components, and provides a very useful abstraction layer from the language of implementation and physical location of a component. Handling of POST requests is relatively easy, with a number of very good implementations (for almost any language). For ad hoc programming, even any web server exposing CGI interface and shell scripts can be used. If performance counts, the component may be easily rewritten to any other computationally efficient language.

In order for components to understand each other's response, a protocol, or data exchange format must be established. It must be stressed that this format is fixed only for input components (query format), whereas data passed further on depends solely on the domain the framework is used in. For example, in our application to search results clustering we specified an XML-based format for exchanging data about snippets, clusters and certain linguistic analysis. Other applications might define their own data exchange specifications, however a large part of the system (like usually the most complex controller component) still remains reusable. A clear and stable format of data exchange ensures that any conforming component may be replaced with other implementation without harming the rest of the system (see Fig. 1).

5   Experiments

In this section we present observations from an experimental application of STC to English and Polish, along with a short discussion of existing approaches to estimating the quality of results in search results clustering.

5.1   Cluster Quality Evaluation

Evaluation of results is perhaps the most difficult part in development of a new search results clustering algorithm. Questions about what constitutes good and what bad clustering remain unanswered. In the past, several approaches have been proposed. Standard IR techniques such as precision and recall have been commonly used [10,6], but they usually require a reference set of documents, for which the clusters are already known. While such databases exist (TREC, OHSUMED, Reuters), their structure is unsuitable for the domain of search results clustering because of the number and lengths of documents. Besides, with predefined collections there is always a danger that the algorithm discovers more subtle, or even better arrangement of groups than humans. According to [12] and also evident in our experiment, humans are rarely consistent both in number, arrangement and structure of a "perfect" clustering. Nonetheless, various forms of comparisons to a predefined structure of clusters have been used [1,10,6]. Especially the measure of cluster quality based on *information-theoretic entropy* [13], used in [1], seems to catch the balance between similarity of the reference set and the clusters being compared. Of course a single value cannot represent all aspects of clustering quality. In our experiments we decided to employ it anyway in order to catch the *trends* and overall view of clusters structure with respect to changing input language and algorithm thresholds, rather than say whether the results are good or bad. It may even be the case that a confident measure of quality will be difficult to express in a mathematical formula; instead an empirical testimony of algorithm's usefulness to final users can be taken as a proof of its value. This approach has also been investigated and used. In [10] and [2], authors compare a standard ranked-list user interface to the clustered one using log analysis from real working systems. Also, explicit surveys have been used to measure users' level of satisfaction. These methods, while providing an excellent feedback from real people, have the drawback of being error prone due to subjectiveness of participants, their ranging level of patience and experience with Web searching.

Interestingly, the first thing the user sees as a results of a clustering algorithm – cluster descriptions – has never been a serious criterion of quality analysis. As suggested by Raul Valdes-Perez, president of a commercial search clustering system – Vivisimo – factors such as label conciseness, accuracy and distinctiveness could be taken into account together with the overall structure of the discovered clusters. In our opinion even light morphological analysis could help greatly in discriminating good (or at least grammatically correct) cluster labels from bad ones.

In our experiments we decided to use a normalized version of Byron Dom's entropy measure, briefly presented in Def. 1. Value of zero denotes no correspondence between the measured clusters and the ground truth set, one means the two are identical.

Definition 1. *Let X be a set of feature vectors, representing objects to be clustered, C be a set of class labels, representing the desired, optimal classification (also called a ground truth set), and K be a set of cluster labels assigned to elements of X as a result of an algorithm.*

Knowing X and K one can calculate a two-dimensional contingency matrix $H \equiv \{h(c,k)\}$, where $h(c,k)$ is the number of objects labeled class c that are assigned to cluster k. Information-theoretic external cluster-validity measure is defined by:

$$Q_0 = - \sum_{c=1}^{|C|} \sum_{k=1}^{|K|} \frac{h(c,k)}{n} \log \frac{h(c,k)}{h(k)} + \frac{1}{n} \sum_{k=1}^{|K|} \log \binom{h(k) + |C| - 1}{|C| - 1}. \quad (1)$$

where $n = |X|$, $h(c) = \sum_k h(c,k)$, $h(k) = \sum_c h(c,k)$.

Byron Dom's measure is defined for flat partitioning of an input set of objects, while STC produces flat, but overlapping clusters. In order to be able to apply the measure, we decided that snippets assigned to more than one cluster would belong only to the one having the highest score assigned by STC.

5.2   Test Data and Results

As a test data set for the experiment we collected real search results (the first 100 hits) to 4 English and 4 Polish queries. Multi-topic queries were selected so that a structure of clusters definitely existed: *salsa, intelligence, merced, logic, knowledge discovery* and certain subqueries such as *salsa sauce, merced lake* or *fuzzy logic*. This data was then clustered manually and independently by 4 individuals. The final ground truth set of clusters for each query was a result of experts discussion and unification of their results. For each query we applied STC in several configurations of input data preprocessing – with and without stemming, lemmatization and stop words removal. We used Porter stemmer for English and our own quasi-stemmer and dictionary lemmatization for Polish [3]. We also ran the algorithm over a wide range of control thresholds. Then we compared the generated clusters to the ground truth set using the above measure of quality.

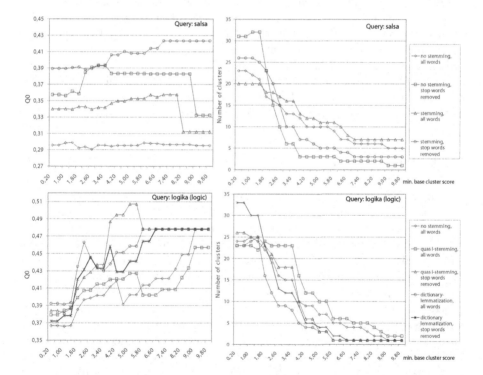

Fig. 2. Quality measure (left) and number of clusters (right) with respect to changing base cluster score and various configurations of input data pre-processing

The positive influence of language pre-processing has been confirmed with reference to our preliminary studies in [3]. Both term conflation algorithms and stop words removal were increasing the chosen measure of quality. However, the gain was not always as optimistic as it can be observed on the *salsa* query in Fig. 2. Sometimes, both in the case of Polish queries (see *logika*), and English queries, the "winning" configuration was not the one with full input data treatment (although it always ranked higher than no pre-processing at all). We expected a much clearer difference in quality between raw and processed input data in Polish because of its rich inflection. Intuitively, without term conflation inflected phrases in Polish will not construct a single base cluster by STC and thus should decrease the overall similarity to the ground truth set. In the light of our analysis it is quite difficult to justify this expectation – the quality distribution over different pre-processing configurations was similar for both analyzed languages. Perhaps a more advanced lemmatization algorithm would bring some noticeable improvements.

As for the significance of STC thresholds, due to the limited space in this paper we cannot graphically depict their distribution. However, we noticed that merge threshold is only slightly affecting the quality of the discovered clusters (similar observation was given in [2]). The minimal base cluster score had a much greater impact as there was a clear relationship between its value and the number of produced clusters. This is natural as it is a cut-off threshold for the merge phase, but there was always a visible and steep drop in the number of clusters around a certain value of this threshold (see Fig. 2). This tendency was translated into a slight, but observable increase in the quality measure. This indicates, that one must be very careful in selecting base cluster score threshold, because even a small change of its value may severely affect the number of discovered clusters.

6   Conclusions

Carrot[2] is characterized by several features, which we think are useful for creating custom web search clustering systems. It defines a clear data-driven process of information manipulation. It decreases the time and effort required for building software and allows performing rapid experiments with search results clustering through component reuse and facilitation of their development. The project is provided as open source[2] and aimed mostly at the research community.

We have performed an experimental evaluation of the impact that the pre-processing of two different languages has on the performance of a representative search results clustering algorithm (STC). According to our best knowledge, such experiments have not been performed so far. As it appears from the results, careful language pre-processing does positively influence the quality of discovered clusters (with respect to the entropy-based measure we used). However, it is difficult to evaluate which of the used pre-processing methods (stemming, lemmatization, stop words removal) had the greatest impact on the measured quality. It is also interesting that in case of Polish, a much simpler technique of term conflation (quasi-stemmer) yielded similar results to the dictionary lemmatization method. We observed that the choice of base cluster score threshold of

---
[2] http://www.cs.put.poznan.pl/dweiss/carrot

the STC algorithm is a crucial issue as it strongly affects the number of discovered clusters.

Our experimental study does not limit the possibilities in measuring clustering quality. In particular, we would like to employ the grammatical structure of cluster labels and use this information to check whether they are understandable and informative to the user.

In terms of Carrot^2's development, we would like to focus on development of new components for linguistic analysis (stemming, lemmatization) and search results clustering algorithms (hierarchical methods in particular).

Acknowledgement. This research has been supported by grant 91-393/03-DS.

References

1. Maarek, Y.S., Fagin, R., Ben-Shaul, I.Z., Pelleg, D.: Ephemeral document clustering for web applications. Technical Report RJ 10186, IBM Research (2000)
2. Zamir, O., Etzioni, O.: Grouper: a dynamic clustering interface to Web search results. Computer Networks (Amsterdam, Netherlands: 1999) **31** (1999) 1361–1374
3. Weiss, D., Stefanowski, J.: Web search results clustering in Polish: Experimental evaluation of Carrot. Accepted for New Trends in Intelligent Information Processing and Web Mining Conference, Zakopane, Poland (2003)
4. Everitt, B.S., Landau, S., Leese, M.: Cluster Analysis. fourth edn. Oxford University Press (2001)
5. Hearst, M.A., Pedersen, J.O.: Reexamining the cluster hypothesis: Scatter/gather on retrieval results. In: Proceedings of SIGIR-96, 19th ACM International Conference on Research and Development in Information Retrieval, Zürich, CH (1996) 76–84
6. Boley, D., Gini, M., Gross, R., Han, S., Hastings, K., Karypis, G., Kumar, V., Mobasher, B., Moore, J.: Partitioning-based clustering for web document categorization. Decision Support Systems **27** (1999) 329–341
7. Hannappel, P., Klapsing, R., Neumann, G.: MSEEC - a multi search engine with multiple clustering. In: Proceedings of the 99 Information Resources Management Association International Conference, Hershey, Pennsylvania (1999)
8. Masłowska, I., Słowiński, R.: Hierarchical clustering of large text corpora. Accepted for New Trends in Intelligent Information Processing and Web Mining Conference, Zakopane, Poland (2003)
9. Dong, Z.: Towards Web Information Clustering. PhD thesis, Southeast University, Nanjing, China (2002)
10. Zamir, O.: Clustering Web Documents: A Phrase-Based Method for Grouping Search Engine Results. PhD thesis, University of Washington (1999)
11. Larsson, J.N.: Structures of String Matching and Data Compression. PhD thesis, Department of Comp. Science, Lund University (1999)
12. Macskassy, S.A., Banerjee, A., Davison, B.D., Hirsh, H.: Human performance on clustering web pages: A preliminary study. In: Knowledge Discovery and Data Mining. (1998) 264–268
13. Dom, B.E.: An information-theoretic external cluster-validity measure. Technical Report IBM Research Report RJ 10219, IBM (2001)

Practical Evaluation of Textual Fuzzy Similarity as a Tool for Information Retrieval[*]

Piotr S. Szczepaniak[1,2] and Marcin Gil[1]

[1] Institute of Computer Science, Technical University of Lodz
Sterlinga 16/18, 90-217 Lodz, Poland
[2] Systems Research Institute, Polish Academy of Sciences
Newelska 6, 01-447 Warsaw, Poland

Abstract. This paper presents a practical evaluation of a document retrieval method based on a certain textual fuzzy similarity measure. The similarity measure was originally introduced in [1] – cf. also [2], and later used in Internet-related applications [3,4]. Three textual databases of diverse level of freedom in the content of documents are used for experiments in the search. In other words, the relation of the documents within each group to the chosen topic is (according to the evaluating person) strong, average, and random. The results of the search coincide with intuition and confirm the expectation that methods based on similarity are advantageous as long as the database contains documents of a relatively well-defined topic.

Keywords: information retrieval, textual documents, fuzzy set, fuzzy similarity measure, text comparison

1 Introduction

Although it undoubtedly contains information that is often structured in a chaotic way or may even be wrong, the Internet has become an information source of unquestionable importance. Consequently, the aspiration to meet an obvious need for effective information retrieval by making improvements in the solutions offered by the popular indexing engines can be observed.

In textual database searching, the methods used so far for text comparison have been based mainly on the classical identity relation, according to which two given texts are either identical or not (assuming that certain simple preprocessing operations are not taken into account). The definition of distance for textual objects is a more complicated task than determination of the distance from a data vector to the prototype; examples like Jaccard, Cosine and Dice Coefficients can frequently be found in

---

[*] This work has partly been supported by the NATO Scientific Committee via the Spanish Ministry for Science and Technology; grantholder – P.S.Szczepaniak; host institution – Politechnical University, Madrid, Spain, 2002/2003.

E. Menasalvas et al. (Eds.): AWIC 2003, LNAI 2663, pp. 250–257, 2003.
© Springer-Verlag Berlin Heidelberg 2003

the literature, e.g. [5–7]. The similarity of two documents is usually determined on the basis of the number of topical terms that appear in both of them.

Novel methods aim at approximate matching of the requirement formulated as a query; an example of an appropriate proposition is described in [4]. Here, the *fuzziness* in the sense of Zadeh [8] is the approach to establish a more sophisticated method for the text similarity analysis [1,2].

1.1 Basic Definitions – Fuzzy Set and Fuzzy Relation

A fuzzy set A in a non-empty space X is a set of ordered pairs

$$A = \{<x, \mu_A(x)>: x \in X \},\tag{1.1}$$

where $\mu_A: X \to [0,1]$ – the membership function.

In other words, to each element of a considered space, a positive real number from the [0,1] interval is added and interpreted as a "membership level (or degree)".
On the basis of (1.1), a fuzzy relation can be defined, cf.[9].

A fuzzy relation R in the Cartesian product of two non-empty spaces X and Y is a set of pairs:

$$R = \{<(x, y), \mu_R(x, y)>: x \in X, \quad y \in Y \},\tag{1.2}$$

where $\mu_R: X \times Y \to [0,1]$ is the membership function. The positive real number $\mu_R(x, y)$ is usually interpreted as a degree of relationship between x and y.

If it has the following properties:

    a)   reflexivity, if and only if

$$\mu_R(x, x) = 1 \qquad\qquad \forall x \in X \tag{1.3}$$

    b)   symmetry, if and only if

$$\mu_R(x, y) = \mu_R(y, x) \qquad\qquad \forall x, y \in X, \tag{1.4}$$

then the fuzzy relation is called a "neighbourhood relation" and can be interpreted as a model of non-transitive similarity.

1.2 Fuzzy Relation for Text Comparison

The fuzzy relation

$$RW = \{(<w_1, w_2>, \mu_{RW}(w_1, w_2)): w_1, w_2 \in W\}$$

on W – the set of all words within the universe of discourse, for example a considered language or dictionary – is proposed in [1,2] as a useful instrument.

A possible form of the membership function μ_{RW}: $W \times W \rightarrow [0,1]$ may be

$$\mu_{RW}(w_1, w_2) = \frac{2}{(N^2 + N)} \sum_{i=1}^{N(w_1)} \sum_{j=1}^{N(w_1)-i+1} h(i, j) \qquad \forall\ w_1, w_2 \in W \qquad (1.5)$$

where:

$N(w_1)$, $N(w_2)$ – the number of letters in words w_1, w_2, respectively;
$N = \max\{N(w_1), N(w_2)\}$ – the maximal length of the considered words;
$h(i,j)$ – the value of a binary function,
   i.e. $h(i, j) = 1$ if a subsequence, containing i letters of word w_1 and beginning
      from the j-th position in w_1, appears at least once in word w_2;
  otherwise $h(i, j) = 0$;
$h(i, j) = 0$ also if $i > N(w_2)$ or $i > N(w_1)$.

Note that $0,5\ (N^2 + N)$ is the number of possible subsequences to be considered.

Example:

Compare two words: $w_1 = $ 'centre' and $w_2 = $ 'center'.
Here, $N(w_1) = 6$, $N(w_2) = 6$, thus $N = 6$.

$$\mu_{RW}(w_1, w_2) = \frac{2}{N^2 + N} \sum_{i=1}^{6} \sum_{j=1}^{6-i+1} h(i, j) = \frac{6+3+2+1}{21} \cong 0,57$$

because in w_2 there are:

 6 one-element subsequences of w_1 (c, e, n, t, r, e);
 3 two-element subsequences of w_1 (ce, en, nt);
 2 three-element subsequences of w_1 (cen, ent);
 1 four-element subsequence of w_1 (cent) − this is the longest subsequence of w_1
                 that can be found in w_2.

Note that the fuzzy relation RW is reflexive: $\mu_{RW}(w, w) = 1$ for any word w; but in general it is not symmetrical. This inconvenience can be easily avoided as follows:

$$\mu_{RW}(w_1, w_2) = \min\{\mu_{RW}(w_1, w_2), \mu_{RW}(w_2, w_1)\}$$

Moreover, RW reflects the following human intuition:
- the bigger is the difference in length of two words, the more different they are;
- the more common letters are contained in two words, the more similar they are.
However, the value of the membership function contains no information on the sense or semantics of the arguments.

Basing on measure (1.5) it is possible to introduce the similarity measure for documents. Here, the document is considered to be a set (not a sequence) of words. The respective formula is of the form [1,2,4]

$$\mu_{RD}(d_1, d_2) = \frac{1}{N} \sum_{i=1}^{N(d_1)} \max_{j \in \{1,...,N(d_2)\}} \mu_{RW}(w_i, w_j)$$

(1.6)

where:

d_1, d_2 – the documents to be compared;

$N(d_1), N(d_2)$ – the number of words in document d_1 and d_2

(the length of d_1 and d_2, respectively);

$N = \max \{ N(d_1), N(d_2) \}$;

μ_{RW} – the similarity measure for words defined by (1.5).

2 Search and Ranking

To make the evaluation as objective as possible, three diverse databases of textual documents were prepared on a local computer. The relation of documents within each group to the chosen topic was (according to the person who performed the preparation) strong, average, and random – see Sect. 3.

Then, the necessary introductory operations of the character standard for identity search (like indexing), or being specific for the applied method – creation of a similarity database – were performed. Apart from all words in the dictionary (built during the standard stage) the similarity database involved also identifiers of the words considered to be similar according to relation (1.5) with an arbitrary similarity threshold. The comparison of all words from the dictionary with one another proved to be the most time consuming procedure – $O(N^2)$ where N is the number of words.

The admissible query involves: single words, operators AND or OR, and option for identity or similarity search.

The ranking was performed according to the following formula:

$$rank(d_i) = \sum_{k=1}^{K} weight\_of\_w_k$$

where w_k $(k=1,2, \ldots, K)$ denotes word w_k found in document d_i, and

$$weight\_of\_w_k = (index\_max - position) \cdot c$$

with *position* standing for the number determining position of the word in the text, and

c denoting a coefficient representing the location rank (e.g. title, keyword).

The idea behind the described construction of the weighting scheme lies in the behaviour of an average user, who generally reads N words forming a few initial paragraphs only and on this basis takes the decision whether a chosen document contains the information that he needs or not. If it does not, the user takes no further effort to continue the reading of the rest of the document. Conclusion: the farther from the beginning of a document a given place is, the fewer are the chances that the user reaches there while reading.

Words in documents are also ranked in terms of importance. As chosen by authors themselves, sets of words that constitute titles of documents can be assumed to be relevant to the whole documents or even to represent them. The same can be claimed about keywords. Hence, coefficient c is applied to enable taking into account the importance of words resulting from where they are found.

The ranking of a given document, denoting its position on a result list presented to the user, is determined on the basis of the ranks of the words found in a particular document.

3   Practical Evaluation

As mentioned, the evaluation was performed on three different textual databases.

Collection I.

Topic is well-defined; the documents deal with a specialised software so the vocabulary is restricted. The original source is "*SleepyCat Software*" [10] that is freely available. The language is English, and the number of documents is 828.

Indexing Parameters.

- indexing subjects: words in the title, keywords and 2000 words from the beginning of the document;
- used length of the document not exceeding 50 000 bytes;
- length of words restricted to range from 3 to 12 characters with shorter words being rejected and longer cut.

Example of Retrieval.

Query: Berkeley AND database AND software.
Identity search: 466 results; documents 1–10 from the obtained list evaluated as fully satisfactory – subjective relevance grade 100%.
Similarity search: 474 results; subjective relevance grade of the documents 1–9 – 100%.

In fact, all the ten documents were the same in both cases; the only difference was one reference to one document of the second list. However, the order of the ranking was different, proving that the similarity search prefers documents having more words similar to those of the query.

Remark. Similarity search proves to work very well. It does not omit important documents; additionally it presents more relevant documents and strongly affects the ranking.

Collection II.

Topic is quite well-defined; the documents are from the field of fantasy; the vocabulary in them is very rich, sometimes even unusual with non-existing words. The documents are written in a natural language and come from many sources in the area of '*role playing games*' and presentations of the world of J.R.R.Tolkien. The language is Polish and the number of documents is 312.

Indexing Parameters. The same as in *Collection I.*

Example of Retrieval.

Query: budowa AND golem.
('budowa' is "structure" in English; golem – a kind of monster)
Identity search: No results.
Similarity search: One result; subjective relevance grade – 100%; ranking – 165 219 points.

The use of inflected forms of the query terms, like 'budowy', 'golema', 'golemów', does not improve the situation. The use of the operator OR results in the retrieval of the right document but its ranking is only 30 427 points.

Remark. Similarity search works well. In particular, it shows to be well suited for languages characterised by rich inflexion of words, like Polish, and is not sensitive to errors. It does not omit important documents; additionally it presents more relevant documents. However, it may sometimes retrieve a wrong document if the words differ only slightly in form but significantly in meaning.

Collection III.

Topic is not defined, while the vocabulary is very rich. The documents are written in a natural language, including local dialects or jargon, and come from different sources, like science fiction, cookbook, sea songs and shanties, navy and yachting. The language is Polish, and the number of documents is 508.

Indexing Parameters. The same as in *Collection I.*

Example of Retrieval.

Query: sernik.   ('sernik' means "cheesecake" in English)
Identity search: three correct results; subjective relevance grade – 100%.
Similarity search: 24 results, most of them wrong, though.

Remark. Similarity search offers many non-relevant documents. The only advantage is that it is well suited for highly inflected languages, like Polish, and is not sensitive to common spelling errors.

For completeness of presentation it is necessary to mention that the retrieval system was implemented on the Linux platform, with the use of Apache server, and C++ programming language.

4 Summary

Comparison of words is an important issue of information retrieval. One of the difficulties that need being overcome is caused by numerous forms of the same word (which is particularly frequent and typical of Slavonic languages). A specific group of problems is due to users making spelling mistakes when formulating their query. A good solution to it would be sending such users back to school; another, perhaps more realistic one, is to equip the computer with a piece of intelligence.

The commonly accepted measure for similarity of words is the Levenshtein distance defined as the minimal number of character deletions, replacements, and insertions needed to obtain identical words. For example, the comparison of the words *"computer"* and *"computing"* results in the distance equal three – one letter to delete (or insert), and two letters to replace. Variations of this basic concept and extensions to longer textual sequences are relatively simple to create.

The presented method does not operate on words by changing their fragments; it computes the occurrence of identical sequences of letters by increasing the length of the compared fragments. Moreover, it is based on concepts having their origin in the fuzzy sets theory. It deals with certain specific quantitative similarity of words and sentences assuming that, to some extent, the presence of identical sequences of letters indicates the possibility of a similar semantic content. Unfortunately, not always is this expectation fulfilled.

Another shortcoming of the method is the long time needed for text comparison, which can sometimes make the real-time application not quite sensible. However, filtering is certainly the task where the method may prove its usefulness.

The method may be applied to a search based on single keywords or groups of words. Moreover, the comparison may also be performed on long textual documents, cf. formula (1.6). The described solution is not sensitive to grammatical mistakes or other misshapen language constructions. As shown, it is particularly well capable of dealing with well-structured and specialised documents related to a well-defined domain in which, despite the domain-restricted specific vocabulary, there exists freedom of the natural language.

References

1   Niewiadomski A. (2000): *Appliance of fuzzy relations for text document comparing*. Proceedings of the 5th Conference NNSC, Zakopane, Poland, pp. 347–352.
2   Niewiadomski A., Szczepaniak P.S. (2001): *Intutionistic Fuzzy Relations in Approximate Text Comparison*. Published in Polish: *Intuicjonistyczne relacje rozmyte w przybliżonym porównywaniu tekstów*. In: Chojcan J. Łȩski J. (Eds.): *Zbiory rozmyte i ich zastosowania*. Silesian Technical University Press, Gliwice, Poland, pp.271-282; ISBN 83-88000-64-0.

3   Niewiadomski A., Szczepaniak P.S., (2002). *Fuzzy Similarity in E-Commerce Domains.* In: Segovia J., Szczepaniak P.S., Niedzwiedzinski M. (Eds.) *E-Commerce and Intelligent Methods.* Physica-Verlag, A Springer-Verlag Company, Heidelberg, New York.

4   Szczepaniak P.S., Niewiadomski A. (2003). *Internet Search Based on Text Intuitionistic Fuzzy Similarity.* In: Szczepaniak P.S., Segovia J., Kacprzyk J., Zadeh L. (Eds.) *Intelligent Exploration of the Web.* Physica-Verlag, A Springer-Verlag Company, Heidelberg, New York.

5   Lebart L., Salem A., Berry L. (1998). *Exploring Textual Data.* Kluwer Academic Publisher.

6   Baeza-Yates R., Ribeiro-Neto B. (1999). *Modern Information Retrieval.* Addison Wesley, New York.

7   Ho T.B., Kawasaki S., Nguyen N.B. (2003). *Documents Clustering using Tolerance Rough Set Model and Its Application to Information Retrieval.* In: Szczepaniak P.S., Segovia J., Kacprzyk J., Zadeh L. (Eds.) *Intelligent Exploration of the Web.* Physica-Verlag, A Springer-Verlag Company, Heidelberg, New York.

8   Zadeh L. (1965). *Fuzzy Sets.* Information and Control, **8**, pp. 338–353.

9   Pedrycz W., Gomide F. (1998): *An Introduction to Fuzzy Sets; Analysis and Design.* A Bradford Book, The MIT Press, Cambridge, Massachusetts and London, England.

10   SleepyCat Software, Inc. BerkeleyDB Documentation;
     http://www.sleepycat.com

Rough – Fuzzy Reasoning for Customized Text Information Retrieval

Shailendra Singh, P. Dhanalakshmi, and Lipika Dey

Department of Mathematics,
Indian Institute of Technology,
Hauz Khas, New Delhi, India – 110016
{lipika,shailen}@maths.iitd.ernet.in

Abstract. Due to the large repository of documents available on the web, users are usually inundated by a large volume of information most of which are found to be irrelevant. Since user perspectives vary, a client-side text filtering system that learns the user's perspective can reduce the problem of irrelevant retrieval. In this paper, we have provided the design of a customized text information filtering system which learns user preferences and uses a rough-fuzzy reasoning scheme to filter out irrelevant documents. The rough set based reasoning takes care of natural language nuances like synonym handling, very elegantly. The fuzzy decider provides qualitative grading to the documents for the user's perusal. We have provided the detailed design of the various modules and some results related to the performance analysis of the system.

1 Introduction

Search engines help users locate information from the World Wide Web. A list of URLs is returned, which is ordered according to the relevance of a document to the user query. The precision of this list is generally very low. This is because usually any two users differ in their perspectives and hence a general relevance computation function cannot satisfy all users simultaneously. Thus, the only viable way to increase precision of retrieval would be to use a client side information filtering system, which can learn the client's perspective and re-order the documents according to a relevance function specific to the client.

In this paper, we have proposed a rough-fuzzy hybridized approach to design a client side system, which can pro-actively filter out irrelevant documents for the user, in a domain of long-term interest to the user. This is a system which when installed on a client – side machine can continuously rate new documents in the domain. To begin with, the user is asked to rank a set of training documents retrieved through a standard search-engine. The user response is then analyzed to form a query which represents the user's interests in a more focused way. This modified query is then fed to the search engine and has been found to retrieve better documents. However, since these documents are also ordered by the ranking scheme of the search engine, they do not reflect the client's preferences. We have, therefore used a rough-fuzzy reasoning

E. Menasalvas et al. (Eds.): AWIC 2003, LNAI 2663, pp. 258–267, 2003.

methodology which ranks these documents and orders them according to the user preferences.

Section 2 presents a brief review of related work on text-filtering system and rough set based document retrieval. Sections 3, 4, 5, 6 and 7 present the details of the various modules of our system and some results.

2   Review of Related Work on Customized Text Retrieval and Rough Set Based Document Retrieval

Significant work has been done towards building client side text retrieval systems based on user ratings. "Syskill & Webert" [1] is a software agent that learns to rate pages on the web to decide what pages might interest the user. Initially, the user is asked to rate a few explored pages on a three-point scale, and the agent learns the user profile by analysing this information. The system converts HTML source codes of a web page into a boolean feature vector of words, indicating presence or absence of words. This system determines the words to be used as features by finding the expected information gain that the presence or absence of a word W gives toward the classification of elements of a set of pages. A Bayesian classifier is used to determine the degree of interest of a new page to the user. "ProspectMiner" [2] is another retrieval system that learns the users' interests based on user rating. The retrieval system suggests better queries, which will fetch more relevant pages. The software agent also takes into account the co-occurrence and nearness of the words. Apart from document rating, the retrieval system requires a term-feedback from the user and maintains a thesaurus with respect to the words present in the initial query. Balabanovic's Fab system [3] recommends web sites to users, based on a personal profile that becomes adapted to the user over time. The user's ratings of pages are used to grow the user's profile adaptively, so that the recommendations gradually become more personalized.

Most of the systems described above have used probabilistic measures for judging the relevance of a document to a user. We will now give a brief introduction to rough sets and also an overview of how rough-set based analysis is used for text information retrieval.

Rough sets were introduced by Pawlak in [4]. A rough set based analysis helps in the extraction of classificatory knowledge, particularly in a domain that sports non-unique classification. Since natural language texts cannot be classified uniquely as "good" or "bad" just by considering the words that are present in the document, a rough set based analysis rather than a crisp logic based one is ideally suited for a text filtering system. The core of all rough-set based reasoning contains an equivalence relation called the indiscernibility relation. The universe is partitioned into a set of equivalence classes.

The equivalence classes obtained from an indiscernibility relation are used to define set approximations. Let $X \subseteq U$. X can be approximated using only the information contained in the equivalence classes formed by the indiscernibility relation, denoted by R. Lower approximation of X denoted by $\underline{apr}_R(X)$ contains those elements whose equivalence classes are wholly contained in X. The upper approximation of X contains elements from those equivalence classes which have non-null intersection with X. Thus the lower approximation of X contains those elements which can be *definitely* classified as members of X, while the objects in $\overline{\text{apr}_R}\left(X\right)$ can only be classified as *possible* members of X. The boundary region contains those objects which lie in the difference of the two approximations. *A set is said to be rough (crisp) if this boundary region is non-empty (empty).* Two rough subsets can be compared to each other for similarity using their approximations.

In the context of text-information retrieval the equivalence relation used is the synonymy relation, which establishes equivalence of two synonymous words. Thus two texts can be considered to be similar if they contain synonymous words and not necessarily the same words. Srinivasan et al. introduced a set of rough similarity measures in [6] to compute document overlaps. Let S_1 and S_2 represent two subsets, which are collections of weighted words. The weight of a word represents the relative importance of the word in the text. Let S_1 represent the words in a retrieved document and S_2 represent the words in a query. One would be interested to find the similarity between the query and the document in order to judge the relevance of the document with respect to the query.

Now, since we have weighted words, a fuzzy approximation to the sets are determined using the weights of the words. A word is considered to be present in a set provided its relevance is greater than a prescribed threshold. Similarly, a synonym is considered to be equivalent to a word provided the degree of synonymy is greater then the threshold.

The approximations for a set S is computed as the union of the approximations of all the words occurring in it. These approximations are then used to find the similarity between two weighted set of words S_1 and S_2, where S1 represents the words in the document and S_2 represents those in the query. Let B_1 denote the *lower approximation* of subset S_2 with S_1 and B_u denote the *upper approximation* of subset S_2 with S_1 The approximations can be used to determine whether a document contains the words or their synonyms present in the query.

The similarity of two subsets S_1 and S_2 is defined in [6] as

$$\underline{\text{Similarity}}_R\left(S_1,S_2\right)=1-\left[\frac{\text{card}(B_l)}{\text{card}\left(\underline{\text{apr}}_R\left(S_2\right)\right)}\right] \tag{1}$$

and

$$\overline{\text{Similarity}}_R\left(S_1,S_2\right)=1-\left[\frac{\text{card}(B_u)}{\text{card}\left(\overline{\text{apr}}_R\left(S_2\right)\right)}\right] \tag{2}$$

where (1) denotes the lower similarity and (2) denotes the upper similarity of S_1 and S_2 considering S_2 as the focus in the comparison. In both the cases the value will be 0 for no match and 1 for maximum match between S_1 and S_2 We will explain in the next few sections how we have used these concepts of rough similarity measures between texts to perform customized text information filtering by our proposed system. Chouchoulas et al describes a rough set based text categorization system in [7] for classifying e-mails. Das Gupta [8] specifies a few more theoretical measures for computing rough similarity of documents.

3 Architecture of the Customized Text Filtering System

Most of the search engines employ a word frequency based function for computing relevance of a document without taking the user feedback into consideration.

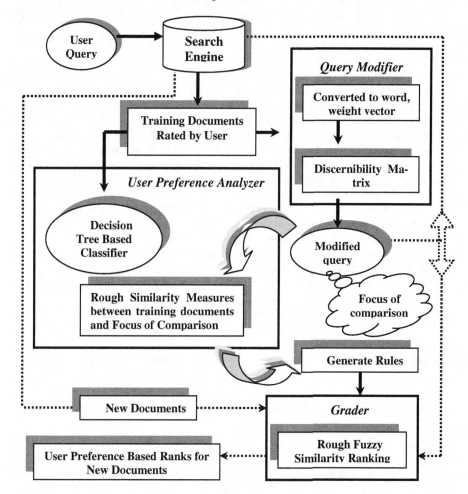

Fig. 1. Schematic view of the Relevant Information Retriever

A rough set based relevance measure can be used for more focused relevance computations with initial feedback from user, which provides the class decision. The most unique aspect of our system is the use of the rough – set theoretic concept of *discernibility* to identify words which help in distinguishing between relevant and irrelevant documents. These words, along with their extracted weights form a modified query for the user indicating the words which should be present or absent in a good document. This query, when fed to the search engine again, is found to yield better documents. However, since the ordering of the new documents is still dependent on the underlying search engine, we have used a rough-fuzzy reasoning scheme to rank these documents for the client. The system is equipped to present both a crisp rank and a fuzzy membership value of the documents to the user. The user can judge the quality of a document from its fuzzy membership and decide whether to read it or not.

Figure 1 gives a schematic view of the complete system. Once the user specifies a query to a search engine, we select a subset of the top ranked documents to act as the training set for the system. The user is asked to rate each training document on a three point scale in which 1 stands for bad, 2 for average and 3 for good. Grossly, the functions of the various modules are as follows:

Query Modifier – Every training document which is rated by the user is converted to a weighted vector of words. A *discernibility matrix* is then constructed based on the user's ranking and the weighted word vector for each training document. This is explained in section 4. The matrix is scanned to extract the set of most discerning words which yields the *modified query*. The words in the modified query may be having positive or negative weights. Words with positive weight help in distinguishing between good and bad documents by their relatively high degree of presence in good ones and a low degree of presence in the bad ones. Words with negative weights have a high degree of presence in bad documents and low degree in good ones. Boolean algebra operators are used to form an effective query. When this modified query is fed to search engine, it is observed that the documents returned are in general better.

User Preference Analyzer – This module uses *rough similarity measures* described in the earlier section, to learn the user preferences for rating of documents. The modified query is the focus of comparison. Lower and upper similarity measures between each training document and the modified query are computed. Fuzzy ranking rules relate the similarity measures to user ratings.

Grader – This module ranks the new retrieved documents using the fuzzy rules extracted by the user preference analyzer. Rough similarity measures between the modified query and each new document is computed, keeping the query as the focus of comparison. The new documents are classified by the fuzzy rules.

4   Forming Modified Query with Most Discerning Words

Every training document is converted to a weighted vector of words appearing in the document using the HTML source code of the pages. Each tag like <B>, <I> etc. are assigned weights. The weighted frequency of each word is then computed as follows:

$$W(x) = \sum_{i=\text{Tag frequency}}^{n} w_i \times n_i$$

where w_i represents the weight of the tag i and n_i represents the number of times the word x appears with the tag i. The weights are normalized by dividing the weight of each word in a document by the maximum weight of a word in that document. Each document is then represented by its top 50 words, since this is found to be sufficient. Using the weighted words and the user ratings, we now construct a *discernibility matrix* to identify discerning words. Suppose documents D_1, D_2 and D_3 have user ratings 1, 2 and 3 respectively. Further, suppose that D_1 has W_1 and W_2 with weights 1.0 and 0.5, $D2$ has W_1 and W_3 with weights 0.5 and 1.0, while D_3 has W_2 and W_3, with weights 0.25 and 1.0. Since W_3 appears in both D_2 and D_3 with a high weight, it cannot distinguish between an 'average' document and a 'good' document. On the other hand, the word W_1 can distinguish a 'bad' document from a 'good' one.

Let the number of distinct documents in the training set be n and the number of distinct words in the entire training set be k. The *discernibility matrix* for this set contains a row for every pair of documents which have different decisions. The weights of every word over all the documents are broken up into intervals and each interval corresponds to a column in the discernibility matrix. Every $(i, j)^{th}$ entry in the matrix indicates whether the mid-point of the jth interval distinguishes the document pair in the ith row, with respect to the word. Table 1 shows the discernibility matrix for D_1, D_2 and D_3.

Table 1. Discernibility matrix

Document	$W_1 (0, .5)$	$W_1 (.5, 1)$	$W_2 (0, .25)$	W_2 (.25,	$W_3 (0, 1)$
(D_1, D_2)	0	1	1	1	1
(D_2, D_3)	1	0	1	0	0
(D_1, D_3)	2	2	0	2	2

[5] states the MD heuristic algorithm for finding the most discerning elements from a discernibility matrix. In that, all entries are binary since all class differences are represented by 1. We have modified this scheme and our (i,j)th entry contains a 0 to indicate no difference and the actual category difference value when there is a distinction. This helps us to identify words that are able to distinguish a 'bad' document from a 'good' one as more discerning than one which differentiate between a good and an average one. Hence, in our proposed modification of the MD heuristic algorithm, we take into account the degree of difference in ranks of the document pairs that are being discerned. The modified MD-heuristic algorithm to find out the words with the highest discerning power now works as follows:

Step 1: Initialize i to the highest class difference
Step 2: If there is no column containing i, then i = i – 1 /* No word which discriminates between the extreme categories */
Step 3: Choose a column with the maximal number of occurrences of i's /* The word which maximally discriminates between documents with wide apart ratings */
Step 4: Delete the word corresponding to the column. Delete all the rows containing i in this column. /* All documents discerned by this word are not considered further */
Step 5: If there are more rows left, then go to step 1. Else stop.

This algorithm takes in the discernibility matrix as input and produces a list of words, which collectively discern all pairs of documents rated by the user. Now, we construct a **modified query** using these words. We feed the modified query to the search engine again. However, this set still contains some irrelevant documents and is also not ordered according to the user preference. In the next section, we will elaborate on how the irrelevant documents can be filtered out from this set.

5   User Preference Analyzer – Learning the User's Basis for Rating

To learn the user's ranking paradigm, we compute rough similarity measures between the modified query and the training documents, using equations (1) and (2), with the modified query as the focus of comparison. We compute the lower and upper similarities between each training document and the modified query treating synonymous words as equivalent up to a specified degree of synonymy. Since there is no apparent unique association between the similarity measures and the user's rating, a decision tree is constructed, which summarizes the relationship as a set of rules. These rules typically relate the rank assigned to a document by the user to its similarity measures. The decision tree is constructed using ID3 algorithm. Here is a sample ranking rule generated for our system: *Rule: If Lower similarity > 0.027 and Upper Similarity <= 0.1111111 then Class = 1 (bad)* (9/2, lift 3.6), where the number of training cases covered by the rule is 9 and 2 of them do not belong to the class predicted by the rule. The lift x is the estimated accuracy of the rule divided by the prior probability of the predicted class.

6   Filtering Out Irrelevant Documents for the User

Finally, the system uses the rules generated by the preference analyzer to filter out irrelevant documents from the new set of documents retrieved. For this we use a fuzzy reasoning scheme which provides both a crisp document rank as well as a fuzzy visualizer, which provides a qualitative idea about the relevance of a document.

Fuzzy reasoning consists of two core activities – editing the fuzzy input and output membership functions. The rules give us an idea about the cut-off values and the membership functions to be used for the input parameters – lower similarity and upper similarity and the class decisions. We have used the triangular function to represent the bad decision class, the gaussian function to represent the average decision class and the sigmoidal function to represent the good decision class. Their relationships with the input parameters are extracted from the rules. Figure 2 (left) shows such an example function which defines the spread of the decision categories. As is obvious, the "badness" of a document decreases as its "averageness" increases, while its "averageness" decreases as its "goodness" increases. The input rules indicate that it is easier to differentiate between a bad and an average document while it is more difficult to differentiate between an average and a good one.

We have used the Fuzzy Reasoning Toolbox of MatLab to implement the fuzzy reasoning scheme. To rank a new document, it is represented as a vector of weighted words. Using the modified query as the focus of comparison, we now compute the lower and upper similarity measures between the modified query and the new document. These similarity values along with the fuzzy membership functions are used to generate the fuzzy membership value of the document to the categories good, average and bad.

Figure 2 (right) shows some sample fuzzy membership values for documents of different categories. A crisp membership value to each individual category may also be obtained and the document may be awarded the class with the maximum membership value.

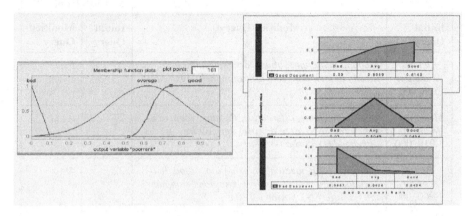

Fig. 2. (*Left*) Editing Membership function for document category in Matlab fuzzy reasoning toolbox, (*right top*) fuzzy membership visualizer for good document, (right centre) average document and (*right bottom*) bad document

7 Results

In this section we will present some performance analysis of our system. Table 2 shows some initial and modified queries we obtained in different domains along with the number of URLs returned. It is obvious that the precision of the system has increased, since the number of bad documents is fewer in the top 50 urls. The same users have been asked to rate the initial and final set of documents to maintain uniform standards of ranking. In all the cases, the users preferred authoritative pages containing good documentation about the topic, to simple link pages.

We have computed the accuracy of the system by comparing the system-generated ranks with user's feedback. Accuracy of system evaluation is defined as

$$\text{Accuracy} = \frac{\text{no. of matches in system rating and user rating}}{\text{Total no. of documents rated by system}} \times 100 \qquad (3)$$

Table 3 summarizes the accuracy of the system's ranking mechanism in various domains, by comparing it with user ranks. Since bad documents can be identified by the system, these can be eliminated from the list presented to the user. In any case, the list is re-ordered, so that the number of bad documents in the top decreases.

Table 2. Modified queries and no. of bad documents in top 50's corresponding to initial and modified query: (-) indicates negative weight

Initial, Modified query & no. of Retrieved Urls using Google		No. of Bad Doc's in Top 50's from	
Initial Query	Modified Query	Initial Query	Modified Query
Alcohol Addiction 528, 000	*Alcohol, addictions, abuse, drugs, treatment, health, description, rehabilitation, help, revised (-) 3270*	25	5
Alternative Medicine 1,910, 000	*Health, medicine, alternative, therapy, yoga, acupuncture, stress, diet, disease, agriculture (-), altvetmed (-), dosha (-) 3940*	27	6
Blood Cancer 1,960, 000	*Cancer, health, medical, information, blood, leukaemia, help, myeloma, alive, symptom, companion (-), safety (-), poison (-) 40*	22	4
Air Pollution 2,180, 000	*Air, Pollution, Health, Carbon, Environmental, Research, Smog, Quality, Rain, Clean 8, 810*	23	5
HIV 6,360,000	*AIDS, Treatment, HIV, Epidemic, Health, Description, Information, Service, Virus, Details (-) 6,150*	36	14
Indian Tourism 695, 000	*India, Tourism, Information, Indian, Pradesh, Indiaworld 190*	38	9

Table 3. Accuracy of system evaluation: comparing system rank vs user rating

Domain	Accuracy
Alcohol Addiction	80%
Alter Medicine	67.74%
Blood Cancer	72.3%
Air Pollution	80%
HIV	85%
Indian Tourism	85%

8 Conclusion

In this paper we have presented a complete client-side filtering system for general text documents. The system uses the rough set theoretic concept of discernibility to find words that can discern between good documents and bad ones by analyzing a set of training documents ranked by the user. This scheme is more powerful than the usual techniques of computing term frequency and inverse document frequency, since it takes into consideration the synonymous words very elegantly. A modified query is built with the discerning words. This query is found to fetch documents which are more relevant to the user. However, since the documents are still fetched by a traditional search engine, the ordering of the returned documents is not customized for the user. Hence, we have proposed a rough-fuzzy reasoning scheme which re-ranks the documents. The system first learns the user's basis of ranking by relating the ranks to rough similarity measures between the training documents and the modified query. These associations are learnt using a decision tree and the classification knowledge is expressed as a set of rules. These rules are used to rank new documents on the basis of rough similarity measures between the new documents and the modified query. To obtain a performance analysis of the system, we requested the users to give their feedback about the retrieved documents also. The system ranking scheme is found to work reasonably well. Currently, we are extending the system to handle more knowledge intensive query processing using an underlying ontology. Rough similarity measures between various related concepts enables intelligent query processing.

References

1. Pazzani, M., Muramatsu, J., Billsus, D.: Syskill & Webert: Identifying Interesting Web Sites. Proceedings of the National Conference on Artificial Intelligence. Portland, OR (1996)
2. http://industry.java.sun.com/javanews/stories/story2/0,1072,1 8628,00.html
3. Balabanoic, M.: An Adaptive Web Page Recommendation Service. First Int. Conference on Autonomous Agents. (2000) 378-85 ACM
4. Pawlak, Z.: Rough Sets. Int. Journal of Computer and Information Sciences, Vol. 11(5) (1982) 341–356
5. Komorowski, J., Polkowski, L., Andrzej, S.: Rough Sets: A Tutorial. http://www.let.uu.nl/esslli/Courses/skowron/skowron.ps
6. Srinivasan, P., Ruiz, M. E., Kraft, D. H., Chen, J., Kundu, S.: Vocabulary Mining for Information Retrieval: Rough Sets and Fuzzy Sets. Information Processing and Management, Vol. 37 (2001) 15–38
7. Chouchoulas, A., Shen, Q.: Rough Set-Aided Keyword Reduction for Text Categorisation. Journal of Applied Artificial Intelligence, Vol. 15(9) (2001) 843–873
8. Das-Gupta, P.: Rough Sets and Information Retrieval. In Proceedings of the Eleventh Annual International ACM SIGIR Conference on Research and Development in Information Retrieval, Set Oriented Models. (1988) 567–581

A Machine Learning Based Evaluation of a Negotiation between Agents Involving Fuzzy Counter-Offers

Javier Carbo and Agapito Ledezma

[1]Computer Science Department, Univ. Carlos III,
28911 Leganes, Madrid, Spain
{jcarbo,ledezma}@inf.uc3m.es
http://scalab.uc3m.es/~jcarbo
http://scalab.uc3m.es/~ledezma

Abstract. Negotiation plays a fundamental role in systems composed of multiple autonomous agents. Some negotiations may require a more elaborated dialogue where agents would explain offer rejections in a general and vague way. We propose that agents would represent their disappointment about an offer through a fuzzy set applied to each attribute of the offer. Fuzziness can also be very useful in order to make user profiles more difficult to acquire. The satisfaction of this intention is evaluated using classification techniques to compare the accuracy of the models that were obtained from the observation of the behaviour of the agents. In order to test how much information may be extracted about the internal preferences of agents, the task of modeling is translated into a classification task solved by a technique that would generate symbolic representations, such as m5.

1 Introduction

In the last decade, the exponential growth of the access to Internet has leaded to an increasing interest in its economic uses. The number of offers available is one of the advantages of Internet, but they also make personal negotiations (through human interaction) impossible. Therefore, automation is desirable in negotiations. It can be achieved through the use of autonomous programs often called 'agents'.

But the success of agents in commercial negotiations did not come up to expectations. The reasons could be the fear of buyers to reveal their shopping profile. They would probably feel more sure delegating in agents, if the behaviour of these agents exhibited intelligence. Intelligence in negotiations is used to evaluate and answer offers according to the particular preferences of the human users. These preferences form the so called 'shopping profile'.

In commercial negotiations, the information that could be collected about an agent has a strategic (end even economical) value. So agents should avoid revealing unnecessary information. They would do it if they could use some ambiguity in negotiating dialogue.

E. Menasalvas et al. (Eds.): AWIC 2003, LNAI 2663, pp. 268–277, 2003.

The next section gives an overview of previous works on agent-mediated negotiations. Section 3 contains a description of the generic negotiation scheme and protocol proposed. The following section details an example of intelligent behaviour from buyers and merchants. Section 5 describes the foundations of machine learning approach applied in Sect. 6 to test the level of improvement of the proposal. And finally, conclusions summarize the results obtained from the experiments hold.

2 Previous Work

Negotiations take place by the exchange of messages that look forward an agreement satisfactory to both parts. Negotiations have been largely studied by Game Theory. [1]. The major issues in whatever negotiation are protocols and strategies. Protocols rule the communication acts allowed in each moment of a negotiation. They should be public and accepted previously by both parts. Strategies rule the particular behaviour of each part in a negotiation. They should be private because they should reflect the personal preferences of the corresponding part.

Game Theory supposes that the negotiating parts have complete knowledge and total rationality. The former means to know the preferences and beliefs of all participants, the latter means the ability of reproducing the computations of any other participant. When we study negotiations from an agent-mediated perspective, these two assumptions are too restrictive in open and dynamic environments of heterogeneous – and possibly malicious- agents [2].

The alternative adopted with agents is based on: a shared ontology of universally accepted terms of the dominion, a protocol publicly known, and private strategies that are not optimal but computed in real time [3].

Among these types, auctions have become the most popular electronic negotiations. They are usually focused in just only one issue (price), with cardinality 1-to-n and a very complex and prefixed interaction [4]. The number of alternatives that could be taken is very limited, so the negotiation space results restricted [5]. In other way, simple protocols as Contract Net [6] have been proposed. In this one, an agent could just accept or reject totally the offer of the merchants. When both parts are able to propose counter-offers, a greater level of sophistication is achieved [7]. The most complex negotiation scheme proposed involves the use of arguments in order to persuade the other part of improving the offer.

Nevertheless auctions are very different from the daily bargain of markets. Most people is not familiar with their rules. If agents intended to reflect the real behavior of society [8], then a human-like negotiation would be searched.

3 Proposed Scheme of Negotiation

We intend agents to hide preferences of the buyer while persuading merchants of improving their offer. Due to this pretension, we propose to use fuzzy sets to express counter-offers in a protocol extremely simple: a sequence of offers and fuzzy counter-offers. The protocol follows the next execution cycle:

- The buyer agent asks for a product/service
- The merchant agent makes an offer
- The buyer agent rejects the offer, sending a fuzzy counter-offer as response.
- Both agents exchange offers and fuzzy counter-offers sequentially.
- Negotiation ends when the buyer agent accepts the offer, or when any of them withdraws the negotiation (possibly when certain number of messages was exchanged).

Reasoning of both agents follows a sample structure of beliefs, plans and intentions, much alike the BDI paradigm [9]. Each KQML [10] typed message has an illocution associated, these are: request, offer, accept, reject, and withdraw. In the next figure we outline the sequence of messages described above, with a state diagram, whose transitions are messages of the protocol.

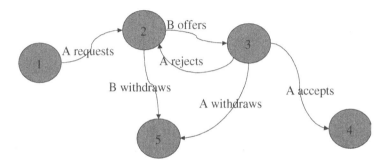

Fig. 1. State diagram of the negotiation protocol proposed

The details of both, offers and counter-proposals, are usually represented by a list of (attribute, value) pairs. However in our protocol, the type of the values, related to the same attribute, are different in offers and counter-offers.

In other words, the merchant agent would fill the attributes with concrete values detailing the agreement proposed. But the buyer agent would explain his rejection through in a general and vague way. This ambiguity reflects the way humans act in popular markets. Buyers give an approach of how much he expects an attribute of the offer to be improved. Commerce should reason with the fuzzy preferences of the user about the desired terms of the agreement. Human reasoning with ambiguity, and vague concepts as tall and young is tackled in Artificial Intelligence with Fuzzy Logic. We propose that only buyer agents would represent their disappointment about an offer through fuzzy values applied to the attributes of the offer.

Fuzzyness can be very useful in order to hide the decision thresholds of the user, and also to increment the expressiveness of his offer rejections. Using a fuzzy set, buyer agents may implicitly transmit a graduation of preferences, together with a measure of their flexibility. We can express these nuances of meaning mathematically with the four squares of a trapezium. The quantity of doubts/ambiguity about what should be considered an acceptable value could be interpreted from the gradient of the trapezium sides.

For instance, fuzziness let agents represent that price is far away from the expected value, and it is also an important attribute, but delivery time is not so much important, and certain modification of this value on both senses would be still acceptable. We can graphically observe two examples of these fuzzy values in the Fig. 2:

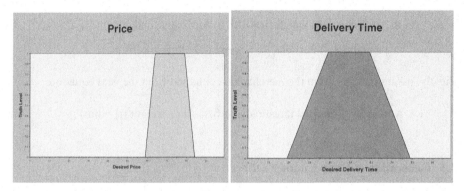

Fig. 2. Fuzzy opinions of the user about price and delivery time attributes

We then conclude that a rejection message express the expected offer with a fuzzy valuation. The list of (attribute, value) pairs in rejections might not be exhaustive. The buyer agent could forgive them because they are already acceptable, or because they are going to be negotiated later. Nevertheless, the offer is composed of an exhaustive list of attributes, and the agent of the merchant is committed with them.

4 Intelligent Behaviour of Agents

In order to test the role played by fuzziness in counter-offers of buyers, the negotiation scheme proposed is compared with a corresponding negotiation where buyers reject the offer of merchants in a concrete way. So the protocol used have to be complemented with the bargaining behaviour of merchants, crisp buyers and fuzzy buyers defined by some preferences function and strategy.

The preferences function of each part consists of a boundary value and a weight for each negotiation attribute. For instance, a buyer may have a positive weight and a minimum threshold value for the attribute 'quality' and a negative weight together with a maximum threshold value for the attribute 'price'. Obviously, the weights of merchants should have opposite sign.

Therefore an agreement is reached when the offer satisfies the next requirements:

$$\forall i \in \text{Attributes, and weigth[i]>0: offer[i] > threshold[i]}, \tag{1}$$

$$\forall j \in \text{Attributes, and weigth[j]>0: offer[j] > threshold[j]},$$

$$\forall k \in \text{Attributes: benefit} > {}_k \text{ weigth[k] } \cdot \text{offer[k]}.$$

The weights and thresholds of each part are chosen with certain random but in a way that agreements are possible, satisfying the next condition:

$$\forall i \in \text{Attributes, and weight[i]>0}, \forall j \in \text{Attributes, and weight [j]<0}: \tag{2}$$

$$| \text{ weight[j] } \cdot \text{ threshold[j] } | > \text{weight[i] } \cdot \text{ threshold[i]}.$$

Finally, the initial offer from the merchant is computed from the next equation:

$$\forall i \in \text{Attributes, offer[i]= threshold[i] + benefit / (weight [i] } \cdot \text{ dim)}. \tag{3}$$

4.1 Generation of Crisp Counter-Offers

Buyers intend two different aims: maximize benefits and minimize the distance with the offer of merchants. Such distance is noted as x and is then used as argument of the goal function z to maximize. Using parameter λ in simplex method in lineal programming with several goals was initially proposed by Zadeh in 1963 [11]. Therefore the definition of goal function z results:

$$\max z = \lambda \ ({}_i \text{ weight[i] } \cdot x_i) + (1-\lambda) \cdot ({}_i -x_i). \tag{4}$$

The restrictions posed over such goal function are obtained from expected benefit from the weighted offer, and from the thresholds of each attribute:

$${}_i \text{ weigth[i] } \cdot x_i >= \text{benefit - } {}_i \text{ weigth[i] } \cdot \text{ offer[i]}. \tag{5}$$

$\forall j \in$ Attributes, and weight[j]>0:

$$x_j >= \max (0, \text{threshold[j]-offer[j]}),$$

$$x_j <= \text{offer[j] } \cdot \lambda \cdot \text{ weight[j] } / (\text{weight[j]-weight[k]}).$$

$\forall k \in$ Attributes, and weight[k]<0:

$$x_k >= \max (0, \text{offer[k]-threshold[k]}),$$

$$x_k <= \text{offer[k] } \cdot \lambda \cdot | \text{ weight[k] } / (\text{weight[j]-weight[k]}) |.$$

Using parameter $0<\lambda<1$ with little values (λ=0.1), benefits are rather less important than the distance with the offer received and it avoids counter-offers very far away from the offer. This approach avoids overreaction and sudden changes in the negotiation. If the problem defined with such λ was infeasible, then λ would be increased until the problem becomes feasible.

4.2 Generation of Fuzzy Counter-Offers

This kind of counter-offers consists of four values for each attribute, representing a piece-wise definition of a trapezium over a dominion of fictitious values. Therefore, merchants could not translate straightforward these values to real values of the dominion corresponding to the given attribute.

However, the shape and relative position of the trapezium should reflect in an indirect way the preferences of the buyer over such attribute. So buyers assign his own scale to the dominion of fictitious values using a value called m. The corresponding dominion results then from offer[i]-m to offer[i]+m. The value m is computed from:

$$m = \max (\,|\text{offer}[i] - \text{threshold}[i]| \,, |\text{benefit} / \text{weight}[i] - \text{offer}[i]|) . \qquad (6)$$

Therefore the four points that define the fuzzy set are the next ones:

$\forall j \in$ Attributes, and weight[j]>0: $\qquad\qquad (7)$

$$x_j^0 = (m + \text{threshold}[j]\text{-offer}[j]) \cdot 100 / m \cdot 2$$

$$x_j^1 = (m + \max (\text{threshold}[j], \text{benefit}/(\text{weight}[j] \cdot \text{dim}))\text{-offer}[j]) \cdot 100 / m \cdot 2$$

$$x_j^2 = 99.999, \ x_j^3 = 100$$

$\forall k \in$ Attributes, and weight[k]>0:

$$x_k^0 = 0, \ x_k^1 = 0.001$$

$$x_k^2 = (m + \min(|\text{benefit} / \text{weight}[k] - \text{offer}[k]|/\text{dim}, \text{offer}[k]) \text{-offer}[k]) \cdot 100 / m \cdot 2$$

$$x_k^3 = (m + \text{threshold}[k]\text{-offer}[k]) \cdot 100 / m \cdot 2x + y = z .$$

On the other hand, merchants have to interpret the fuzzy set received, scaling the dominion with their own weights, expected benefit and thresholds.

5 Machine Learning Based Evaluation

This section describes the experimental sequence needed to obtain a symbolic model m from an agent a_1 (buyer), which is considered as a black box, than can be used by an agent a_2 (merchant). To do so, we have carried out two phases: an agent's negotiation phase between a_1 and a_2, and a modeling phase for obtaining a model m of a_1, that can be used in future by a_2. During the negotiation, the transactions between the agents are recorded.

Once the logs of negotiations has been acquired, the knowledge that tries to model the behaviour of a_1 is obtained by a regression tree modeler ([12], continuous outputs). The detailed steps for training a_2 are as follows:

1. Several negotiations between agent a_1 and agent a_2 are performed. At every transaction, the merchant offers (inputs) and the buyer counter-offer (outputs) are logged to produce a trace of the reactive behaviour of the agent$_1$. From this trace it is straightforward to obtain a set of examples T so that a_2 can learn and model a_1.

2. Let T be the whole set of available examples from a_1 inputs and outputs. Each example t_i in T is made of two parts: an n-dimensional vector representing the attributes $a(t_i)$ and a value $c(t_i)$ representing the class it belongs to.

3. The set T is used to generate the symbolic model m using a learning technique. As the class part of the examples in T are a_1 outputs, the rules generated should model the behaviour of a_1. That is, a_2 can use the model m to predict the output of a_1.

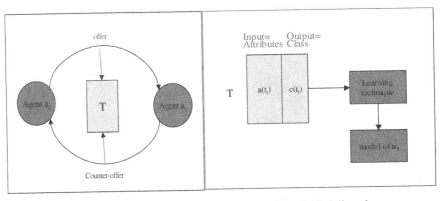

Fig 3. Negotiation phase   **Fig. 4.** Modeling phase

Now, we have to determine how closely m models a_1 behaviour. To do so, we carry out ten-fold cross-validation. M5 use the correlation coefficient to measure the model error. The correlation coefficient is the measure of the correlation between the predicted values and the real values of test instances. If correlation coefficient is 1, the predicted and real values are perfectly correlated. If the correlation coefficient value is close to 0 there is no correlation. A -1 value means that they are inversely correlated

6   Experimental Results

For evaluation purposes, we have considered 242 interactions a long 100 negotiations (4 experiments) between crisp buyers and merchants, and other equivalent 485 interactions a long 100 negotiations (4 experiments) between fuzzy buyers and crisp merchants. In each of these 100 negotiations, buyers and merchants use different preferences functions (essentially weights and thresholds of the negotiation attributes). It is also stated that negotiations fail after a sequence of 10 pairs of offers and counter-offers.

We have test an illustrative example with only two attributes to negotiate: price and quality. One of them (quality) has a positive weight in the preferences function of the buyer, and the other (price) has a negative influence over the possibility of accepting the offer.

Since when the weight of a given attribute is positive, the two first values of the piece-wise definition of the fuzzy set (x^1 and x^2 of quality) are always equal to 0 and 0.001 (Eq. 7), these values are not considered in the evaluation. In the same way, when the weight of the attribute is negative, the two last values of the fuzzy set (x^3 and x^4 of price) are not relevant because they are always equal to 99.999 and 100 (Eq. 7).

Table 1. Correlation coeficient of crisp counter-offers from buyers

No. Experiment	Quality in crisp counter-offer of buyer	Price in crisp counter-offer of buyer	No. Interactions
1	0.8289	0.9679	68
2	0.9343	0.983	73
3	0.6624	0.9854	28
4	0.8187	0.9479	73
Total	0.8937	0.9806	242

Table 2. Correlation coeficient of fuzzy counter-offers from buyers

No. Experiment	x^3 of fuzzy quality	x^4 of fuzzy quality	x^1 of fuzzy price	x^2 of fuzzy price	No. Interactions
1	0.8491	0.8193	0.6333	0.6439	133
2	0.9091	0.7215	0.77	0.7702	104
3	0.8661	0.797	0.5971	0.5974	76
4	0.9011	0.8978	0.8029	0.8028	172
Total	0.9074	0.8013	0.7616	0.7673	485

As we can see in Table 1, for the crisp negotiations we obtained a high correlation coefficient for the two predicted classes (quality and price). Namely, the models acquired from the negotiations logs have a high probability to predict the buyer counter-offer given a merchant offer. On the other hand, for fuzzy experiments (Table 2) we obtained high correlation coefficient for the values corresponding to the quality counter-offer but worse results for the values corresponding to the buyer price counter-offer. These results show us that is more difficult to predict the buyer counter-offer if this use fuzzy answer to merchant offer.

7 Conclusions

Our proposal first intends to make negotiation dialog more human, and second, it also intends to make user profiles more difficult to acquire. Both intentions are tackled by fuzziness in the counter-proposals generated by users. This idea was previously proposed in [13,14] combined with the anonymous use of arguments in persuasive negotiations.

In this paper, a realistic scenario was defined with two different kinds of buyer. One of them uses fuzzy sets to suggest improvements in the offer of the merchant. The other type of buyer uses concrete values to reply with a crisp counter-offer. An illustrative example of a possible behaviour of both of them, and of merchants, is described and justified in this document.

The main contribution relies on the application of machine learning techniques to compare the privacy of preferences function using fuzzy sets as counter-offers with the classical alternative based on concrete values. Machine learning algorithm, M5, is used to model the behaviour of two type of buyers (crisp vs. fuzzy) considered as a black box. From the experimenal results we can conclude that it is more difficult to predict the buyer counter-offer with a fuzzy answer to the merchant offer.

References

1. Von Neumann, J., Morgenstern O.: The Theory of Games and Economic Behaviour. Princeton University Press (Princeton, 1944)
2. Rosenchein, J. Genesereth, M.: Deals among rational agents, Int. Joint Conf. on Artificial Intelligence (Los Angeles, 1985) 91–99
3. Binmore, K., Vulkan, N.: Applying game theory to automated negotiation. Netnomics 1-9, Baltzer Science Publishers BV (1999)
4. Rosenchein, J. Zlotkin G.: Rules of Encounter: Designing conventions for automated negotiation among computers, MIT Press (Massachusetts, 1994)
5. Sandholm, Lesser: Issues in automated negotiation and electronic commerce. Proceedings International Conference on MultiAgent Systems (San Francisco, 1995)
6. Sierra C., Jennings N.R., Noriega P., Parsons S.: A framework for argumentation-based negotiation. Intelligent Agents IV, number 1365 in LNAI, Springer-Verlag (Berlín, 1997) 177–192
7. Smith R.G., David R., Frameworks for cooperation in distributed problem solving., IEEE Trans. on Systems, Man and Cybernetics, 11(1) (1981) 61–70
8. Gasser: Social conceptions of knowledge and action: DAI foundations and open systems semantics. Artificial Intelligence, 47 (1991) 107–138.
9. Rao A.S., Georgeff M.P.: Modeling rational agents within a BDI architecture. Procs. 2nd Int. Conf. on Principles of Knowledge Representation and Reasoning, R. Fikes and E. Sandewall Eds., Morgan Kaufmann, (1991) 473–484.
10. Finin T., McKay D.,Fritzson R., McEntire, R.: KQML: an information and knowledge exchange protocol. Procs. Int. Conf. on Building and Sharing of Very Large-Scale Knowledge Bases (Tokyo, 1993).
11. Zadeh L.A.,: Fuzzy Sets Information and Control, n° 8, (1965) 338–353.

12. Quinlan, J.R.,: Combining Instance-Based and Model-Based Learning. Procs. 10th Int. Conf. on Machine Learning. Amherst, MA, (1993) 236–243.
13. Carbo, J., Molina, J.M., Davila J.: Augmenting Users' Confidence in Agent-mediated Commerce Negotiations. In Procs. 20th Int. Conf. on Artificial Intelligence and Applications (Innsbruck, 2001) 388–393
14. Carbo, J., Molina, J.M., Davila J.: Argumentative Negotiations with Anonymous Informer Agents. Int. Journal on Information & Security, Vol. 8, Number 2 (2002) 194–208

Autonomous Agents to Support Interoperability and Physical Integration in Pervasive Environments

Marcela Rodríguez[1,2] and Jesus Favela[1]

[1]Departamento de Ciencias de la Computación, CICESE, Ensenada, México
[2]Facultad de Ingeniería, UABC, Mexicali, México
{marcerod,favela}@cicese.mx

Abstract. Ubiquitous computing is the method of augmenting and improving work practices and knowledge sharing, by making computers of all scales, available but invisible throughout the physical environment, while amplifying human-to-human communication. Personal systems, such as PDAs and cell phones, give users access to computing resources regardless of their location. Handheld computers are being transformed from personal electronic agendas into mobile communication devices with intermittent network connectivity. Thus, they are becoming a natural medium to tap into an ubiquitous computing infrastructure. However, handhelds most often operate disconnected from the network thus reducing the opportunities for spontaneous interoperation with other peers or web services, which is a desirable feature of ubicomp environments. Autonomous agents can enable spontaneous collaboration by representing users, as well as devices or services available through the Web, which has become an ubiquitous medium for information sharing. An agent acts on behalf of the user while he is disconnected, and represents services added to the environment, thus allowing the physical integration and interoperability of these entities. We present the SALSA framework, which allows developers to implement simple agents for ubicomp systems. These agents use an expressive communication language based on XML, which provides protocols for locating and interacting with Web services even when the user is disconnected.

1 Introduction

Ubiquitous computing (ubicomp) is the attempt to modify the traditional desktop interaction paradigm by distributing computers, of all scales, into the environment surrounding the user to augment and improve work practices and knowledge sharing while amplifying human-to-human communication. Thus, the notion of ubiquitous computing allows greater user mobility. Mobile computing devices, such as Personal Digital Assistants (PDAs) and smart cell phones, are becoming extremely popular. As new services and more powerful devices reach the market, this tendency will certainly continue in the near future. Thus, these devices are becoming a natural medium to tap into an ubiquitous computing infrastructure.

Handheld computers are being transformed from personal electronic agendas into mobile communication devices with intermittent network connectivity. Ubicomp environments allow mobile users to interact with other users and with devices that provide almost constant access to information and different kinds of services (print-

E. Menasalvas et al. (Eds.): AWIC 2003, LNAI 2663, pp. 278–287, 2003.
© Springer-Verlag Berlin Heidelberg 2003

ers, whiteboards, cameras, etc.). However, handhelds most often operate disconnected from the network thus reducing the opportunities for spontaneous interoperation with other peers or services, which is a desirable feature of these environments.

Handhelds provide alternatives for network connectivity, yet they are often inactive and even when in use they are most of the time disconnected from the network, which severely limits their use for ubiquitous interaction with the environment's entities. Autonomous agents can be integrated to ubicomp environments in order to enhance the collaborative activities of mobile users and allow their interoperation with other devices. Thus, we can envision a multi-agent system where autonomous agents act on behalf of the users while disconnected. In this case, an autonomous agent might be able to maintain a limited user presence and execute actions on his behalf while he is disconnected or inactive by performing actions, such as making decisions. Other agents can represent services added to the environment to allow their opportunistic utilization by users. These agents allow users to access computing resources available through the Web which has become an ubiquitous medium for information sharing.

We present the SALSA framework, which allows developers to implement simple agents for ubicomp systems. These agents use an expressive communication language based on XML, which provides protocols for locating and interacting with services, users and other agents using Web technology and standards protocols.

Our framework is developed from the premise that the Web provides a strong basis for pervasive mobile computing [4]. This premise is based on the web's potential to realize ubiquitous access and its lightweight software requirements.

Before we present the SALSA framework, we first discuss in Sect. 2 a couple of use scenarios to motivate the need for autonomous agents, and we describe in Sect. 3 the requirements of the software infrastructure that we have identified from these scenarios. Then, in Sect. 4 we introduce the architecture of SALSA. In Sect. 5 we describe the behavior, structure, and the communication means of the agents. Sect. 6 presents a particular scenario of an ubiquitous collaborative application implemented with SALSA. Finally, in Sect. 7 we present our conclusions.

2 Autonomous Agents in Ubiquitous Collaborative Applications

In order to lay the foundation of the proposed framework, we first present a couple of scenarios that describe the use of autonomous agents in ubiquitous collaborative applications. This analysis helped us determine key issues to be addressed in the development of the framework we are presenting. The applications analyzed and their associated use scenarios are described next.

2.1 Conference Scheduling Agent

A user attends a conference with multiple simultaneous tracks. On her handheld device she fills a form in which she specifies her main interest within the scope of the conference. While she registers at the conference she connects her handheld to a point of presence provided by the conference to send her profile. This will launch an agent that communicates with another agent in the conference server to build for her a recommended personalized schedule given the user preferences. Once the schedule is generated it will be stored in the server to be downloaded to the handheld the next time the user is connected to the network. The data will be integrated in the calendar application in the handheld.

As the conference progresses users could add notes or grade the talks they attend. If these notes are marked as being public they will be downloaded to the server when the user connects to a point of presence in the conference. Public notes from other users will be transmitted to the connected user, as will updates to the schedule based on recommendations by other users with similar profiles [9]. Users could also exchange notes and recommendations using their handheld computers without requiring a connection to the network.

2.2   An Agent That Deals with Shared Resources

A user is co-authoring a research paper with a couple of colleagues and he needs to incorporate his final contributions and send the paper today. However, the latest version of the paper is currently locked in a shared repository by one of his co-authors who has left town to attend a conference for the week. The user sends a message to his co-author's agent who will decide, based on the context and the trust he has on the author making the request, whether or not to liberate the resource.

In [8], Moran et al. describe a tool named Doc2U that could be the basis for supporting this scenario. With Doc2U shared resources are added to the roster of an instant messaging and presence awareness application. A user then can be aware of the state of resources, such as a document being locked. An instant message can be sent directly to a co-author or to a resource in the form of a command. In this case the decision to unlock a resource is left to the user, but he could have configured an agent to act on his behalf when he is disconnected or inactive. An agent can be seen in the roster of a handheld-based instant messaging application, such as Doc2U, as another user to which one can send messages or commands such as "launch". When the device has no access to network resources, all events generated are stored by the handheld application and later sent, when access to the network is provided or a synchronization process is performed. A similar approach is used for information flowing from the application server to the mobile device, if the device is not accessible, all messages and other events are blocked until the exchange of data is possible.

3   SALSA Development Framework's Requirements

The SALSA (Simple Agent Library for Sope Applications) development framework must enable developers to build autonomous agents that act on behalf of a user. An agent might be able to maintain a limited user presence and execute actions on the user's behalf while he is disconnected or inactive. These two main characteristics, "acting for another" and "autonomy", and the proposed use scenarios were used as the basis to discover and define all the characteristics that an agent living in an ubiquitous environment must have. These attributes are described next.

Proactivity: Bradshaw uses the word proactivity as synonymous of autonomy, which means goal-directedness and self-starting behavior [1].

Temporal Continuity: An agent will live in its environment until it has reached its goals, by maintaining its persistence and state over long periods of time. SALSA provides an agent life cycle and considers that the agents reside in a trusted server or a desktop computer.

Reactivity: an agent perceives its environment and responds in a timely fashion to changes that occur in it [11]. Ubiquitous computing environments contain components, which are fixed or mobile, such as PDAs, that enter and leave routinely. Thus, an agent allows users to become aware of the available services or users with whom to interact.

Collaborative Behavior: An agent can work in concert with other agents to achieve a common goal [1]. Thus, an agent is part of a multi-agent system.

Communication Ability: The agent must be able to communicate with the user or the device that it represents, and with other agents in order to collectively tackle problems that no single agent can handle, individually. Then, for agents to communicate with each other they need a common language.

We identified the following functional requirements for the SALSA architecture in order to support users in ubiquitous computing applications:

Provide an *infrastructure of services* that enable the naming, registration, authentication, and localization of agents, and a *simple API* to develop autonomous agents with the above characteristics.

Support for *disconnected mode of operation*. An agent acts on behalf of the user when he is disconnected or inactive.

Allow the *interoperation* between users and devices by notifying the presence and status of new devices offering services and allowing the interaction with them.

Authentication: By the authentication of the user's handheld, the agent recognizes the user that it represents when he gets connected to the network or any user with whom it should interact according to its action plan.

Users should be able to *launch agents explicitly* or they could be *launched automatically* when certain conditions are met.

Agents might be able to *communicate* with its user and with other agents in other desktops or a server. Additionally, agents can read and write to the repository where the user's personal information is stored (agenda, to-do list, preferences, etc.).

4   SALSA's Architecture

The architecture and functionality of SALSA to support agents living in a pervasive computing environment is illustrated in Fig. 1, in which the main components of a SALSA application are the following:

A Terminal or Desktop Computer That Acts as an Access Point. This computer is used to access both networked information and the handheld device. Wireless connectivity to the access point is increasingly a viable option with the proliferation of devices that support the Bluetooth and IEEE 802.11b standards. The access point runs an HTTP server to handle XML/HTML communication with the handheld. In addition, it stores the Agent Directory to which agents representing services and users will register.

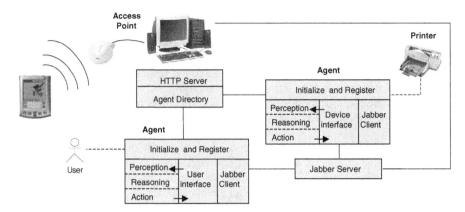

Fig. 1. Architecture of a ubiquitous computing environment created with SALSA

Jabber Server. Jabber is an open instant messaging and presence awareness system. This server (http://www.jabber.org) is used to notify the state of people and agents, and to handle the interaction between people, agents and devices through XML messages. All communication between the handheld and the agent will go through this server. The information in the user's handheld is synchronized with the server every time the device is connected to a point of access.

Agents. There are two kinds of agents that can be implemented with SALSA: agents that represent users and agents that represent devices. These agents might run in the access point or any other computer with connectivity to the access point. They can be launched explicitly by the user or automatically when certain conditions are met. An agent contains several components: a *protocol to register* into the Agent Directory; an *interface* to the device that acts as a wrapper to query its status and interact with it or an interface that allows the user to introduce information by which the agent learns his interests; a Jabber client to notify the device's status to all interested users and receive XML messages through which remote users, user's agents and device's agents interact; and finally, the subsystem that implements the agent's intelligence that contains components for *perception, reasoning* and *action*. The perception module obtains knowledge (from interfaces to environment's sensors or getting information of users, other agents or devices through the Jabber server, such as their state), and feeds the reasoning subsystem, which governs the actions, including deciding what to perceive next. Among the actions that can be triggered by an agent are included sending a message to the user or creating a new agent with a predefined subgoal. The reasoning component can be implemented as a simple action/perception rule or with a more sophisticated algorithm, which is left to the user based on his application's logic.

Devices. These are appliances that offer services and are connected to the local network. Communication with the device is made through its agent. Devices define possible states, the services it offers, and the protocol used to interact with them.

5 Agent Development Framework

5.1 Agent's Behavior

Agents are computer programs that have goals and methods to achieve these goals. They are implemented to assist a user in accomplishing a task. An agent can be used to search for information, schedule a meeting or perform actions on behalf of the user. Agents exhibit autonomous behavior in the sense that they use internal mechanisms to make decisions as to how to reach their goals.

Pattie Maes identified two issues to be dealt with in designing and implementing autonomous agents: competence and trust [7]. Competence related to the mechanisms used by the agent to acquire knowledge and make decisions. Agents normally acquire competence by observing and imitating the user and receiving feedback from it, thus adapting their behavior to conform to the user's expectations. The issue of trust relates to the confidence that the user has on the agent to delegate work on him. Trust is build over time based on the agent's response to the tasks assigned to it.

5.2 Agent's Life Cycle

A SALSA agent has a life cycle, which, as shown in Fig. 2, includes these states:

Activated. This is the original state of an agent when it is created. This is a super-state that contains different sub-states that an activated agent can present.

Learning. It is the initial sub-state. An agent acquires knowledge of its environment in different ways. For example, by explicitly receiving information from the user, a service or another agent, from a sensor's interface that detects a new device/service added to the environment, or thru learning. An agent gets into this state if its action plan requires it. That is, it moves from the executing state to the learning state.

Thinking. The agent analyzes the obtained knowledge in the *learning* state in order to establish its goals and an action plan to reach these goals.

Executing. In this state the agent performs the action plan proposed previously.

Communicating. The agent interacts with one or more agents in order to get information necessary to fulfill its goals. An agent can get into this state if it is dictated by his action plan or because the agent needs to request specific knowledge.

Suspended. An agent in this state is alive but it is not performing any activity. It is waiting to be activated again. For example, if an agent is waiting from information that it has requested to another agent, then it changes from the communicating state to the suspended state, and when contacted by the other agent, its state returns to communicating.

Deactivated. If the agent has fulfilled its obligation, then it is deactivated and consequently killed.

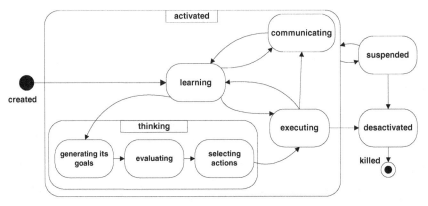

Fig. 2. The life-cycle of an agent

5.3   Agent Communication

An ACL (Agent Communication Language) provides agents with the means to exchange information and knowledge through a set of communicative acts. The purpose of these acts is to convey information about the agent's own mental state with the objective to affect the mental state of the communication partner [6]. We usually hear agents mentioned within the context of the Web, and the Internet is the arena in which we generally expect them to compete. But ACL's. such as, KQML and FIPA ACL have followed a path away from the mainstream Internet technologies and standards [5]. They also do not cover the entire spectrum of what agents may want to exchange. The content of the message (beliefs, desires, intentions) is expressed in other languages, such as, KIF, Prolog, etc. [2].

The SALSA development framework must provide an expressive language that enables the exchange of different kinds of objects between agents (such as actions, beliefs, goals, or simple messages), between agents and users (such as the user's profile), and between agents and services (such as the service's state). This information must be exchanged through the Web, which permits ubiquitous access to resources and information. The Web is an appropriate platform for the support of pervasive computing because it is accessible from a large and rapidly growing number of places [4]. The Web relies on the HTTP protocol, which can be implemented on a vast variety of devices, such as devices that the user carries, e.g. personal digital assistants (PDAs) and laptops, and devices that provide specific services, such as digital cameras and printers. Furthermore, the Web supports mobile users through its flexible global addressing scheme, allowing them transparent access to resources outside their current environment. Finally, the form of interaction with particular devices and other entities, such as autonomous agents, can be encoded using XML (eXtensible Markup Language) [4].

A number of researchers have suggested that ACL messages and its content ought to be encoded in XML because it offers several advantages over traditional ACLs, e.g. KQML and FIPA ACL, which are based on Lisp-like encoding [6]:

1. XML describes data in a human-readable format
2. It is a database-neutral and device neutral format. Data marked up in XML can be targeted to different devices using the eXtensible Style Language (XSL).
3. XML-encoding is easier to develop parsers. One can use off-the-shelf tools for parsing XML, instead of writing customized parsers to parse the ACL messages.
4. Makes the ACL more WWW-friendly, which facilitates the development of software agents.
5. Using XML will facilitate the practical integration with a variety of Web technologies.
6. XML incorporates links, which allow to interface the ACL message to the knowledge repository that is the WWW.

Our proposal for the SALSA development framework is to use a more Internet friendly agent language taking advantage of XML to encode any kind of message. Thus, SALSA provides developers an API that facilitates the composition, sending, and receiving of messages between agents, agents-services, and agents-users. However, the code for every content message type of the communicative act is left to the programmer, because it depends on the application logic and the details of the agent system of the ubiquitous collaborative environment.

5.4   SALSA's Library

The SALSA library consists of a set of abstract classes such as, **Agent, Goal, Knowledge** and **Action.** The Agent class provides the methods to **create** and control the life cycle on an agent. Thus, an agent can be created with a specific goal, which is specified in an object **Goal**. The agent first invokes the **learn** method which the developer needs to specialize to implement a simple or complex learning mechanism, such as, a decision tree or a neuronal network that will create a **Knowledge** object. Then, the **think** method is invoked to create an **Action** object that contains the action plan, which the agent will execute. The Agent class contains others methods, such as **authenticate** that is used to recognize the represented user each time he connects to the network, or any other user that should be contacted by the agent, and the **send** and **receive** methods to exchange XML messages with other agents or users. Agents also include attributes, for instance, the **agentKind** attribute specifies if the agent represents a user or a device, the **Identification** object contains information about the user or device that the agent represents (its localization and id), the **AgentDirectories** object contains information of all the agent directories where the agent is registered.

The contents of the Goal, Knowledge and Action objects can be specified using first order logic statements or simple statements and conditions. It depends of the application's complexity and logic. Next we describe how an agent can be implemented to enhance an ubiquitous application.

6 A Sample Application

To illustrate how the components of a SALSA's application interact, we show in Fig. 3, a sequence diagram based on the scenario introduced in Sect. 2.2, and we present in Fig. 4 the sample application, which is describe next.

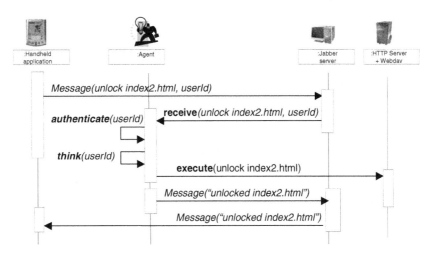

Fig. 3. Sequence diagram of a sample ubiquitous computing application

When the user connects to an environment's point of presence to send to his co-author Hiroshi a message requesting to liberate the document index2.html, than the message is intercepted by the co-author's agent because he is not available. The agent analyzes the user's request and **authenticates** the user by checking a predefined list of co-authors and accessing the Webdab to obtain information of the user's rights on the document. Than, the agent executes the method **think,** which will analyze the context of the situation in order to generate an action plan. The agent, by a mechanism of action/perception rule, decides to liberate the document considering that the requester is the main author, the dateline is very close, and that it doesn't know when Hiroshi will be available to attend this request. Finally, the agent sends a message to the authors notifying that the document has been unlocked.

7 Conclusions

In this paper we describe the SALSA architecture which uses a combination of the instant messaging paradigm and agent technology to support the disconnected mode of operation of users and the opportunistic interoperation with services. Autonomous that agents act on behalf of the user and reside on a desktop computer or trusted server, can maintain a limited user presence and execute commands or make decisions on his behalf while he is disconnected or inactive. Developers that wish to add a new agent to represent a user or a device in a pervasive computing environment need only

Fig. 4. Handheld's client of the ubiquitous computing application

to program an interface to the device or user by defining an XML document to specify the interaction with them, and overwrite some methods of the abstract Agent class according to the application's logic.

References

1. Bradshaw, J.: Software Agents. AAAI Press/MIT Press, 1997, pp. 3-49.
2. Finin, T., Fritzson, R., McKay, D., McEntire, R.: KQML as an Agent Communication Language. Proceedings of the Third International Conference on Information and Knowledge Management, 1994, pp. 456–463.
3. Glushko, R., Tenenbaum, J., Meltzed, B.: An XML Framework for Agent-based E- commerce. Communications of the ACM, March 1999, Vol. 42, No. 3
4. Kindberg, T., Barton, J.: A Web-based Nomadic Computing System. Computer Networks, Special Edition on Pervasive Computing, Elsevier. HP Labs Technical Report #2000-110.
5. Labrou, Y., Finin, T., Peng, Y.: Agent Communication Languages: The Current Landscape. IEEE Intelligent Systems, March/April 1999, Vol. 14, No. 2, pp. 45–52.
6. Labrou, Y.: Standardizing Agent Communication. Proceedings of Advanced Course on Artificial Intelligence (ACAI-01). Springer-Verlag, 2001.
7. Maes, P.: Agents that Reduce Work and Information Overload. Communications of the ACM, July 1994, Vol. 37, No. 7, pp. 30–40
8. Moran, L., Favela, J., Martinez, A., Decouchant, D.: Document Presence Notification Services for Collaborative Writing. Proc. of the Seventh International Workshop on Groupware 2001, pp. 125–133.
9. Sarwar, B.: Using Filtering Agents to Improve Prediction and Quality in the GroupLens Research Collaborative Filtering System. Proc. of ACM Conf. on CSCW 1998, pp. 345–354
10. van Ejic, R.: Semantics of Agent Communication: An Introduction. UKMAS 1996-2002, LNAI 2403, 2002, pp. 152–168.
11. Wooldridge, M., and Jennings, N.: Intelligent Agents: Theory and Practice. Knowledge Engineering Review, Cambridge University Press 1995, Volume 10 No. 2, pp. 115–152.

Feature Selection Algorithms to Improve Documents' Classification Performance

Pedro A. C. Sousa[1], João Paulo Pimentão[1],
Bruno René D. Santos[2], and Fernando Moura-Pires[3]

[1] Universidade Nova de Lisboa, Faculdade de Ciências e Tecnologia, Caparica, Portugal
{pas,pim}@fct.unl.pt
http://www.fct.unl.pt

[2] UNINOVA Instituto de Desenvolvimento de Novas Tecnologias, Caparica, Portugal
brd@uninova.pt
http://www.uninova.pt

[3] Universidade de Évora Departamento de Informática, Évora, Portugal,
faje@di.uevora.pt
http://www.uevora.pt

Abstract. This paper presents a study where feature selection algorithms were evaluated in order to improve documents' classification performance. The study was made during the project DEEPSIA, IST project Nr. 1999-20 283, funded by the European Union. The need to improve documents recognition was imposed by the need to increase the overall performance of the Framework for Internet data collection based on intelligent agents, used within the project. The Framework is briefly described and the learning techniques used are presented. The focus of this paper is on the feature selection algorithms, where the most relevant work was the use of Conditional Mutual Information, estimated using genetic algorithms, since the computational complexity of C_k^N invalidated an iterative approach. Methods, techniques and comparative results are presented in detail.

Keywords: text learning, multi-agents systems, feature selection, information retrieval

1 Introduction

In the near future, huge network infrastructures and new information and telecommunication technologies will be some of the most basic and important tools for all business processes in organizations ranging from the industrial sector, through services and government, to financial institutions. However, the proliferation of information, already evident in recent times, is starting to cause considerable problems both to individuals and to organizations [1]. In consequence, tools to enhance the results of the traditional procedures of acquiring data, substituting them by electronic processes,

E. Menasalvas et al. (Eds.): AWIC 2003, LNAI 2663, pp. 288–296, 2003.

are mandatory. The "Framework for Internet data collection based on intelligent agents", offers a user-friendly interface customized through a user's-personalized catalogue, which is automatically updated with information gathered from available web sites.

The catalogue stores, under a pre-selected ontology, the data collected from different web sites, avoiding manual useless visits to several sites. The process of presenting the catalogue's-collected data is ergonomic and automates the user's most common tasks.

The autonomous data collection and semi-automatic catalogue updating is executed by a Multi-Agent System (MAS), relieving the end-user from all the "hard work" (i.e. interfacing the web and the private databases). The agents increase their performances, taking advantage of text learning methods, dedicated to Internet information retrieval.

1.1 The DEEPSIA Project

The project DEEPSIA "Dynamic on-linE IntErnet Purchasing System, based on Intelligent Agents", IST project Nr. 1999-20 283, funded by the European Union has the generic aim of supporting Small and Medium Enterprises (SME) usual day-to-day purchasing requirements, via the Internet, based on a purchaser-centred solution and tailored to meet individual needs.

The procurement process is no exception in trying to find relevant information on an information-overloaded phenomenon magnified by the myriad of new commercial sites that are made available everyday.

DEEPSIA's purpose is to provide a purchaser centred solution, available on the user's desktop and tailored to the individual's requirements, rather than a supplier centred marketplace.

The reduction of time in collecting data will be achieved by presenting the user with a catalogue of the set of entries that he/she is looking for, avoiding having to browse through a wide range of web pages and links that are not related to his/her needs.

The developed DEEPSIA's prototype, based on a "Framework for Internet data collection based on intelligent agents", worked as a test bed for the proposed architecture.

2.2 The Adopted Framework

The adopted framework is composed by three subsystems, responsible for performing specific tasks, and interacting with each other through data and information flows. The three basic modules are a Dynamic Catalogue (DC) [2], responsible for data maintenance and presentation; a Multi-Agent System (MAS), responsible for autonomous data collection, and semi-automatic catalogue update; and an optional Portal Interface Agent (PIA), responsible for a privileged interface with the web data suppliers [3].

Focusing in the MAS there are several types of agents that accomplish subsidiary tasks contributing to the ultimate goals of the system. The tasks performed by the different agents include, among others: message processing, name resolution service, web page discovery, web page classification, web page content recognition, etc.

The most relevant agents, concerning text learning, are the Crawler (CA), in charge of user themes identification; the Miner (MA) in charge of object content identification and cataloguing; and the Tutor (TA), responsible for the learning procedures. To keep the Agent's simplicity, all the learning processes (feature selection, classifiers creation, DSS-Decision Support System definition) are performed by the Tutor, and the achieved results (mapped to XML) are then communicated, using FIPA messages,[1] to the respective agents (the Crawler and Miner). The basic behaviour of all agents is based on a bootstrap knowledge, complemented in time, by the Tutor Agent whenever new conclusions are achieved.

The Crawler Agent is the responsible discovering and deciding if a page contains product information or not. The Miner Agent is responsible for the product identification and for determining the promotion's associated conditions (price, quality, etc).

3   The Tutor Agent (TA)

The Tutor Agent's role is to perform all the text learning tasks, in an off-line process, in order to create DSSs for the Crawler and the Miner.

As in all supervised learning processes, knowledge is extracted from a set of classified observations that is stored on a database. The database creation is made using a dedicated user's interface, in a very simple, but very tedious process, that consists of browsing representative web sites and classifying every page either as a relevant or a non-relevant page.

After collecting a meaningful number of pages (usually more than 20.000), the TA has the capability to create its training, validation and test sets.

The TA's role is, in an off-line process, to perform the classical learning tasks:

- **Feature Selection:** identification of the most relevant words to be selected for the vector in order to reduce the vector's size, usually superior to 30.000 dimensions (one dimension for each word found in the dictionary).

- **Creation of Classifiers**: the creation of several possible classifiers in order to produce alternative classification procedures. The classifiers are produced using the pre-selected features vector. The methods studied were the K nearest neighbour, K weighed – NN [4], C4.5 [5] and Bayesian classifier [6].

- **Setting Up a Decision Support System**: the creation of rules in order to perform the classification task. The setting up of the DSS is finally defined based on the available classifiers and the analysis of their performance. The selected DSS is the rule of majority applied to the classifications assigned by the selected classifiers.

---

[1] FIPA – Foundation for Intelligent Physical Agents – www.fipa.org

- **Creation of the Equivalent Decision Support System (EDSS) for Performance Optimisation**. In order to enhance the system global performance an effort was made on the creation of an EDSS, which is explained in detail in [7].

4 Feature Selection

This section presents the available TA's behaviour dedicated to feature selection, and a comparative performance analysis of its use applied in a case scenario with real data.

The objective is to identify the best method to determine the list of features (S) that best descriminate the class (C) under analisys. That is, being $\Delta = \left\{ A_1, \cdots, A_{|\Delta|} \right\}$ the set of all features, and $C: A_1 \times A_2 \times \cdots \times A_{|\Delta|} - C$ a relation, where A_i takes a set of discrete and finite values of $\left\{ a_{i,1}, \cdots, a_{i,|A_i|} \right\}$ and $C = \left\{ c_1, \cdots c_{|C|} \right\}$, find the best process to define $S = \left\{ S_1, \cdots, S_K \right\} \subseteq \Delta$, which is the subset of k features from the complete universe Δ that best supports the classifier's induction. The features ordering is performed by using (1):

$$M\left(S_1;C\right) \ge M\left(S_2;C\right) \ge \cdots \ge M\left(S_K;C\right) \ge M\left(Z;C\right) \quad \text{for all } Z \in \Delta - S \qquad (1)$$

where M is the method used to score the features.

4.1 The Corpus

The corpus, used for the experimental results, was created during the DEEPSIA project. The corpus was built using web site pages, from an arbitrary Internet site selection. The corpus included a total of 3166 documents, tagged as selling or non-selling samples. Unlabelled documents, or double document tagging (i.e. one document classified in both categories) were not allowed. The corpus included 2294 selling documents and 872 non-selling documents. Each document is represented as a vector $\vec{p} = (p^1, p^2, ... p^N)$, so that similar documents have analogous vector representation, according to a similarity metric. Each p^i element represents a word Wi and N is the number of words considered. Each p^i element is a binary feature that states whether the word is in the page or not. At this stage, the corpus included more than 30.000 features, which implies the need to reduce its number prior to classifier induction.

The first step consisted in removing all the features included in the stop list DTIC/DROLS. This list retains most of the words in the standard Verity Stop List and adds the words from the DTIC/DROLS stop word list (the full list can be found at `http://dvl.dtic.mil/stop_list.html`).

After stop list features elimination, 8393 features are present in the selling class documents, with an average feature's occurrence of 7.187, however 87% of the features have 5 or less incidence. In the non-selling documents, the total of features is 12234, the average feature's occurrence is 19.816, but also, 72.2% of the features have 5 or fewer incidences.

4.2 Methodology for Evaluating the Effectiveness

The corpus was used based on the following strategy division, training, validation and test set. The test set can only be used for classifier performance analysis, and the training and validation sets are used to induct the classifier, and test it, respectively.

For evaluating the effectiveness of the category assignments by the inducted classifiers, created using the different feature rankings, the recall, precision and F_1 measures were used. Recall (R) is the obtained dividing the correct selling assignments by the total selling documents, using the test set. Precision (P) is obtained dividing the correct selling assignments, by the total selling assignments, using the test set. [8] The F_1 measure, presented by van Rijsbergen in [9], combines precision and recall in the following equation:

$$F_1 = \frac{2RP}{R+P} \tag{2}$$

The measures used were computed to the document selling assignment, and the values obtained are an average of the values calculated using the k-fold cross-validation [10]. In k-fold cross-validation, the corpus is divided into k subsets of (approximately) equal size. The classifier is inducted k times, each time leaving out one of the subsets from training, and using only the omitted subset to compute the presented measures.

4.3 Methods for Feature Selection

The methods for feature selection under analysis were Mutual Information (MI), defined as $MI(S_i;C) = H(C) - H(C|S_i)$, and Chi-Square ($\chi^2$), defined as

$$\chi^2_{avg}(S_i;C) = \sum_{j=0}^{1} P_r(c_j)\chi^2(S_i,c_j).$$

These two methods do not eliminate correlated features. In fact, correlated features have the same score, which means that if one of the features is selected, its correlated features are also strong candidates to be selected. This situation is obviously not desirable, since the use of correlated features does not contribute to further document discrimination. With the intention to eliminate correlated features, the Conditional Mutual Information, defined as $CMI(C;S) = H(C) - H(C|S_1, \cdots, S_K)$, was also analysed. In this case, the generic Equation 1 is not applicable, being selected the set S of features that maximizes CMI(C;S).

For the CMI method calculation, Genetic Algorithms (GA) were used, since the computational complexity of c_k^N invalidate an iterative approach. Although GA do not guarantee the best solution, they provide a viable approach to achieve good results.

4.4 Comparing Results

The study consisted in comparing the three proposed methods, increasing the number of features (from 10, up to 100 with steps of 10). For each step, a C4.5 classifier was induced with the set of features returned by each method. The C4.5 was chosen since it has the best performance on our corpus among the tested classifiers.
The k-fold cross-validation was used to evaluate the methods, with a k equal to 10.
The results achieved for the precision, recall and F_1, using the different feature raking obtain by the MI, CMI and the χ^2 (X2) methods, are presented in Fig. 1, Fig. 2, and Fig. 3, respectively.
    A first analysis indicates that all the results achieved are very encouraging, since they are above the usual values for text learning. Nevertheless, it must be noticed that the corpus used, dedicated to selling and non-selling documents, is a special case and extrapolations must be done very carefully. Intuitively it is expected that selling pages could be very easily identified by focusing on a small set of words (e.g. price, reference, product), which is not that obvious in other scenarios.

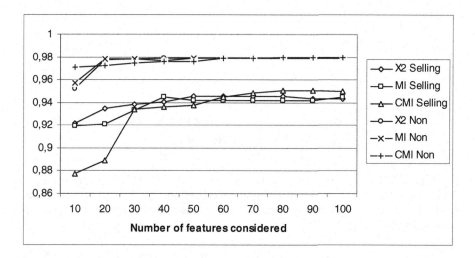

Fig. 1. Graphical presentation of the average precision measure achieved with the inducted classifiers C4.5 using Mutual Information, Conditional Mutual Information and Chi-Square features rankings. The x-axis shows the number of features considered in each step and the y-axis shows the achieved precision

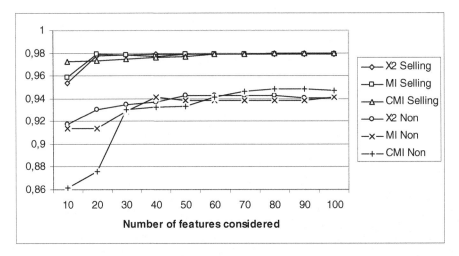

Fig. 2. Graphical presentation of the average recall measure achieved with the inducted classifiers C4.5 using Mutual Information, Conditional Mutual Information and Chi-Square features rankings. The x-axis shows the number of features considered in each step and the y-axis shows the achieved recall

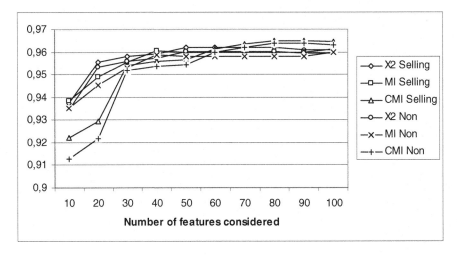

Fig. 3. Graphical presentation of the average F_1 measure achieved with the inducted classifiers C4.5 using Mutual Information, Conditional Mutual Information and Chi-Square features rankings. The x-axis shows the number of features considered in each step and the y-axis shows the achieved F_1

The detailed analysis shows that the best ranking method is the Conditional Mutual Information, even if the methods have similar performance. Chi-Square and MI have very similar results, which were expected because of the analogous base principles involved. The slight improvement achieved by the CMI (more perceptible in Figure3, above 60 features), derives from the elimination of the correlated variables, which does not happen on the other methods.

For the non-selling documents the precision measure analysis scores better, on the other hand the recall measure analysis is poor. For the selling documents the perform-ance is the opposite. Taking to account that the classifiers are used to identify the selling pages, this is the adequate behavior, since the non-recognition of selling pages represents loss of relevant information. Mistaking non-selling pages as relevant repre-sents a decrease of global system performance but does not incur in loss of informa-tion.

5   Conclusions

The framework was under extensive tests in the DEEPSIA's project, and the achieved results were very positive rising above the consortium's expectations. For further information about the project, the latest achievements and access to the prototype please consult the DEEPSIA's web site on http://www.deepsia.org.

The "Framework for Internet data collection based on intelligent agents" is a ge-neric approach; its context definition is done using the training process of the Crawler and of the Miner agents.

Although the used corpus is dedicated e-procurement, the global results achieved are encouraging and the framework is now under testing with other corpus.

Regarding feature selection methods, the focus of this paper, the best method was the Conditional Mutual Information, because of its capability to eliminate correlated features. The Genetic Algorithms had a good performance, even if they do not guar-antee the best solution.

In order to improve the global performance of the Framework, the C4.5 classifier was used because it has the best results. Since, C4.5 already eliminates correlated features, the slight improvements achieved are more relevant. The use of CMI for feature selection with classifiers that are not so efficient as C4.5 in eliminating corre-lated features may produce better results.

References

1. Bokma, A.: CogNet: Integrated Information and knowledge management and its use in virtual organizations. In: E-business and Virtual Enterprises Managing Business-to-Business cooperation, Luis Camarinha-Matos, Hamideh Afsarmanesh, Ricardo Rabelo, Kluwer Academic publishers, ISBN 0-7923-7205-0 (2000)
2. Sousa, P., Pimentão, J., Garção, A.: Deepsia – From supply chains to supply webs. In Intelligent Engineering Systems through artificial neural networks, Cihan H. Dagli, Anna L.Buczak, Joydeep Ghosh, Mark J. Embrechts, Okan Ersoy, StephenHercel, Volume 11, ASME PRESS, NEW YORK, ISBN 0-7918-0176-4, (2001) 1019–1024

3. Sousa, P., Pimentão, J., Garção, A.: DEEPSIA – focusing e-commerce on the purchaser's side. In International ICSC Congress on Computational Intelligence: Methods and Applications (CIMA'2001), Ludmila l. Kuncheva, Friedrich Steimann, Christian Haefke, Mayer Aladjem, Vilem Novak, ICSC Academic Press, Canada, ISBN 3-906454-26-6 (2001) 436–442

4. Yang, Y., Liu, X.: A re-examination of text categorization methods". In Proceedings of ACM SIGIR Conference on Research and Development in Information Retrieval (SIGIR'99) (1999) 42–49.

5. Quinlan, J.: C4.5: Programs for Machine Learning. Morgan Kaufmann, San Mateo, CA: (1993)

6. Hastie, T., Tibshirani, R., Friedman, J.: The elements of statistic learning, Data Mining, Inference, and prediction, Springer Series in Statistic, Springer-Verlag, ISBN 0387952845, (2001)

7. Sousa, P., Pimentão, J., Pires, M.,Garção,A. A Framework for Internet Data Collection based on Intelligent Agents: The Methodology to produce equivalent DSS, Intelligent Engineering Systems through artificial neural networks, Volume 12, Dagli, C., at al (ed), ASME Press, New York, ISBN 0-7918-0191-8, (2002) 147–151

8. Junker, Markus, Hoch Rainer, Dengel Andreas, On the Evaluation of Document Analysis Components by Recall, Precision, and Accuracy in Fifth International Conference on Document Analysis and Recognition, page 713, 1998

9. Rijsbergen, C. J. v.: Information Retrieval. London, Butterworths (1979)

10. Warren Sarle: What are cross-validation and bootstrapping?
    http://www.faqs.org/faqs/ai-faq/neural-nets/part3/section-12.html
    (2003)

ROSA – Multi-agent System for Web Services Personalization

Przemysław Kazienko[1] and Maciej Kiewra[2]

[1] Wrocław University of Technology, Department of Information Systems, Wybrzeże
S. Wyspiańskiego 27, 50-370 Wrocław, Poland
kazienko@pwr.wroc.pl
[2] Fujitsu España General Elio, 2 – entlo. dcha. – 46010 Valencia, Spain
mkiewra@mail.fujitsu.es, matixy@wp.pl

Abstract. Automatic and non-invasive web personalization seems to
be a challenge for nowadays web sites. Many web mining techniques
are used to achieve this goal. Since current web sites evolve constantly,
web mining operations should be periodically repeated. A multi-agent
architecture facilitates integration of different mining methods and permits the discovered knowledge to be verified and updated automatically.
We propose ROSA (Remote Open Site Agents) — a system that may
be easily incorporated into an existing web site. It consists of multiple
heterogeneous agents such as: User Session Monitor, Crawler, Content
Miner, Usage Miner, Hyperlink Recommender, Banner Recommender,
etc., that are responsible for specific web mining and personalization
tasks. They integrate various mining techniques using common representation of documents in the vector space model in order to recommend hyperlinks and banners. Verification process is represented by a task graph.
ROSA agents not only detect when their information should be verified,
but they are also able to coordinate knowledge update operations (using
method presented in this paper). The practical part describes the usage
of FIPA- RDF0 and ACL languages.

1 Introduction

Personalization is one of the most important techniques used for increasing the
number of clients. Developers can create web sites that use efficient and automatic personalization techniques that do not require any user's intervention.
Those systems acquire information about clients' behaviour in order to provide
content adapted to individual necessities [16]. Hyperlinks to probably interesting documents [14,18] or to commercial offers (e.g. banners [1,11]) are the most
typical examples.

1.1 Personalization Problems

As the information about individual interests and preferences is hidden among
a huge volume of data, web mining techniques are very useful in personalization

E. Menasalvas et al. (Eds.): AWIC 2003, LNAI 2663, pp. 297–306, 2003.
© Springer-Verlag Berlin Heidelberg 2003

issue. These techniques are grouped in accordance with the type of analysed data into [13]: *web usage mining* (analysis of navigation patterns and other data related to users' activity) [12,14,18] and *content mining* (where documents' content is mined) [2]. Both web mining branches can complement each other in order to provide more effective personalization [15]. Our system ROSA (Remote Open Site Agents) also integrates web usage and content mining (by means of vector structure) in one coherent system that can be incorporated into every web site [9,10].

Since the web mining process consists of many time-consuming steps, it was originally divided into two parts. The former consisted of operations that could be performed off-line (data cleaning and selection, clustering, etc.). The latter was composed of tasks that must take place on-line (current user session classification, ranking list creation, etc.). Since the current sites evolve constantly (the site content and users' activities are changing), the off-line operations should be periodically repeated to update the mined information. Typically off-line operations are up to the site administrator who had to decide when and how often the whole process should be performed again.

Obviously, the update will be quite trivial, if the web site is small, but it may be a real headache in case of professional huge portals. Manual monitoring of changes can be very tedious administrative duty. The more data a web site generates, the longer the update process is and the greater probability of system inconsistencies is. Therefore, a strict data coordination method is required. Additionally, the off-line operations should be carried out when the users' activities are minimal.

1.2   Multi-agent System

For all these reasons, ROSA has been evolved towards multi-agent system, whose expert-agents cooperate with one another and may be distributed among many hosts [5]. Every agent is responsible for a single web mining task, so it encapsulates specific functions that would be available for the rest of the system. Agents not only interchange information, but they also possess their own knowledge.

ROSA can be included in every web site. From the end-users' point of view, ROSA is an assistant that facilitates the site navigation. The current version is able to recommend hyperlinks and banners using information about site content, previously visited pages and typical web usage patterns. Moreover, it provides a search engine and some administration tools (e.g. statistics and association rules discovering).

2   ROSA Agents in Personalization Process

Every ROSA expert-agent possesses its own characteristics related to personalisation process (Fig. 1).

Crawler retrieves the site content using HTTP, extracts terms from documents and counts the document-term frequency (*itf*). This capability is also

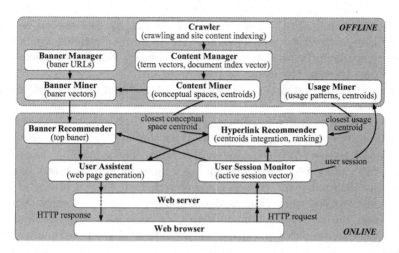

Fig. 1. Personalization process

supplied as a service (used for example by Banner Miner). Crawler is also responsible for a periodical web site monitoring and deciding whether changes are serious enough to start the update process. Crawler takes the first step in the personalization process.

Content Manager creates term vectors using *itf* indices generated by Crawler. For every term t_i a N-dimensional vector $c_i^t = \langle w_{i1}^c, w_{i2}^c, \ldots, w_{iN}^c \rangle$ is created. w_{ij}^c denotes the weight of the term t_i in the document d_j. N is the number of documents. As vector representation is common for the whole system, Content Manager stores URL index that assigns vector coordinate to the specific URL address (*document index vector*).

Content Miner clusters term vectors. Each cluster corresponds to a thematic group denoted *conceptual space* [9], which is represented by the term vector denoted *centroid*. Not all terms are used in the clustering process, only the best content descriptors are chosen by means of the information of their occurrences in documents and queries sent to the Search Engine [9].

User Session Monitor captures users' HTTP requests and groups them into sessions using JSP servlet session mechanism [8]. For every session s_i a N-dimensional vector $c_i^t = \langle w_{i1}^s, w_{i2}^s, \ldots, w_{iN}^s \rangle$ is created. The coordinate w_{ij}^s has non-zero value, if the document d_j was visited in the session s_i [9]. User Session Monitor possesses historical sessions and active user sessions (sessions of the users who are currently on-line). Since it is able to estimate the number of requests per time, it informs the Host Manager about WWW server overload.

Usage Miner clusters historical sessions into typical usage patterns. Each pattern is represented by the mean cluster vector — *centroid*.

Hyperlink Recommender is responsible for creating hyperlink ranking lists. It receives the current user's session vector from User Session Monitor and sends it to Usage Miner and Content Miner. The former finds the closest usage pattern centroid and the latter — the closest conceptual space centroid, using cosine similarity measure [17]. Both centroids and the current user session vector are joined together by Hyperlink Recommender. It forms a ranking list according to the algorithm presented in [9]. n top documents from the ranking list are presented to the user (by means of User Assistant).

Banner Manager is responsible for removing, adding and modifying banner related data.

Banner Miner creates a banners' vector $b_i = \langle w_{i1}^b, w_{i2}^b, \ldots, w_{iM}^b \rangle$ for every conceptual space, where w_{ij}^b corresponds to the similarity between i^{th} conceptual space and j^{th} banner; M is the number of banners. The value of w_{ij}^b is calculated using terms common for the conceptual space and the banner target page.

Banner Recommender chooses a banner that should be presented to the user on the current page. Banner Recommender relays to Content Miner the current user session vector obtained from User Session Monitor. Content Miner returns the closest conceptual space centroid. Next, Banner Recommender asks Banner Miner for the b_i vector corresponding to the conceptual space. Banner Recommender creates a banner ranking list using the b_i^{th} vector coordinates, each banner life-time and the number of times the banner must be exposed (according to the advertise contract conditions). Additionally, the information about m-last exposed banners is stored for each on-line user in order to prevent the same banner to be showed too many times.

Search Engine finds and ranks the documents that fulfil query's criteria. It extracts terms from the query and asks Content Manager for a list of corresponding term vectors. The vectors are joined together in a result vector in accordance with the operators placed between terms in the query. The result list is created from the result vector: documents are ordered by corresponding result vector's coordinates. Additionally, the frequencies of queried terms are stored in order to permit Content Miner to select appropriate conceptual space descriptors.

User Assistant sends requests to agents and generates ROSA page area.

Every host on which ROSA agents reside has an auxiliary *Host Manager* agent. It is responsible for mediation between agents that try to use system resources from the same host simultaneously.

3   Knowledge Verification Method

The knowledge of an agent depends on other ROSA agents' knowledge. Therefore, the update process can be represented as a directed acyclic *task graph* where knowledge verification tasks performed by single agents are modelled by nodes and dependency between nodes are represented by directed arcs (Fig. 2). Task graphs are widely used especially in parallel and distributed computing [3,4]. Changes in the knowledge of an agent implicate a necessity of knowledge update in its all explicit and implicit dependent nodes. Agents that start and manage the update process are called *Update Managers*. There are four Update Managers, thus the whole task graph can be divided into a four overlapped task graphs (Fig. 2). By chance, only trees are presented on the Fig. 2, but it is not a system restriction. It is possible to add an agent whose knowledge would depend

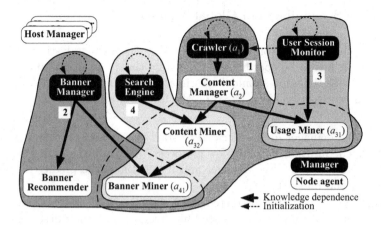

Fig. 2. Task graphs for knowledge verification

on Content Miner's and Usage Miner's knowledge. For commodity, the "tree nomenclature" (parent, child, leaf) is applied to this paper.

The update is the four-stage process that consists of:

1. Initialisation — detection of needs for knowledge updating and approval
2. Time scheduling and global time-out estimation
3. Acquisition and propagation of knowledge changes
4. Synchronization — the acceptance of changes carried out by agents.

3.1   Initialisation

Some agents may suggest to Update Manager that external knowledge has changed significantly. Such initialising agent may but does not have to belong to the task graph. Verification suggestions were marked with dotted arrows (Fig. 2):

- User Session Monitor detects non-existing pages and suggests to Crawler reindexing the site content. When User Session Monitor finds many new sessions in its database, it initiates the recalculation of usage clusters by itself.
- Crawler discovers changes in the site content (new pages, updates and deletion) on the grounds of periodically made sampling.
- Banner Manager is responsible for banner insertion and erasing, thus it suggests updating the knowledge related to banner recommendation process.
- Search Engine possesses statistics of user queries and may initialise an update of content mining data with the new most frequently asked terms.

The detected need is sent to the Update Manager with specific parameters, e.g. list of unavailable pages. The manager verifies the necessity of update (accepts or rejects it) according to the premises obtained from initialization agent, the build-in decision rules, its previous experiences and its own knowledge.

3.2   Time Scheduling and Global Time-Out Estimation

Since the whole verification process consists of various long-lasting and dependent steps, it has to be coordinated. The start time, and duration of each step and the global time-out should be estimated. The below description of time scheduling process (Fig. 3) is based on the first task graph (Fig. 2):

1. After the manager a_1 has decided to start the update process, it sends the predicted duration d_1 of its own process (determined on the basis of its experience) to its Host Manager and it negotiates the predicted best start time t_0 and finish time t_1.
2. Manager a_1 sends the predicted finish time t_1 to all its children with the questions concerning the suggested finish time for all their descendants. The children (a_1 has only one child a_2) negotiate with their Host Managers a start time (closest after t_1) and calculate their finish times. They relay the question to their children with the negotiated time (a_2 sends t_2). If an agent had two or more parents it would ask the Host Manager for the time period after $\max(t_{p1}, t_{p2}, \ldots)$ where t_{pn} is the estimated finish time of the nth parent.
3. Leaves a_{31} and a_{41} return responses to their parents. Answers include only their predicted finish time (t_{31} and t_{41} respectively). Parents relay their children replies upwards in the graph. If an agent has more than one child, it will return the greatest value, i.e. a_2 will return t_{41}.
4. The global time-out is equal to the latest time returned to the manager (t_{41}).

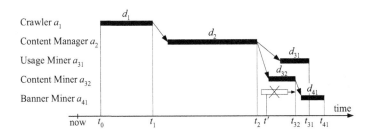

Fig. 3. Knowledge verification suggested timeline for the graph No. 1

Please note that, every agent may have already been engaged in an update process P' of another task graph, e.g. Content Miner a_{32} might be executing the process from the fourth graph. In this case, the agent asked P' Update Manager (Search Engine), through their ascendants, for the whole time-out t' of the process P'. The agent a_{32} will seek for its starting time after t' (Fig. 3). Generally, an agent must not start second process, until the first one finishes. It prevents processes from overlapping each other.

3.3   Acquisition and Propagation of Knowledge Changes

The manager and all other agents wait for the answers (concerning global time-out) only for a short time. If not all answers come to the root, the whole process is cancelled. Otherwise the manager sets up the global process time-out. At the time t_0 the manager (Crawler) begins indexing web pages. None of the involved agents overwrite its *current data*. New information are stored in the *new data*. After the manager has finished, it sends an appropriate message to its children. If any node detects that no data was changed, its children obtain a *nothing-changed message*. If a child receives a *nothing-changed message* from all its parents, it sends the same message downwards in the graph. Otherwise it starts its own verification. The process repeats recursively. As soon as a leaf agent finishes, it reports this to its parents, which once having answers from all its children relay them upwards.

If another update request (from another task graph) comes while processing, an agent waits for the first process to be finished and remembers the processes' order.

3.4   Canceling

If the whole process does not end until the global time-out (t_{41}), the manager keeps waiting. However if another initialisation suggestion comes, it cancels the unfinished process after taking decision about the new process. The cancel message is sent downwards. An agent which obtains such a message deletes all unnecessary data.

Any agent may break its process down for any reason before finishing, informing the manager about it. In such case the manager cancels the whole process similarly to the previous case. The manager informs the system administrator (e.g. by sending e-mail) every time the process is cancelled.

3.5   Knowledge Synchronization

If the manager has obtained positive responses form all its children, it begins synchronization process, sending *lock request* to all dependant nodes with short t_{lr} time-out. The agents wait for *lock report* from their children. All agents from the graph after *lock request* works in default mode (not based on *current data*) during the personalization process. If the manager does not obtain the *lock report* from all its children until t_{lr} time-out, it will cancel the process (roll it back) and it will try again after a long t_r time-out. Otherwise, the manager sends *change data request*. All agents backup *current data* to *old data* and rewrite *new data* into *current data*. Next, they report it to their parents. The manager sends *finish request* to all agents after receiving reports from its children. Agents from the task graph delete *old data* and unlock *new data*. Initialisation agents reset their parameters used for initialisation.

If two verification processes are performed in the same time and there is at least one agent that is involved in both of them, the second process must not be carried out in the conflictive node until the first is totally finished.

4   ACL and FIPA-RDF0 Usage

Each multi-agent system needs a communication language that provides a framework for every communicative act defining some standard types of messages: (inform, request, accept, etc.) and a content language that permits agents to express their world (objects, propositions, and functions). Agent Communication Language [6] can be used as the former and FIPA-RDF0 [7] as the latter. Since ROSA architecture is thought to be easily extended, task graphs are created dynamically by means of ACL messages. For example, if an agent a_1 wants to be an element of knowledge dependency graph it must request it (sending the following message):

```
(request
 :sender agent_a1
 :receiver agent_a2
 :content (<?xml version="1.0"?>
   <rdf:RDF xmlns:rdf="http://www.w3.org/1999/02/22-
                       rdf-syntax-ns#"
           xmlns:fipa="http://www.fipa.org/schemas#">
     <fipa:Action rdf:ID="unique-identifier">
       <fipa:actor>agent_a2</rdf:actor>
       <fipa:act>join-to-graph</rdf:act>
       <fipa:argument>
         <rdf:bag> <rdf:li>agent_a1</rdf:li> </rdf:bag>
       </fipa:argument>
     </fipa:Action>
   </rdf:RDF>)
 :language fipa-rdf0)
```

Every agent that provides any information should store a list of its knowledge dependant nodes (children and parents). Initialisation and the global time-out estimation is presented on Fig. 4, as an example of a communication language usage. Message content (*KnowledgeVerification*, *ProcStarted*, *FinTime*, etc.) is

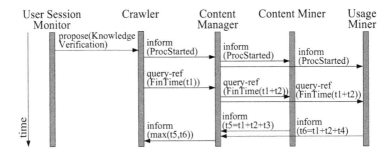

Fig. 4. Sequence diagram with ACL commands used for time scheduling

expressed in FIPA-RDF0 language. For clearness, the communication between agents and corresponding host administrators was omitted.

5   System Implementation

Agents and their communication were developed in Java. Although the server part of ROSA was implemented using JSP/Servlet technologies ROSA can be incorporated into every web site (Fig. 5). It results from that User Assistant adds only a simple HTML frame into the current page returned by the web server. The small java script code is attached to every site page in order to capture user activities by User Session Monitor.

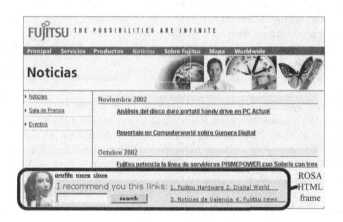

Fig. 5. ROSA HTML frame incorporated into a web page

6   Conclusions and Future Work

Usage and integration of information coming from different sources (web usage mining, site content mining, search-engine statistics), especially when the site evolved rapidly, has many inconveniences. First of all, the process of verification of discovered knowledge is very tedious. Moreover, manual update can lead to periodical system inconsistency. Multi-agent architecture, apart from encapsulation of typical web mining tasks in heterogeneous entities, solves those problems. ROSA agents not only detect when their information should be verified, but they are also able to coordinate knowledge update tasks. Additionally, they treat local system resources like limited goods that should be shared in an effective way.

Since presented system is quite easy to expand, the future works will concentrate on implementation of new agents, extending personalization functionality of ROSA. It is considered to include Shop Miner – an agent that would recommend the products from an internet shop and give some advice for the hesitating customers. Another challenge is to develop an agent that would be responsible for prompting sponsored hyperlinks (during the search result presentation).

References

1. Aggarwal C.C., Yu P.S.: An Automated System for Web Portal Personalization. 28th VLDB Conference, Morgan Kaufmann (2002).
2. Boley D., et al.: Document Categorization and Query Generation on the World Wide Web Using WebACE. Artificial Intelligence Review 13 (5-6) (1999) 365–391.
3. Casavant T.L., Kuhl J.G.: A Taxonomy of Scheduling in General-Purpose Distributed Computing Systems. IEEE Transactions on Software Engineering, 14 (2) (1988) 141–154.
4. Coffman E.G., Graham R.L.: Optimal Scheduling for Two-Processor Systems. Acta Informatica, 1 (1972) 200–213.
5. Ferber J.: Multi-Agent Systems. Addison Wesley Longman (1999).
6. FIPA Agent Communication Language Specification. Foundation for Intelligent Physical Agents (2000).
7. FIPA RDF Content Language Specification. Foundation For Intelligent Physical Agents (2001).
8. Java Servlet Specification Version 2.3, `http://java.sun.com`.
9. Kazienko P., Kiewra M.: Link Recommendation Method Based on Web Content and Usage Mining. New Trends in Intelligent Information Processing and Web Mining Conference Proceedings, Advances in Soft Computing, Springer, to appear.
10. Kiewra M.: Web Management Using Users' Data and Activities. Wrocław University of Technology, M.Sc. Thesis (2002).
11. Langheinrich M., Nakamura A., Abe N., Kamba T., Koseki Y.: Unintrusive Customization Techniques for Web Advertising. Computer Networks 31 (11-16) (1999) 1259–1272.
12. Lin W., Alvarez S.A., Ruiz C.: Efficient Adaptive-Support Association Rule Mining for Recommender Systems. Data Mining and Knowledge Discovery 6 (1) (2002) 83–105.
13. Madria S.K., Bhowmick S.S., Ng W.-K., Lim E.P.: Research Issues in Web Data Mining. Lecture Notes in Computer Science 1676 Springer (1999) 303–312.
14. Mobasher B., Cooley R., Srivastava J.: Automatic personalization based on Web usage mining. CACM 43 (8) (2000) 142–151.
15. Mobasher B., Dai H., Luo T., Sun Y., Zhu J.: Integrating Web Usage and Content Mining for More Effective Personalization. EC-Web 2000, Lecture Notes in Computer Science 1875 Springer (2000) 156–176.
16. Perkowitz M., Etzioni O.: Adaptive Web sites. CACM 43 (8) (2000) 152–158.
17. Salton G., McGill M.J.: Intruduction to Modern Information Retrieval. McGraw-Hill Book Co. (1983).
18. Yao Y.Y., Hamilton H.J., Wang X.: PagePrompter: An Intelligent Agent for Web Navigation Created Using Data Mining Techniques. RSCTC 2002, Lecture Notes in Computer Science 2475 Springer (2002) 506–513.

Supporting Software Maintenance in Web Repositories through a Multi-agent System

Aurora Vizcaino[1], Jesús Favela[2], Mario Piattini[1], and Felix García[1]

[1]Escuela Superior de Informática. Universidad de Castilla-La Mancha
13071, Paseo de la Universidad, 4, Ciudad Real, Spain
{avizcain,mpiattini,fgarcia}@inf-cr.uclm.es
[2]CICESE, Ensenada, México
favela@cicese.mx

Abstract. Software Maintenance (SM) is a knowledge-intensive activity. A suitable management of this knowledge could decrease the high costs (economic and in effort) of software maintenance tasks.
The challenge of managing this knowledge increases as the distributed development of software becomes more popular, and developers as well as knowledge are distributed worldwide. Increasingly web repositories are being used for the coordination of development tasks among software and maintenance engineers. Thus, an appropriate technical solution to this problem should be based on a web architecture and associated protocols.
On the other hand, in order to work with all the concepts related to SM is advisable to establish different levels of abstraction, thus the complexity of the concepts, and their management, are simplified. This work presents a system that, by storing information in XMI documents, manages the data and metadata generated during SM, facilitating the work of SM engineers.

1 Introduction

Many studies [7,15,18] provide evidence that the majority of the overall expenses incurred during the life-cycle of a software product occur during the maintenance stages. Thus, in recent years researchers have focused their attention on proposing methods and techniques which help increase the efficiency of the Software Maintenance Process (SMP).

One way to improve maintenance quality and decrease software maintenance costs is to reuse previous information and knowledge [10]. However, for information to be usable it needs to be modeled, structured, generalised and stored in a reusable form, to allow for effective retrieval [1].

In order to decrease the efforts and cost in the SMP we developed a knowledge management system called KM-MANTIS. The system is in charge of storing and reusing information, knowledge and expertise generated during the SMP. KM-MANTIS is based on the experience factory concept [4,5] since it is known that an organizational memory must be maintained by an organizational unit separate from the project organizations because it is mainly concerned to keeping schedules and cost constraints, and proving knowledge would imply an extra effort for the project organizations employees.

E. Menasalvas et al. (Eds.): AWIC 2003, LNAI 2663, pp. 307–317, 2003.

KM-MANTIS is a multi-agent system where different types of agent manage the diverse types of information generated during SMP. Agents interchange data and take advantage of the information and experience acquired by other agents.

The main feature of KM-MANTIS is that it stores data and metadata in XMI (XML metadata interchange) [13] documents. It is critical to manage diferent levels of abstraction to carry out an integral management of a software process. Moreover, being XMI an open format fosters the interchange of data between distributed and heterogeneous repositories which also use XMI.

The contents of this paper are divided as follows. Section 2 discusses the importance of managing the knowledge generated during the software maintenance process. Section 3 describes the features of KM-MANTIS. Section 4 explains how and why information is stored in a XMI repository, and shows, through an example, the use of the system. Finally, conclusions are presented in Sect. 5.

2 The Need for Knowledge Management in Software Maintenance

Software maintenance is an activity where different kinds of knowledge are generated from different sources. This knowledge comes not only from the expertise of the professionals involved in the process, but it is also intrinsic to the product being maintained, and to the reasons that motivate the maintenance (new requirements, user complaints, etc). Moreover, the diverse types of knowledge are produced at different stages of the maintenance process. For instance, [6] claims that during Initial Development the maintenance staff acquires knowledge about the application domain, user requirements, roles of the application, solutions and algorithms, data formats, strengths and weaknesses of the program architecture, operating environment, etc. In the Software Evolution stage new users and environmental requirements arise and changes are produced which generate new knowledge, and this process continues in the rest of the stages.

Furthermore, this knowledge is used by different persons at different stages. Each person has partial information that is required by other members of the group. If the knowledge only exists in the software engineers and there is no system in charge of transferring the tacit knowledge (contained in the employees) to explicit knowledge (stored on paper, in files, etc) when an employee abandons the organization a significant part of the intellectual capital goes with him/her.

One of the five factors that have been identified as having a major impact on the productivity of software maintenance is the expertise of the staff members [2]. It has been found that systems maintained by relatively inexperienced programmers average significantly higher error rates [3].

Another well-known issue that complicates the SMP is the scarce documentation that exists related to a specific software system. Even if detailed documentation was produced when the original system was developed, it is seldom updated as the system evolves. For example, legacy software written by other units often has little or no documentation describing the features of the software.

In addition, organizations still lack a culture of reuse and information sharing. As [12] claims, companies only use a quarter part of its intellectual capital.

On the other hand, thanks to technology advances it is frequent for maintenance teams to be geographically distributed, which implies:

- Coordination of distributed work.
- Providing access to knowledge to the different sub-units.
- Managing experience compiled from previous projects and making it available and reusable for new projects.

A knowledge management system could satisfy these needs so as to avoid some of the issues commented previously. For instance, if organizations store their information and knowledge in a KM system, they would own this intellectual capital. Therefore, even if experts left the organization their expertise would remain within the companies.

In addition, a suitable storage of information facilitates its reuse. For these reasons we decided to develop a KM system where the diverse kinds of knowledge generated from different stages of SMP were stored, analysed, shared and reused.

Another advantage of a KM system is that staff may also be informed about the location of information. A critical factor for maintenance engineers is to have access to the knowledge the organizations have. In [22] a study was conducted, which found that the number one barrier to knowledge sharing was "ignorance": the sub-units are ignorant of the knowledge that exists in the organizations, or the sub-units possessing the knowledge are ignorant of the fact that another sub-unit needs such knowledge. Sometimes the organization itself is not aware of the location of the pockets of knowledge or expertise [11].

3 The KM-MANTIS Multi-agent System

This section describes the features of KM-MANTIS and its architecture. However, before presenting the system we explain why a multi-agent architecture for the management of information was chosen.

3.1 Why Agents?

Previous works such as [21, 19] have used agents for knowledge management. There are several reasons why agents are recommendable for this task. First of all, agents can manage both distribute and local information. This is an important feature since, as it was explained in Sect. 2, the software maintenance information is generated by different sources and often from different places.

In a distributed architecture each agent knows about its local environment, and it is close to the place where the information is generated. When global knowledge is required the agents can act together and share knowledge. The alternative will be to have a centralized system that knows "everything". However, this is more difficult to implement and also less robust.

An aspect related to the previous one is that agents may cooperate and interchange information. Thus, each agent can share its knowledge with others or ask them advice, benefiting from the other agents' experience. Therefore, there is reuse and knowledge management in the architecture of the system itself.

Another important issue is that agents can learn from their own experience. Consequently the system is expected to become more efficient with time since the agents have learnt from their previous mistakes and successes.

On the other hand, agents may utilize different reasoning techniques depending on the situation. For instance, they can use ID3 algorithms to learn from previous experiences and use case-based reasoning to advise a client how to solve a problem.

3.2 The KM-MANTIS Architecture

The system is formed of a set of agent communities which manage different types of knowledge. When the ontology to represent the maintenance domain was developed different types of information were detected, thus the system has a community per type of information detected since each one has its specific features. The three more relevant types of information identified were: information related to the products to be maintained; information referent to the activities to perform in order to maintain the products; and, peopleware involved during software maintenance process [23].

Therefore, KM-MANTIS has three communities: a community termed "products community", another called "activities community", and the last community denoted "peopleware community". In what follows, we describe each community in more detail.

Products Community: This community manages the information related to the products to be maintained. Since each product has its own features and follows a specific evolution this community has one agent per product. The agents have information about the initial requirements, changes made to the product, and about metrics that evaluate features related to the maintainability of the product (this information is obtained from different documents such as modification requests, perfective, corrective or preventive actions performed or product measurements). Therefore, the agents monitor the product's evolution in order to have up to date information about it at each moment.

Each time an agent detects that information about its product is being introduced or modified in KM-MANTIS (the agent detects it when the product identification number that it represents is introduced or displayed in the interface of KM-MANTIS) the agent starts to work analysing the new information (in the case of there being any), or comparing it to that previously held in order to detect inconsistencies, or checking the differences and storing the relevant information in order to have up-to-date information.

Besides information relevant to each product, which is stored in a database that each agent has, general information about products such as type of products that the system manages should be considered. This information which can be considered as metadata is stored in a XMI repository common for the community, called "community repository" (see Fig. 1). The decision to use XMI documents based on the MOF (Meta Object Facility) standard (they are described in more detail in Sect. 4) makes it possible for agents of this community to have access to the different levels of information that they need to process and classify their information.

Thus, products and activities communities have a common repository where general information and metadata are stored. For instance, an agent can detect that whenever a change labelled "A" is demanded another change called "B" is required. This knowledge learnt by the agent will be stored in the community repository and thus it will be shared with the rest of the product agents. In a previous design of this system a single agent was in charge of this repository but this fact increased considerably the traffic of messages between agents, and so it was eliminated, producing thereby an improvement in the speed of the system.

Besides the repository that each community has, agents can also consult a general repository where the documents generated during the SMP are stored in format XMI. This repository is usually used when agents need additional information for answering queries or performing their tasks. Later, in Sect. 4, we provide examples of this.

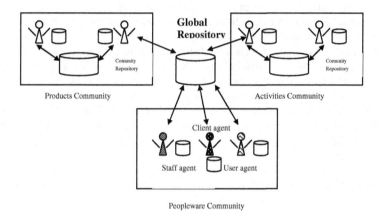

Fig. 1. KM-MANTIS architecture

Activities Community: Each new change demanded implies performing one or more activities. This community, which has one agent per activity, is in charge of managing the knowledge related to the different activities such as methods, techniques and resources used to perform an activity.

Activities agents can also obtain new knowledge from their experience and learning. For instance, an activity agent can learn what person usually carries out a specific activity.

As in the previous case each agent has a database to store its information, and a community repository to access it. This repository contains metadata and data important for all the community. For instance, a taxonomy of activities.

Peopleware Community: Three profiles of people can be clearly differentiated in MP [16]: the maintainer, the customer and the user. The Peopleware community has three types of agent, one per profile detected. One agent is in charge of the information related to staff (maintainers). This is the staff agent. Another manages information related to the clients (customers) and is called the client agent. The last one is in charge of the users and is termed the user agent.

The staff agent knows the personal data of the employees, in what activities they have worked, and what product they have maintained. Of course, the agent also has current information about each member of the staff. Therefore, it knows where each person is working at each moment.

The agent can utilise the information that it has to generate new knowledge. For instance, the staff agent may calculate statistics that indicate the time that an employee took to perform a task or calculate the performance graph of each member.

The client agent stores the information of each client, their requirements (even the initial requirements if they are available) and requests. The client agent also tries to obtain new knowledge. For instance, it tries to guess future requirements depending on previous requirements or it estimates the costs of changes that the client wants to make, warning him for instance of the high costs associated with a specific change request.

The user agent is in charge of knowing the requirements of the users of each product, their background and also their complaints and comments about the products. New knowledge could be generated from this information, for example by testing to what degree the users' characteristics influence the maintenance of the product.

Each type of agent has a database but in this case there is not a community repository because there is no data common to the three types of agents. However, as arrows indicate in Fig. 1 agents can access the global repository.

Agents exchange information by using ACL (Agent Communication Language). This language provides agents with the means to share information and knowledge through a set of communicative acts.

The platform used is JADE (Java Agent Development Framework) since it simplifies the implementation of multi-agent systems through a set of tools that supports the debugging and deployment phase.

4   Web Repositories of Information

The World Wide Web has moved from its origins as a medium for the dissemination of information to a middleware platform for the development of sophisticated distributed applications. This trend has given rise to a new branch of Software Engineering, named Web Engineering, concerned with establishing sound principles, techniques, and tools for the development and maintenance of systems, services and applications over the Web.

As the web becomes the preferred medium for the deployment of software applications several CASE tools have migrated to the web and several others have been developed. The use of the web as a platform for the support of software development offers several advantages:

- Ubiquitous access. Web repositories can be accessed from any computer connected to the Internet, including portable devices.
- Simple integration of tools. The web is based on simple, open protocols that can be easily integrated in CASE tools to allow their interoperability. At the lowest level of integration a tool can export content to HTML or semantically richer XML documents.
- Support for distributed software development. Large-scale software systems are increasingly being developed by distributed teams of specialists that need to communicate and coordinate their activities. The web offers a simple middleware for the deployment of workflow and groupware tools that support collaboration.

Of particular interest to us is the use of web servers as repositories for product and process information. This information is not only essential to the production of software, but to its maintenance as well. The centralized storage of this information facilitates configuration management, quality control, project tracking, and the management of requirements.

An important effort in this area is the IETF's DeltaV project [24], an effort to extend the WebDAV and HTTP protocols to support document versioning and configuration control for shared web documents and resources.

On the other hand, applications manipulating Web data require both, documents or information retrieved from the Web, and metadata about this information [8]. In order to specify and manage meta-data we used the standard MOF proposed by the OMG [13].

This standard defines four conceptual levels (see Table 1): the base level, called M0, is where the instances or real data are. For example in the KM-MANTIS repository at this level we find the concrete changes that have been performed. Data managed in this level are instances of the concepts defined in the superior level called M1. The specific model that we used in level M1 is based on the MANTEMA methodology [17] and on a set of techniques adapted to maintenance, such as effort or risk estimations [20]. An example of information at this level are the different types of *support activities* that exist according to MANTEMA. The next level is the M2, which corresponds to the meta-models, in our case to the software maintenance process meta-model. And the last level, M3, is where the meta-meta model is represented, this is the MOF model itself.

Table 1. Conceptual levels in MOF and KM-MANTIS

Level	MOF	KM-MANTIS
M3	MOF model (Meta-metamodel)	MOF Model
M2	Meta-model	SMP metamodel
M1	Model	MANTEMA
M0	Data	SMP instances (products, activities)

An example will help illustrate this classification. The generic concept "Maintenance Activity" represents the correspondence between M3 and M2 (see Fig. 2). This concept is instantiated in a specific type of activity in the correspondence M2 and M1. For instance, in "Urgent Corrective Intervention" activity. When we have real instances of this type of activity it will be stored in the level M0, for example "Intervention number 3 performed in the project Counts.

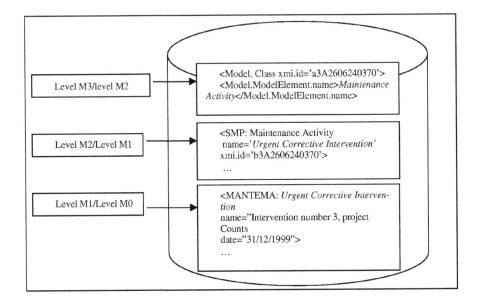

Fig. 2. Example of the XMI repository

As Fig. 2 shows, data from an Mi level are converted into metadata in the inferior level Mi-1. Thus, "Maintenance Activity", that is a piece of data in the XMI document which represents the correspondence between M3-M2, is converted into a label (metadata) in the XMI document which represents the correspondence between the levels M2 and M1.

Using XMI enables us to represent different levels of abstraction and their relationships. Knowing the relationship between these levels helps to deduce new knowledge from the previous one. Moreover, XMI permits to obtain information from other repositories, systems or information sources which support XMI [14]. And it also facilitates the interchange of information between agents since all use the same information representation.

In order to demonstrate how agents use the repositories we describe a scenario. Suppose a user consults in KM-MANTIS, when and by whom the intervention number 3, which was an Urgent Corrective Intervention, was performed. In this case the agent in charge of this type of activity should act. As Fig. 3 shows, the urgent corrective intervention agent will consult in its database the date and name of the person who carried out the intervention number 3. If a second query was performed asking the name of the maintenance activities the agent would have to consult the community repository where the information requested is. This type of information is in a higher level in the MOF standard, which corresponds to M2-M1, therefore XMI documents of this representation would be consulted in order to find all the names of maintenance activities.

To show an access to the global repository, imagine that a user needs to see the intervention number 3 request document. In this case the agent will access the global repository in order to get the XMI document that represents that request document.

A last example showing collaboration between agents is exposed. Once it is known who performed the intervention number 3 the user asks for more information about this person. The agent would contact the staff agent which will answer this request providing all information related to John Cruise such as telephone number, e-mail, his office location, etc.

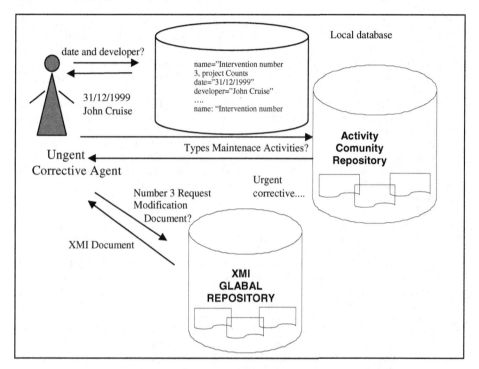

Fig. 3. Example of consults in KM-MANTIS

5   Conclusions

The complexity of the SM process demands a model of the information with a suitable level of abstractation for dealing with the different concepts that the process involves. XMI and MOF enable us to define and store a model with different levels of metadata and data. Several examples have clarified how agents utilise the levels and how diverse abstraction queries can be solved.

A future work will be the evaluation of KM-MANTIS following the DESMET [9] method. DESMET proposes a technique of evaluation divided into two types: Evaluation focused on the measurable effects of using a method or tool and the second evaluation centred on establishing criteria to measure in what degree a method or tool is suitable for a orgnisation taking into account its necesities and its culture.

References

1. Althoff, K-D, Birk, A., and Tautz, C. : The Experience Factory Approach: Realizing Learning from Experience in Software Development Organizations. In proceedings of the 10th German Workshop on Machine Learning (FGML 1997), University of Karlsruhe, (1997), 6–8

2. Banker, R.D., Datar, S.M. and Kemerer, C.F. A model to evaluate variables impacting the productivity of software Maintenance Project. Management Science 37 (1), (1991), 1–18

3. Banker, R.D., Datar, S.M. and Kemerer, C.F., and Zweig, D. Software Errors and Software Maintenance Management. Journal of Information Technology & Management. Pirkul, N., and Vargheses S.J (Eds.). Vol. 03. ISSN 1385-951X. Kluwer Academic Publichers, (2002) 25–41

4. Basili, V.R., and Rombach, H.D. The TAME project: Towards improvement-oriented software environments. IEEE Transactions on Software Engineering, SE-14(6):(1988). 758–773

5. Basili, V.R., Caldiera, G., and Rombach, H.D.: Experience Factory. In John J. Marciniak (Ed.) Encyclopedia of Software Engineering, v. 1, pp. 469-476. John Wiley & Sons.(1994)

6. Bennet K.H., and Rajlich V.T. Software Maintenance and Evolution: a Roadmap, in Finkelstein, A. (Ed.), The Future of Software Engineering, ICSE 2000, June 4–11, Limerick, Ireland, (2000) 75–87

7. Card, D.N., and Glass, R.L. Measuring Software Design Quality. Prentice Hall, Englewood Cliffs, NJ (1990)

8. Gomes, D., Campos, J.P., Silva, M.J: Versus: A Web Repository. Workshop on Distributed Data and Structures (WDAS) (2002)

9. Kitchenham, B. Evaluating Software Methods and Tools Using the DESMET Methodology. In Proc. Of Empirical Assesment in Software Engineering (EASE), University of Keele, U.K. (1997).

10. de Looff, L.A., Information Systems Outsourcing Decision Making: a Managerial Approach. Hershey, PA: Idea Group Publishing, (1990)

11. Nebus, J. Framing the Knowledge Search Problem: Whom Do We Contact, and Why Do We Contact Them? Academy of Management Best Papers Proceedings, (2001) h1–h7

12. Nonaka, Ikujiro and Takeuchi, Hirotaka.; The knowledge creating company. Oxford University Press. ISBN 0-19-509269-4. (1995)

13. OMG Meta Object Facility (MOF) Specification, v. 1.3 RTF, Sep. 1999. In http://www.omg.org.

14. OMG XML Metadata Interchange (XMI), v. 1.1, Nov-2000

15. Pigoski, T.M.: Practical Software Maintenance. Best Practices for Managing Your Investment. Ed. John Wiley & Sons, USA, (1997)

16. Polo, M., Piattini, M., Ruiz, F. and Calero, C.: Roles in the Maintenance Process. Software Engineering Notes; vol 24, no. 4, 84–86. ACM., (1999)

17 Polo, M., Piattini, M., Ruiz, F. and Calero, C.: MANTEMA: A Complete Rigourous Methodology for Supporting Maintenance based on the ISO/IEC 12207 Standard. Third Euromicro Conference on Software Maintenance and Reengineering (CSMR'99). Amsterdam (The Netherlands). IEEE Computer Society, (1999) 178–181

18. Polo, M., Piattini, M., and Ruiz, F.: Using a Qualitative Research Method for Building A Software Maintenance Methodology. In Software Practice & Experience. John Wiley and Sons. Vol. 32, No. 13, (2002): 1239–1260

19. Rasmus, D.W. Mind Tools: Connecting to Groupware. PC AI, September/October, (1996) 32–36

20. Ruiz, F.; Piattini, M.; Polo, M.; Calero, C.; Audit of Software Maintenance. In "Auditing Information Systems". Idea Group Publishing, USA (2000)

21. Silverman, B.G., Bedewi, N. and Morales, A. Intelligent Agents in Software Reuse Repositories. CIKM Workshop on Intelligent Information Agents. Baltimore, (1995)

22. Szulanski, G.,: Intra-Firm Transfer of Best Practices Project. American Productivity and Quality Centre, Houston, Texas, (1994) 2–19
23. Vizcaíno, A., Ruíz, F., Favela, J., and Piattini, M. A Multi-Agent Architecture for Knowledge Management in Software Maintenance. In Proceedings of International Workshop on Practical Applications of Agents and Multiagent Systems (IWPAAMS'02), Salamanca, Spain 23–25 October, (2002) 39–52
24. Whitehead, J. "The Future of Distributed Software Development on the Internet." Web Techniques, Vol. 4, No. 10, October, (1999), 57–63

A Hybrid Method for Patterns Mining and Outliers Detection in the Web Usage Log

Mikhail Petrovskiy

Computer Science Department of Lomonosov Moscow State University,
Building 2, MSU, Vorobjovy Gory, Moscow, 119899, Russia
michael@cs.msu.su

Abstract. This paper presents a novel approach to mining patterns and outliers detection in the Web Usage log. This approach involves kernel methods and fuzzy clustering methods. Web log records are considered as vectors with numeric and nominal attributes. These vectors are mapped by means of a special kernel to a high dimensional feature space, where the possibilistic clustering method is used to calculate the measure of "typicalness" of vectors. If the value of this measure for a particular record is less than specified threshold this record is labeled as an outlier. The records with high "typicalness" are considered as access patterns of user activity. The performance of the approach is demonstrated experimentally.

1 Introduction

Cooley et al. in [1] defined Web Mining "as discovery and analysis of useful information from World Wide Web". They outlined the following three major tasks: mining Web structure, mining Web content and Web usage mining. This paper is devoted to the latter task. Web usage mining was firstly introduced as "automatic discovery of user access patterns from Web access logs" and initially included four techniques – simple statistical analysis of Web traffic (e.g. collecting statistics like the most visited pages, average daily hits, etc.); association rules mining (e.g. finding the relationships between URLs visited by a user during single session); sequential patterns mining (e.g. discover time ordered sequences of hits); clustering (e.g. partitioning URLs into natural groups according to users behaviors). Though all these techniques provide powerful tools for Web log analysis, there is another one task, which has not been widely discussed in the Web mining literature yet. It is outliers detection in the Web usage log. This technique can be used on a pre-processing step to cleanup Web usage log for further analysis and as independent procedure, for example, for anomaly detection in users behaviors. This technique is useful in Web Personalization systems and especially in Intrusion Detection systems.

In this paper a novel approach for outlier detection is presented. In Sect. 2 the geometric framework for outliers detection in HTTP access logs is proposed. The log records are considered as fixed length vectors of numeric and nominal attributes,

E. Menasalvas et al. (Eds.): AWIC 2003, LNAI 2663, pp. 318–328, 2003.

which are implicitly mapped by means of the special kernel into the high dimensional feature space. In Sect. 3 modern algorithms for outliers detection in the feature space are briefly discussed and the novel fuzzy algorithm is presented. This algorithm allows calculate the measure of "typicalness" for log records. Records with small value of "typicalness" are considered as outliers and with high "typicalness" as access patterns. Section 4 is devoted to experiments and achieved results are presented.

2 Feature Space for Outlier Detection in the Web Usage Log

In the suggested approach we work with HTTP server access log as a data source for Web usage mining. Though the approach can be applied for other types of logs, for example, proxy level or client site logs. We assume that HTTP log satisfies Common Log Format and may contain fields: user id ('-' for anonymous), HTTP request method (GET, POST, etc.), path (URL), status code, processing time, number of transmitted bytes, etc. First of all, we split the set of source log records into subsets where all records in the particular subset belong to the same user. Such subset is considered as input space, and every user has own input space. From this moment and below we will denote as X the input space of log records for some user.

2.1 Feature Spaces and Kernels

One of the key ideas of suggested approach is mapping data instances from the input space X to a feature space H. The non-linear mapping is performed implicitly by means of a kernel function K. This technique is widely used in machine learning methods, e.g. in SVM, kernel PCA, kernel Fisher Discriminant and others [3]. Usually the feature space is a vector space of high or infinite dimension, or more generally it is a Hilbert space. The feature map φ is defined as:

$$\varphi : X \to H \tag{1}$$

This map associates with every x from the input space the image $\varphi(x)$ in the feature space. The kernel function corresponds to dot product in the feature space:

$$K(x, y) = \langle \varphi(x), \varphi(y) \rangle \tag{2}$$

This definition of kernel function allows define a distance metric as:

$$d(x, y) = \sqrt{K(x, x) - 2K(x, y) + K(y, y)} \tag{3}$$

The main advantages to use kernel-based approach in the Web usage mining tasks are as follows. Foremost, it allows deal with log records geometrically, and thus it allows applying in Web log analysis geometrical algorithms, working in terms of distance metric and dot product. Secondly, the kernel function K can be considered as a similarity measure for records in the input space. The freedom to choose the feature map φ and corresponded kernel function K enables us to design a large variety of similarity measures and analysis algorithms. It is also called "kernel trick", when given an algorithm which uses distance metric or dot product and one can substitutes the distance metric in this algorithm by "kernelized" distance metric or replace the dot product by another kernel function and as a result get the new algorithm with new properties and possibly better performance. Thirdly, using kernels allows us do not determinate the feature map explicitly, and thus we do not need to calculate and store in memory high dimensional vectors of images $\varphi(x)$.

2.2 Kernel for Outlier Detection in the Web Usage Log

The choice of the feature space, i.e. the choice of the kernel function is application specific and greatly depends on the ability of the feature space to capture the information, relevant to the application domain. Smola, Vapnik et al. in [3,4] investigated this problem for several application domains and suggested that for outlier detection the good performance could be achieved with Gaussian kernel:

$$K(x, y) = e^{-q(x-y)^2} \tag{4}$$

where q is a parameter, controlling the kernel width.

It is obvious that Gaussian kernel cannot be applied directly for the input space of Web usage log data, because of two reasons. First of all, there are nominal attributes like HTTP request method, URL, status code, etc. For nominal attributes we use standard approach: each nominal attribute that takes n different values from its domain we consider as n numeric (actually binary) attributes from the domain {0,1}. The second problem is that attributes may have different ranges of values. For example, the number of transmitted bytes may vary from zero bytes to several megabytes, on the other hand, the value of processing time attribute may vary in the range of several seconds. To avoid such problem we use data-dependent normalized kernels. All attributes values are normalized to the number of standard deviations away from mean. Taking it into account we can define the kernel for Web usage log records as a product of kernels, defined for each attribute:

$$K(x, y) = \prod_{d=1}^{D} K_d(x_d, y_d) \tag{5}$$

where $x \in X$ is a Web log record, i.e. a composite structure; x_d are "parts" of it, $x_d \in X_d$, K_d is a proper kernel defined on $X_d \times X_d$.

As a result we suggest to use the following normalized data-dependent kernel:

$$K(x, y) = \prod_{i \in Num} e^{-q_i \frac{(x_i - y_i)^2}{\sigma_i^2}} \prod_{j \in Discr \wedge x_j \neq y_j} e^{-\frac{q_j}{N_j^2} \left(\frac{1}{(P(x_j)(1-P(x_j)))^2} + \frac{1}{(P(y_j)(1-P(y_j)))^2} \right)} \tag{6}$$

where x_i is a value of i-th attribute of record x; Num is the set of indexes of numeric attributes; $Discr$ is the set of indexes of nominal attributes; $P(x_j)$ is a probability of the value $_i$ for j-th nominal attribute; N_j is a size of the domain for j-th nominal attribute, $_i$ is a dispersion of the i-th numeric attribute and q_i is a kernel width parameter for i-th attribute. It is important to note that q_i can be considered as an importance weight of i-th attribute, since it controls how the deviation of the attribute affects the overall deviation of K. It is easily can be shown that formula (6) is a correct kernel function.

3   Outliers Detection in the Feature Space

Algorithms for detecting outliers in the feature space are based on the assumption that some unknown probability distribution generated the data exists and the feature map is topologically correct, i.e. high density regions from the input space are mapped into high density regions in the feature space. The elements from the input space are labeled as outliers if their images in the feature space lie in low-density regions [3,6]. That is, the idea of the most outliers detection algorithms in the feature space is to examine the image location whether or not it lies in sparse region. The "kernelized" versions of standard geometrical outliers detection algorithms can be used in the feature space. For example, it could be k-nearest neighbor algorithm, which labels as outliers the points having "small" number of "neighbors" or it could be crisp cluster-based algorithm, which labels as outliers the points lying "far" from centers of "big" clusters. The only difference in applying these methods in the feature space is using distance metric (3).

3.1   Support Vector Clustering Algorithm for Outliers Detection

One of the most effective algorithms for detecting outliers in the feature space is Support Vector Clustering algorithm discussed in [4]. It computes the binary function, which is supposed to capture regions in input space where the probability density is in some sense large; i.e. the function is nonzero in a region where most of the data located. Informally the idea of this algorithm can be described as follows. The data instances from the input space are mapped by means of kernel function into high dimensional feature space where the algorithm search the sphere with "soft margin" and minimal radius enclosing "the most part" of images of data. The size of this "most part" is controlled by the special parameter v. The data instance which image lies outside the sphere is labeled as an outlier. The mathematical formulation of the problem is:

$$\min_{\xi \in \mathfrak{R}^m, R \in \mathfrak{R}, a \in H} \left[R^2 + \frac{1}{vN} \sum_{i=1}^{N} \xi_i \right] \tag{7}$$

$$subject\,to\,\|\varphi(x_i) - a\|^2 \le R^2 + \xi_i, \forall i \in [1, N]$$

where R is radius and a is a center of the sphere in the feature space; N is a number of points in X; $0 < v \le 1$ is a quantile, controlling the number of outliers; ξ_i are slack variables for "soft margin". The problem (7) leads to the dual problem, formulated in terms of the Lagrangian:

$$\min_{\beta} \sum_{i,j} \beta_i \beta_j K(x_i, x_j) - \sum_i \beta_i K(x_i, x_i) \qquad (8)$$

$$subject\ to\ 0 \le \beta_i \le \frac{1}{\nu N}\ and\ \sum_i \beta_i = 1$$

and the solution is

$$a = \sum_i \beta_i \varphi(x_i) \qquad (9)$$

with decision function

$$f(x) = \mathrm{sgn}\left(R^2 - \sum_{i,j} \beta_i \beta_j K(x_i, x_j) + 2\sum_i \beta_i K(x_i, x) - K(x, x) \right) \qquad (10)$$

where β_i are Lagrange multipliers, the solution of (8). They are equal to $(1/\nu N)$ for outliers; nonzero and less than $(1/\nu N)$ for point on the sphere's border, i.e. for support vectors; and equal to zero for points inside the sphere.

3.2 Kernel-Based Fuzzy Clustering Algorithm for Outliers Detection

The main drawback of Support Vector Clustering algorithm from our point of view is crisp decision function (10). As it was shown in [4] and in [3], the algorithm performance strongly depends on the value of the quantile ν and it is quite difficult task to estimate it. One of the solutions suggested in [4] leads to the necessity of invoking the algorithm several times increasing the value of the quantile, and choose the one with best performance on the particular dataset. It starts from $\nu = 1/N$, which means no outliers, and iteratively increases ν while some criteria are not satisfied. This stopping criteria as well as a value of increasing step for ν are heuristic and the question how to determine them is open [4]. Because this approach requires running the SVM clustering algorithm several times, we have to solve quadratic programming problem (8) several times with different values of ν. Though effective optimization methods like Sequential Minimal Optimization [3] have been proposed for solving quadratic programming problems for SVM in large datasets, it is not much helpful in case of iterative quantile ν estimation for SVM clustering, because we have to apply it several times with new parameters. Another drawback is not related to the size of dataset, though it is the result of crisp decision function (10) too. The SVM algorithm cannot be used for access patterns mining straightforwardly, since all non-outlier records are of the same "quality" from the point of view of the algorithm. Their Lagrange multipliers are all equal to zero.

To avoid these problems we suggest using fuzzy approach. The suggested method is hybrid method involving the kernel methods and fuzzy methods both. Recently several works in this direction have been published, for example, the Fuzzy SVM method for multi-class classification problem [7], or EM fuzzy clustering algorithm in the feature space [5]. In our approach instead of finding the crisp sphere in the feature space we suggest to find fuzzy sphere including all images of data from the input space. This problem can be considered as finding single fuzzy cluster in the feature space using possibilistic fuzzy clustering approach [2]. In this case the fuzzy membership can be also interpreted as a measure of "typicalness" of data instances. The Web usage log records with low "typicalness" are considered as outliers, the records with high "typicalness" are considered as access patterns, the thresholds are set by user. Changing thresholds or in other words changing the outlier's criteria does not require recalculating the model as it is for SVM clustering algorithm. Mathematically the problem is formulated as follows:

$$\min_{U,a} J(U,a) \tag{11}$$

$$J(U,a) = \sum_{i=1}^{N} (u_i)^m (\varphi(x_i) - a)^2 - \eta \sum_{i=1}^{N} (1 - u_i)^m \tag{12}$$

where a is a center of the cluster in the feature space; N is a number of points in X; U is a membership vector, where $u_i \in [0,1]$ is membership of the image $\varphi(x_i)$ to the fuzzy sphere and besides the "typicalness" of datum x_i; m is fuzzyfier and η determinates the distance at which the membership of a point becomes 0.5. It is necessary to note that unlike traditional possibilistic fuzzy clustering approach in the input space [2] neither cluster center a nor $\varphi(x_i)$ can be calculated directly, but it can be shown that $J(U,a)$ can be minimized by simple iterative algorithm, formulated in terms of kernels. Setting to zero the derivative of J with respect to a and u_j we get:

$$a = \left(\sum_{i=1}^{N} u_i^m \phi(x_i) \right) \Big/ \sum_{i=1}^{N} u_i^m \tag{13}$$

$$u_j = \left[1 + \left((\phi(x_j) - a)^2 / \eta \right)^{m-1} \right]^{-1} \tag{14}$$

The distance in (14) can be calculated according to (3):

$$(\phi(x_j) - a)^2 = (<a,a> + K(x_j,x_j) - 2 <a, \phi(x_j)>) \tag{15}$$

where dot products $<a,a>$ and $<a,x>$ can be calculated using (13):

$$< a, a > = \left(\sum_{j=1}^{N} u_j{}^m \sum_{i=1}^{N} u_i{}^m K(x_i, x_j) \right) \bigg/ \left(\sum_{i=1}^{N} u_i{}^m \right)^2 \tag{16}$$

$$< \phi(x_j), a > = \left(\sum_{i=1}^{N} u_i{}^m K(x_i, x_j) \right) \bigg/ \left(\sum_{i=1}^{N} u_i{}^m \right) \tag{17}$$

Kernel-Based Fuzzy Clustering Algorithm for Outliers Detection

```
Initialize membership vector U
Initialize the parameter 1
/* 1 - iteration counter*/
Repeat
  For all x calculate dot product <a,x> using (17)
  Calculate dot product <a,a> using (16)
  Update U using (14) and (15)
Until ‖U^l - U^{l-1}‖ < ε
```

In comparison to SVM clustering our algorithm has advantages and drawbacks both. As we have discussed above, the main advantage is that there is no crisp decision function any more. That is why changing of outlier's criteria in our algorithm does not require to run it again on the same data, since outlier's criteria is just a threshold and does not affect the calculating of the measure of "typicalness". Our algorithm does not use quantile v and that is why it does not require step-by-step executing to find a suitable solution. Another advantage is that our algorithm is quite simpler from computational point of view in comparison with SVM clustering, which requires solving the several quadratic programming problems (8).

But out algorithm has weakness too. The first one is that our algorithm depends on initialization of U and parameter η. Lets discuss it more in details. We propose two different methods for initialization of our algorithm. The first and the simplest one is following. The initial cluster center is set to the center of gravity, hence all $u_i^0 = 1/N$. η can be initialized by a constant, for example, it can be the squared maximal distance between all images in the feature space, or some other method, developed for estimating this parameter in possibilistic clustering approach can be applied. Details on different methods of setting and estimating η are discussed in [2]. Another approach for parameters initialization is using as a preprocessing stage the only one iteration of SVM clustering, for example, in no outliers mode, i.e. with quantile $v = 1/N$. After that the initial center of fuzzy cluster is supposed to be the same as the center of sphere, calculated in SVM. η is set equal to the square of the radius of the sphere. In this case:

$$u_i^0 = \left(1 + (R^2(x_i)/R^2)^{m-1} \right)^{-1} \tag{18}$$

After that our algorithm is run. It iteratively improves the position of the cluster center.

Another important question is algorithm performance on very large datasets. In this case we use sampling. We run our algorithm on sampled data and after that it can be shown that the membership for any new record x can be estimated using memberships of sampled records by the formula:

$$u(x) = \left[1 + \left(\frac{\sum_{j=1}^{N} u_j^{m} \sum_{i=1}^{N} u_i^{m} K(x_i, x_j)}{\eta (\sum_{i=1}^{N} u_i^{m})^2} - 2 \frac{\sum_{i=1}^{N} u_i^{m} K(x, x_i)}{\eta \sum_{i=1}^{N} u_i^{m}} + \frac{K(x, x)}{\eta} \right)^{m-1} \right]^{-1} \quad (19)$$

where N is a number of sampled records; u_i is membership of the sampled record x_i.

This approach allows deal with very large datasets, though the precision of the solution becomes worse of course. It is important to outline that the sampling can be used with SVM clustering too, but for the same size of sampled dataset our approach is less computationally expensive than SVM.

4   Experiments

In this section we describe the simple experiment demonstrating the capability of the algorithm to discover outliers in the Web usage log. Unfortunately, since the problem of outliers detection in Web usage logs has not been broadly discussed in the literature, there are no special well-studied datasets, which might be used to test the algorithms performance. That is why we used for the experiment the EPA-HTTP dataset [8] and included in it several artificial outliers to test our algorithm. The EPA-HTTP access trace contains a day's worth of all HTTP requests to the EPA WWW server located at Research Triangle Park, NC. The log is an ASCII file with one line per request, with the following columns: host making the request, date in the format [DD:HH:MM:SS]; request given in quotes; HTTP reply code; bytes in the reply. The logs were collected by Laura Bottomley (laurab@ee.duke.edu) of Duke University and may be freely used and redistributed.

4.1   Experiment Setup

For the experiment the additional preprocessing of the dataset was done. The HTTP request was parsed and split into three fields: HTTP request method, URL and extension of the requested file (e.g., html, gif, zip, etc.). Six invalid records were deleted from the log. After that processing the structure of the log became as follows. Every record contains the key attribute identifying the source host (e.g. "sutr.novalink.com", etc.), one numeric attribute – transmitted bytes and four nominal attributes: HTTP request method, URL, URL file extension and request status. After that we selected top two active hosts. They are "e659229.boeing.com" and "sandy.rtptok1.epa.gov". To check the capability of our algorithm to find outliers we added to the logs of each of these hosts two additional requests, which simulate a virus activity or intrusion. Exactly the requests are: "GET /MSADC/root.exe", status code 403, transmitted bytes 3458; and "/winnt/system32/cmd.exe", status code 404, transmitted bytes 3415. The algorithm was initialized using the center of gravity approach, i.e. without SVM. All kernel width parameters q_i are set to 0.1. For comparison we run the SVM algorithm on the same data. We used libsvm tool [9] with following settings. All nominal attributes were converted into set of binary attributes; the normalization was performed using svmscale utility from libsvm package. We used RBF kernel with default gamma value for training SVM. We started from quantile equal to 0.01 and increased it by 0.02 every time SVM running.

4.2   Experiment Results

The experiment demonstrates that the algorithms have nearly similar accuracy. But SVM clustering required three executions to discover intrusion – it was run with quantile equal to 0.01, 0.03 and 0.05. While our algorithm was executed only once and setting threshold was used for intrusions filtering without algorithm re-execution.

Table 1. The results of the experiment using SVM are presented in the table

Source host	Quantile	Outliers / total requests	Discovered Intrusions
sandy.rtptok1.epa.gov	0.03	3/296	1/2
sandy.rtptok1.epa.gov	0.05	9/296	2/2
e659229.boeing.com	0.03	1/294	1/2
e659229.boeing.com	0.05	6/294	2/2

Table 2. The results of the experiment using our algorithm are presented in the table

Source host	Fuzzy threshold	Outliers / total requests	Discovered Intrusions
sandy.rtptok1.epa.gov	0.181133	2/296	2/2
e659229.boeing.com	0.201254	4/294	2/2

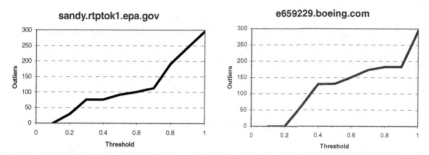

Fig. 1. These charts demonstrate how in our approach the number of outliers depends on the value of threshold for experimental dataset.

5 Conclusions and Future Work

This paper presents a novel approach for outliers detection and access patterns mining in the Web usage log. The geometric framework for outliers detection in the Web usage log is proposed. In this framework the HTTP log records are considered as fixed length vectors of numeric and nominal attributes, which are implicitly mapped by means of the kernel into the high dimensional feature space. The special data-dependent kernel is designed for that purposes. In the feature space a novel algorithm is applied to find outliers and access patterns. This algorithm is based on ideas of SVM clustering algorithm [4], though instead of margin estimation it involves a possibilistic fuzzy clustering approach in the feature space to calculate the measure of "typicalness" for log records. The records are considered as outliers if their "typicalness" is smaller than a specified threshold and as access patterns if their "typicalness" is higher than another specified threshold. The benefits and drawbacks of the suggested approach in comparison to SVM clustering algorithm are discussed in the paper and demonstrated in the simple experiments. The algorithm was implemented as OLEDB for Data Mining provider and can be used by various analysis applications. Besides, the algorithm has been applied for several real world's logs. For particular, for IIS access logs and TCP-dump logs. It demonstrated very promising results there. Future work in this direction involves further investigating and formal proof of properties of the suggested algorithm; finding new and more efficient initialization methods; experimental comparison with state-of-the-art outliers detection and access patterns mining algorithms.

References

1. Cooley, R., Mobasher, B., Srivastava, J.: Web Mining: Information and Pattern Discovery on the World Wide Web (A Survey Paper), in Proceedings of the 9th IEEE International Conference on Tools with Artificial Intelligence (ICTAI'97)

2. Krishnapuram, R., Keller, J. M.: A Possibilistic Approach to Clustering. IEEE Trans. Fuzzy Systems. Vol. 1. No. 1 (1993), 98–110

3. Scholkopf, B., Smola, A., J.: Learning with kernels: Support Vector Machines, Regularization, Optimization and Beyond. The MIT Press Cambridge, Massachusetss (2000)

4. Ben-Hur, A., Horn, D., Siegelmann, H.T., Vapnik, V.: Support vector clustering. Journal of Machine learning Research, Vol. 2, (2001), 125–137

5. Girolami, M.: Mercer Kernel Based Clustering in Feature Space. I.E.E.E Transactions on Neural Networks, 13 (4), (2001), 780 –784

6. Eskin, E., Arnold, A. , Prerau, M., Portnoy, L., Stolfo, S.: A Geometric Framework for Unsupervised Anomaly Detection: Detecting Intrusions in Unlabeled Data. Applications of Data Mining in Computer Security, Kluwer, (2002)

7. Takuya Inoue, Shigeo Abe: Fuzzy Support Vector Machine for Pattern Classification. In Proc. of IJCNN, (2001) 1449–1455

8. Bottomley, L.: Dataset: A day of HTTP logs from the EPA WWW Server. Duke university (1995) http://ita.ee.lbl.gov/html/contrib/EPA-HTTP.html

9. Chih-Chung Chang, Chih-Jen Lin: LIBSVM – A Library for Support Vector Machines. http://www.csie.ntu.edu.tw/~cjlin/libsym

Analysis of User's Behaviour in Very Large Business Application Systems with Methods of the Web Usage Mining – A Case Study on SAP® R/3®

Jorge Marx Gómez, Gamal Kassem, Claus Rautenstrauch, and Markus Melato

¹Otto-von-Guericke-Universität Magdeburg, Germany
{kassem,rauten}@iti.cs.uni-magdeburg.de
²Technical University Clausthal, Germany
gomez@informatik.tu-clausthal.de

Abstract. Navigation opportunities and options in modern business application systems¹ are numerous and complex. Here users leave navigation traces, which can be pulled up as a basis for a user behaviour analysis. Based on results of the analysis the application systems can be (re-) configured or (re-) customized in order to be more favourable for a user. In the field of web applications similar analyses have been successfully executed by methods of Web Usage Mining. Therefore, these methods can be considered as a basis for the analyses in the field of business application systems. Proceeding from this, an aim of the present paper is a definition of approaches for a user behaviour analysis in the field of business application systems. This aim and approach definition should be derived from significant differences between web applications and business application systems. In this case study as an example of a widespread ERP-system the software product SAP R/3² is used. These methods should be derived from differences between web applications and business application systems. As a research in this field is not finished, this article is a research-in-progress paper.

1 Introduction

ERP-systems³ are a subject of continuous extension and today they widely cover all tasks of an enterprise. However, with the implementation and usage of these systems the complexity level also rises. The systems become more incomprehensible because of the functions and capabilities surplus. ERP-systems offer an enormous amount of

---

¹ Business application system means an installed software product, which serves the support of task settings in the business field.
² SAP and R/3 are trademarks of SAP AG, Systems, Applications and Products in Data Processing, Neurottstr. 16, 69190 Walldorf, Germany. The authors gratefully acknowledge SAP's kind permission to use its trademark on this publication. SAP AG is not the publisher of this paper and not responsible for it under any aspect of press law.
³ The abbreviation "ERP" means Enterprise Resource Planning. This limits the application spectrum of the considered software to economical task settings in an enterprise and to the public administration [4].

E. Menasalvas et al. (Eds.): AWIC 2003, LNAI 2663, pp. 329–338, 2003.

navigation possibilities for the users, which enable them to perform tasks purpose-fully. Nevertheless, navigation through such a system is not trivial. During navigation users leave traces in the form of log, protocol and trace data. These data can be pulled up and used as a main data source for user behaviour analysis. The main aspect of a user behaviour analysis is to discover and analyse interesting pattern from this data. The results of the user behaviour analysis should support the correctness of the business processes structure examination of the enterprise on the ERP-system and the system settings (Customizing[4]). They also should simplify the personalization[5] of the system for the user as well as enabling the investigation of user's behaviour with regard to work efficiency. In the field of web applications[6] the methods of the Web Usage Mining [1] are successfully used for investigation of user's behaviour. The overall purpose of users' behaviour analysis is to support system designers in custom-izing and personalization towards a more user friendly appearance of the system.

Therefore, it is rather possible to use these methods also in the field of business ap-plication systems, because here basically the same principles apply. Separating the examination of the user's behaviour in the business application systems from the Web Usage Mining, the concept of "Application Usage Mining" is introduced here. At the same time the term indicates the relationship and similarity of both research fields. In order to designate the requirements for a user behaviour analysis in the field of busi-ness application systems, first of all, the methods of the Web Usage Mining are pre-sented and then explicitly described. Based on this, the description of the Application Usage Mining and, finally, a subsequent comparison between web applications and business application systems take place. This comparison should allow to decide, what aims can be reached by the help of this analysis. Finally a summary of SAP concepts that play a crucial role for the user's behaviour investigation is given. In addition, the navigation opportunities, screen and dialog program as well as SAP transactions[7] are mentioned. In the concluding chapter a summary and conclusions of future research activities in this field are given.

2   Web Usage Mining

For the better understanding of Application Usage Mining first of all an introduction to the concepts and methods concerning the acquisition of information by Web Usage Mining is given. In principle all web servers collect data about user interactions [1]. These data are stored in form of listed entries in the respective server log file. The analysis of web access protocols of different web pages can contribute to a better understanding of user's behaviour. Thereby, a best possible exploit of resources as

---

[4] The customizing in SAP terminology [6] enables the customer to select and parameterize, on the basis of his aims and demands, the desired processes with the appropriate functionality from the various solutions of functions and processes.

[5] Personalization means to adjust the system to meet the work requirements of specific users or user groups. Personalization aims to accelerate and simplify the business transactions of sys-tem processes.

[6] Applications in the field of E-Commerce are considered as web applications.

[7] SAP transactions are the smallest units which can be executed directly by the user. They implement a set of actions, which belong to a certain business procedure and can only be executed completely or not.

well as the design improvement of an extensive web application structure can be reached [12]. Thus, suitable goods and customized services can be offered to the visitors of a web page [9].

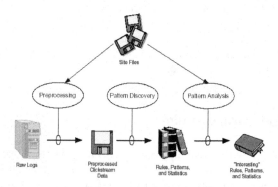

Fig. 1. Web usage mining process

Web Usage Mining as an independent and separate research field is an important component of the Web Mining [2] research area. It deals mainly with the application of Data Mining technology on protocols [1], which allow information and interpretation of the user's behaviour in the web. This kind of data processing applies different algorithms in order to detect structures and clusters in the navigation behaviour of the visitor that is characterized by the time spent online and visiting sites. These structures and clusters can explain and elucidate user's groups and segments. At present Web Usage Mining develops in the direction "General Access Pattern Tracking" as well as "Customized Usage Tracking".

In Web Usage Mining three essential steps have to be conducted (cf. Fig. 1). At the beginning the data are pre-processed, i.e. irrelevant data are deleted from the outset. This procedure is called Data Cleaning. Afterwards, before the irrelevant pattern are finally eliminated by means of the pattern analyses, different Mining algorithms are applied. These algorithms will be described more in detail in the course of this paper.

Web Usage Mining provides techniques for information extraction. In particular the following techniques and methods are concerned:

- *Path Analysis*: This is applied to determine frequently used paths within a web page.
- *Association Rule Analysis*: With the aid of the association rule analysis one tries to make certain conclusions about the sequence of certain events. If an event takes place, transfer to another certain event is automatically released. The considered site "A" pulls compulsively site "B". The association rule analysis helps to understand, which sites of a web application are linked to others. The aim of this analysis is to achieve a better understanding of the consumer's behaviour.
- *Sequential Pattern Analysis*: It serves the evaluation of the user's accesses over a certain period of time in order to be able to predict future patterns of the user's behaviour. At the same time, it should be analyzed what is the navigation path composition from the customer's point of view, i.e. how the operating

ability of the site can be improved and whether there are some areas to be re-
dundant or improved.

- *Cluster Analysis*: By means of the cluster analysis the users are grouped into
  clusters on the basis of similar characteristics (e.g. a similar searching behaviour).
- *Classification Rules*: Applying classification rules the allocation of users to
  certain user classes with associated attributes (as for example age, place of residence, etc.) will be facilitated.

3 Application Usage Mining

The attempt to apply the basic approaches and methods of the Web Usage Mining
in the field of business application systems and especially in ERP-systems shows
some significant differences, having direct influence on aims of user's behaviour
analysis in the area of business application systems. These differences are caused by
the fact that there are some logical as well as technical differences between a web
application of e.g. electronic shopping and a business application system. In a web
application the connection between a guest and provider is not binding. The visitor
has the freedom to navigate through the providers' web pages. Moreover, he can
access information and contents of the site and perhaps he buys goods or services.
However, there are some differences perceivable using a business application system. In this case, an employee of the enterprise operating in the company's interests
is considered rather than a visitor or customer. Along with the usage of a business
application system the employee should optimally perform the assigned tasks and
business processes of the enterprise. These different intercommunications influence
the application's concepts to a great extend. Table 1 illustrates the comparison between web applications and business application systems with their belonging attributes.

The following essential differences were identified during the comparison of the
applications:

1. *System Access*: In the web area the user stays anonymously while accessing the
   web pages. However, in Web Usage Mining it is very important to recognize
   and to identify users. In order to be able to examine their deserted traces over a
   long period of time, a system registration is essential and is urgently required
   not only for safety reasons. For this purpose several applications can be implemented. So, the users' IP addresses can be identified, e.g., by registration and
   with the help of the HTTP protocol. This is not completely trouble-free, because a computer can be used by several people or a proxy server is used for
   the allocation of temporary and dynamic IP addresses. Another possible solution would be to check and to evaluate the usage of cookies. Although, there
   are some disadvantages. As for instance, cookies can be deleted every time or
   legal regulations as far as the use of cookies is concerned are not eliminated
   completely. By contrast in business application systems a user's identification
   takes place every time.

Table 1. Web usage mining process

Attribute	Web Application	Business Application System
System access	The visitor can stay anonymously	The user must be identified
Authorization	Usually, the visitor does not need an authorization	The user receives a certain authorization according to function's allocation in the enterprise to perform certain tasks
Protocol	Standard http	No standards
Software	Web application; (most of them) based on HTML-documents	Different software platforms are available
User's behavior	Free	Execution of predefined tasks and business processes
User's objective	Not defined	Optimal performance of tasks and business processes
Application's aim	There is a possibility to reach a lot of visitors and customers	Efficient execution and automation of business processes

2. *Authorization*: In a provider/customer relationship within a web application the role of the user is defined from the start, i.e. all visitors obtain the same authorization concept. In exceptional cases only some certain actions and sites, which the user can perform or see correspondingly, are allowed to access. In some cases a group of users can execute several actions or visit also additional pages if they e.g. have been registered. Basically, however, the web page of the provider is a shop window for all users who want to get information or buy goods or services from the provider. In business application systems like for example SAP R/3 each user must receive a certain authorization profile assigned in accordance with his function or role within the enterprise.

3. *Protocol*: In the web area the HTTP protocol has a specific meaning and purpose. The starting point of the analysis in the Web Usage Mining represents all data, which describe the behaviour of the web visitor. In comparison to this there are different application services, which are provided by WWW server. Now dominant application services are the Hypertext Transfer Protocol (HTTP) that serves the transfer of HTML pages. During the usage of business application systems several protocols can be implemented. In the application field the required data can be mainly collected from the existing data in the business application system trace-, log- and various protocol files. The information content and format of the data differ from system to system.

4. *Software*: Web engineering methods [8], which are applied to develop web applications, are usually based on HTML, Java and XML technology. In the area of

business application systems different software platforms and software technologies of different system providers can be applied. Therefore, it might be difficult to obtain standardized software technologies for all business application systems in the future.

5. *User's Behaviour, Goals and Application Aims*: If the customer retrieves the web pages of a certain provider, he automatically shows his interest in the site's contents. At this point it cannot be yet determined what goals the customer pursues and what motivated him to visit the appropriate site. This can be only a curiosity or, for example, the customer opened the site just by chance. However, the goal of the provider is clear and unambiguous. By supplying the web pages he wants to wake the customer's interest in the goods and services in order to sell them afterwards. By means of this incentive the provider aims that the customers view a variety of products on different sites and come up to a decision which product to buy. Thus, structure and presentation of web pages play an crucial role. With the aid of Web Usage Mining methods the patterns of the customers' behaviour is analysed and evaluated in order to facilitate and to support the design of the providers' pages according to the costumer demands.

The differences specified above have some influence on the aims and the procedure of the user's behaviour analysis in the area of business application systems. Because the user should perform tasks serviceable and purposefully, two aspects of the aim definition should be considered here:

1. *Behaviour of the Users during the Performance of the Work Procedures*: Analyzing the user's behaviour by applying Data Mining methods in order to enable the user to perform his tasks serviceable and purposeful. In this manner a significant step can be made towards an application personalization.
2. *Correctness of the Execution of a Business Process and Its Activities*: Another important goal of the analysis is the examination and if necessary an optimization of the business processes. By observation of the users' navigation behaviour the business process trend can be analyzed and evaluated.

During the analysis it must be clarified, which process execution levels of the business processes have to be examined and whether it refers to partial processes or the whole business processes.

4   SAP R/3 – Case Study as an Example for an ERP-System

For this case study an examined business application system must fulfil some fundamental requirements. Here, among other things, the possibility of navigation, availability of system wide log data and user's trace data should exist. Furthermore, multi user capabilities and openness of systems should be concerned. The ERP-system SAP R/3 fulfils these assumptions. It also offers additional auxiliary and monitoring tools. In this case study the SAP concepts for the representation and support of the user's activities in SAP R/3 are examined in detail. Moreover, it is shown how the Application Usage Mining can be applied to SAP R/3.

4.1   SAP R/3 Concept for the Presentation and Support of User's Actions

In difference to the Web area, as far as the navigation in a business application system is concerned, the work procedures[8] which the user works on are subject of focusing and not the user himself. The Application Usage Mining examines how the user treats these operations. Consequently, with regard to the user's behaviour the system can be better interpreted, understood and arranged in order to organize the interaction between the users and the system more effectively. In terms of management science a business process is an operation, which is a bundle of one or more input activities and produces the value (output) for the customer [11].

From the viewpoint of computer science (technical aspect) not the actual purpose of a business process stands in the foreground, but which activities are implemented and how these are connected. Here business processes are based usually on several (sub-)programs that implement business process activities and provide for each case specialized services [10]. In the SAP R/3 terminology these programs are called a dialog-oriented application as explained below:

- *SAP Transactions*: The process activities are implemented in the SAP R/3 system as transactions [7]. Transactions form the core of the SAP R/3 program treatment. They are the smallest units, directly executable by the user. They implement a set of actions, which belong to a certain business procedure and can only be executed completely or not. They are like a bowl at the real program. Every transaction is identified by its unique transaction code. In SAP R/3 different kinds of transactions are distinguished, e. g. batch or dialog transactions. The most frequently used kind of transactions is the dialog transaction, which makes possible the execution of dialog-oriented applications.

- *Dialog-Oriented Applications in SAP R/3*: Dialog oriented applications [7] process data are caused by the interactive users' work with the system. In the SAP R/3 system the dialog applications are based on the so-called "screen". A screen consists of the combination of an input form and a program code, which is assigned to this input form. The program code processes data that are given in this form. The screens determine only the appearance of the work surface, first of all, kind and number of input elements and their behaviours. The connection between screen and a program takes place through the process logic. The processing logic is a short source code where only modules of the so-called module pool are accessed. These modules can be generally considered as sub-programs. The modules, which are implemented before the announcement of the screen, are called Process Before Output (PBO). There, for example, initializations or dynamic modifications are specified. Modules, which are implemented directly after completion of the data input, are called Process After Input (PAI). Here, the test and processing of the data take place.

A dialog transaction is associated to a program of a so-called module pool and to attributes like transaction type, number of the start screen and, also, the name of the program. The program task is to provide screens and their assigned subprograms, here named modules. An executable dialog application (transaction) consists of several

---

[8] Work procedure [5] is a procedure in an organization which function is that participants cooperative achieve given results at work.

screens (dialog steps) and an ABAP-Program (cf. Fig. 2), which contains the processing modules (module pool). An executable dialog application (transaction) consists of several screens (dialog steps) and an ABAP-Program (cf. Fig. 2), which contains the processing modules (module pool).

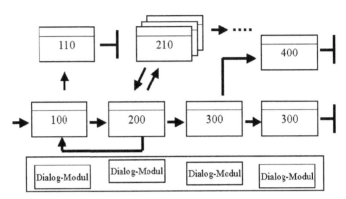

Fig. 2. Web usage mining process

The SAP R/3 transaction is also called LUW (Logical Unit of Work), which is a consequence of logically coherent dialog steps with a subsequent updating of the database. These dialog steps can be extended to several dialog programs. A protocol record will be produced if business process dialog transactions and programs are assigned to it. This concerns the special booking tables for the database updating, which are processed after the termination of the dialog part. First of all, while processing this protocol record (update) the changes produced by the transaction are realized in the database [3].

4.2   Application Usage Mining and SAP/R3

In Application Usage Mining applied to SAP R/3 two essential aspects should be considered. On the one hand the analysis depth for the examination of the user's behaviour at different transaction execution levels in SAP R/3 should be determined (vertically). On the other hand, the realization of the Application Usage Mining phases in the SAP R/3 system should be defined. Application Usage Mining operates on three analysis levels due to transaction, business process and mode[9] data. At the lowest level the executed transactions are analyzed. Here the coherence between screens and events caused by the users like input of data and clicks on buttons are examined. At the medium level the relations between the separate transactions are examined. Transactions are considered here as business process activities. At the highest level the interactions between transactions, which were executed by the same user in several modes simultaneously, are analyzed.

---

[9] A mode is a window where the user can process a specific task. After a successful login to the R/3 system, a session will be initiated. Six sessions at the same time can be opened.

Similarly to Web Usage Mining, Application Usage Mining consists of three essential phases:

- *Pre-processing*: During the pre-processing phase the relevant data from different sources, as for example user trace data, workflow protocol data and log data are extracted. These are structured and stored. At the latest stage of this phase the data are transformed to the next phase in suitable formats.
- *Pattern Discovery*: During the pattern discovery phase different methods of the Data Mining are used. The applied methods should help to disclose certain coherences. Different techniques can be used, which are already known from the Web Usage Mining. During the path analysis the used paths are determined with the help of a system in order to clarify, for example, the following questions:

  1. At which places of the same users access path does a mistake message appear?
  2. At which places of the users access paths are transactions frequently cancelled?
  3. At which places of the access paths dead-end streets could encountered?

  With the aim of the association analysis the connection between events (e. g. input of data and clicks on buttons) and the running of a screen sequence should be stated. Here the customizing of the system is checked for rightness. For example, the deviations of the user access paths from the ideal access path of this business process should be analyzed. In the sequence analysis time-related data are considered. Among other things the efficiency of the users contacts with the system should be examined here:

  1. How fast becomes a new user familiar with the system?
  2. How long does it takes for a user to perform a task?

- *Pattern Analysis*: Pattern analysis is the final phase of the whole Application Usage Mining process. The aim of this phase is to remove irrelevant patterns, which were found during the pattern discovery phase. A database query language like SQL (Structured Query Language) is the most common form of the pattern analysis. Another method like OLAP (Online Analytical Processing) can be used to analyze the multidimensional databases.

5   Summary and Conclusions

Our decision to use Web Usage Mining methods in the field of business application systems is based on the following fact: During the last years modern business application systems like SAP/R3 were introduced to the market which offer users a lot of navigation opportunities in order to support the user during tasks and operation treatments. Hence, examination of the user's behaviour can help to understand and adjust the system, just like in the Web Usage Mining. However, at an early stage of our research we found out that web application and business application systems differ logically and technically. Therefore, the aims of the analysis in the Application Usage Mining and in the Web Usage Mining differ.

We are at the beginning of our research, thus this contribution is concerned as a research-in-progress paper. The next stage of this research work would be the recording and examination of the student's behaviour at the Otto-von-Guericke-Universität in Magdeburg during their practice and usage of SAP R/3.

References

[1]   Berendt, B.: Detail and Context in Web Usage Mining: Coarsening and Visualizing Sequences – Lecture notes in computer science. Springer, Berlin 2002.

[2]   Chang, G.: Mining the World Wide Web: an information search approach. Boston, Kluwer Academic, 2001.

[3]   Cooley, R.; Pang-Ning, T.; Jaideep S.: Measuring Interestingness in Web Usage Mining - Discovery of Interesting Usage Patterns from Web Data. Springer, Berlin 2000.

[4]   Hufgard, A.: Definition und Abgrenzung des Begriffs ERP/ERM-Standardanwendungssoftware. IBIS Prof. Thome AG, Würzburg 2000.

[5]   Jablonski, S,; Böhm, M.; Schulze, W.: Workflow-Management: Entwicklung von Anwendungen und Systemen. dpunkt-Verlag, Heidelberg 1997.

[6]   Keller, G: SAP R/3 prozessorientiert anwenden: Iteratives Prozess-Prototyping mit Ereignisgesteuerten Prozessketten und Knowledge Maps. Addison-Wesley, Bonn 1999.

[7]   Matzke, B.: ABAP/4 – Die Programmiersprache des SAP-System R/3. Addison-Wesley, München 1999.

[8]   Murugesan, S.; Web Engineering: Managing Diversity and Complexity of Web Application Development. Springer, Berlin 2001.

[9]   Saeuberlich, F.: KDD und Data Mining als Hilfsmittel zur Entscheidungsunterstützung. Karlsruhe, Univ., Diss, Frankfurt am Main 2000.

[10]   Schuldt, H.: IS-Infrastruktur und SAP, Swiss Federal Institute of Technology, Zürich 2001.

[11]   Schnetzer, R.: Business Process Reengineering (BPR) und Workflow-Management-Systeme – Theorie und Praxis in der Schweiz, Shaker, Aachen 1997.

[12]   Spiliopoulou, M.; Faulstich, L. C.; Winkler, K.: A Data Miner Analyzing the Navigational Behaviour of Web Users. Proceedings of workshop on Machine Learning in User Modelling of the ACAI'99, Creta, Greece 1999.

Automation of the Deep Web with User Defined Behaviours

Vicente Luque Centeno, Carlos Delgado Kloos, Peter T. Breuer,
Luis Sánchez Fernández, Ma. Eugenia Gonzalo Cabellos, and
Juan Antonio Herráiz Pérez

Departamento de Ingeniería Telemática
Universidad Carlos III de Madrid
Avda. Universidad, 30, E-28911 Leganés, Madrid, Spain

Abstract. Giving semantics to Web data is an issue for automated Web navigation. Since legacy Web pages have been built using HTML as a visualization-oriented markup for years, data on the Web is suitable for people using browsers, but not for programs automatically performing a task on the Web on behalf of their users.

The W3C Semantic Web initiative [16] tries to solve this by explicitly declaring semantic descriptions in (typically RDF [19] and OWL [23]) metadata associated to Web pages and ontologies combined with semantic rules. This way, inference-enabled agents may deduce which actions (links to be followed, forms to be filled,...) should be executed in order to retrieve the results for a user's query.

However, something more than inferring how to retrieve information from the Web is needed to automate tasks on the Web. Information retrieval [3] is *only* the first step. Other actions like relevant data extraction, data homogeneization and user definable processing are needed as well for automating Web-enabled applications running on Web servers.

This paper proposes two programming languages for instructing assistants about how to **explore Web sites** according to the user's aims, providing a real example from the legacy deep Web.

Keywords: agents, web exploration, deep web, automation of tasks on the web

1 Introduction

The World Wide Web has rapidly expanded as the largest human knowledge repository. Not only information sources, but also Web-enabled applications, like e-mail, auctions, intranet applications, online stores, hotel reservations or even procedures involving government forms have to be repeatedly used by millions of users who daily sit in front of their browser-enabled computers to spend a lot of effort by filling in forms and usually cutting & pasting small chucks of data through different windows in order to perform tasks that have to be repeated once and again over the same forms. Most of the information they deal with is usually stored at Web enabled databases that are not fully exploited. Web

E. Menasalvas et al. (Eds.): AWIC 2003, LNAI 2663, pp. 339–348, 2003.

browsers have traditionally been the main tool for Web navigation, though this is not necessarily true [18]. Web browsers are great for presenting multimedia pages to users and collecting their data into form fields interactively, but they don't care of managing that data intelligently according to user definable rules.

Fortunately, it is possible to build task oriented Web clients that automate these tasks for the user. These programs need to automatically select and follow links and fill in forms emulating a human user behind a browser, but presenting only the final results for her, requiring less user's interactivity. These Web clients, referred as **Web Navigation Assistants (WNA)**, can be used to automate tasks performed over well known Web sites, specially those involving a large amount of data or navigation paths which need some steps to be followed. WNA are also suitable for data integration across heterogeneous information sources.

WNA are quite different from search engine robots. The task of search engine robots is to follow almost every link encountered in order to index as much pages as possible in a database according to the words contained within those pages. Pages containing user's defined keywords can then be obtained as a result of their queries. However, these final results are just URLs of whole documents, not *fine grained* expected results, so further computation still has to be performed in order to extract appropriate data from those documents and perform computations with them.

WNA can intelligently manage data from the Web according to automated actions programmed to perform specific tasks for the user. By manipulating Web data automatically, imitating users, large amounts of data can be easily managed without overwhelming the user with lots of screens to be seen. By intelligently selecting which links need to be followed, WNA may navigate through the *deep Web* [14] and manipulate data from online databases in a large amount of hyperlinked pages without getting lost exploring non needed documents.

In order to navigate a browser-oriented Web, navigation platforms executing these assistants need to be able to manage all those low level details which are usually hidden by browsers. In other words, cookies, HTTP redirections, internal reconstruction of badly formed pages and other issues, like JavaScript based navigation, should be transparently managed by the navigation platform where assistants will be executed. Any low level feature not supported by the platform, should be explicitly considered by actions programmed within the WNA. Figure 1 shows main differences between manual and automatic navigation. During manual navigation, the user has to interactively select links to be followed. However, during automatic navigation, a user-defined assistant executed on a navigation platform may autonomously decide which links should be followed without requiring user interaction.

However, not only developing these assistants, but maintaining them operative, is rather expensive. In this paper, we present two languages for specifying and building WNA. These high level descriptions can be used to represent robust navigation paths to be followed by Web agents navigating through the *deep Web* and user defined behaviours to be performed over the data found in those pages. The first of these languages, called **XPlore**, is based on the **Message Sequence**

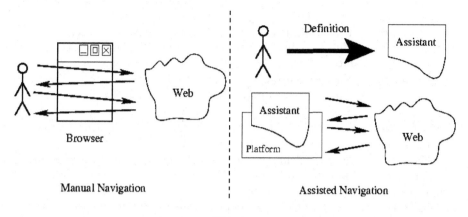

Fig. 1.

Charts (MSC) [7], a formal method defined by the ITU (International Telecommunication Union) for specifying behaviours in distributed middleware systems. XPlore can be used to express navigation paths to be surfed in the *deep Web*. The second of these languages, called **XTendedPath**, is an extension of the W3C XPath 2.0 Working Draft [22] for defining data extraction rules and simple user definable computing over data retrieved from visited pages. A platform providing execution support for these two languages has also been implemented and successfully tested.

2   XPlore: A Language for Web Navigation Path Specification

XPlore is a specification language for specifying Web navigation paths that may automate user's tasks in the World Wide Web. Web tasks specified in XPlore language result simple and robust. XPlore can define complete user sessions hiding message details, but also low level HTTP details for requests and responses, if required. In both cases (whole HTTP sessions and single HTTP transactions), XPlore just needs a few lines of code. XPlore is a language which defines a sequence of conditions to be tested and actions and transactions to be executed, allowing the user to specify the control of this execution with loops (*while-do-done* and *foreach-in-do-done*), conditional branching (*if-then-else-end*), variables, user defined functions and full access to machine resources, like files, external programs, timers, threads and synchronizing methods like locks. The language is both expressive and concrete, so it is applyable to a wide range of problems, but also being able to be translated to an executable if all the needed information is provided.

XPlore has been defined as a Web-client-oriented adaptation of the textual representation of MSC. MSC have been traditionally used for specifying behaviours and communications within components of distributed systems which communicate by exchanging messages. MSC have both graphical and textual representations. Since their birth in 1992, MSC have periodically been expanded with new powerful functionality. A MSC easily allows defining expected dialogs between remote software, as well as defining error conditions, repetitive and conditioned behaviour, concurrency, timers or defining and calling functions. All these features can be used to improve the construction and maintenance of wrapper programs [9] by properly using them in a specification language, directly translated to an executable, instead of reviewing a large amount of code written in a common programming language.

The approach of easily defining both HTTP requests and HTTP sessions in a single line of code may result difficult when using well known programming languages like C, Perl or Java. None of these languages provide the right level of abstraction required to keep the required amount of code to the minimum and are not oriented to be robust to changes on the Web pages. Since every HTTP transaction or filling in a form field, involves one XPlore line (perhaps two or three when data schema gets complex), maintaining these applications is not very expensive, since the amount of lines to review when a modification is required is small.

3   XTendedPath: A Language for Web Data Processing Specification

The extraction of relevant data from visited pages is modelled as MSC *actions* performed only at the client side between network transactions. These actions could be implemented by calling user defined routines which can be written in any programming language managed by the user. Semi-structured data retrieval techniques for this purpose have been proposed in the literature [2,5,6,11,10]. However, most of them are not focused on getting simple robust expressive data extraction rules and try to solve this issue by applying lexical analyzers and parsers based on regular expressions, which is a difficult to understand, low level yet powerful solution that can't offer by itself all the needed functionality and is usually difficult to understand and maintain by non specialized users.

Recent projects [12,15,1] prefer to approach this issue by applying XML techniques, like DOM [21] programming or XSLT [20] transformation rules, to dynamically XML-ized Web pages. XSLT is then used to transform any incoming XML-ized Web page into a well formed document that can be processed further. This is a higher level approach than treating pages as plain text, like regular expressions do, but something more than simple XML transformation is needed. In fact, better than well formed XML documents, structured data directly processable by user defined computation routines are often preferred. XSLT can be considered as a good solution in order to get a uniform set of documents representing the different collections of data obtained from different servers. However, XSLT can't be considered to do efficient manipulations on small parts of incoming pages, specially if they need to be repeatedly performed over a single document. DOM is a much more powerful solution which can solve this issue, but since it has a lower level of abstraction, a lot of lines of code are required to be developed and to be maintained when a simple modification in the markup design of a Web site may appear, as explained at [17]. However, XPath has been specifically designed as a language for addressing parts of XML documents by using simple expressions. XPath expressions may easily fit in a single line and are well understood by many people. XPath 1.0 is a good option for selecting nodes in a document only if no complex processing need to be specified, so it becomes a good option for XSLT. More complex treatments can be specified with the new XPath 2.0 draft, but most of its new capabilities, have not been completely defined yet.

As an alternative to this option, XPlore programs can directly call data extraction primitives defined over XTendedPath, a XPath 2.0 [22] extension. XPath 2.0 is a W3C Working Draft for data addressing in XML documents. Unlike regular expressions, XTendedPath extraction rules do take into account the document's tree-like structure. This is possible since HTML pages obtained from Web servers by our platform are given XML syntax *on the fly* when retrieved, by using the *Tidy* [13] tool to repair HTML pages.

The main purpose of XTendedPath is to give structure to data embedded in HTML pages and store them in programmable repositories (typically memory variables or files) so that WNA may find them suitably available. Besides the usual programming data-types like integers, floats, booleans, strings, lists, structured records or arrays, XTendedPath includes specific data-types for documents and selected ranges within a document.

XTendedPath may apply alternative extraction rules when Web pages present changes in their structural markup, so WNA can be given robustness to unexpected changes. This is achieved by providing XTendedPath constructors of *service combinators* [4] for the treatment of execution errors. Because of XTendedPath simplicity and standard adoption, most changes suffered by a Web based information source can be solved by changing a single line of code when robustness oriented rules fail.

3.1   Data Processing

When the amount of extracted data is small and the computation over them is reduced to simple comparisons, the user can happily perform her task manually with a browser. However, when the amount of data is large, or there are some pages that have to be explored, or processing that data involves some logic or mathematical calculi, the user behind a browser becomes overwhelmed and error prone, perhaps trying to cut & paste small pieces of data through different windows, trying to memorize too much information and repeatedly clicking on some links. Unfortunately, browsers can't be explicitly told about user's purposes, neither whatever is relevant for the user and whatever is not, so they can't offer better support for those user *impetuous* actions. However, this processing is indeed a major reason for data extraction. Data management is not finished when matching selected data against expected patterns, but letting the programmer read and manipulate retrieved data through well known programming data types, like lists, arrays, trees or structured records which can be easily further processed by user defined routines. Comparing elements in a list or performing a user defined action over selected elements in a document can be efficiently programmed if document extracted data are located at well known data types.

Once all relevant data are available at structured local repositories, further computing is often required to be performed over them, like comparisons, accumulations, re-orderings, or any kind of semantic reasoning which may decide things like which link should be followed next or whether an information retrieval process is near from being concluded. Though this computations can be easily programmed with any imperative programming language, Web site navigation skills need to be considered as well. XTendedPath is also well suited for defining user defined behaviours to be performed over data obtained from extraction rules.

4   Platform Support

XPlore programs are not directly compiled or interpreted as other programming languages. Though this could be possible, a more effective solution has been found by translating XPlore programs into well known programming languages which will indeed implement the required functionality in programmed libraries. Traducing XPlore programs to almost any programming language, like C or Java, is not difficult if good support is provided at system libraries. Our current prototype is able to translate XPlore programs to the WebL programming language [8]. WebL has been chosen because its good support for HTTP management. However, translation to other languages could also be possible.

One major lack of our platform nowadays consists in its lack of support of JavaS cript execution. This has been solved by letting assistants to emulate JavaScr ipt defined behaviour within their own code. This results in a major development effort, since JavaScript inverse engineering needs to be performed, though this is not always needed. However, XPlore and XTendedPath expressions can be easily used to emulate these actions.

5   Commented Example: Yahoo! Mail

A commented example showing XPlore usability is found in this section, where a pr ogram for listing messages from Yahoo! mail spool and cleaning it from spam is implemented. The program starts by declaring some variables and a four argument function called `myconnect`, which receives the login and password for the e-mail user account, and the subjects an senders of those messages that have to be deleted from the incoming spool. Each variable corresponds to a page or a part of a page which has been considered relevant for this task. The number at the end of the variable names is used for documenting the numbered order of the page which is being treated.

```
LET(myconnect,FUN((login,passwd,sender,subject),

VAR(P1); VAR(P2); VAR(P3); VAR(P4); VAR(P5); VAR(a1);
VAR(form2); VAR(redir); VAR(a4); VAR(table5aux);
VAR(table5); VAR(tr5); VAR(form5); VAR(keepon);
```

The first line of this piece of the program is used to store the retrieved Yahoo! main page at the P1 variable. XTendedPath parenthesized code appear preceded with the equivalent non parenthesized XPath version in a comment for better reading. Functions C and D refer to Child and Descendant nodes, whereas F is used for declaring predicates. AT is used for having access to attributes and O is used for function composition. In this case, the first link element of P1 containing the word "Correo" (mail in Spanish) is stored at the a1 variable. This link is used to get the second page, which contains a form for getting identified at Yahoo! site. This form is stored at form2 variable.

```
GET(P1,"http://www.yahoo.es/",nil);

/* a1 = $P1//a[match("Correo", text())][1] */
a1 = F(1)(F(O(XFSTRMATCH("Correo"))(TEXT))(D("a")(P1)));

GET(P2,AT("href")(a1),P1.URL);

/* form2 = $P2//form[@name="login_form"] */
form2 = F(O(EQ("login_form"))(AT("name")))(D("form")(P2));
```

In order to have access to the user mail box, form fields are properly filled in, and some links are followed. Notice that no matter how many further transactions can be performed, P4 variable stores the welcome page and contains links for performing other actions apart from checking the Inbox. P5 contains the incoming spool of e-mails.

```
/* $form2//input[@name="login"]/@value=$login */
SET("value")(login)
    (F(O(EQ("login"))(AT("name")))(D("input")(form2)));
/* $form2//input[@name="passwd"]/@value=$passwd */
SET("value")(passwd)
    (F(O(EQ("passwd"))(AT("name")))(D("input")(form2)));

POST(P3,form2,P2.URL);

redir = F(O(EQ("Refresh"))(AT("http-equiv")))(D("meta")(P3));
GET(P4, LET(content, AT("content")(redir),
 XFSUBSTRING(content, XFSTRINDEXOF("=", content) + 1,
   XFSTRINGLENGTH(content))), P3.URL);

/* a4 = $P4//a[match("Bandeja entrada", text())] */
a4 = F(1)(F(O(XFSTRMATCH("Bandeja entrada"))(TEXT))(D("a")(P4)));

GET(P5,AT("href")(a4),P4.URL);
```

Since user's Inbox contained at P5 may contain more messages than the maximum allowed in one single page, these need to be paginated in an a priori unknown number of similar pages which will have to be checked sequentially. This can be performed with a *while* loop, which will have to be abandoned when the final page has been visited. For each visited page, messages are presented in rows within the most internal table (external tables are used for layout) that contains the word "Remitente". The number of messages and the text of these rows is printed on the standard output.

```
keepon = XFTRUE();
WHILE keepon DO
    /* table5aux = $P5//table[match("Remitente", text())] */
    /* table5 = $table5aux[not(descendant::$table5aux)] */
    /* tr5 = $table5/tr[position() != 1 and position() != last()] */

    table5aux = F(O(XFSTRMATCH("Remitente"))(TEXT))(D("table")(P5));
    table5 = F(NOT(D(table5aux)))(table5aux);
    /* tr5 = C("tr")(table5); */
    tr5 = F(COND(a,CONDPOS(a) > 1 AND CONDPOS(a) < CONDLAST(a)))(C("tr")(table5));
    /* tr5[1] and tr5[last()] are invalid (headers and buttons) */

    PRINTLN("Number of e-mails: " + TOSTR(XFCOUNT(tr5)));
    FOREACH i IN TOSEQ(tr5) DO
        PRINTLN("#@@@@@@@@@@@");
        PRINTLN(XFNORMALIZESPACE(XFSTRREPLACE(TEXT(i), '\n', ' ')));
    END;
```

Since every message in the table comes with a check-box field for selecting messages, a for-each loop is then used to check all messages that should be deleted, that is, those matching expected subject and sender received as arguments. If any message with these characteristics is found, it will be deleted by using the *Delete* button of the form and next page will be requested. However, if no such message is found at the current page, the program finishes.

```
    keepon = XFFALSE();

    /* form5 = $P5//form[@name="messageList"] */
    form5 = F(O(EQ("messageList"))(AT("name")))(D("form")(P5));

    /* FOREACH i IN $tr5[match($sender, td[3]/text()) and
        match($subject, td[6]/text())] DO */
    FOREACH i IN TOSEQ(F(COND(a,XFSTRMATCH(sender,
    TEXT(F(3)(C("td")(a)))) AND
    XFSTRMATCH(subject, TEXT(F(6)(C("td")(a))))))(tr5)) DO
        /* $i//input[@type="checkbox"]/@checked="checked" */
        SETATTR("checked")("checked")
        (F(O(EQ("checkbox"))(AT("type")))(D("input")(i)));
        keepon = XFTRUE();
    END;

    IF keepon THEN
        /* I want to Delete: (as extracted from JavaScript code) */
        /* $form5//input[@name="DEL"]/@value="1" */
        SETATTR("value")("1")(F(O(EQ("DEL"))(AT("name")))(D("input")(form5)));
        POST(P5,form5,P5.URL);
    END;
END /* WHILE */

),myconnect(ARGS[1],ARGS[2],ARGS[3],ARGS[4]));
```

6   Conclusions

Information retrieval is only the first step towards Web task automation. Once all relevant pages are retrieved, further computing needs to be applied to the data embedded in those pages. Integrating data from Web pages into a program requires giving structure to those data, according to extraction rules which are usually based on markup regularities. These extraction rules, which enclose some semantics for the task of the user, can be easily broken when expressed in general formalisms, like regular expressions. XML related standards like XPath have been defined to solve many issues, but they can be poorly applied to define complex computing. In this paper, a well known formal method (Message Sequence Charts) has been adapted for the construction and maintenance of Web clients that automate the Web, which is a recent kind of application for which no formal method has been proposed. The language has been successfully used at several well known Web servers for user defined tasks. Our experience shows that the effort of updating these applications for common minor modifications (which use to appear by one or two months periods) gets reduced to a few minutes, when prior technologies required some hours or days to be repaired.

References

1. P. Atzeni, G. Mecca, and P. Merialdo. Semistructured and structured data in the web: Going back and forth. In *Workshop on Management of Semistructured Data*, 1997.
2. A. S. F. Azavant. Building light-weight wrappers for legacy web data-sources using w4f. *International Conference on Very Large Databases (VLDB)*, 1999.
3. R. A. Baeza-Yates and B. A. Ribeiro-Neto. *Modern Information Retrieval*. ACM Press / Addison-Wesley, 1999.
4. L. Cardelli and R. Davies. Service combinators for web computing. *Software Engineering*, 25(3):309–316, 1999.
5. S. Chawathe, H. Garcia-Molina, J. Hammer, K. Ireland, Y. Papakonstantinou, J. D. Ullman, and J. Widom. The TSIMMIS project: Integration of heterogeneous information sources. In *16th Meeting of the Information Processing Society of Japan*, pages 7–18, Tokyo, Japan, 1994.
6. C. P. David Buttler, Ling Liu. A fully automated extraction system for the world wide web. *IEEE ICDCS-21*, April 16-19 2001.
7. ITU-T. Recommendation z.120: Message sequence chart (msc). In *Formal description techniques (FDT)*, Geneva, Switzerland, 1997.
8. T. Kistler and H. Marais. Webl - a programming language for the web. In *Proceedings of the 7th International World Wide Web Conference*, pages 259–270, Computer Networks and ISDN Systems 30, 1998.
9. N. Kushmerick, D. S. Weld, and R. B. Doorenbos. Wrapper induction for information extraction. In *Intl. Joint Conference on Artificial Intelligence (IJCAI)*, pages 729–737, 1997.
10. L. Liu, C. Pu, and W. Han. XWRAP: An XML-enabled wrapper construction system for web information sources. In *ICDE*, pages 611–621, 2000.
11. I. Muslea, S. Minton, and C. A. Knoblock. Hierarchical wrapper induction for semistructured information sources. *Autonomous Agents and Multi-Agent Systems*, 4(1/2):93–114, 2001.
12. J. Myllymaki. Effective web data extraction with standard XML technologies. In *World Wide Web 10th Conference, Hong Kong*, pages 689–696, 2001.
13. D. Raggett. Clean up your web pages with html tidy. *Poster 7th International World Wide Web Conference*.
14. S. Raghavan and H. Garcia-Molina. Crawling the hidden web. In *Proceedings of the Twenty-seventh International Conference on Very Large Databases*, 2001.

15. H. Snoussi, L. Magnin, and J.-Y. Nie. Heterogeneous web data extraction using ontology. In *Third International Bi-Conference Workshop on Agent-orienter Information Systems (AOIS-2001)*, Montreal (Canada, 2001.

16. J. H. T. Berners-Lee and O. Lassila. The semantic web. In *Scientific American*, May 2001.

17. A. Tost.   Xml   document   processing   in   java   using   xpath   and   xslt. www.javaworld.com/javaworld/jw-09-2000/jw-0908-xpath.html.

18. W3C. Policies relating to web accessibility. `http://www.w3.org/WAI/Policy/`.

19. W3C. Resource description framework (rdf). www.w3.org/RDF.

20. W3C. Xsl transformations (xslt) version 1.0. *W3C Recommendation 16 November 1999*, 1999.

21. W3C. Document object model (dom) level 2. *W3C Recommendation 13 November, 2000*, 2000.

22. W3C. Xml path language (xpath) 2.0. *W3C Working Draft 15 November 2002*, 2002.

23. W3C. Web ontology language (owl) reference version 1.0. In *W3C Working Draft 21 February 2003*, `http://www.w3.org/2001/sw/`, 2003.

Author Index

Lecture Notes in Artificial Intelligence (LNAI)

Vol. 2443: D. Scott (Ed.), Artificial Intelligence: Methodology, Systems, and Applications. Proceedings, 2002. X, 279 pages. 2002.

Vol. 2445: C. Anagnostopoulou, M. Ferrand, A. Smaill (Eds.), Music and Artificial Intelligence. Proceedings, 2002. VIII, 207 pages. 2002.

Vol. 2446: M. Klusch, S. Ossowski, O. Shehory (Eds.), Cooperative Information Agents VI. Proceedings, 2002. XI, 321 pages. 2002.

Vol. 2447: D.J. Hand, N.M. Adams, R.J. Bolton (Eds.), Pattern Detection and Discovery. Proceedings, 2002. XII, 227 pages. 2002.

Vol. 2448: P. Sojka, I. Kopecÿek, K. Pala (Eds.), Text, Speech and Dialogue. Proceedings, 2002. XII, 481 pages. 2002.

Vol. 2464: M. O'Neill, R.F.E. Sutcliffe, C. Ryan, M. Eaton, N. Griffith (Eds.), Artificial Intelligence and Cognitive Science. Proceedings, 2002. XI, 247 pages. 2002.

Vol. 2466: M. Beetz, J. Hertzberg, M. Ghallab, M.E. Pollack (Eds.), Advances in Plan-Based Control of Robotic Agents. Proceedings, 2001. VIII, 291 pages. 2002.

Vol. 2473: A. Gómez-Pérez, V.R. Benjamins, Knowledge Engineering and Knowledge Management. Proceedings, 2002. XI, 402 pages. 2002.

Vol. 2475: J.J. Alpigini, J.F. Peters, A. Skowron, N. Zhong (Eds.), Rough Sets and Current Trends in Computing. Proceedings, 2002. XV, 640 pages. 2002.

Vol. 2479: M. Jarke, J. Koehler, G. Lakemeyer (Eds.), KI 2002: Advances in Artificial Intelligence. Proceedings, 2002. XIII, 327 pages. 2002.

Vol. 2484: P. Adriaans, H. Fernau, M. van Zaanen (Eds.), Grammatical Inference: Algorithms and Applications. Proceedings, 2002. IX, 315 pages. 2002.

Vol. 2499: S.D. Richardson (Ed.), Machine Translation: From Research to Real Users. Proceedings, 2002. XXI, 254 pages. 2002.

Vol. 2504: M.T. Escrig, F. Toledo, E. Golobardes (Eds.), Topics in Artificial Intelligence. Proceedings 2002. XI, 432 pages. 2002.

Vol. 2507: G. Bittencourt, G.L. Ramalho (Eds.), Advances in Artificial Intelligence. Proceedings, 2002. XIII, 418 pages. 2002.

Vol. 2514: M. Baaz, A. Voronkov (Eds.), Logic for Programming, Artificial Intelligence, and Reasoning. Proceedings 2002. XIII, 465 pages. 2002.

Vol. 2522: T. Andreasen, A. Motro, H. Christiansen, H. Legind Larsen (Eds.), Flexible Query Answering. Proceedings 2002. XI, 386 pages. 2002.

Vol. 2527: F.J. Garijo, J.C. Riquelme, M. Toro (Eds.), Advances in Artificial Intelligence – IBERAMIA 2002. Proceedings 2002. XVIII, 955 pages. 2002.

Vol. 2531: J. Padget, O. Shehory, D. Parkes, N. Sadeh, W.E. Walsh (Eds.), Agent-Mediated Electronic Commerce IV. Proceedings, 2002. XVII, 341 pages. 2002.

Vol. 2533: N. Cesa-Bianchi, M. Numao, R. Reischuk (Eds.), Algorithmic Learning Theory. Proceedings 2002. XI, 415 pages. 2002.

Vol. 2541: T. Barkowsky, Mental Representation and Processing of Geographic Knowledge. X, 174 pages. 2002.

Vol. 2543: O. Bartenstein, U. Geske, M. Hannebauer, O. Yoshie (Eds.), Web Knowledge Management and Decision Support. Proceedings, 2001. X, 307 pages. 2003.

Vol. 2554: M. Beetz, Plan-Based Control of Robotic Agents. XI, 191 pages. 2002.

Vol. 2557: B. McKay, J. Slaney (Eds.), AI 2002: Advances in Artificial Intelligence. Proceedings 2002. XV, 730 pages. 2002.

Vol. 2560: S. Goronzy, Robust Adaptation to Non-Native Accents in Automatic Speech Recognition. Proceedings, 2002. XI, 144 pages. 2002.

Vol. 2569: D. Gollmann, G. Karjoth, M. Waidner (Eds.), Computer Security – ESORICS 2002. Proceedings, 2002. XIII, 648 pages. 2002.

Vol. 2577: P. Petta, R. Tolksdorf, F. Zambonelli (Eds.), Engineering Societies in the Agents World III. Proceedings, 2002. X, 285 pages. 2003.

Vol. 2581: J.S. Sichman, F. Bousquet, P. Davidsson (Eds.), Multi-Agent-Based Simulation II. Proceedings, 2002. X, 195 pages. 2003.

Vol. 2583: S. Matwin, C. Sammut (Eds.), Inductive Logic Programming. Proceedings, 2002. X, 351 pages. 2003.

Vol. 2586: M. Klusch, S. Bergamaschi, P. Edwards, P. Petta (Eds.), Intelligent Information Agents. VI, 275 pages. 2003.

Vol. 2592: R. Kowalczyk, J.P. Müller, H. Tianfield, R. Unland (Eds.), Agent Technologies, Infrastructures, Tools, and Applications for E-Services. Proceedings, 2002. XVII, 371 pages. 2003.

Vol. 2600: S. Mendelson, A.J. Smola, Advanced Lectures on Machine Learning. Proceedings, 2002. IX, 259 pages. 2003.

Vol. 2627: B. O'Sullivan (Ed.), Recent Advances in Constraints. Proceedings, 2002. X, 201 pages. 2003.

Vol. 2631: R. Falcone, S. Barber, L. Korba, M. Singh (Eds.), Trust, Reputation, and Security: Theories and Practice. Proceedings, 2002. X, 235 pages. 2003.

Vol. 2636: E. Alonso, D, Kudenko, D. Kazakov (Eds.), Adaptive Agents and Multi-Agent Systems. XIV, 323 pages. 2003.

Vol. 2637: K.-Y. Whang, J. Jeon, K. Shim, J. Srivastava (Eds.), Advances in Knowledge Discovery and Data Mining. Proceedings, 2003. XVIII, 610 pages. 2003.

Vol. 2639: G. Wang, Q. Liu, Y. Yao, A. Skowron (Eds.), Rough Sets, Fuzzy Sets, Data Mining, and Granular Computing. Proceedings, 2003. XVII, 741 pages. 2003.

Vol. 2663: E. Menasalvas, J. Segovia, P.S. Szczepaniak (Eds.), Advances in Web Intelligence. Proceedings, 2003. XII, 350 pages. 2003.

Lecture Notes in Computer Science